*Gardening
in a
Hot Climate*

ACKNOWLEDGEMENTS

My grateful thanks and acknowledgement are due to the following for their help with this book.

George Green, The Anthurium Nursery
Peter Young, Birdwood Nursery
Birkdale Nursery
Greg Braun, Kempsey
Brindley Bros. Nurseries
The Bunker family, Redlands Greenhouses Holdings
Fairhill Native Plants Nursery
Col Harding, Nursery Traders
Hawkins Garden Centres, Brisbane
Dennis Hundscheidt, Palmyra Landscaping and Design
Impact Grass, Sydney
Jan Iredell
Jimboomba Turf, Brisbane
Vic Levey's Nurseries
Ross McKinnon
Monica Mead
Nuway Landscaping Supplies
Barry Paget, Orchidworld
Ray and Diane Parker, Parkers Place Nursery
Mr and Mrs Ray Punter
The Queensland Department of Primary Industries
The Queensland Hibiscus Society
Roseworld, Redland Bay
The Shade Centre, Stafford, Brisbane
Graham and Wendy Snell, The Vireya Nursery
Terry Keogh, Wellington Point Nursery
John Waller
Ian Wicks
Yuruga Nursery

Especial thanks to Ralph Bailey, to Joy Lane, and to Harry Oakman whose life and work have long been an inspiration to many gardeners in a hot climate. I would also like to acknowledge the great contribution made by members of the Queensland nursery industry without whose affectionate support and encouragement this book could not have been written.

Thomas C. Lothian Pty Ltd
11 Munro Street, Port Melbourne, Victoria 3207

First published 1996
Copyright © Julie Lake 1996

National Library of Australia
Cataloguing-in-Publication data:
Lake, Julie.
    Gardening in a hot climate.
    Bibliography.
    Includes indexes.
    ISBN 0 85091 640 2
    1. Gardening. 2. Gardening - Tropical conditions.
    I. Title.
635.952

All photographs by the author
Line drawings by Julia McLeish
Designed by Jo Waite
Printed in Hong Kong by South China Printing Co., Ltd

Gardening in a Hot Climate

— JULIE LAKE —

Lothian
BOOKS

Contents

Acknowledgements 2

An introduction to gardening in a hot climate 7
  How to use this book • Beating the heat • What is hot? • Tropical and sub-tropical

1 Creating a garden in a hot climate 13
Designing your hot-climate garden 14
  Planning • Hard surfaces • Time and money • Planning with colour • Very small gardens and courtyards

2 Directory of garden styles 23
A low-maintenance garden 24
  Planning essentials • To mow or not to mow • Design ideas
A shady garden 26
The tropical touch 29
  Water features • Truly tropical plants • A tropical idyll
A tropical rainforest garden 34
Pools, ponds and swimming pools 37
  Types of ponds and pools • Running water • Planting in the water • Maintaining the pool • Swimming pools
A seaside garden 43
  Soil • Protection • General care
The natural look 50
Hot and dry gardens 51
  Soil • General care • Lawns • Plants for hot and dry gardens
An instant garden 56

3 Garden design challenges 61
Planning for problem areas 62
  Narrow side areas • Steep banks • Gullies • Damp spots • Stormwater runoff
Storm warning! 66
  Wind • Rain • Stormproofing your garden
Fire protection 69

4 Plant directory 71
Trees 73
  Hot-climate conifers • *Tropical treats: Lilly pillies*
Palms 88
  Cultivation • Pests and diseases • Landscaping with palms
Shrubs 94
  Shrubberies • Shrubs at a glance • *Tropical treats: Hibiscus, Vireyas*
Climbers 115
  Tropical treats: Bougainvilleas
The flower garden 126
  Perennials • Annuals • Lilies and lily-like plants • Roses • The rockery • *Tropical treats: Orchids*

Foliage and fillers 146
    Ferns • Staghorns and elkhorns • Ornamental grasses • Bamboo
    • Cycads, zamias and bowenias • *Tropical treats: Bromeliads*

5 Walls 'n' floors 161

Hedges and screens 162
    Hedges • Care and cultivation • Screens
Lawns and groundcovers 165
    Lawns • Drainage • Soil base and levelling • Planting • Lawn care
    • Improving an existing lawn • Lawn alternatives

6 A productive garden 171

Fruit 172
    Frost protection • Pests and diseases • Other fruits
Vegetables 179
    Design and preparation • Planting • Making a seedbed • Cultivation
    • Protection • Growing vegetables in containers • Organic growing
    • No digging • Frost • Planting guide for seed-grown vegetables
Herbs and spices 187

7 Pottering about 191

Gardening in containers 192
    Container plants outdoors • Sun or shade • Pots • Potting mixtures and
    fertilisers • Hanging baskets • Window boxes • Container plants indoors
    • Temperature • General care • Light • Light requirements for indoor
    plants • Day-length requirements for flowering • Indoor plant problems
Shadehouses and garden sheds 203
    • Shadehouses • Ferneries • Sheds
Propagating your own plants 205
    Seeds • Cuttings • Suckers • Leaf cuttings • Layering • Division

8 Caring for your garden 211

Before you start: the importance of soil and drainage 212
    The good earth • Drainage
Planting 214
    Selecting plants • Planting seeds and seedlings • Trees and large shrubs
    • Palms • Transplanting • Plant protection
Watering, feeding and mulching 218
    Watering • Conserving water • Fertiliser • Types of fertilisers
    • Fertilising facts • Compost • Mulching
Pruning 224
    Fruit trees • Ornamental shrubs and young trees • Tip-pruning
    • Renovation • Natives • Removing suckers
The plant clinic 226
    Recognising insect pests & diseases • Insect types • Diseases • Organic pest
    & weed control • Integrated pest management • Natural weed control
    • Biological methods • When all else fails — chemical control • Weeds

Index of botanical names 235
Index of common names and general topics 239

An introduction to gardening in a hot climate

I GREW UP IN A HOT CLIMATE, near the equator, where the garden was as richly colourful as a Gauguin painting throughout the year. Bougainvillea spilled over the white garden wall, yellow allamanda covered the verandah, quisqualis threaded its way through the neem tree by the kitchen door, hibiscus lined the driveway, a vast, pink, spreading *Cassia javanica* overhung the front gates and the persistent rustle of palm fronds enticed us down to the nearby beach. To this day, the tree which I associate with Christmas is not the pine but the poinciana, which proudly produces its great scarlet sprays of blossom every December.

Over the years I have returned often to this garden in my mind, and its memory has inspired me to create many other gardens in its image. This is why, though I love all plants, and every sort of garden, it is the flamboyantly flowering shrubs and climbers of the tropics and sub-tropics which remain dearest to my heart. Through this book I hope to introduce more people to the sheer joy of gardening with these plants, which give so much reward for so little effort.

Gardening in a hot climate offers many such rewards. For one thing, the range of suitable plants is so very large. Some of the world's most beautiful plants originate in the tropics and sub-tropics. These include many Australian natives, in particular the splendid plants from the rainforests. Many familiar perennials and annuals commonly grown in cooler climates thrive in hot climates. The climate also allows gardening all year round, with just enough seasonal change — as well as a satisfying number of winter-flowering plants — to make the garden always interesting. The permanently warm weather makes it possible to spend plenty of time outdoors and enjoy the garden at any time of the year.

But gardening in a hot climate *is* different in many ways from the traditions forged in a cold climate. Plant growth habits, appropriate methods of cultivation, the types of problems encountered, the very climate itself, offer different challenges to those faced by cold-climate gardeners. It was these challenges which motivated me to write this book.

Not so very long ago, gardening in a hot climate was all about taking a stalk of frangipani or bougainvillea from someone else's garden and sticking it in the ground. It grew. This resulted in gardens which were easy to grow but very limited in scope. Today, there is a bewildering range of plants from which to choose, as well as products to protect plants and enhance growth.

We need to know more, not only about the plants we want to grow, but how we should grow them. We need to be able to manage our gardens just as we manage other aspects of lives — so that we can get the best out of them. This book is written to help people do just that. It is written for those who love gardening and enjoy the work involved; and for those reluctant weekend-only gardeners who want to know how to make the private space around their house look as attractive as possible without too much effort. It is written for experienced gardeners who are always happy to learn something new, and for the many young, keen, novice gardeners who are building homes in outer suburbs where the starting point is a block of bare ground. It is written for those who have moved from cooler places and are thus unfamiliar with growing plants in a hot climate, and for those who have gardened in hot climates all their lives but are still timid about trying new plants and new techniques.

A poinciana in full bloom is a glorious sight. This summer-flowering tree originates in Madagascar and has become a popular street and garden specimen in hot climates throughout the world. Distinguishing features are the wide flat canopy and the vivid red flowers which can cover the tree in season. See page 81.

HOW TO USE THIS BOOK

In order to satisfy the needs of so many different gardeners, a book like this has to contain a lot of information. In a sense, a comprehensive gardening book is like a modern garden centre, packed with such a variety of plants and associated products that it can appear confusing and even a bit intimidating at first sight. I have tried to make *Gardening in a Hot Climate* as informative as necessary without being indigestible; and, as it is intended to serve the reader as a faithful gardening companion for many years to come, I have tried to present information in such a way that it won't become quickly outdated. For example, throughout the book brand names for gardening products have mostly been avoided because new products are frequently being introduced. This same principle has been applied to plant varietal names. In the plant lists and schedules only species names are mentioned for the most part, the exceptions being those few varieties which have become so familiar that gardeners ask for them by name, rather than the species. So many new cultivars are introduced every year that it is difficult to keep listings up-to-date. At the same time, while many old favourites are retained, others are no longer produced, usually because they have been replaced by varieties with improved qualities.

The book differs from others in that the method of listing plants by name is slightly unorthodox. With most entries we have followed the usual procedure of putting the plant's botanical name first, followed by its common name in brackets. However, where it is apparent that the common name is so familiar to readers that they will have difficulty finding the plant otherwise, the common name has been placed first, with the botanical name following. Oleander, poinsettia and poinciana are three plants which fall into this category. The aim of this book is to make gardening information as easily accessible as possible; it is first and foremost a gardening book, not a botanical treatise, and it is hoped gardeners will feel comfortable with this approach. All listings are in alphabetical order and indexes of botanical and common names appear at the end of the book.

Heights given for plants are approximate only. It must be appreciated that the height of individual plants in the garden varies not only with the habits of different cultivars bred from original species but also with climate and conditions. Cold and lack of water stunts the growth of hot-climate plants; conversely plants from cooler climates have been known to run riot in height and spread when grown in a warmer area. Poor soils limit root growth and therefore stunt plant growth. Plants, like people, are individuals and while selective breeding leads to a certain consistency and uniformity in factors such as height (dwarf shrubs, for example, do not grow into giant trees — or even medium-sized shrubs), no gardening book can tell you exactly how an individual plant will grow in *your* garden.

Finally, all temperate climes experience hot summers. Thus most of the information about how to garden in a hot climate will be as much of interest to gardeners in temperate zones as it is to those in the more tropical.

BEATING THE HEAT

Gardeners in a hot climate need to look after themselves as well as their plants. The very sun which makes plants grow so profusely in the tropics and sub-tropics, and which makes gardening possible all year round, can also make a gardener's favourite pastime very uncomfortable.

High temperatures cause humans to wilt as well as plants, and for the same reason. They become dehydrated, sometimes dangerously so. Gardeners undertaking heavy tasks during very hot weather should make sure they replace lost moisture with frequent drinks. Drinks which replace electrolytes and salts are particularly valuable. In other words, make sure you put back what you sweat out! Heat exhaustion is not something to take lightly and even the very fit and healthy can suffer from it. By far the majority of regular gardeners, however, are over the age of forty, and they are the most susceptible to the ill effects of working in excessive heat.

As a general rule, major gardening endeavours such as digging beds, building sheds or other structures, installing watering systems, building ponds, making paths, and so on, are best done during the three cool-season months of June, July and August. If work must be done in summer then it should be done before, say, 10 a.m. and after 3 p.m. — though late afternoons in northern areas can be very hot. If mad dogs and Englishmen are known for going out in the midday sun, hot climate gardeners most emphatically should not! Experienced gardeners have learned to take advantage of the cool, dew-damp dawns when plants seem at their best and tough tasks seem easiest.

Sun protection in a hot climate is very important. Even in the cooler months the sun can damage exposed skin; in summer during the hours between 8 a.m. and 4 p.m. gardeners should cover as much of their bodies as is comfortable. Hats with brims large enough to protect the face and back of the neck should be worn. Loose, light clothes with long sleeves are cool, comfortable and offer maximum protection not only against the sun but against scratches, rashes, chemical sprays and insect stings or bites. Sunscreen lotions are a wise extra precaution, though perspiration can reduce the effectiveness of some brands so they need frequent renewing. Sunscreens can be used on the face (but not above or close to the eyes because perspiration can make them run into the eyes). They will also protect the backs of hands for those tasks which are difficult to do when wearing gloves.

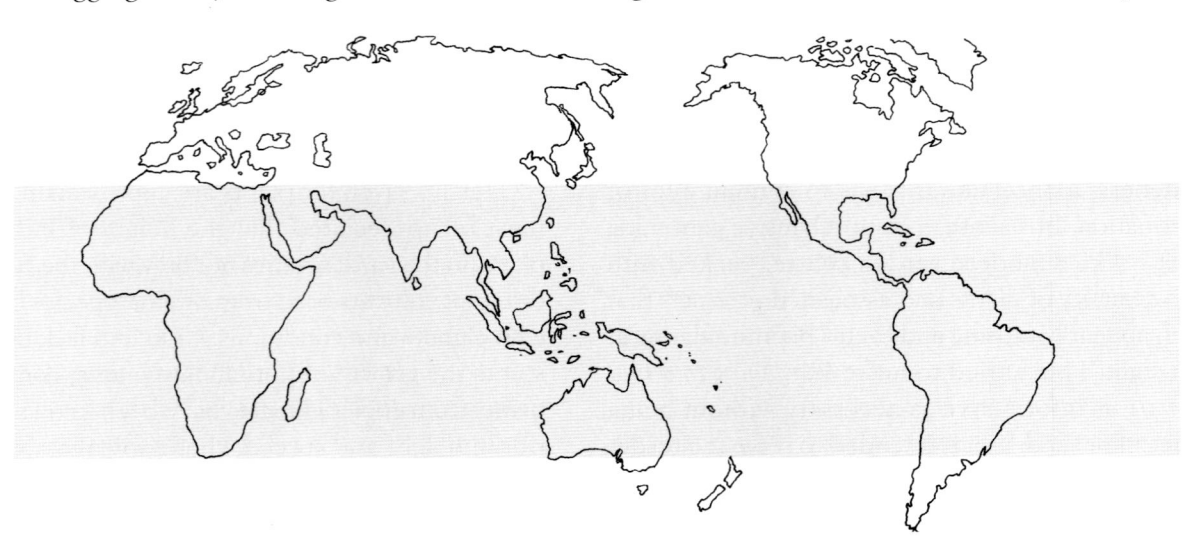

People who live in hotter parts and who spend long hours in the garden without adequate protection against sun are in the high risk group for skin cancer. Australia, for instance, is said to have the highest incidence of skin cancer in the world per ratio of population. Besides this, too much sun causes the skin to dry out and age prematurely.

Taken all-in-all, gardening in a hot climate is generally easier and more pleasant than gardening in areas where winters — and often summers too — are cold and wet. The few commonsense precautions outlined here are all it takes to cope with the obvious problems. Throughout the book there are further hints to make hot-climate gardening easier for those who want maximum enjoyment from their gardens for a minimum amount of work.

WHAT IS HOT?

What exactly is meant by a 'hot' climate? For the purposes of this book, a hot climate is defined very simply as one in which summer temperatures frequently rise above 30°C and cool season temperatures rarely go below 10°C. In the southern hemisphere this applies to the sub-tropical and tropical regions of Australia's east and west coasts, the tip of the North Island of New Zealand, much of low-lying southern Africa, the coastal areas of southern United States. 'Tropical' is easy to define in Australian terms because it refers to the areas north of the Tropic of Capricorn. 'Sub-tropical' is a looser term; for Australian readers it can be taken to include Sydney and Perth because, despite lower winter temperatures, most sub-tropical plants (and some from the tropics) will thrive there and basic gardening conditions are the same.

Temperature

Most plants will survive drops in temperatures markedly lower than those common to their natural habitats for brief periods. They may not, however, withstand frost. So if you live in an area where frosts occur, play safe and avoid very tender plants or give them adequate protection. At the other end of the scale, as very high temperatures often go hand-in-hand with extremely dry conditions, all but desert plants are likely to die if temperatures exceed 40°C for a prolonged period. They will only survive if given large amounts of water to replace moisture loss. Fortunately for gardeners in areas where these conditions are not uncommon, there are many plants which are adapted to them. Many are listed in this book, in the chapter on hot and dry gardens, page 51.

Rainfall

Sub-tropical and tropical regions get most of their rain in summer, though rainfall can occur throughout the year. This ranges on average from 1000 mm (southern end of the sub-tropics) to 1500 mm (tropics) a year, with scattered pockets of higher and lower rainfall depending on local conditions. Concentrated deluges are not limited to the tropics; the highest recorded rainfall in one hour, 97 mm, occurred in Sydney. There are very few places, even those with the highest rainfall, which do not experience drought. Then many Australian native plants, including many rainforest species, come into their own for they have a built-in ability to go without water for long periods or to recover rapidly from drought damage.

TROPICAL AND SUB-TROPICAL

It is useful to know the climatic origins of plants. Tropical land areas are characterised by high rainfall, predominantly warm temperatures showing minimal seasonal change, and a day-length which varies little all year round. Plants from these regions require such conditions in order to thrive. Some are so specialised that they will only grow elsewhere if given an environment which closely emulates their natural habitat — this generally means indoor growing. Others are remarkably tolerant of all but very cold, exposed or dry conditions. Selective plant breeding over generations has made many modern garden plants much more adaptable to conditions outside their natural habitat.

Sub-tropical plants are probably the most adaptable of any because they originate in areas immediately north of the Tropic of Cancer or south of the Tropic of Capricorn, where compared with the tropics there is more variation in temperature and day-length, yet the climate is predominantly warm, with high rainfall. Sub-tropical plants often tolerate climates colder than their natural habitat while at the same time doing well in the tropics. Some plants designated as 'tropical' or 'sub-tropical' actually come from highland regions where temperatures are quite cold. This means they will do well in climates where winter temperatures are low; with such plants day-length is often more important than temperature.

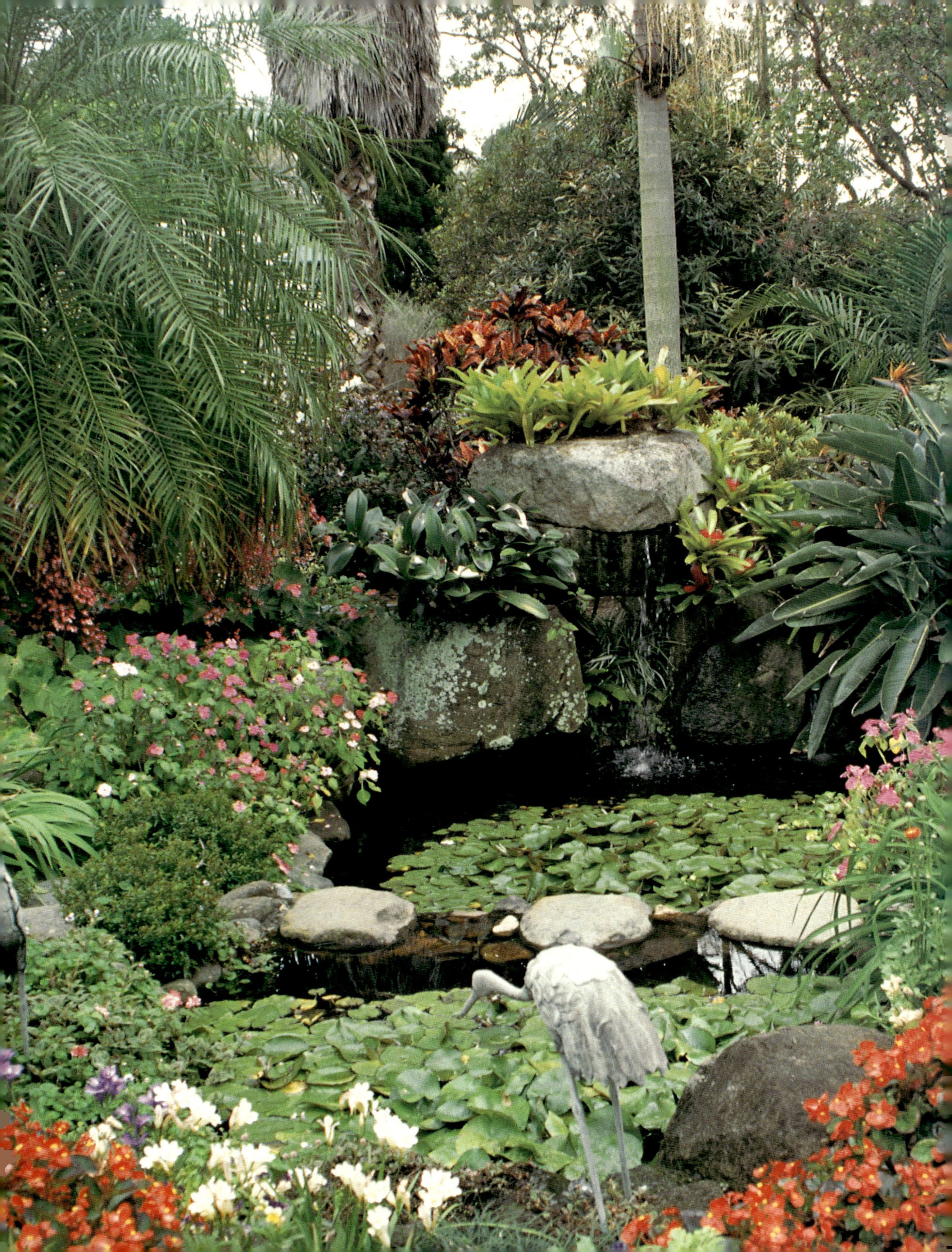

1

Creating a garden in a hot climate

This prize-winning garden perfectly blends all the ingredients essential to gardening in a hot climate — lavish colour, green shade and cool water. Palms, treeferns and foliage plants form a tropical-style shrubbery beneath a canopy of mature trees. This provides a backdrop for the masses of flowering shrubs around a large pool which has been designed to merge naturally into the landscape. A dramatic touch is added by the large strelitzia or BIRD OF PARADISE *plant (at right of picture), see page 132; colourful plants include begonias in the foreground, plenty of impatiens around the water's edge, crotons behind the waterfall and the red 'throats' of bromeliads growing out of the rocks. The palm on the left draped gracefully over the pool is a* DWARF DATE PALM *(Phoenix roebelenii), see page 91.*

Designing your hot-climate garden

At the simplest level, a garden is the outdoor area which surrounds our house and where we grow plants in imitation of nature. Beyond that, gardens are different things to different people and what we do with them is a very individual decision. So, the first decision to make when designing or re-designing a garden is what kind of garden do you want? Do you want to turn your garden into a rainforest or do you prefer uncluttered space, with plenty of lawn and a few shrubs? Do you wish to grow plants in containers? Have you time to plant and care for a display of annuals? Do you like plenty of colour or do you prefer a soothing predominance of green? Do you want to grow fruit or vegetables or even herbs?

Some people have a very clear vision right from the start of how they want their garden to look. They will thoroughly plan it down to the last plant — sometimes to the actual cultivar and flower colour required for a particular effect. Others are content to sketch in a few basic details and let the garden develop haphazardly; adding a shrub here, a flowerbed there, as the fancy takes them. I would suggest that most of us are of this latter breed. Furthermore, some of us are haphazard in our approach but belong also to the 'I must...' school of plant lovers: 'I *must* have at least one poinciana...I *must* grow some annuals...I *must* have a herb garden.' It doesn't matter which type of gardener you are, a haphazard developer or an ultimate planner, provided you follow some of the basic principles outlined in this chapter you will be able to create a garden that satisfies your particular needs.

Conventional garden design wisdom has generally dictated that planning a garden from scratch, that is, a patch of bare (or fairly bare) earth around a brand new home, is easier than trying to re-design an existing garden. This convention should be challenged because it is easier for those without formal training in garden design to envisage changing or enhancing existing features than to visualise a garden where none exists at all. Nor, usually, is there the same sense of urgency to create some sort of a garden in a hurry, which often leads to making silly mistakes. Most people buying an established home consider the garden as part of the overall package when choosing one home over another. This means that if they think the garden needs change or improvement it will be because it doesn't come up to their particular expectations.

PLANNING

Whether your garden is old or new, the fundamental design principles remain the same. We are not talking here about the finer points of landscape architecture but about commonsense measures which ensure that your garden is a comfortable and pleasant place. If your ideas for a garden are very ambitious, if you have very specific needs but don't know how to design them, if your site is very difficult, then it will certainly pay you to employ a landscape architect or designer — the initial cost will be money well spent. But this is beyond the means of most home buyers and, fortunately, it is not too difficult to come up with a perfectly workable and attractive design for the average suburban block — or even the larger garden.

Gardening writers always advise making a sketch plan when planning a new garden. This is sound advice, but unfortunately most gardeners appear to ignore it. Some people are just too impatient to bother with a plan, others are too intimidated by the prospect of formalising their ideas on paper. A plan need only be very simple. Unless you are artistically inclined, or a very thorough and dedicated gardener indeed, don't worry about drawing it to scale or transposing it on to graph paper. The idea is merely to sketch in the following:

- The approximate shape of the garden
- Major internal features (existing trees, buildings, etc.)
- Major external features (roads, street trees, very tall close-by buildings)
- Direction of north, south, east and west
- Location of services and utilities: drains, powerlines, position of garbage bin, washing lines, shed (existing or proposed)
- Outdoor living areas (existing or proposed)
- Swimming pool and other water features (existing or proposed)
- Direction of any views
- Planned plantings of trees, shrubberies and flowerbeds.

If you plan a more ambitious garden, sketch in fruit trees and herb and vegetable gardens, and other feature plantings. You may also sketch in, if you consider them applicable:

- Prevailing wind direction
- Desirable placements for shade
- Garden structures such as pergolas
- Shaded areas caused by building features such as house walls and overhangs

When you have even the roughest sketch before you it is much easier to visualise your garden ideas and foresee problems and this is helpful to even the most haphazard of garden developers. Indeed, you may draw up several plans before you find one that suits. But don't make too much of it all; the main benefit of a plan may have less to do with how the garden will eventually look than with avoiding serious and costly mistakes at the outset.

In a hot climate, two aspects of planning are particularly important — shade and coolness. The northern side of the house is exposed to the sun most of the day. Wind from this direction is not prevailing, so shade trees will not block necessary breezes which come mostly from the south-east. The western side of the house nearly always needs summer shade because it becomes very hot in the afternoon, without cooling breezes. In winter, south of the Tropic of Capricorn and inland, this side will be chilled by westerlies. Thus shade trees on the western side of the house will screen hot afternoon sun in summer and help to deflect westerly winds in winter. Unless required for screening, it is not a good idea to plant trees with dense canopies on the eastern and south-eastern side of the house because they will block both prevailing breezes and early morning sun. Palm trees, for example, will provide a lighter shade. Homes perched high on land by the sea will receive almost constant strong south-easterly winds which may necessitate screen plantings to make the house and garden more comfortable. As you can see, planning for shade and coolness in a hot climate is fairly clear cut:

- Establish where prevailing winds come from, and where shade is required
- Ensure that your shade trees don't block your breezeway (unless your house and garden are just too breezy and need protection).

Views are the other aspect to be considered when planting trees or large shrubs in a garden. Obviously it makes no sense to plant a large, bushy tree right where it will block a pleasant view. At the same time, a view can be enhanced by framing with trees. Again, palm trees make very effective frames for tropical views; a view of sea or mountain can look very romantic part-seen through the foliage of a eucalypt or poinciana.

At its simplest level, planning needs to allow for services such as power, telephone and water lines and drainage. Trees should not be planted where they will grow up and interfere with overhead powerlines, nor should they be planted directly over drains or where there is a danger of digging into underground power or telephone lines. Access points to grease traps and septic tanks must be kept reasonably clear. The garbage bin should be located where it is readily accessible from the house and easily pushed to its roadside collection position. A clothesline or hoist is best placed where it receives plenty of sun and wind; clothes won't get any morning sun if the hoist is too close to the southern or western side of the house.

Soil and Topography

Understanding the soil and topography of your garden is an important part of planning. Advice on improving soil is included in the garden care section, page 212; however it is not always feasible to improve the soil over a large area of garden, at least in the short term. This will certainly be necessary if you want to grow annuals and vegetables; and to this end small areas can be cultivated. Otherwise, an understanding of the soil type should lead you to selecting plants suited to it, perhaps with some minimum improvement to the immediate planting area to help the plant establish.

For example, the very light, sandy soils common to many coastal areas will need plenty of additional humus to grow almost any plants other than those indigenous to the area. A less obvious problem is posed by the rich, red soils found in some areas of the coast and adjacent mountain ranges. These grow very good vegetables and some fruits such as strawberries but, despite their fertility, it can be hard to establish many garden plants in them. Pawpaw, frangipani, citrus and many Australian natives from areas with lighter soils are just some of the plants which find this kind of soil rather heavy around their roots. Once established, they do very well, but will be hard-put to survive at first unless the soil is lightened with sand or compost. It is very frustrating to design your garden and then find that many of the plants on which the design depends are just not suited to the local soil type. You then have no choice but to go to the expense of improving or changing the soil or, more sensibly, changing your plant selection.

> Garden design is to a large extent dictated by whether your block is flat, gently sloping, very steep or a mixture of all three. A block which is steep overall is not necessarily more expensive or troublesome to develop than a flat block; it just depends on what you want to do with it. It can be terraced with rocks, railway sleepers or retaining walls of block or brick. Restructuring a slope with earthworks and rocks is cheaper and often more effective than building a retaining wall, particularly on very uneven sites. Another alternative is to leave the natural slope as it is, with perhaps a few shrub and tree plantings, and the placement of a rock or two. If the slope, or a substantial part of it, lies above the house then drainage is particularly important. Don't think that house sites on slopes can't flood; they can and do! In heavy rain, water can pour down in a great volume from the road above or from adjacent land. This can bank up around the house slab for a short but damaging period, unless it is channelled away.

IT CAN BE MORE DIFFICULT to manage a block which has one or two non-level areas which demand attention. Gentle slopes may be grassed or mulched and planted; steep slopes may need some kind of management, such as retaining walls or terracing, if they are likely to collapse or create problems by shedding water on to other areas of the garden during heavy rain. It is obviously best to assess these problems when a new garden is being planned; they can then be considered in the overall design so that possible negatives can be turned into positives. After all, a flat garden can be rather dull; a few uneven features are an easy way of creating visual interest. Banks, for example, lend themselves to a multi-layered effect impossible to achieve in a flat garden. Terraced areas are a great place for growing herbs, rockery plants and many other species which require extra good drainage, particularly if the natural garden soil is heavy. A bank can also be turned to advantage by terracing it into flowerbeds which can be worked without having to bend over — a big plus for older people and those with bad backs.

On a steep or otherwise difficult site, even if you plan to do the work yourself, it is wise to consult a professional first, to avoid mistakes which can be costly to put right.

Hardwood sleepers have been used to dramatise the beginning of a rainforest garden pathway. The natural timber complements the surrounding foliage which includes dracaenas (at right), bromeliads and palms.

Points to ponder

The following chapters cover a variety of garden styles and approaches. However, whatever the style of garden you are planning, a few simple design points are worth noting:

- ❖ Think of your garden as an extension of the house. Even the smallest house is made more liveable by the provision of outdoor living and playing areas. A well-planned children's play area, easily visible from the main living area, will keep children out of the house and off the streets. A small, secluded section off the main bedroom can make a quiet cool retreat for harassed parents or for elderly people who live with their families.
- ❖ Lawns (or lawn substitutes) and vegetation are cooler than hard surfaces. If your house is located on, say, the western side of a ridge it will require more vegetation to cool it than one which is on the eastern side of a ridge, close to the sea. Heavy vegetation does, however, raise the humidity level.
- ❖ Light-coloured stone and concrete reflect heat. Dark-coloured gravels and brick paving absorb it.
- ❖ Despite the work involved, a lawn provides the softest

and safest surface on which children can play. Even a small lawn is worth having in a family garden though it must be kept free of bindiis and thistles. If a common, exotic lawn grass is for some reason unsuitable or unwanted, consider some of the alternatives discussed on pages 168–70. A shaded lawn will not grow unless a shade-tolerant species is chosen.

- Make sure you know a plant's ultimate size before planting or you will find yourself having constantly to trim plants which are too big for their position or even remove them altogether. In a hot, wet climate plants easily become rampant.
- Tall and dense plantings on the boundaries give privacy but they can also give a closed-in feeling to the garden and make it seem smaller. Conversely, low plantings or fences allow the garden to blend in with the outside world, giving a feeling of space.
- A garden will seem larger and more interesting if it cannot all be seen at once. Hedges, screens and off-set shrubbery plantings which conceal or part-conceal another area beyond will help create a feeling of mystery. A curved path with its ending hidden from immediate view adds to the effect.
- If a new building block retains some of the indigenous vegetation, try to preserve these plants by integrating them into your garden design. Even if they look unkempt, a little care will work wonders. Whether you wish to make them the basis of a native garden, or whether you blend them into a mixed planting of natives and exotics, you will not only help conserve our local flora, but also cultivate interesting plants which may not be readily available in nurseries.

HARD SURFACES

The type of surfacing you choose will, of course, depend on cost and individual taste. Often, a clearly visualised garden design will influence your choice: for example, a sawdust or other soft-surface path may look good in a rainforest garden but it will not suit a cottage garden where brick or paving may be more in keeping. As a general principle, it is always worth spending money on good quality, long-lasting surfaces for hard areas such as driveways, paths and outdoor living areas. After all, you have to live with them for a long time.

Driveways

Suitable surfacing materials for driveways include plain reinforced concrete (perhaps with a brushed or patterned surface), stamped concrete, pebble aggregate (which comes in varying qualities), bitumen, gravel, paving and brick. Driveways can contribute to erosion because they are impervious to stormwater runoff. There should be a shallow drain on the lower side, or better on both sides, covered with grass or pebbles of sufficient size and weight that they can't be washed away. On long driveways, simple water diverters such as flat stones raised slightly above the surface will slow down the speed of rushing water. The surface should be smooth and kept weeded to avoid the build-up of soil particles which may block the free flow of water and cause it to back up.

Pathways

Suitable surfacing for pathways includes gravel, bark mulch, sawdust (for a natural look), slate, sand, sawn log pavers, stone paving, brick or concrete pavers, and reinforced or brushed concrete. Gravel should not be used on steep pathways where there is any chance of soil washing down them during heavy rain, because soil particles can collect up against the gravel and prevent water flowing freely.

Gravel, bricks and pavers of all kinds should be laid on a well-compacted bed of crushed gravel or sand; laying them on a reinforced concrete slab makes them more proof against movement or subsidence in heavy rain, but this is really a job for the professional, unless you are very skilled.

Other paths need some kind of undersurface to suppress weeds; geotextile fabric is best because soft mulch material tends to slide off plastic sheeting. If possible, make your pathways wide enough for two people to stroll side by side, that is, at least 1.2 m wide. If paths are needed as drainage channels during heavy downpours, as is often the case in the tropics, they should be slightly depressed towards the centre so that runoff cannot cause damage on either side. Otherwise, make them slightly higher than lawns and surrounding planting areas, and the resulting quick runoff will make it easy to walk on them in wet weather.

Treated hardwood sleepers can be laid to surface small areas such as those around a garden bench or path intersections.

Outdoor living areas

Outdoor living areas can be surfaced with plain concrete, stamped or brushed concrete, aggregate, paving, slate, bricks or timber decking. Before you decide on the material, consider what type of use the area will have. For example, if food is to be eaten there frequently the floor will need regular cleaning so it is best to choose a surface which is easy to sweep and wash. Mould and moss build up quickly in shaded areas in a humid climate; they can be difficult to remove from rough surfaces such as brick.

Steps

Steps can be made of cut stone or slate, brick, reinforced concrete, stamped concrete, pavers or hardwood sleepers. Each surface should be level and they should not be too steep. Remember that the proportion of tread to riser should be comfortable. The general rule is that the shallower the rise, the longer the tread, varying from the ideal of 175 mm high rise to 250 mm wide tread. Long flights of small steps should be laid by a professional but large, shallow steps are quite easy to construct.

Walls

Suitable materials for garden walls include brick, cement blocks (rendered or unrendered), cut stone or rock. A wall gives a home a great feeling of permanency and seclusion but it is a lot more expensive than fencing and should be professionally constructed.

Edging

Lawns look best and are easier to maintain if they are neatly edged. The edging should be adequate to prevent grass invading nearby flowerbeds or shrubberies. Popular methods include bricks laid end to end or placed upright at a slant, rocks, timber edging or continuous concrete edging. Much depends on the style of garden but the edging should be even enough so that the mower and whipper-snipper can operate hard up against it. Avoid very sharp angles as they make mowing difficult.

Use straight lines and geometric shapes if you are aiming for a formal garden; free-flowing lines for a more natural look.

Raised garden beds

Consider the advantages of raised garden beds, built of brick, stone or timber. Provided they suit your garden style, they are easy to work, particularly for older or disabled people. It is, for example, possible to cultivate and weed a raised bed while sitting in a chair or wheelchair. In areas where there is heavy monsoonal rain, raised beds (provided they are well-constructed to drain from the bottom) drain far more efficiently than those at ground level and can be used to grow plants which are susceptible to root problems due to waterlogging. Raised beds surrounded by a hard surface are an easy way of providing greenery and colour in a low-maintenance garden. They don't have to be rectangular in shape but can be built in a circle, U-shape, cross-shape or any design which offers easy access.

A COMBINATION OF MATERIALS in driveways, paths, outdoor living areas and steps can look very attractive and may also work out more cheaply — for example if you can't afford an all-brick path you can alternate bricks with concrete. Hardwood can also be used as cross sections in concrete or brick paths — or vice versa. Slate and timber go well together.

In damp, shady areas mould or slime can make smooth surfaces very slippery so design for this with a textured surface if you want to avoid the need to remove growths regularly. A final point worth remembering about hard surfaces in the garden is that in a hot climate people are likely to go barefoot. Therefore the best surfaces are those which cannot scratch, cut or splinter.

TIME AND MONEY

If you are sensible enough to bother drawing up a design sketch, you will also be well-advised to draw up a rough budget. By some strange quirk in the nature of things, gardeners very rarely cost out the plants they require, yet a trolley-load from the garden centre will always cost more than you expect. This tends to mean a fits-and-starts approach to plant buying which can leave unattractive gaps in the garden or some plants lonely for company.

When you visit a garden centre, you will not only get an idea of the kind of plants to grow but also how much they cost. Try to work out the number of plants you need for an immediate planting project and, if possible, for the long term. Take an average costing per plant and add them up — the result will probably be a nasty shock! Nonetheless, it gives you a chance realistically to assess just how much you will need to spend. If necessary, you can then modify your design ideas to accommodate a reduced expenditure. Some gardeners do this on a plant (or planting project) plan per month or per week, costed into the household budget. The commonest mistake, when on a budget, is to buy too few of a particular plant where borders or similar mass plantings are required. This is false economy and bad gardening practice; it is much better to spend money on getting sufficient plants at the one time and postpone buying, say, that tree or shrub you want for a particular corner.

It is also important to be realistic about the time you have available to spend in the garden. If you are working full-time at a demanding job and have several other interests, or travel a lot, then keep your garden design simple. Gardening can be an important antidote to stress, but not if an over-ambitious design has resulted in a garden so time-consuming to maintain that it becomes a burden.

PLANNING WITH COLOUR

As you can see, the advice here is about the practical aspects of design. Your choice of style is very much up to you — one person's good taste can be another person's poison. Again, however, a few guiding principles about colour are worth noting:

- Colour theming adds dramatic effect to the garden. When flowers of one colour are planted in a mass display, the effect is of course multiplied many times over and the result is far more eye-catching than a variety of different colours. The exception to this is massed plantings of the same flower in different colours, for example petunias. Even then, the shades are usually complementary to one another.
- If you are aiming for coolness, the many mauve, white and blue-flowering plants, and those with grey, silver or bluish foliage, will help achieve this effect. These colours seem to recede into the distance, adding depth to the part of the garden in which they are planted.
- Yellow reflects the colour of sunshine and psychology tests show it has a cheering effect. Masses of yellow flowers give a friendly, sunny feel to a garden, even on the gloomiest day.
- Don't ignore foliage when creating colour effects. Blue-grey, silver, gold and variegated yellow-green leaves give colour all year. Many Australian rainforest plants are noted for their brilliantly coloured new foliage growth, ranging from softest pinks to mauves, bronze, copper and shining black.

Of course, you may prefer a garden which is a patchwork of many colours, freely mixed. It is surprising how colours which are usually considered non-compatible in clothes and household furnishings work well together in the garden. This is particularly true of a hot-climate garden full of tropical and sub-tropical flowering plants. However, such diversity does not work so well with hard surfaces; the materials used for walls, driveways, paths and outdoor living areas should be in harmony, with each other, and with the house itself. A jumble of brick, timber, stone and concrete looks fussy and unattractive.

Insect deterrents

In outdoor living areas, scented plants can be used to deter insects such as mosquitoes and flies. The effectiveness of such plants should not be exaggerated; they are mild deterrents only and will not drive away hordes of irritating insects, but they do help a bit. The more plants you use, the better the effect. For example, plantings alongside and close to a patio can consist of insect-repelling plants, enhanced by pots of the same plants on the hard surface. Certain scents seem particularly undesirable to mosquitoes; notably lemon and aniseed. Plants which have proved reasonably effective at deterring flies and mosquitoes include the following. Insects will certainly be repelled if you crush the leaves of these plants and rub them on your skin.

Insect repelling plants
Artemisia SPP. (e.g. wormwood, southernwood, mugwort)
Backhousia anisata
Backhousia citriodora
BASIL (flies hate it)
FENNEL
LAVENDER
Lemon-scented geraniums (and most other scented geranium
LEMON-SCENTED TEA-TREE (*Leptospermum petersonii*)
LEMON VERBENA
Mints (particularly pennyroyal and eau-de cologne mint)
PYRETHRUM

A courtyard serves as an outdoor room and can be designed to complement the interior decor. Here an effect of traditional European elegance is achieved by setting an outdoor fountain against a high, rendered wall, softened by the surface-hugging creeper, Ficus pumila, *see page 118.*

VERY SMALL GARDENS AND COURTYARDS

Because very small gardens and courtyards are nearly always enclosed, it is important to keep the south-eastern side as open as possible to take advantage of summer breezes. Shade should be planted on the northern and north-western sides. Or else it can be provided by one large tree in the centre, around which the rest of the courtyard or garden is developed. The tree can provide shade for a barbecue and outdoor sitting area; brachychitons, poincianas and jacarandas are particularly good because of their spreading habit and their brief deciduous or semi-deciduous period which lets in sunlight during the cool season. If their spread at maturity is going to be too large for a small courtyard, choose a smaller tree with a spreading canopy.

If privacy is important, use climbing plants on upright supports or trellis to provide a screen. These will take up less room than trees or large shrubs, and are less likely to cause problems to the neighbours. Otherwise, plant slender-growing, non-messy trees such as palms or conifers.

Very rarely, in an enclosed courtyard, will sun be available to plants all day. This will be a problem for annuals and many flowering shrubs, so check the amount of shade throughout the day before planting. Where only about half a day's sun is available, choose plants which thrive in part shade, for example, many small or dwarf rainforest plants, such as cordylines, ferns. Whatever plants you choose, select ones with non-aggressive root systems, for footings and drainage lines are very vulnerable in small areas.

2
Directory of garden styles

A low-maintenance garden

IS THERE A GARDEN WHICH REQUIRES NO WATERING, no feeding, no weeding, no pruning — no care at all? Of course there isn't! People who really don't want to be bothered with gardening work should live in apartments. It is possible, however, to design and establish a garden which requires only a minimum amount of work to keep it in good shape.

There are really two types of low-maintenance garden. The first is the wilderness garden, in which a profusion of plants are allowed to grow as they please, with little or no interference from the gardener. This kind of garden may not suit the average suburban block and, like the tropical rainforest garden discussed on page 34, it is hard work during the early years. What I am talking about here is how to create a garden which does not require too much work at the establishment stage as well as being low in maintenance.

The low maintenance garden starts with a clean, weed-free block which has soil good enough to grow a selection of undemanding plants. After that, it is a question of good planning. A low maintenance garden can very easily become a boring and neglected garden if it is not well-planned in the beginning. Putting right mistakes will take time and effort — and isn't this what we are trying to avoid?

PLANNING ESSENTIALS

- Surround the entire block with the best quality fencing you can afford. This will keep your boundary tidy and unwanted visitors such as neighbours' dogs at bay. Choose a material which doesn't need repainting.
- Cover much of the ground with easy-care paving or stamped concrete, in the form of wide driveways and outdoor living areas. Ensure that these are adequately drained to prevent erosion or other problems from water runoff. Sweeping outdoor hard surfaces is hard work so beware of overhanging trees or untidy shrubs. Remember, too, that these hard surfaces can become very hot; and even reflect heat on to the house, so trees which don't litter, or some other form of shade, will help beat the heat.
- Keep it simple. A few well-chosen and well-placed shrubs can constitute a garden just as effectively as a profusion of species. There is no room in the low-maintenance garden for annuals or fussy flowerbeds.
- Put in an irrigation system with automatic timers.
- If you have plants with high water needs such as palms, group them in one area.
- Demarcate any borders with a continuous long-lasting kerbing of pine, bricks or perhaps least aesthetically pleasing but most economical concrete. This will eradicate the need to trim the edges — if necessary a speedy whippersnip will quickly tidy the border. It also makes mowing easier (if you have a lawn) and helps prevent certain weeds spreading.
- Weeds: Leave no bare ground anywhere. Hard (pebble, gravel) or soft (pinebark, nutshells) mulches will help suppress weeds; dense plantings will be even more effective. Don't put down black plastic sheeting because it is bad for the soil, bad for plants, groundcovers won't grow over it and it looks terrible when exposed as inevitably happens. Spraying weeds with weedkiller is safe and easy.
- Fertilising: If this seems like too much work, select plants with very low fertiliser requirements. All plants benefit from being fed once a year and the easiest method is with a controlled-release fertiliser. Even the lowest-

maintenance garden needs the soil structure maintained with a dressing of compost or animal manure once every couple of years.

TO MOW OR NOT TO MOW

A very simple garden can be created with just a lawn and shrubs around the sides. This looks cool and uncluttered, and unless the lawn is very large it is not usually a major job to mow it if there are no other garden jobs to be done. Or take the easiest solution and consult the local paper for advertisements from people willing to mow lawns at a reasonable cost.

The other possibility is to do without a lawn at all. Instead, thickly mulch any unpaved surfaces and pathways with pine bark or a similar coarse material, and plant densely with tidy shrubs, filling any gaps with groundcovers and prostrate-growing plants such as some of the junipers and grevilleas.

DESIGN IDEAS

Here are just a few simple themes which can serve as the bases for low-maintenance garden designs.

- Renaissance: Earth-toned paving, white gravel or quartz, a couple of shrubs in tubs, a few conifers, at least one paved terrace and a wrought-iron or timber bench in traditional style. A pond, with wall fountain and *Ficus pumila* growing up the wall behind.
- Mediterranean: Lots of pale paving (or earth-tones), a couple of citrus trees in pots, dwarf date palms, stark-looking plants like *Dracaena draco* and perhaps a cycad or two. A brick-edged bed or two full of upright and trailing geraniums (which aren't much work) will add colour.
- Mexican: A courtyard effect with walls and paving in earth-tones. A sabal, fan or dwarf date palm as a feature and to give shade; cacti in high, well-drained beds; yucca or agave as feature plants.
- Naturalistic: Large boulders, gravel. Plants with relaxed informal shapes; native plants are particularly good for this. Grevilleas, callistemons and acacias as well as some small flowering plants are suitable.
- Japanese: Small boulders, a simple stone lantern. A pond. Spreading, low-growing conifers. Any small-leaved, neat plants which don't require much care. Mondo and other ornamental grasses. (The idea here is for a Japanese *theme* because of its simplicity; a traditional Japanese garden is a lot of hard work.)
- Seaside: Natural vegetation where possible. Horizontal junipers for a windblown look, coprosma, westringia, groundcover daisies. Add large pieces of driftwood.
- Typically Aussie: Lawn. Shrubberies either side of a mixture of large shrubs which don't require any care. *Buckinghamia celsissima*, grevilleas, callistemons, murrayas, metrosideros, leptospermums, durantas, syzygiums, acacias, acalyphas are amongst the more popular choices.
- Queenslander: Mostly lawn, frangipani, lagerstroemia, brunfelsia, crotons, a palm corner lush with foliage, understorey plants and a rainforest tree or two, traveller's palms by the gate. Poinciana on the footpath.

Trees and large shrubs for the low-maintenance garden

Acacia SPP. (need some pruning to prolong life)
Acalypha SPP.
Backhousia citriodora
Buckinghamia celsissima
Callistemon SPP.
Conifers
Coprosma SPP.
Cycads
Grevillea SPP.
Hakea SPP.
Lepidozamia SPP.
Leptospermum SPP.
Lilly pillies
Melaleuca SPP.
Metrosideros SPP.
Murraya paniculata
Palms
POINCIANA (if room permits)
WESTRINGIA
Xanthorrhoea SP.
Tree ferns

Climbers for the low-maintenance garden

Allamanda cathartica
BOUGAINVILLEA
Cissus antarctica
HONEYSUCKLE
JASMINE
Pandorea SPP.
Pyrostegia SPP.

A shady garden

IN HOT CLIMATES, SHADE ADDS A DESIRABLE COOL FEELING to the garden, but it does present a challenge in selecting plants which will thrive without full sunshine. Fortunately, there is a wide range of shade-loving plants which need year-round warmth to grow. So whether your own challenge is to plant up a narrow passageway deprived of sun by a wall, or to provide an attractive understorey beneath the natural shade of trees, there is no shortage of exciting plants from which to choose.

The majority of what we think of as shade-loving garden plants require light or part-shade where they receive some direct sunlight, or plenty of filtered sunlight, for several hours a day. It is important to assess the amount and type of shade when selecting plants. This is particularly vital when shade is provided by a structure: the area concerned may be in quite deep shade for much of the day but still exposed to hot, direct sunlight for a short period. Such exposure would be enough to damage plants which originate in deep-shade conditions. Sunburn is not the only problem here. Plants which grow in shade are able to maximise low light levels for photosynthesis; thus the deeper the shade in which they naturally occur, the lower the light level required for photosynthesis. This highly specialised adaption means that photosynthesis in these plants does not operate so efficiently where light levels are high — quite simply, the plants will not grow well, if at all.

Characteristic features of shade-loving plants which achieve photosynthesis at low levels include large, fleshy, deep green, often shiny leaves and, not uncommonly, fleshy stems. These are, of course, characteristic of the plants familiar to us all as indoor plants such as spathiphyllums, calatheas, dieffenbachias and philodendrons. In hot climates, these plants can be used outdoors to fill large, shade areas of the garden and create a truly tropical effect.

A common misconception is that shady gardens lack colour. Apart from those plants which flower in shade, such as justicias and clivias, there is a wide variety with gorgeous, glowing foliage. The lists in this section are just a small selection of the many shade-loving plants which are also colourful. It goes without saying — but I will remind you anyway — that most shade-loving plants are also suitable for growing in shadehouses and indoors.

Plants which originate in rainforests obviously grow well in shade in the home garden. Many rainforest species are therefore included in the following lists.

Shade-loving plants

Flowering

AFRICAN VIOLET (*Saintpaulia* SPP.)
Alpinia SPP.
Alocasia SPP.
Anthurium SPP.
Azaleas (filtered shade or morning sun)
Begonia rex and *B. semperflorens* (bedding begonia, light shade only, preferably with some morning sun)
BLUE SAGE (*Eranthemum pulchellum*)
Bromeliads
BUSY LIZZIE (*Impatiens* SPP.)
Clivia SPP.
Curcuma australasica
Dianella SPP.
Eugenia reinwardtiana
Eupatorium megalophyllum
Eupomatia laurina (NATIVE GUAVA)
Gingers (ornamental types such as hedychiums, alpinias and *Tapeinochilus ananassae*)
Hydrangea SPP. (best on southern side, or with morning or afternoon shade)
Ixora SPP.
Jacobinia carnea syn. *Justicia*
Kohleria eriantha
Lepidozamia SPP.
Orchids
Pentas lanceolata
Randia SPP.
Spathiphyllum SPP.
Vireya SPP. (part shade)

Foliage

Acalypha SPP.
Aglaeonema SPP.
Ardisia SPP.
Bromeliad SPP.
Calathea SPP.
CAST-IRON PLANT (*Aspidistra elatior*)
Codiaeum (CROTON) SPP.
Coleus SPP.
Cordyline SPP.
Ferns including BIRD'S NEST (*Asplenium nidus* and other aspleniums), MAIDENHAIR (*Adiantum* SPP.), Hare's Foot (*Davallia* SPP.), RASP FERN (*Doodia* SPP.), FISHBONE FERN (*Nephrolepis cordifolia*)
Fittonia SPP.
Hosta SPP.
Iresine herbstii
JADE PLANT (*Portulacaria afra*)
Lilly pillies (small-growing forms)
Maranta leuconeura
Nautilocalyx lynchii
Peperomia caperata
Phaleria clerodendron
Philodendron SPP.
Platycerium bifurcatum (ELKHORN) and *P. superbum* (STAGHORN)
POLKA DOT PLANT (*Hypoestes sanguinolenta*)
SACRED BAMBOO (*Nandina domestica*)
Tree Ferns (*Cyathea* and *Dicksonia* SPP.)

Groundcovers

JAVANESE VELVET PLANT (*Gyneura sarmentosa*)
Hemigraphis SPP.
MINT (*Mentha* SPP.)
Syngonium SPP.
Tradescentia SPP.
Viola hederaceae

Climbers

Cissus antarctica
Clematis aristata
CLIMBING (OR CREEPING) FIG (*Ficus pumila*)
CUP AND SAUCER VINE (*Cobaea scandens*)
Dipladenia varieties (part shade)
Hardenbergia violacea
IVY (*Hedera* SPP.)
Monstera deliciosa
Philodendron SPP.
Pandorea SPP.
WAX PLANT (*Hoya australis* and *H. carnosa*)

For palms for shady gardens, see page 93.

OVERLEAF
A curving path entices the eye deep into the shade of a rainforest garden, where a cunningly placed statue adds a touch of jungle magic. This type of rainforest garden, with its emphasis on fast-growing palms and tropical foliage plants, matures quickly and is easy to maintain thereafter. The plants with yellow and green variegated leaves, above and around the statue are Pleomele reflexa, *one of the lesser known plants which add beauty to gardens with a tropical theme.*

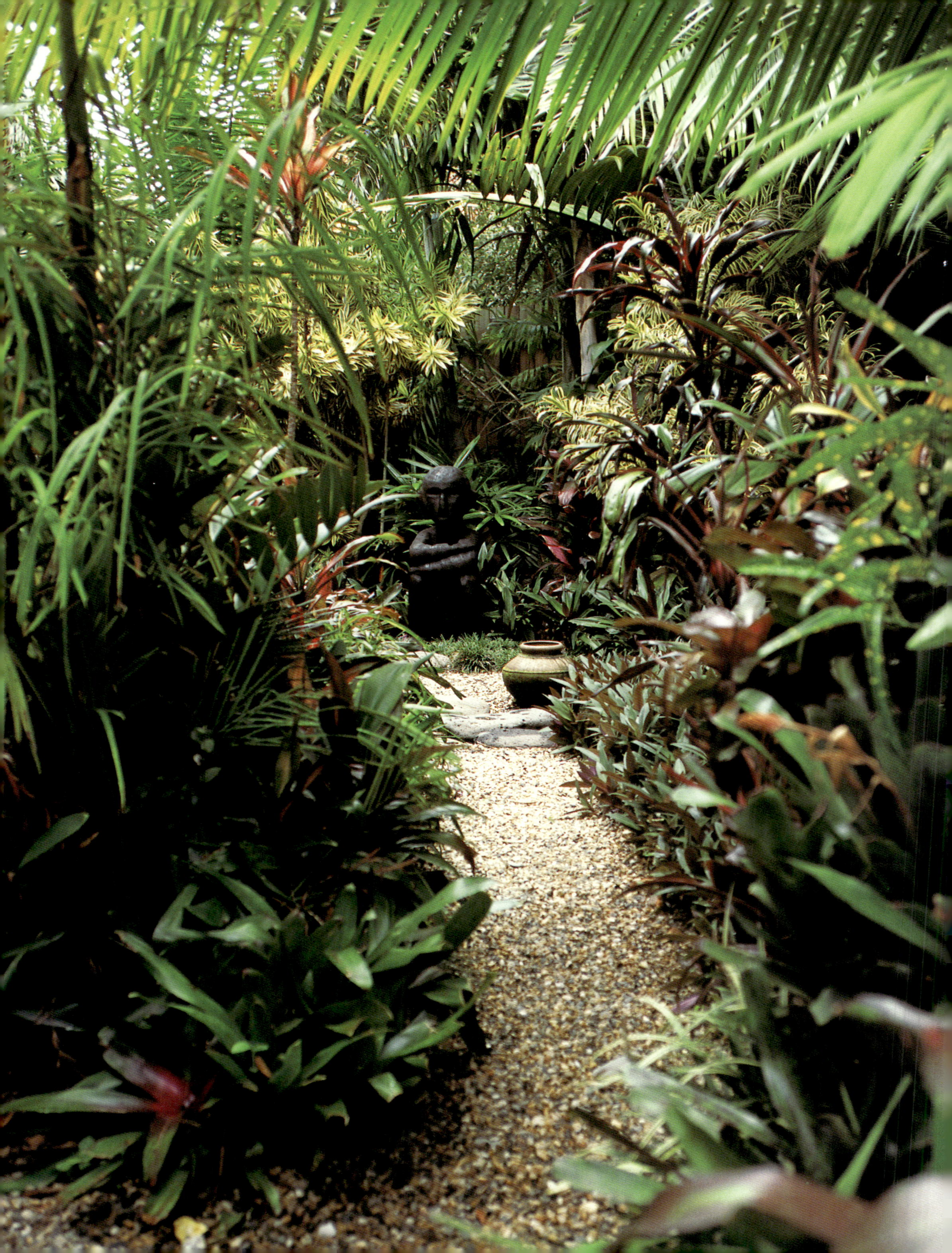

The tropical touch

'TROPICAL' IS A STATE OF MIND as much as a geographical definition. To the gardener it conjures up visions of cool, green lawns studded with brightly flowering bushes, low-spreading, shady trees, clumps or rows of palms, and shrubberies filled with fleshy-leaved plants. The ideal tropical garden is vibrant with colour throughout the year, offsetting areas of deep, mysterious shade. It should appeal to all the senses, with plenty of day and night fragrance, and water features to please both eye and ear. Flowering plants with strong sometimes overpowering fragrance are characteristic of the tropical garden and some of the best known include gardenia, brunfelsia and night jasmine.

The truly tropical garden is essentially informal in style, which makes it relatively easy to plant and maintain. What distinguishes it from other informal gardens is merely the choice of plants. Not all the plants which we have come to think of as 'tropical' actually originate in that zone between the tropics of Cancer and Capricorn (though most do) and there tends to be some confusion between 'equatorial' and 'tropical'. Here I deal with plants which thrive in a warm climate where rainfall is plentiful, humidity high, frost danger low or non-existent and the sea never very far away. Names such as bougainvillea, frangipani, allamanda, hibiscus and poinciana immediately spring to mind. And, of course, palms, ferns, climbers and epiphytes. These are the foundation of the typically tropical garden.

WATER FEATURES

It is the sound as well as the sight of water in a tropical garden that seems to cool the atmosphere so effectively. Therefore water features should be selected so that they can be clearly heard plashing, purling or trickling. A naturalistically designed swimming pool particularly suits the informal tropical style and can be made to represent a rainforest pool. The most obvious way of making the pool seem even more tropical is to plant palms nearby, or all around. Tall growing, single-stem palms will provide some light shade but if they are planted close to the pool, or its surrounds, make sure you choose types which don't drop a lot of messy fruit or fronds in season (the odd frond in the pool won't matter much).

Clumping palms such as Golden Cane also look tropical but you should allow plenty of room as this palm grows large quite quickly in a hot climate. When mature, it makes a good screen or windbreak for pool areas. Other attractive tropical poolside plants include crotons, dracaenas, cordylines, heliconias, strelitzia, Traveller's Palm (*Ravenala madagascariensis*), pandanus and *Acalypha wilkesiana* (see pages 40–2 for more plants).

Baroque or similarly elaborate fountains would look out of place in a tropical garden. Simple bubbling fountains or waterfalls look better. Ornamental pools should be free-form and naturalistic and, as suggested above, watercourses through ferneries or other shaded areas can be easily made to look like rainforest streams.

TRULY TROPICAL PLANTS

Flowering shrubs

The spectacular flowering ability of many of the larger tropical shrubs and small trees is usually best seen to advantage when they are planted as individual specimens in the garden. Smaller-growing species, and those with smaller flowers, are best planted in groups. Hibiscus, gardenia, medinilla, bougainvillea grown as a standard, gordonia, mussaenda, ixora, allamanda, tibouchina, *Caesalpinia gilliesii*, brunfelsia, randia, alloxylon and buckinghamia are all examples of plants which can be allowed to bloom in solitary splendour.

Shrubs which look best when grouped include *Streptosolen jamesonii* (syn. *Browallia*), galphimia, pentas, barleria and shrub bauhinias. No rules need apply here; it all depends on the effect which you want to create. Shrubs can be grouped in species, to create mixed or single colour effects, in beds, in shrubberies with larger plants, or in rows as borders, hedges or dividers. They also provide backdrops for smaller shrubs and herbaceous plants.

Bedding plants

Flowerbeds in the tropics should be free-form rather than in squares, rectangles or perfect circles. This is not a hard and fast rule but the free-flowing appearance seems to suit the relaxed tropical style. Probably the most colourful, reliable and commonly grown bedding plants in hot climates are cannas (*C. indica*) which come in a vast range of colours, with tall-growing and dwarf sizes. They tolerate almost any conditions and put up a good show for much of the year. Equally versatile and easy to grow are day lilies, and the colours are gorgeous. Other plants which look good in hot climate beds include heliconias, strelitzias, begonias, megaskepasma, alpinias, bedding (wax) begonias, *Pachystachys lutea* and *Crotalaria agatiflora*.

Flamboyant foliage

There are some hot climate plants with large, colourful foliage which look good in the tropical garden, either as feature plants, backdrops, screens or hedges. They include crotons (*Codiaeum* spp.), coleus, cordylines and acalypha.

Hedges and climbers

The truly tropical hedge is one which has plenty of flowers for much of the year. Two of the most reliable are calliandra (with fluffy red or pink and white flowers), or *Plumbago auriculata* which has white or blue-mauve flowers. (The variety 'ROYAL CAPE' has a more vivid blue flower.) Hibiscus can make a spectacular hedge but its susceptibility to insect attack makes it somewhat risky and demanding. The Australian native *Hibiscus tiliaceus* makes a good screening hedge for large gardens in coastal areas, though if water is readily available it will eventually grow into a tree. *Barleria cristata*, with its dainty mauve trumpet flowers makes an attractive small hedge in the tropics; in the sub-tropics (and tropics too) *Murraya paniculata* and *Tecomaria capensis* (if trimmed to prevent rambling) are popular choices. Other plants used for informal hedges include *Streptosolen jamesonii* and *Bauhinia galpinii*. Oleander (Nerium) is a popular choice but its foliage is rather sparse. Perhaps the most spectacular hedge for a hot climate is bougainvillea, either in a single colour or two (or more) colour combinations.

Any tough, large-growing plant can be used to screen out anything you don't want to see. Clumping palms, for example, are very effective in a tropical garden. But undoubtedly the densest, hardiest and most attractive screen is provided by one of the tropical-growing bamboo species, particularly one which is not too invasive in a small garden, see page 155–6. Some of the bamboos have the advantage of being very fast growing and make excellent windbreaks.

Climbers most readily associated with tropical gardens include bougainvillea, allamanda, quisqualis, *Thunbergia mysorensis*, solandra, dipladenia and mandevilla. Monstera and philodendrons help give a jungle effect in shady areas. Climbers are valuable to provide needed shade over pergolas, for example, and look effective when allowed to climb naturally through the branches of large trees just as they would in the rainforests where many originate.

PLANTS WHICH ADD THE TRULY TROPICAL TOUCH TO YOUR GARDEN

FO — colourful foliage rather than flowers

Trees

Barklya syringifolia
GOLDEN PENDA (*Xanthostemon chrysanthus*)
GOLDEN SHOWER (*Cassia fistula*)
Jacaranda mimosifolia
Palms (self-cleaning types are best)
PINK CASSIA (*Cassia javanica*)
POINCIANA (*Delonix regia*)
Schotia brachypetala
Tabebuia SPP.
YELLOW POINCIANA (*Peltophorum pterocarpum*)

Shrubs

Acalypha SPP. FO
Allamanda neriifolia
Brunfelsia SPP.
Dichorisandra SPP. FO
Frangipani (*Plumeria* SPP. often grown as a tree)
Galphimia glauca
Gardenia SPP. exotic and native
Hibiscus rosa-sinensis (and other types of hibiscus)
Hosta SPP. FO
Ixora SPP.
Lagerstroemia indica (PRIDE OF INDIA) — better grown as a shrub than allowed to develop into a tree
Mussaenda SPP.
Pachystachys lutea
Pentas SPP.
POINSETTIA (*Euphorbia pulcherrima*)
SINGAPORE HOLLY (*Malpighia coccigera*)
Streptosolen jamesonii syn. *Browallia*
Tecomaria capensis (shrub or climber)
Tibouchina SPP.

Climbers

Allamanda cathartica
Beaumontia grandiflora
Bougainvillea SPP.
Cissus antarctica
Dipladenia SPP.
Faradaya freycinetia
GOLDEN CUP VINE (*Solandra maxima*)
Hoya SPP.
Ipomoea horsfalliae var. 'BRIGGSII'
Mandevilla SPP.
Philodendron SPP.
Pyrostegia venusta
Quisqualis indica
Tecomanthe hillii
Thunbergia mysorensis

Fragrant

Bouvardia humboldtii
Brunfelsia SPP.
Cestrum nocturnum
Clerodendrum fragrans
Gardenia SPP.
Murraya paniculata
Phaleria clerodendron
Randia SPP.

Other plants

Aphelandra SPP.
Bromeliad SPP.
Canna indica
Clivea miniata
Heliconia SPP.
Ornamental gingers (*Alpinia*, *Hedychium*, *Zingiber* SPP. and *Tapeinochilas ananassae*)
Strelitzia reginae
Vireyas

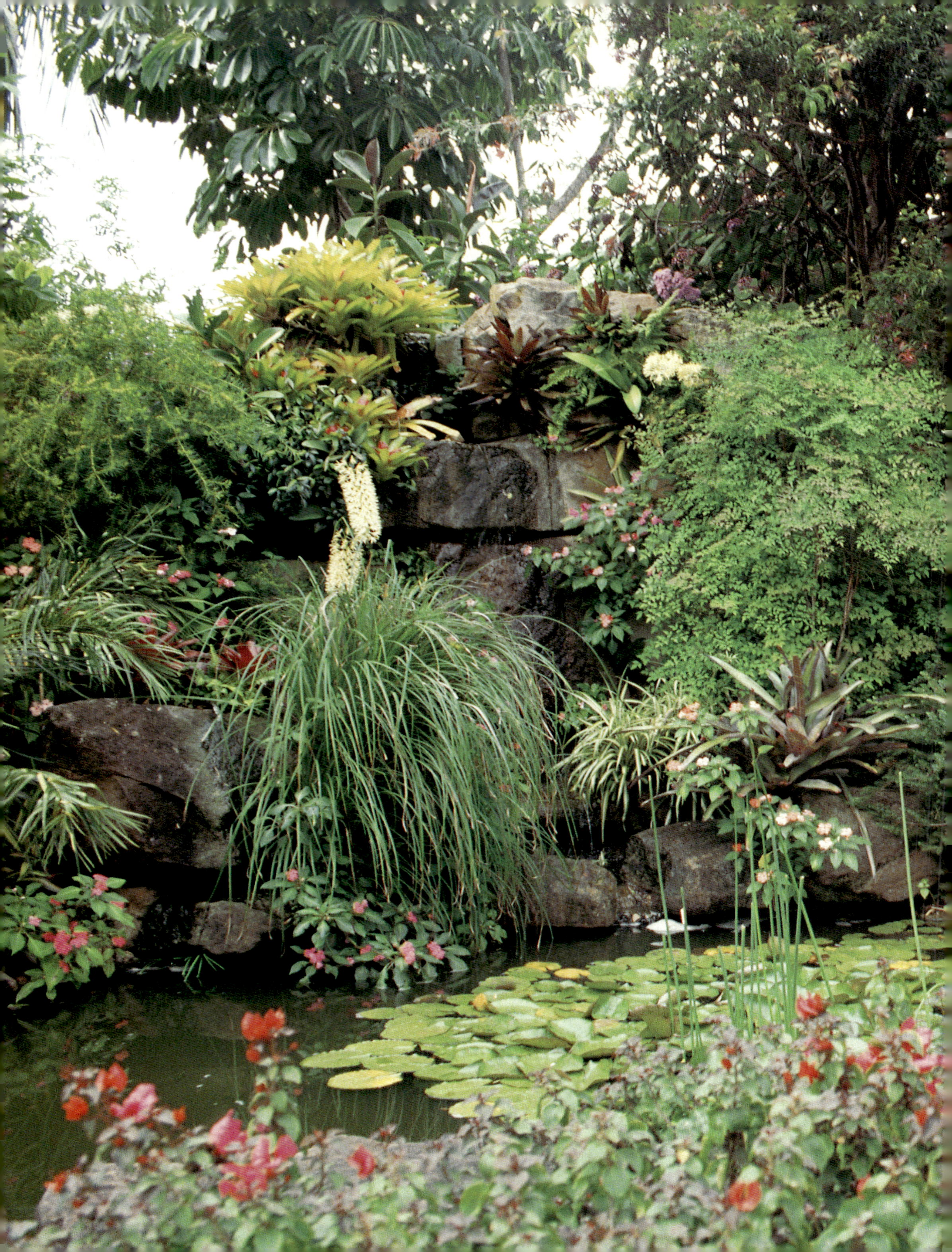

No truly tropical garden is complete without a water feature. This splendid cascade and pool looks very natural but it was actually constructed by the owner of the garden. Bromeliads sprout from the rocks, ferns cascade softly, king orchids add a touch of spring, impatiens and coleus add splashes of colour. The tree, top left, is an UMBRELLA TREE (Schefflera actinophylla).

A TROPICAL IDYLL

Just for fun, let's dream up a typically tropical garden. The street outside would be lined with poincianas, glowing red with blossom at Christmas. A stately palm would stand either side of the gateway, continuing up the long driveway, which would be bordered with a hedge of alternating white and salmon pink, gold or scarlet bougainvillea. Beyond the hedge, the sweeping lawn would be dotted with flowering trees and shrubs; frangipani would certainly be there, as would tibouchina and *Lagerstroemia indica*. The focal point of the front garden would be a large, ornamental tree; perhaps a jacaranda, fig or the gorgeous, pink-flowering *Cassia javanica*. There would be seating here, and perhaps some shade-loving plants to add ground-level greenery. Poinsettias would be massed around the base of the house, with brunfelsia and night jasmine planted nearby to give fragrance. Allamanda, quisqualis and other tropical twiners would ramble here and there over pergolas or up the verandah posts. There would be a swimming pool, surrounded by palms and tubs of small-growing flowering shrubs. The back boundary and corners would be turned into a true jungle of trees, shrubs, fleshy-leaved plants, climbers, epiphytes and ferns, with a small and very natural-looking stream gurgling through it. To add interest there might be a collection of a particular kind of plant; perhaps bromeliads or orchids or, in gardens higher up in the coastal ranges, the exquisite vireyas. And perhaps our garden might be large enough to feature some of the more unusual tree specimens, such as *Kigelia pinnata* with its large, curious, sausage-like pods. As a final touch — for remember this is our tropical ideal — the sea would be at the bottom of the garden.

With such a garden as this, there would be no need to yearn for holidays on a tropic isle. You would have it all right there on your doorstep.

The Tropical Touch • *33* •

A tropical rainforest garden

NATURE'S ULTIMATE TROPICAL GARDEN is undoubtedly the rainforest and it is very easy to turn an average suburban block into a jungle full of mystery and cool shade. Australian rainforest plants from northern areas can be used here to good effect, as well as those from rainforests in other parts of the world, including many foliage plants which we usually associate with indoor growing such as calatheas, spathiphyllums and aglaeonemas. These can be grown under a canopy of trees and tall shrubs. In large gardens, bamboo can be used to provide an appropriate backdrop, particularly if protection from exposure is required. Water in the form of a shallow pond or water course, dark and mysterious or with a pale sandy bottom, will simulate the pools and streams of the rainforest and help maintain humidity. It should be constantly recycled because mosquitoes breed in stagnant water.

Palms are usually the first choice for anyone creating a rainforest or jungle garden, because they combine the two concepts of 'rainforest' and 'tropical' more than any other plant. They are fast-growing, soon providing shade for other plants, and their straight, vertical, slender trunks support a sheltering foliage cover without taking up too much horizontal space below. This also allows for a great variety of palms to be grown in a small space and they look particularly good when planted in groups. Tree ferns need similar growing conditions to palms and do well alongside them.

Palm and treefern trunks provide vertical growing surfaces for climbing plants such as philodendrons and Kangaroo Vine (*Cissus antarctica*). At ground level, ferns and tropical foliage plants can be allowed to grow at will. The dominant greenery of the rainforest floor can be enlivened by the rich, glowing reds of cordylines and bromeliads. Other colour contrast is provided by the variegated dwarf umbrellas (*Schefflera arboricola*).

This kind of garden is the ultimate in low maintenance. Once established it looks after itself — and there is no lawn to mow. An automatic irrigation system is essential to provide the necessary humidity as well as to save time.

A rainforest garden is a cool and private refuge which gives the illusion of being far from the everyday world. For those people who may find such a proliferation of greenlife overwhelming, or who believe that it makes the house too dark, a good compromise is to set aside part of the garden as a rainforest retreat, not too close to the house and possibly where its density is desirable to block out unwanted sights and sounds on an otherwise vulnerable boundary.

Rainforest plants from the ground up

Hemigraphis SPP.
Syngonium SPP.
Bird's Nest Ferns (*Asplenium* SPP.)
Bromeliads
Cordyline SPP.
Aglaeonema SPP.
Caladiums (Elephant Ears)
Calathea SPP.
Colocasia SPP.
Croton (*Codiaeum* SPP.)
Dieffenbachia SPP.
Maranta SPP.
Monstera deliciosa (can be grown as climber) and the more delicate *M. friedrichsthalii*
Lepidozamia peroffskyana and *L. hopeii*
Pleomele reflexa
Orchids (terrestrial)
Philodendron scandens (vine)
Palms
Schefflera actinophylla and *S. arboricola* 'JACQUELINE' and 'MADELEINE'
Tree ferns

Australian rainforest trees and shrubs

(Some of the best-known are included in the other lists)
Acmena SPP.
Agathis robusta
Alloxylon flammeum
Alocasia macrorrhiza (CUNJEVOI)
Alpinia SPP.
Ardisia pachyrrhachis
Barklya syringifolia
Bowenia serrulata (BYFIELD FERN) and *B. spectabilis*
Caldcluvia australiensis
Cissus antarctica (vine)
Curcuma australasica (CAPE YORK LILY)
Darlingia SPP.
Dianella SPP.
Diploglottis SPP.
Doryanthes palmeri (SPEAR LILY)
Eupomatia laurina
Faradaya splendida (vine)
Maidenhair ferns (*Adiantum* SPP.) and other native rainforest ferns including KING FERN (*Todea barbara*)
Mugravea SPP.
Ochrosia elliptica
Phaleria clerodendron
Pothos longipes (climber)
Randia SPP.
Schelhammera multiflora
Staghorns and elkhorns
Stenocarpus SPP.
Syzygium SPP.
Waterhousea SPP.
Tetrastigma nitens (vine)
Xanthostemon chrysanthus (GOLDEN PENDA)

OVERLEAF
*Bird's Nest ferns (*Asplenium nidus*) are epiphytes which occur naturally in our rainforests. In the home garden they require little care and can be grown on trees, as they are here, to simulate their natural environment. They can also be grown on the floor of a rainforest garden.*

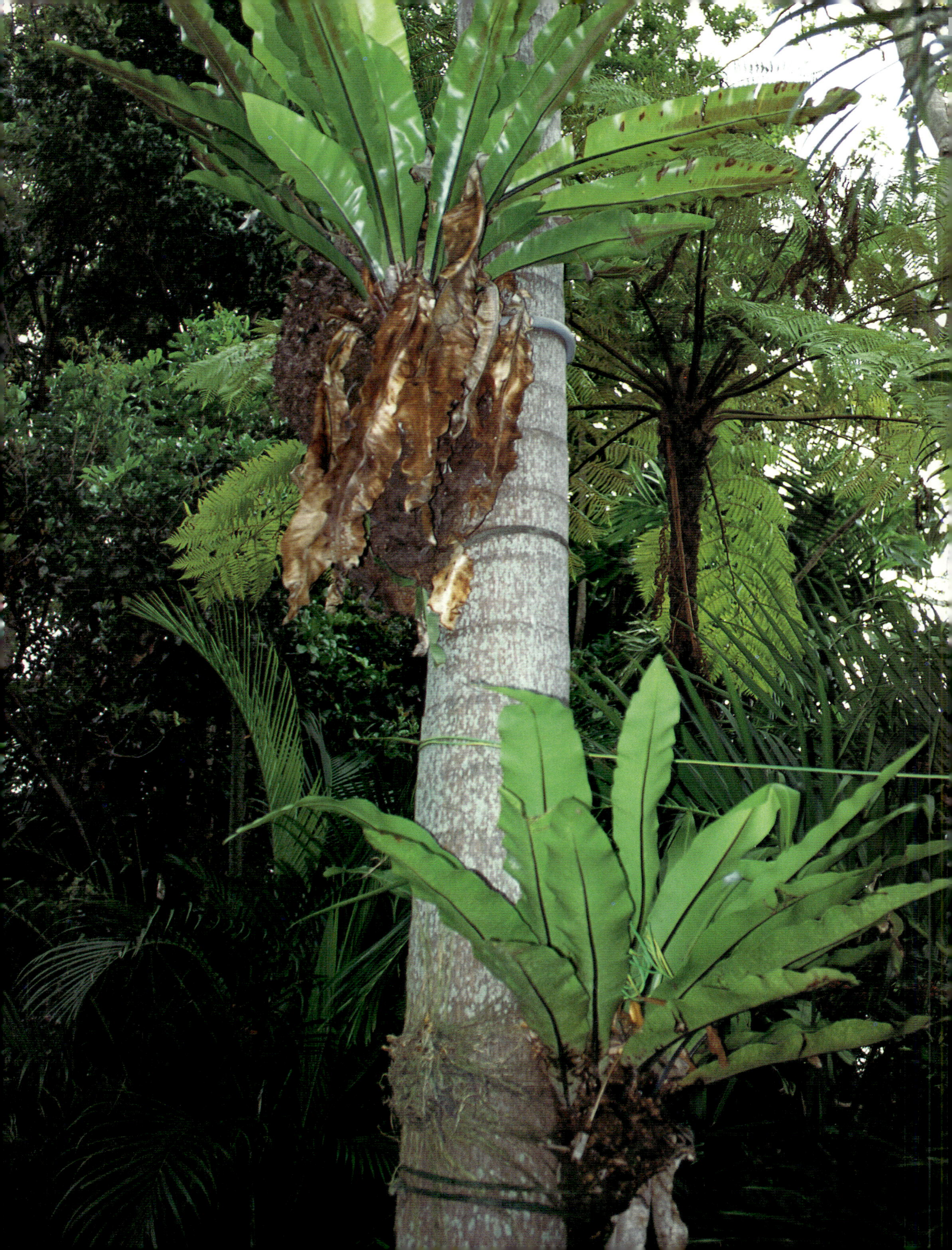

Pools, ponds and swimming pools

EARLY GARDENERS SUCH as the Babylonians and Persians knew the value of water for creating coolness in the garden. The Moors later developed water gardening to a fine art, as can be seen to this day in the Alhambra Palace at Granada in Spain, which is surrounded by hot, dry countryside. Water not only looks, feels and sounds cool, it actually does help cool the surrounding atmosphere. Every hot-climate garden should have at least one small water feature.

TYPES OF PONDS AND POOLS

Garden pools need to be lined; the methods used to make earth or clay farm dams are not suitable because of the small surface of water involved. Pool linings come in four basic types: reinforced concrete, prefabricated fibreglass mould, plastic or vinyl, butyl rubber.

Choice depends on the style of your garden, your personal taste and cost. Shallow pools lined with vinyl or butyl are often all that is necessary in an informal garden where a very natural appearance is desired. For a more formal garden a regular shaped pool is more suited—a square, rectangular, round or oblong—and a concrete-lined pool will probably be necessary, though there are some suitably shaped preformed fibreglass moulded pools.

Whether your pool choice is formal or informal, concrete is the most versatile lining material as well as the most permanent. You can dig a hole to any depth or shape required; round, square, rectangular or free-form, and line it with concrete. Unless the pool is very tiny, it should be reinforced with steel rods and mesh. A very large pool is best lined with the specially strengthened and waterproofed concrete used for swimming pools. Very large pools, and formal pools with corner angles, are in any case best built by a contractor, and you will, of course, need to obtain the necessary council permits. If you wish to do the work yourself, make sure you hire or purchase the correct tools and get the right advice from the supplier. Buying or borrowing a book on concreting or garden construction is a good idea also.

The concrete liner should be a minimum 10 cm thick, with a minimum cover of 5 cm over the reinforcing. Corners should be strengthened with extra reinforcing. Cement causes water to become alkaline, and may contain other toxins, so the pool must be cured before use. Traditionally this was done by filling the pond with water, allowing the lime to leach out for a couple of weeks, then emptying and refilling the pond. Today it is faster and easier to use an appropriate sealant, though this must be done thoroughly. Fill the pond as quickly as possible after sealing; this makes the concrete stronger. Whichever method you use to cure your pond, it is safer to wait a couple of weeks longer before introducing plants and fish.

A concrete pool can also be lined with a mixture of cement and fibreglass mixed together; the fibreglass compound is available from hardware stores and large garden centres which stock pool products.

Concrete ponds are often finished with a render, which, though not necessary, looks good and enhances the waterproofing. Renders come in various coloured plasters, mixed with cement. A vinyl liner can also be laid over the concrete.

Pools raised above the ground offer certain advantages, apart from an attractive appearance. They require less digging and you can sit on the edge and dangle your hand in the water, or feed the fish. Such pools have a concrete base and stone, brick or block edges. Building raised pools is a job for the contractor rather than the home gardener.

Prefabricated fibreglass moulds come in a variety of shapes and sizes and are very easy to install. If you invert the pool you can mark out the shape to be dug on the ground, digging the hole a little larger than the outline. In heavy soils it is best to fill a much larger hole with sand and use this as a bed for the mould. The pond must sit level with its rim at soil height. Once installed, alternately add water to the pool and backfill around the edge, a bit at a time, until the pool is filled and the backfilling completed.

Plastic or vinyl lined pools are very easy to build yourself and lend themselves to any informal size and shape. They are obviously not suited to formal pools with sharp corners. The liner can be laid straight into a hole, though, with very hard-to-work soil, an additional layer of sand will help to fill cracks and bumps and make a good bed for the liner.

To calculate the amount of liner required: add the maximum width of the pool to twice its depth to get the width; to get the length, add maximum length to twice the depth; then add at least 15 cm to both width and depth to extend around the edge; more if required. With thin plastic, at least two and preferably three layers are needed.

The pool hole should have gently sloping slides so that soil doesn't collapse inwards. While slowly filling the pool with water, continually pull the liner into place to keep it as smooth and wrinkle-free as possible. Hold the edges in place with bricks or rocks, then spade soil around the rim to disguise the edges and integrate the pool with the garden.

Vinyl is stronger and more durable than plastic sheeting and, though more costly, you will need only one layer rather than two or more. Both can easily be ripped by stones, sharp implements or animal claws. So be careful when planting, replanting, placing rocks in the pool, and cleaning. And keep dogs and wildlife out of the pool.

Butyl rubber is a synthetic rubber which is more UV resistant than plastic or vinyl and is also tougher and less liable to rip. It is laid in the same way.

Siting

A garden pool should be constructed in a natural depression or on a level site. Sloping sites involve extra work. Pools look very attractive in the shade but will also become filled with tree litter. Direct sunlight encourages algae growth.

- Always ensure that the hole is free of rocks, stones, tree roots and other obstructions. The surface should be as smooth as possible.
- Make sure the pool is level; use the correct equipment such as spirit levels. Prefabricated pools can be particularly difficult to keep level during installation.
- While the pool surface must be level, it is more interesting if there are different depths in the pool for this will allow you to grow a wider range of aquatic plants. Prefabricated pool moulds often have different depths; if you are using concrete or a fabric liner, dig different depths in the pool hole and fit the lining accordingly.
- Hide the lining at the edges of informal pools with stones, rocks and/or gravel. Leave an area clear, either paved (a couple of large, smooth stones laid flat will do) or concreted, so that you (and possibly wildlife) can have easy access for plant care and pool maintenance.
- If you want your pond to look natural, leave a surrounding area close to the rim free for planting with appropriate species.

Finishing off

Fountains are an attractive addition to any pool. Some send up a gentle jet of water which splashes down into the pool, others send up a powerful spray. The effect is cooling and also discourages mosquitoes which breed in still water. Fountains come in a variety of designs, many of them quite elaborate. Simple fountains, in which only the jet of water rather than any elaborate statuary is seen, are best for informal gardens. Rocks, tree stumps and large, ornamental pieces of driftwood add a natural touch and provide a perching place for birds.

RUNNING WATER

There is no end to the ways in which water can be used in the garden. Instead of one pool, a series of connecting pools can be created using recycled water driven by a pump. Other water features include waterfalls and streams. With time and imagination, it is not too difficult to create a whole system of pools, streams and waterfalls all around the garden. The small, shallow pools and streambed are easy to construct; waterfalls can be made with a few carefully arranged rocks. Moulded fibreglass waterfalls are available. Once the system is in place, the water can be constantly recycled through it at a very moderate cost in electricity.

Equipment

Once a pool and water system has been built, one or more electric pumps will be needed to drive waterfalls, fountains and artificial streams. The pump should be submersible — and also silent. Buy the best pump you can afford, powerful enough to do the job required, and with waterproof fittings and cable. Installation of electrical equipment in the garden should be done by a qualified electrician, particularly where water is concerned. If you must do the job yourself, it is safest to select a low voltage pump with adaptor. Make sure any equipment is installed according to the manufacturer's instructions.

PLANTING IN THE WATER

Some aquatic plants just float on the surface of the water and are thus very easy to establish. Others need to be anchored in containers; waterlilies come into this category. Traditionally they are planted in a mix of one part well-rotted animal manure to three parts earth but nowadays especially formulated aquatic potting medium is available which holds firm under water and doesn't release too many polluting nutrients. As waterlilies are heavy feeders, controlled-release or another phosphorus-rich fertiliser can be added to the mix; this is not necessary with other deep-water plants. The plant and mix is placed in a container which has plenty of holes so that the soil can 'breathe'. Special containers are available but laundry baskets (for several plants in one container), wicker baskets (which break down in time) and even buckets and ice-cream cartons are suitable provided they are given a couple of holes. As the top of the plant must be on the surface of the water, the containers may need to be placed on bricks or some other object to hold them at the right height.

Marginal plants which grow at a fairly shallow depth around the edge of ponds and lakes are planted in the same way as deep-water plants, but at shallower depths around the edge, so that at least two-thirds of their vegetation is above the surface of the water.

MAINTAINING THE POOL

Like soil, a pool needs to be in good health, with the right chemical balance for plants to grow well there and fish (if you have them) to thrive. To maintain a pool with clear, clean water, free of algae bloom, you should note the following points:

- Don't overfill with plants. If the surface of the pond is covered with an untidy tangle then you are likely to have problems. By contrast, waterlilies can be allowed almost to cover the surface, provided they are not choked with other plants. If a pool looks overcrowded, it is.
- Don't overstock with fish. If in doubt, reduce the numbers. Books on fishkeeping will give information about the best type of fish for the garden and the optimum number for a given body of water.
- The right amount of plants and fish are usually enough to keep a pool clean and healthy. If you don't want to grow anything in the pool then you may need to install filters and even chlorinators to keep the water clear.
- Try to protect the pool from stormwater runoff which can cause contamination by pollutants. These can include fuel and cleaning chemicals, garden chemicals and fertilisers. Chemicals can poison fish and plants; fertiliser encourages algae to form. If contamination occurs, flush out with a hose.
- Biological filters which use bacteria to convert problem elements in the pond to usable plant food are also available. These are particularly useful in large ponds which contain fish. They solve algae problems and keep the water very clear. Other systems are also available which filter out solids from the water in stages, using coarse, absorbent materials.
- An algae build-up can be cleared with chemical products available from hardware stores, pool shops and large garden centres. Otherwise, remove algae regularly by hand. You might also try a very old English country remedy which works wonders in an otherwise well-managed garden pool. Buy a bale of barley straw and use it at the rate of about 10 g of straw per m^2 of water — or more if that is convenient. As it rots, the straw produces an algae-inhibiting chemical. Keep the straw tied together in a bundle, bale or enclosed in mesh; in a very large pond it is more effective if distributed at different points. The treatment will need renewing about once a year, preferably in spring. Wheat straw or hay will also work, but not as effectively as barley straw.

Deep-water plants

T — suited to tropics
Ceratopteris SPP.
Myriophyllum aquaticum (PARROT FEATHER)
Nuphar SPP.
Nymphoides SPP.
SACRED LOTUS (*Nelumbo nucifera*)
WATERLILY (*Nymphaea* SPP.)
WATER TRUMPET (*Cryptocoryne beckettii*)
Victoria amazonica (T)
Villarsia reniformis (RUNNING MARSHFLOWER)

Oxygenators

(These are particularly efficient at maintaining the correct oxygen levels so necessary to pool life)
Anacharis SPP.
Ceratophyllum demersum
EEL GRASS (*Vallisneria spiralis*)
Egeria densa
Limnophila indica
Potamogeton SPP.
Ranunculus aquatilis
 R. trichophyllus
Vallisneria SPP.
WATER STARWORT (*Callitriche* SPP.)
Utricularia australis (YELLOW BLADDERWORT)

Surface floaters

Azolla SPP.
Ceratopteris thalictroides (WATER FERN)
Heteranthera SPP.
Marsilea SPP. (NARDOO)
Najas SPP. (BUSH PONDWEED)

Marginal plants

Baumea articulata (JOINTED TWIG RUSH)
Carex SPP.
Cyperus alternifolius
 C. exaltatus
Iris laevigata
 I. pseudacorus
MARSH MARIGOLD (*Caltha palustris*)
Orontium aquaticum (GOLDEN WATER CLUB)
PICKEREL RUSH, PICKEREL WEED (*Pontederia cordata*)
Restio SPP.
Thalia dealbata

Warning: Beware of bringing plants into your garden from dams and streams outside. Some may be declared weeds which will take over your pond and possibly spread elsewhere. Gardeners should be aware that almost any plant in the warm and humid lushness of tropical waters can become a problem, so do consult the local nursery or the botanic gardens before you give or accept gifts of strange plants.

The combination of lush foliage, clear water, skilfully placed rocks and a pale aggregate surface resembling sand makes this swimming pool in a small suburban garden look just like a tropical island hideaway. Palms and foliage plants provide welcome shade without dropping litter into the pool. Crotons and cordylines add colour at right.

SWIMMING POOLS

The largest body of water in a hot climate garden is usually the swimming pool, which is also the focus of family entertainment. Whether the pool is rectangular and formal, or free-form and resembling a natural pool in the forest, plantings must be compatible with people (i.e. not prickly), must permit human traffic around the edge and must not drop debris into the pool. Self-cleaning palms are ideal for this purpose, as are large-leaved foliage plants (where there is shade) and many neat shrubs with tidy habits. Avoid plants with fruit which becomes messy underfoot, or with light and fluffy seedheads which blow into the pool, as well as those with thorns, very sharp edges and heavy seasonal leaf-shedding.

Make sure plantings are far enough away from the pool not to be affected by splashing; the salt or chlorine solutions used to keep pools in healthy condition are damaging to plants, including lawn. Tall palms, succulents and salt-resistant plants are less susceptible than most shrubs and plants with soft foliage such as coleus and rex begonias.

Sun warms the surface of the water, but a pool which is in full sun all day is less pleasant than one which receives shade for part of it, preferably in the afternoon. Trees planted on the northern, north-western and western boundaries (but sufficiently distant from the pool not to cause problems) will provide shade. Trees on the western side will also protect against winter westerlies.

Plants in containers provide greenery and colour without being able to spread their roots and make a mess, which means they can be placed fairly close to the water. Be careful, though, when watering, to avoid washing dirt and fertiliser into the pool.

One way of adding a really tropical effect to a pool is to house the filter pump in a grotto or disguise it with a waterfall which recycles water into the main swimming pool. These can be planted with ferns and other 'tropical'-looking plants.

Plants for poolside plantings with a tropical look

Trees

Barklya syringifolia
Buckinghamia celsissima
FRANGIPANI
GOLDEN PENDA
Grevillea baileyana
Melicope elleryana syn. *Euodia*
Palms (self-cleaning, in tubs or in-ground)
Tipuana tipu syn. *speciosa*
UMBRELLA TREE (*Schefflera actinophylla*)

Trees in tubs

Figs
Palms

Shrubs and foliage plants

(These can be grown in-ground or in tubs.)
SH — shade
Allamanda SPP. (shrub forms)
Alocasia macrorrhiza SH
Alpinia SPP. SH
BYFIELD FERN (*Bowenia serrulata*) SH
Bromeliad SPP. SH
Calathea SPP. SH
Colocasia SPP. SH
Cordyline SPP. SH
CROTON (*Codiaeum* SPP.)
Cycas revoluta
Dianella SPP.
Dieffenbachia SPP. SH
Dietes bicolor
Dracaena SPP.
Duranta SPP. (low-growing gold and variegated leaf species)
DWARF UMBRELLA TREE (*Schefflera arboricola* cultivars)
Hosta SPP. SH
Ixora SPP. (part shade)
Lepidozamia peroffskyana
Lomandra SPP.
Mussaenda SPP.
Ornamental grasses
Pentas SPP.
Poinsettia SPP.
Randia SPP.
ZAMIA FERN (*Bowenia spectabilis*) SH

Screens

Acalypha SPP.
BAMBOO (non-invasive)
Calliandra SPP.
Duranta SPP.
Mussaenda SPP.
Plumbago SPP.
Tecomaria SPP.

A seaside garden

GARDENING BY THE SEA presents special problems because of generally sandy soils, wind, salt spray and sandblasting of tender stems and leaves. At the same time it offers the compensation that tangy sea breezes have a freshening effect on plants, helping to prevent fungal diseases and deterring many insect pests. Many vegetables do better by the sea, seeming to benefit from some exposure to sea winds. Most other plants can be grown at the coast provided that they are given enough protection.

Much depends on just how far from the sea your garden is located, and what stands between in the way of protection. Tall buildings, high sand dunes or a belt of trees will all act as barriers against wind and salt spray, but strong on-shore breezes can carry salt spray a surprising distance inland. During gales, plants up to several kilometres from the seashore can suffer salt burn. When this occurs the garden will benefit from a thorough hosing of all susceptible plants, just as a safeguard.

SOIL

It is often wrongly assumed that coastal sand dunes lack nutrients. In fact they are quite richly endowed with decaying matter from the vegetation growing there, as well as minerals. Many such soils support large stands of littoral rainforest; others resemble heathland, with a profusion of wildflowers in spring. Even the frontal dunes carry some vegetation, though they are less rich in nutrients than those further back from the sea.

However, dune plants are especially adapted to their habitat and are very efficient at obtaining nutrition; whereas garden plants which have been bred over many years to depend on very high nutrition levels for good performance need heavier, richer soil. Once the original plant cover is destroyed on sandy soils, their nutrient level drops dramatically and must be artificially supplemented.

The main problem with coastal sand dunes is that they are very free-draining. Nutrients are leached out quickly and water does not stay long enough around plant roots. Therefore the gardener has to build the soil structure up to provide a growing medium which can hold plants firmly in place, feed them adequately and retain moisture. Soil can be improved with the addition of organic matter such as leaf litter, rotted sawdust, animal manures, grass clippings, straw, sugarcane trash, bagasse and whatever suitably organic products and by-products are available in your area. Compost made from a variety of matter, either purchased or home-made, is the best material of all. If you are not in a hurry to establish your garden, the organic matter can just be left on the surface of the sand and allowed to rot down. But if you want things to happen more quickly, it will need to be dug in.

The other obvious way of improving sandy soil is to bring in good soil from elsewhere. If large trees and shrubs are to be established, any imported soil will need to be well dug in and if the garden is large it may be worth having this done with mechanical

Grevillea 'Honey Gem', one of the most popular varieties for home gardens. Many grevilleas will thrive in coastal areas, provided they have light, slightly acid soil and good drainage (see page 100).

digging equipment. For small plants, a layer of topsoil added to the sand will be sufficient to give them a start, after which the regular addition of compost, and mulching of the surface, will keep them growing.

Mulching is beneficial to all gardens, but for coastal gardens it is particularly important. Regular applications of organic mulch not only enrich and improve the structure of the soil beneath, they also prevent moisture loss and keep the soil surface from becoming too hot.

Coastal soils may be either acid or alkaline. Those which are peaty, or support littoral rainforest, will certainly be acid and will need sweetening with dolomite if you want to grow many annuals, perennials and vegetables. Soil acidifiers such as chelated iron and other products available from garden centres can be added to alkaline soils around acid-loving plants such as azaleas, but this will only temporarily acidify the immediate area. In the long term, the addition of organic matter to the soil will lower the pH level to the satisfaction of most plants. A simple pH test with a kit bought from the garden centre or hardware store will tell you whether your soil is acid, alkaline or nicely neutral.

As with any garden, a richer and better quality soil is needed to grow annuals and vegetables; in coastal areas this will almost always need to be purchased initially, and its quality maintained with annual additions of compost and a thorough mulching regime.

Not all coastal soils are sandy. Some, particularly those high on headlands, are rocky. This poses a different problem of insufficient soil to anchor plant roots and provide adequate moisture and nutrition.

Soil can be built up or imported to a depth sufficient to create the garden you desire. Or, you can make the best of the location and plant shallow-rooted species which thrive by making use of every crevice. With plants that need to get their roots down, even if their habit is spreading, a reasonably deep hole should be made, or an existing crevice enlarged as much as possible, and filled with soil or potting mix. This will give plants sufficient stability and nutrition to start with; after that they should be able to manage on their own. A light application of fertiliser now and again will help but most plants which thrive in rocky soil should not be fed too much or too often; they are extremely efficient at obtaining nutrition from what is available naturally. For the same reason, light mulching only is desirable. Plants which are designed to scramble over rocky surfaces cannot do so if their way is blocked by heavy mulch.

Plants for rocky ground

- *Bauera rubioides*
- *Boronia megastigma*
- *Brachyscome* spp. (daisies)
- *Canavalia rosea* (COAST JACKBEAN)
- *Dampiera* spp.
- *Darwinia* spp.
- *Erigeron karvinskianus* (COASTAL DAISY)
- *Frankenia pauciflora*
- Grevilleas (some prostrate forms are suitable)
- *Hibbertia scandens* and other *Hibbertia* spp. if available
- *Howea longifolia* dwarf
- *Kennedia* spp.
- *Kunzea* spp.
- *Leptospermum flavescens* prostrate form
- *Melaleuca incarna* dwarf
- *Mesembryanthemum* spp.
- Paper daisies
- *Portulaca* spp.
- ROSEMARY (prostrate form)
- *Scaevola* spp. (FAN FLOWERS)
- *Thryptomene saxicola*
- THYME (*Thymus* spp.)

PROTECTION

If you study what is left of the natural vegetation along the sea shore, you will see that there is a first line of defence consisting of tough, tall-growing plants. The leaves are usually narrow and hard-surfaced and they are resistant both to strong winds and salt spray. Casuarinas and banksias are typical of such plants. This first line of defence needs to be established in the home garden; behind it other plants will be able to flourish. The screen should be several metres thick if room permits; if the garden is right at the beach edge then it is advisable to use native species such as casuarinas and banksias in the forefront. Other tough, wind-resistant and salt-tolerant species can then be planted behind them to form a shrubbery. Planting should be graduated from tallest species nearest the shore to smallest species towards the house and garden. If room is limited then a thinner line of the hardiest species only can be planted. When establishing a screen planting in any garden it is always wise to use a variety of species. This means if any don't thrive, or suddenly die, then there is still plenty of cover.

wind direction

on the leeward side protection is afforded for thirty times tree height

still air banked up against windbreak gives five times tree height protection to windward

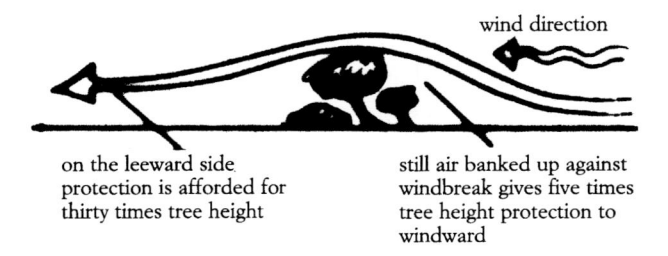

Windbreaks in seaside gardens follow the same rules as for all windbreaks, except that salt-tolerant, bushy, wind-resistant species should be planted on the outside to meet the prevailing wind. Note that height should suit garden scale; extreme height is not needed as protection extends to thirty times the height of trees on the leeward side, and five times the height on the windward side due to wind-lift over still air.

— *A Seaside Garden* • 45 •

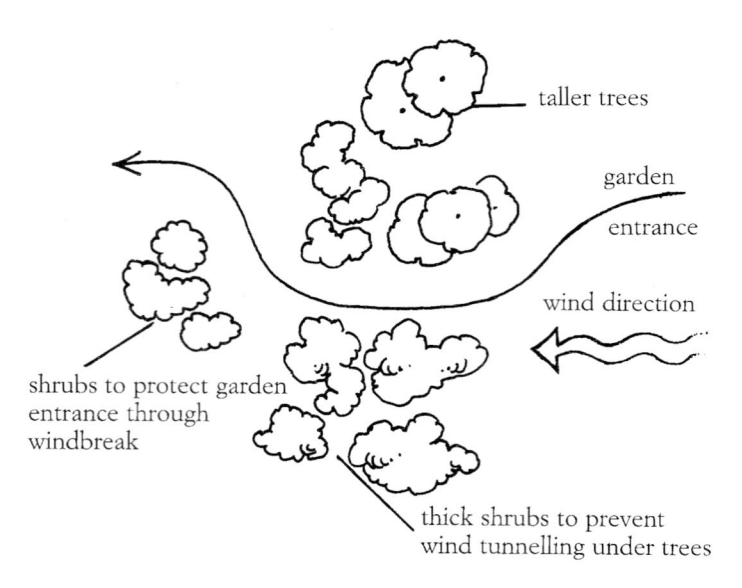

Diagram labels:
- taller trees
- garden entrance
- wind direction
- shrubs to protect garden entrance through windbreak
- thick shrubs to prevent wind tunnelling under trees

Plants for the first line of defence

These plants are tough enough for the most severe coastal conditions and should make up the frontline section of your screen.

Acacia sophorae (COASTAL WATTLE)
Allocasuarina verticillata
Atriplex cinerea (GREY SALTBUSH)
Banksia SPP. e.g. *B. integrifolia*, *B. robur* and *B. serrata*
Casuarina equisetifolia
Correa alba
Hibiscus tiliaceus
Leptospermum laevigatum (COAST TEA TREE)
Melaleuca quinquenervia (PAPER BARK)
Metrosideros excelsa
  M. thompsonii (NEW ZEALAND CHRISTMAS TREE)
Pandanus pedunculatus
Rhagodia SPP. (SALTBUSH)
Westringia fruticosa (COASTAL ROSEMARY)
Yucca filamentosa

Plants for coastal screening

The following plants grow well very close to the sea but need some protection by other plants such as those listed above. Place them among or just behind trees and shrubs in the front line of your screen:

Acacia concurrens
  A. longifolia
Acmena smithii
  A. hemilampra syn. *Eugenia*
Acronychia imperforata
Alectryon coriaceus
Banksia ericifolia
Callitris glaucophylla (BRIBIE ISLAND PINE)
Casuarina glauca
Cupaniopsis anacardioides
Elaeocarpus obovatus
Eugenia reinwardtiana (BEACH CHERRY)
Euroschinus falcatus
Glochidion ferdinandii (CHEESE TREE)
Grevillea banksii (various forms)
Lagunaria patersonii (NORFOLK ISLAND HIBISCUS)
Macaranga tanarius
Melaleuca quinquenervia (PAPERBARK)
Melia azederach (WHITE CEDAR)
Syzygium banksii

COASTAL SCREENING PLANTS HAVE A HARD LIFE so they need to become accustomed to their tough conditions. Very young plants are better able to do this than larger specimens, because they have time to adapt. When they come fresh from the nursery, they should be left in their pots for a week or two, with regular watering, so that they have a chance to harden before planting. After establishment, don't spoil them with too much fertiliser or water; if the roots are forced to forage for food and moisture they will spread out, and downwards, to anchor the plant strongly. Plants which receive large amounts of fertiliser and water may become too sappy and tender instead of developing the hardiness necessary for surviving constant exposure.

Although most of the plants suitable for screening are fast growing, it will still take two years or more for even the fastest growing to be large enough to form a barrier. As an interim measure, you can make screens of shadecloth or

> hessian to shelter the young screen plants and help them grow faster, while the rest of the garden is being established. It is, however, difficult to put up screens high enough to keep out salt spray.
>
> Instead of a plant barrier, you may prefer artificial screens of a permanent material. If you can't afford a wall, a tall timber or brushwood fence, or timber lattice can be used. Beautify latticework with creepers which will also increase the screening cover. These constructed screens will not usually be high enough to keep out salt spray, though it depends on the position of your land, so a few tall-growing species will enhance the protective effect of a wall or fence.

GENERAL CARE

Watering

Gardens on sand will require more watering than most because of the free drainage. In a hot climate, this can add up to considerable water use. The addition of organic matter to the soil will improve its ability to hold water but lawns, trees, shrubs and shallow-rooted flowering plants will still require watering several times a week. The most effective method is drip irrigation which reaches the roots of plants instead of evaporating quickly on the surface of the sand and possibly never reaching the roots at all. A cheap solution is to use plastic bottles pierced sufficiently to ensure a steady drip; thrust into the sand at the base of plants and fill periodically.

Other options are soaker hoses with perforations along their length, or leaving the ordinary hose running to drench thoroughly. Your watering regime will depend on plants and conditions; the usual rule applies — if the soil is dry below the surface, water is needed.

Gardeners in coastal areas can add to the available town water supply by putting in rainwater tanks, or bores if groundwater is not too saline. These are particularly useful on days when the use of sprinklers is banned, and also reduce water costs. It is not too difficult to connect these to ponds in which water can be recycled for ornamental purposes, while being available for garden use during dry periods.

Fertilising, mulching and weeding

The relative infertility of sandy soils from which natural cover has been removed means that they require plenty of fertiliser if exotic plants are to grow there. Any standard fertiliser can be used, but the feeding regime must contain some organic bulk fertilisers such as animal manure, nutrition-enriched compost or blood and bone to build up the soil.

Mulching is a must on sandy coastal soils to reduce soil moisture loss and overheating. Use organic materials so that when they break down they improve soil structure. See pages 222–3. Most coastal gardens today are established with a cover of pinebark or similar coarse material which is slow to break down, so other mulches will help. Remove weeds as quickly as possible as they will compete with garden plants for whatever water and soil is available.

Shrubs for coastal gardens
T or ST — best suited to tropics or sub-tropics only
Acacia longifolia (SYDNEY WATTLE)
Akocanthera spectabilis
Austromyrtus dulcis (MIDGEN BERRY)
Baeckea 'SPARKLES'
Coprosma repens (MIRROR PLANT)
Correa alba
DIOSMA (*Coleonema* SPP.) ST
Elaeagnus angustifolia
Grevillea SPP.
Hakea florulenta and *H. gibbosa*
Hibiscus SPP.
Metrosideros SPP. and varieties
Murraya paniculata (MOCK ORANGE)
OLEANDER (*Nerium oleander*) normal and dwarf forms
PINEAPPLE GUAVA (*Feijoa sellowiana*)
Plumbago auriculata
Raphiolepis indica and *R. × delacourii*
Russelia juncea syn. *equisetiformis*
Tamarix SPP. (TAMARIND)
Viburnum tinus
Vitex trifolia (silvery leaves, blue flowers)
Westringia fruticosa (COASTAL ROSEMARY)

Low shrubs and groundcovers

Acanthus mollis
Actinotus helianthi (FLANNEL FLOWER)
Brachyscome SPP. (daisies)
Cistus varieties (ROCK ROSE)
CONDAMINE COUCH (*Phyla nodiflora*)
Coprosma × kirkii 'VARIEGATA'
Erigeron karvinskianus (COASTAL DAISY)
Gazania ringens
Hibbertia scandens (TWINING GUINEA FLOWER)
JUNIPER (*Juniperus* SPP.)
Lantana montevidensis
Leptospermum scoparium 'HORIZONTALIS'
Mesembryanthemum SPP.
Osteospermum ecklonis (gazania-like flowers)
Paper daisies (*Chrysocephalum apiculatum* syn. *Helichrysum* SPP. and *Bracteantha bracteata*)
Portulaca SPP.
Sedum rubrotinctum (STONECROP, JELLY BEANS)
Sempervivum SPP.
Viola hederacea (NATIVE VIOLET)
WANDERING JEW (*Tradescantia fluminensis*)

Perennials and small flowering plants

Agapanthus SPP.
Alpinia SPP.
Babiana stricta
BIRD OF PARADISE (*Strelitzia reginae* and other strelitzias)
CANNA varieties
Clivia miniata (for shade)
Crinum pedunculatum (SWAMP LILY)
GERANIUM (*Pelargonium* SPP.)
Hedychium SPP. (GINGER LILY)
KANGAROO PAW (*Anigozanthos* SPP.)
Limonium sinuatum (STATICE)
MARGUERITE daisies (*Chrysanthemum frutescens*)
SALVIA (flowering ornamental sages)
Scaevola SPP. (FAN FLOWERS)
Stokesia laevis (STOKES' ASTER)

Trees

Angophora costata
Callistemon salignus and *C. viminalis*
FRANGIPANI (*Plumeria* SPP.)
Grevillea robusta
Lagerstroemia indica (CREPE MYRTLE, PRIDE OF INDIA)
Melicope elleryana syn. *Euodia*
Melaleuca SPP. suited to coastal situations
NORFOLK ISLAND PINE (*Araucaria heterophylla*, too large for most gardens)
PLUM PINE (*Podocarpus elatus*)
POINCIANA (*Delonix regia*)
RED-FLOWERING GUM (*Corymbia ficifolia* syn. *Eucalyptus*)
Scolopia braunii (good windbreak plant)
Syzygium oleosum (LILLY PILLY) and *S. paniculatum*

Palms

It is a popular misconception that all palms can be grown by the sea. In fact, most of them come from tropical rainforests and cannot tolerate exposure to wind and salt spray. Some of these can be grown in seaside gardens if given adequate protection. Those which do well without protection include:
BANGALOW PALM (*Archontophoenix cunninghamiana* which is more tolerant of coastal conditions than its close relative, the popular *A. alexandrae*; however the latter will do well enough if given protection from salt winds.)
CARPENTARIA PALM (*Carpentaria acuminata*)
Chamaerops humilis (EUROPEAN FAN PALM) ST
Chrysalidocarpus SPP. (often wrongly labelled as Areca palms)
COCONUT PALM (*Cocos nucifera*)
COTTON PALM (*Washingtonia robusta*) ST
Livistona australis (needs protection while young)
  L. chinensis

Phoenix canariensis (Canary Island Date Palm) st
Ptychosperma spp.
Palmetto (*Sabal* spp.) st
Queen Palm (*Syagrus romanzoffianium* syn. *Cocos plumosa*)

Climbers

Bougainvillea
Dipladenia spp.
Hoya australis
Jasmine
Pandorea spp.
Petrea volubilis
Pyrostegia spp.
Solandra spp.
Solanum jasminoides
Tecomanthe hillii (Fraser Island Creeper)
Tecomaria capensis

When the sun is hot and the temperature high, a well-planned garden can provide a cool refuge. Deep verandahs, shaded by a profusion of greenery, is the traditional way of keeping the heat at bay; it also helps integrate the house with the garden. Syagrus palms provide a tropical frame; tree ferns provide privacy around the verandah. The plant with small yellow flowers beyond the palm at right is Thevetia peruviana, *see page 82.*

Other Plants

Cycads (*Cycas* and *Zamia* spp.)
Grass Trees (*Xanthorrhoea* spp.)

— *A Seaside Garden* •49•

The natural look

Although the plants that grow there look tough, coastal dunes and heathlands are very vulnerable to the changes brought about by housing development. Developers tend to clear subdivisions of all the natural vegetation, a practice we should all discourage. And even if they don't, the householders who arrive from elsewhere want to impose their own gardening notions upon the natural landscape. This has several adverse effects:

- ❖ The natural bushland which once graced our coastlines is fast disappearing except in a handful of national parks.
- ❖ Fertilisers (chemical or organic) used on lawns and garden plants wash down into adjacent bushland, or swamps, and destroy plants which are adapted to obtaining nutrients from sandy coastal soils. This can mean the death of entire ecosystems of which these plants are an integral part.
- ❖ The vast amounts of water needed for traditional gardening in coastal areas is expensive and often environmentally damaging to supply. Lawns are particularly heavy water users.

Gardeners who value our environmental heritage, and who want to make things easy on themselves, might well consider maintaining and enhancing the natural vegetation on a seaside housing block. Houses can be designed and built so that plants receive minimal disturbance. A relatively undisturbed block can be left in its pristine condition; a partly cleared block can be revegetated. This is not easy with many hard-to-grow dune and heathland species; expert help may be needed or else you may concentrate only on those plants which are easy to obtain and grow. Creating and preserving such a garden can be an interesting and worthwhile exercise because it becomes a showcase for indigenous vegetation.

If this challenge doesn't excite you, then consider preserving as much of the existing vegetation as possible, maybe adding to it a bit, and mixing in some exotics which require little or no fertilising and minimum water. Many plants on the coastal garden lists (pages 46–9), and those from arid areas, are suitable. You may even grow your herbs, vegetables, roses and other garden favourites in containers around the house, leaving the rest of the garden in its natural state. Many interesting compromises and combinations are possible; the main aim being to have a beautiful garden which complements rather than harms the surrounding environment. Most of our now heavily populated coastal regions have at least one good native plant nursery which sells indigenous species; staff will be able to advise on planting and care.

Hot and dry gardens

CREATING A GARDEN WHERE TEMPERATURES are high for most of the year and rainfall is low is certainly a challenge. However, there are some advantages. For instance, pests are usually fewer (though when they come they tend to do so in plague proportions) and fungal disease is less common than in humid, coastal regions.

Much depends on how much water is available. The dry inland boasts relatively few large rivers which flow all year. Where they exist, some magnificent gardens have been created even in areas where rainfall is low. Farmers and graziers usually rely on bore and dam water; the first is often unsuitable for many plants and there is rarely sufficient dam water to waste on the garden. As for those who live in towns, the water supplies are often inadequate during droughts to meet gardening needs. And there are few sights sadder for gardeners than a garden dying of thirst.

It makes sense, therefore, to concentrate your gardening efforts on plants which are adapted to hot, dry conditions. A small area might be set aside for growing vegetables, flowers and a few shrubs and other plants with fairly high water requirements which can perhaps be supplied from tanks or some other storage, or town water if available. But the bulk of the garden should consist of species with low water needs, which are efficient at storing water, or can go without water for long periods provided there is adequate seasonal rainfall and perhaps some additional water from the domestic supply in between. As these plants usually have low fertiliser needs, your workload will be fairly light once the garden is established. The drier your area, the more limited your choice of plants.

SOIL

Some areas which regularly experience long, dry periods also have deep, loamy soils. For the most part, however, inland soils are shaly, sandy and infertile, rich but hard and heavy red volcanic soils, or the dark, cracking clays which make gardening very hard indeed. They will all benefit from the addition of organic matter to improve their tilth; this is mandatory with very sandy soils (see page 43). Clay soils will be opened up for penetration by plant roots by adding gypsum. Most of these soils are very hard to dig. Of course, topsoil can be brought in from elsewhere, and this may be a good idea for small sections such as a vegetable or rose garden, but it will be very expensive for large areas. If time permits, much the best solution in the long term is to improve the soil by heavy mulching until the surface is easy to dig over for beds or dig into for planting holes. The no-dig method (pages 184–5) can be used for establishing small plants or you can get in a mechanical digger and have planting areas thoroughly dug over to the required depth for planting your larger species.

If you are in a hurry to establish a garden in soil which is hard to dig, holes for trees and shrubs will

The striking flowers of Strelitzia reginae *strongly resemble the heads of large birds with long, pointed beaks and colourful crests, which is why this plant is commonly known as* BIRD OF PARADISE *or* CRANESBILL *(see page 132). It can withstand long periods without water which makes it an excellent choice for hot, dry gardens.*

need to be wide and fairly deep, so that plant roots have a chance to develop in earth which has been broken up, before they have to tackle the tough stuff. Imported good quality soil or potting mix in the hole will give the plants a good start. If you have the time and the energy you could dig up your own soil heap in a corner of the garden; piling it up and working it until it is a good tilth, perhaps improving it with potting mix or compost. This soil could be used to make beds or place in planting holes.

Whatever method you use, you don't have to dig up the *whole* garden. Shrubberies and beds can be established, with the areas in between turned into paths, paved areas or open space clothed in a tough groundcover adapted to local soils and conditions.

When creating garden beds, whether for flowering plants or as the basis for shrubberies of larger species, mound them up if possible. This not only looks attractive by adding topographical interest to a flat garden but ensures excellent drainage. Even in sandy areas, the soil surface may form a hard pan on which water tends to lie rather than drain freely. Grevilleas and many other plants will develop root rot if their roots are waterlogged even for a short period.

GENERAL CARE

Watering

Obviously the conservation and best use of available water is particularly pertinent to gardeners in dry, inland areas. Again, I emphasise that drip-soaking of plant roots is the most efficient and economic use of water. And, as with coastal gardens, plastic bottles or other containers filled with water can be used to drip water on to plant roots so that it will be taken up as needed rather than just drain uselessly away. This is particularly useful during establishment, or when the gardener is away. The aim is to create a garden which, once established, needs no water (or very little) except that which comes from the sky.

Fertiliser

Many plants can be grown without fertiliser, particularly those indigenous to an area, but as we generally require garden plants to look better than those in the bush, most are lusher and flower better if given an occasional feed. In drier areas, this should be done sparingly, perhaps slightly reducing the amount recommended on the packet. Plants in dry soils are not able to take up nutrients easily and roots may suffer damage if they are exposed to heavy doses of chemicals or even manure. Controlled-release fertilisers are excellent but they need to be well watered in as they need a certain amount of moisture to break down and release their nutrients as required. Animal manures are better able to release their nutrients in poor soils, though their nutrition level will be unreliable. Another reason for being sparing with fertiliser is that plants in a dry, hot garden will grow tougher and more drought hardy if left to learn to forage for their own food. A third factor to consider is that many native plants such as banksias and grevilleas in the Proteaceae family don't like fertilisers high in phosphorus. Whichever fertiliser you do use, it is best applied during or just before rain, so that it can be well watered into the soil.

Weeding

Weeds are less prolific in hot, dry areas than in more humid areas; nonetheless they can be a nuisance as they use up whatever precious water is available. Get rid of them — but before declaring any plant a weed, make sure it is not a naturally occurring species which can be turned to good account as a groundcover or 'living' mulch. If it is decorative, not too invasive and seems to live well with other garden species then you may not consider it a weed at all even though it is so designated in a book. When in doubt let such a plant grow for a while, observe its habits and decide accordingly. If it proves troublesome, out it comes, or hit it with weedkiller!

Pruning

Plants in a hot, dry garden need plenty of foliage to provide shade and to go about their essential business of photosynthesis and transpiration. At the same time, the production of lush foliage needs a lot of water, which can put a strain on plant plumbing. Hard pruning is not recommended, unless a plant has suffered illness or a severe insect attack and needs pruning to recover, in which case it will also need additional water during that period. Generally speaking, plants will benefit from a light, overall pruning in a dry period. This will maintain form (particularly as many Australian native plants can develop a leggy appearance if left unpruned) and get rid of dead and dying branches (the latter will still use up valuable water). If the plant is very straggly or shows signs of stress from lack of water, reducing the vegetative top growth will help reduce its water needs.

LAWNS

Lawns consume a great deal of water if they are to remain green. Yet they do provide a cool contrast in a hot, dry landscape. Some Australian grasses make acceptable lawns yet do not require much watering. They include WEEPING GRASS (*Microlaena stipoides*); RED LEG GRASS (*Bothriocloa macra*), which will need some watering in very long, dry periods, WALLABY GRASS (*Danthonia setacia*) for low wear areas, and *Dryarna fluvius* which does best if given some water in summer. Or you could consider the lawn lookalike CONDAMINE COUCH (*Phyla nodiflora*).

PLANTS FOR HOT AND DRY GARDENS

The plants listed in this section have been selected as appropriate to most dryland gardens, but not extreme desert conditions. They will grow in an annual rainfall as low as 500 mm–750 mm; those marked DT (drought tolerant) can get by on less than that. Most of them require additional water in very long, dry periods and some, like cannas, tolerate wet and dry conditions.

There are a great number of Australian plants which are particularly suited to these conditions but which do not appear here because they are little known, difficult to obtain or hard to grow. They are, however, often obtainable from specialist nurseries or your local Society for Growing Australian Plants group, and some at least should be available from nurseries in areas where such plants are indigenous. In the case of acacias and eucalypts, there are so many species which either occur naturally or will thrive in dry areas that it would be pointless to list just a few. These include trees and shrubs from tropical regions which are not well known further afield. The most popular and most suitable acacias and eucalypts should be available from local nurseries. If you want a particular species, ask the nursery to order it, or else get hold of the catalogue of a large production nursery and order direct.

Some species of trees and shrubs which are not readily obtainable from nurseries may be available from Forestry Departments.

Plants for hot, dry gardens

Trees

DT — drought tolerant (below 500 mm annual rainfall)
Acacia SPP. DT
Backhousia anisata and *B. myrtifolia*
Banksia SPP. DT
BOTTLE TREE (*Brachychiton rupestris*) DT
Brachychiton gregorii DT
Callistemon SPP.
Casuarina cristata (BELAH) and *C. littoralis*
Ceratonia siliqua (CAROB BEAN)
Eucalypts
Erythrina vespertilio (BAT'S WING CORAL TREE) DT
Flindersia collina and *F. maculosa*
Gleditzia triacanthos (HONEY LOCUST)
GOLDEN RAIN TREE (*Koelreuteria paniculata*, down to about 750 mm annual rainfall)
Grevillea SPP.
Harpullia pendula
Jacaranda mimosifolia
Leptospermum SPP.
Melaleucas (dryland spp.) DT
Paulownia tomentosa
Schinus areira syn. *Schinus molle* (PEPPER TREE) DT
SILKY OAK (*Grevillea robusta*)
TAMARISK (*Tamarix aphylla*) DT
Terminalia aridicola DT
Willows (plant around dams or near water courses and soaks)
WHITE CEDAR (*Melia azedarach*)

Palms

All palms require water; even palms in the desert grow mainly around oases. The following can be grown if they can get their roots down into groundwater and are best planted around dams or along watercourses. They will need watering during establishment and an occasional deep soaking during long droughts if underground water is inadequate.
Chamaerops humilis (EUROPEAN FAN PALM)
MAZARI PALM (*Nannorrhops richiana*)
Phoenix SPP. (date palms, especially *P. dactylifera* and *P. reclinata* (SENEGAL DATE PALM)
Sabal domingensis
Washingtonia robusta and *W. filifera*
See also palms, page 93.

Conifers

Callitris columellaris (WHITE CYPRESS PINE) DT
Cupressus arizonica (ARIZONA CYPRESS) and *C. sempervirens* (MEDITERRANEAN CYPRESS, PENCIL PINE) DT
Juniper (*Juniperus* SPP.) — spreading, horizontal types will withstand long, dry periods)
Pinus canariensis (CANARY ISLAND PINE) DT
  P. halepensis (ALEPPO PINE) DT
  P. mugo (spreading shrub habit)
  P. pinnaster (CLUSTER PINE)
  P. pinea (STONE PINE) DT

Shrubs — over 2 m

Abelia grandiflora (needs some water in dry periods)
Acacia SPP.
Artemisia SPP.
Banksia dentata DT
Bauhinia galpinii
Buddleia SPP.
Caesalpinia gilliesi (DWARF POINCIANA)
Callistemon SPP.
Chamelaucium uncinatum
Elaeagnus angustifolia
Elaeocarpus reticulatus
Grevillea SPP.
Hakea trineura
Lagerstroemia indica (CREPE MYRTLE, PRIDE OF INDIA)
Leptospermum SPP.
Melaleuca SPP.
Protea SPP. (provided some water can be supplied)
Santolina chamaecyparissus DT
Viburnum tinus
Vitex SPP. DT
Westringia fruticosa DT and var. 'WYNYABBIE GEM'

Shrubs — under 2 m

Baeckea virgata
Cotoneaster horizontalis DT
Dillwynia sericea (SHOWY PARROT PEA)
Dryandra SPP. Most dryandras dislike alkaline soil.
Grevillea 'NED KELLY'
Leptospermum SPP. (low growing forms such as 'PINK CASCADE')

LAVENDER (*Lavandula* SPP.)
Melaleuca compacta
ROSEMARY (*Rosmarinus officinalis*) DT
SAGE (*Salvia officinalis*) DT
YARROW (*Achillea* SPP.)

Hedges

Hedges are not easy to grow and maintain in good condition where rainfall is low. Here, species are limited to those which require little water throughout the year or are adapted to making particularly good use of whatever water is available. Supplementary water is needed in very long, dry periods.

Many Australian shrubs and small trees such as acacias, callistemons, grevilleas, hakeas and melaleucas make very satisfactory informal hedges for dry, inland areas.

Allocasuarina torulosa
Backhousia myrtifolia
Cytisus linifolius (BROOM)
  C. racemosus
LAVENDER (*Lavandula* SPP.)
ROSEMARY (*Rosmarinus officinalis*)
Westringia fruticosa, particularly 'WYNYABBIE GEM'

Groundcovers

Aloe vera
CONDAMINE COUCH (*Phyla nodiflora*)
Dampiera SPP.
Dolichos lab lab and *D. lignosus* (will also climb)
Echeveria SPP. DT
Gazanias
Hovea acutifolia
Myoporum parvifolium
NASTURTIUM (*Tropaeolum majus*)
Scaevola SPP.
Sedum SPP. (STONECROP) DT
Sempervivum SPP. DT
SNOW-IN-SUMMER (*Cerastium tomentosum*) — good for banks
STURT'S DESERT PEA (*Clianthus formosus*) DT
THYME (*Thymus* SPP.) DT

Annuals

Amaranthus SPP.
Anthemis SPP.
Calendula officinalis (POT MARIGOLD)
CALIFORNIA POPPY (*Eschscholtzia californica*)
Chrysanthemum SPP.
Coreopsis SPP.
Dianthus chinensis
Everlasting daisies (e.g. helichrysum, helipterum and gomphrena) DT
Gypsophila elegans (BABY'S BREATH)
MARIGOLD (*Tagetes* SPP.)
Phlox drummondi
Portulaca grandiflora
Rudbeckia selections
Senecio cineraria (daisy)
Zinnia SPP.

Climbers

Bougainvilleas
Campsis grandiflora (syn. *Bignonia grandiflora*, CHINESE TRUMPET VINE)
Celastrus orbiculatus (ORIENTAL BITTERSWEET)
Clematis microphylla
Euonymus fortunei DT
Hardenbergia violacea
Hibbertia scandens
Kennedia rubicunda (DUSKY CORAL PEA) DT
NASTURTIUM (*Tropaeolum majus*)
Pyrostegia venusta

Other plants

Agave SPP. DT
Ajuga reptans (CARPET BUGLE)
ALYSSUM (*Lobularia maritima*)
Cactus (most available species) DT
Canna SPP. (although moisture-loving, they will equally tolerate long, dry periods but will do better if given some water)
CROWN OF THORNS (*Euphorbia milii*)
Erigeron SPP. (daisies)
Grass Tree (*Xanthorrhoea* SPP.) DT, but must be watered well for three months if transplanted)
KANGAROO GRASS (*Themeda triandra*) DT
KANGAROO PAW (*Anigozanthos* SPP.)
LARGE TUSSOCK GRASS (*Poa labillardieri*)
Macrozamia moorei
Pennisetum alopecuroides (SWAMP FOXTAIL) — plant in mulch
SUNFLOWER (*Helianthus* SPP.)
Yucca gloriosa and *Y. aloifolia* DT

Plants which tolerate alkaline soils

Where soils are strongly alkaline, limited areas can be gradually neutralised by continuous mulching, adding organic matter to the soil (particularly pine needles which are strongly acid) and applications of lime sulphate or 'flowers of sulphur'. You can also grow those plants which are tolerant of alkaline soil.

Acacia harphopylla
  A. melanoxylon
Banksia integrifolia
Calothamnus SPP. (NET BUSH)
Cassia artemisioides
Clematis microphylla
EMU BUSH (*Eremophila* SPP.)
Eucalyptus forrestiana
  E. leucoxylon
  E. platypus
Hakea leucoptera
Koelreuteria paniculata
Melaleuca armillaris
Myoporum floribundum
Pittosporum phillyreoides
Scaevola SPP. (FAN FLOWER)
Stenanthemum scortechinii (SNOWBALLS)
TAMARISK (*Tamarix aphylla*)

Fragrant plants for arid inland areas

Eucalyptus citriodora
LAVENDER
PINEAPPLE SAGE
Prostanthera SPP. (mint bushes)
ROSEMARY
SAGE
THYME

An instant garden

IT ISN'T NECESSARY TO WAIT YEARS to create a garden which gives pleasure and looks good from the outside. In a hot climate, where many species grow quickly and the weather is kind, it is possible to establish an 'instant' garden which has immediate appeal while serving as the foundation for better things to come. In many new suburbs, it is not unusual to see gardens spring into being almost overnight. Often the work has been done by landscape contractors, but it is quite easy to do it yourself.

There are two secrets to creating an instant garden: one is to select plants which have a mature look while still young; the other is to plant them in sufficient quantities so that they provide plenty of cover from the start. A scattering of lonely plants in a mass of bare ground will not do at all, and the aim should be to cover the ground as quickly as possible to avoid erosion in a tropical downpour.

Young plants which have a mature look when purchased from the nursery include palms, dwarf conifers, rush-type clumping plants and shade-loving plants with large, fleshy leaves. These, in some sort of combination, form the basis of a garden which can be bought and established in a few days, a weekend or even a day, depending on the site, the size of the garden, and the number and energies of the people doing the work. A middle-aged couple with an average-sized suburban block should be able to establish an instant garden in a few days. This is provided that the block offers no particular landscaping challenges, such as a very steep bank, and has reasonable garden soil. For the purpose of this section, I'll assume that any improvements to the soil and the physical shape of the garden will have been done already.

If you can afford it, buy advanced tree specimens which quickly transform a bare block into a garden. Some trees, even huge figs, can be successfully transplanted even when a few years old. Palms are probably the best-known example of mature trees which are readily available — at a price. Mature specimens of pandanus can often be seen transplanted for landscaping purposes, but these have become too expensive for most gardeners. It may be worth investing in one, perhaps two, large specimens to give immediate interest. But it is not necessary; a perfectly attractive instant garden can be made using the larger sizes of plants commonly found in nurseries.

One of the most 'instant' features of any garden is the lawn, because turf can be laid quickly. The next step is to mulch the rest with a deep layer of pine bark or some similar coarse material which looks tidy, suppresses weeds and has the effect of integrating and drawing the rest of the garden together. Organic 'soft' mulches (as opposed to hard mulches of pebbles or gravel) will break down in time; they may no longer be as necessary because sufficient cover will have grown up, but they can easily be renewed.

If the block already has some trees and shrubs growing on it, these can be used to support hanging baskets and epiphytic plants such as staghorns and bird's nest ferns. The latter can also be placed on the ground. The shaded area beneath the larger plants can be used immediately for mass plantings of large-leaved species such as caladium and alocasia, and other shade-loving foliage plants such as hostas.

If the block is bare, and you wish to establish some shade-loving plants at once, put up temporary structures of shadecloth on timber stakes, to serve as cover until fast-growing trees or shrubs can take over. Or make permanent, attractive structures which will provide instant shade and possibly future supports for climbing plants. Such structures might form part of the house, for example, a covered patio or pergola.

Use instant plants to create features; for example to line a pathway or driveway, to make a border either side of steps, or to frame an entrance. This will help give the garden a finished look; more so than if plants

Pachystachys lutea (GOLDEN CANDLES, see page 104) is a fast-growing plant which is ideal for shrubberies where its bright yellow flowers provide colour throughout spring and summer. For a truly spectactular effect, combine it with plantings of Pachystachys coccinea which has red flowers. In an instant garden both are excellent choices for filling in shaded areas after the initial planting has been completed.

are just stuck in at random. Group them in one large, feature bed, or in smaller beds. Place them around the base of upright supports such as porch pillars, patio posts and car ports. Use them to mark the border of the property. As with any garden, a plan (however rough) should be drawn up first so that you know exactly what effect you wish to create, where you want foliage plants, and where you want plenty of colourful flowers, which features need accentuating, and so on.

The denser the planting, the more finished the garden will look. This is particularly important where a lot of plants are needed to create an effect, such as a border or low hedge. Allowing for the fact that individual plants must have space to grow, large gaps between such plants as cannas will take a while to fill. If you want an instant garden, you must be prepared to buy enough plants to do the job.

Spacing depends on the effect you wish to create. Dense plantings of palms and other fast-growing species will still need some room for individual expansion. Dwarf upright conifers are very slow-growing but sufficient space must be left between them at the start to allow for their eventual width. This is even more important with horizontal-growing cypresses and junipers. Such plants don't need to be crowded together; they have a very 'old' look to start with, rather resembling bonsai specimens, and look better isolated rather than surrounded by a clutter of other plants. Here, pebbles, a few rocks or gravel make a more effective groundcover than pine bark.

Rocks, the larger the better, give an established look to the instant garden and suit its spare, uncluttered landscape. Other features with instant eye appeal include imaginatively laid logs, tree stumps, ponds, fountains and statuary. Container-grown plants, the more the merrier, are a quick and easy way of filling in space. They can be moved elsewhere, if desired, as the garden develops.

Of course, the whole garden does not have to be given the instant treatment. You may wish, for example, to create an instant garden at the front, which is most visible from the street, while taking your time about developing the back.

An instant garden is best planted in late spring or early summer, to take advantage of summer rainfall and the main growing period. A bonus is that many plants are in flower at this time and will give instant colour. If you have to establish your garden at another time of year, plan to have at least one plant which flowers at that time.

Secondary plants, that is, fast-growing species which do not have the immediate mature appearance of the instant garden plants, can be established at the same time or soon after. Then, as the third and last step, add slow-growing species gradually within the existing framework. This is only necessary if you want a garden with a great variety of plants. Some people are so content with the simplicity of their instant gardens that they never add another plant.

Plants for an instant garden

Trees

Palms (most palms look good from the start; Alexandra and Queen Palms are particularly fast-growing)
Dwarf conifers
Horizontal and procumbent conifers, e.g. some junipers and cypresses
Pandanus SPP.

Shrubs

(Even when young, these can be massed or arranged to give a good show)
Alocasia SPP.
Azaleas
BUSH BASIL, PERENNIAL CREEK BASIL (*Ocimum obovatum*)
Caladium bicolor
Coleus SPP.
CROTON (*Codiaeum* SPP.)
Cuphea SPP. (e.g. 'MAD HATTER')
Duranta repens gold and green-gold varieties
GRASS TREE (*Xanthorrhoea* SP.) (If transplanted, these will need to be watered every day for about three months. When you buy check that the grass tree, which has become very popular in landscaping and in domestic gardens, although it is rather slow growing, has been grown from seed. Some mature specimens are taken from the bush by licensed operators; it is an offence for anyone without a licence to remove grass trees and most other native plants from the bush.)
Grevillea SPP.
Hostas
Hydrangeas (when in mid-summer bloom)
Oleander (dwarf)
Poinsettia

Climbers

These are either very fast-growing or look good even when young.
Dipladenia varieties (make attractive small shrubs which will climb if desired)
BLACK-EYED SUSAN (*Thunbergia alata*)
Monstera deliciosa (shade or part shade)
Philodendron SPP. (shade)

Groundcovers

Grevillea spp. (prostrate, ground-covering types)
Ferns (for shady areas)
Junipers (prostrate, procumbent forms)
Leptospermum 'Pacific Beauty'
Mondo grass (*Ophiopogon* spp.)

Other plants for instant gardens

Agapanthus
Agave spp.
Bedding Begonia
Bird's nest ferns (*Asplenium* spp.) — on ground or trees/supports
Brachyscome daisies
Canna
Clivia (for immediate winter colour; in shade)
Dianella
Dietes bicolor
Ixora spp. (in light shade)
Geraniums
Kangaroo Paw (*Anigozanthos* spp.)
Lomandra longifolia (Matt Rush)
Staghorns and elkhorns (*Platycerium* spp.)

Fast-growing plants

Once the instant garden is established, these are a good choice for quickly filling in spaces and adding interest.
Acacia macradenia (Zig Zag Wattle) very fast-growing but short-lived
Acacia — other species
Antigonon leptopus (Coral Vine)
Aristolochia elegans (Dutchman's Pipe) — climber
Bougainvillea (as shrub, standard, hedge or climber)
Buddleia spp.
Calliandra spp.
Callistemon spp.
Galphimia glauca
Helipterum spp.
Hymenosporum flavum (Native Frangipani)
Lagerstroemia indica (Crepe Myrtle, Pride of India)
Marguerite Daisy (*Chrysanthemum frutescens*)
Oleander (larger form)
Pachystachys lutea
Paper daisies (*Chrysocephalum apiculatum* syn. *Helichrysum* and *Bracteantha bracteata*)
Plumbago
Pyrostegia venusta (Orange Trumpet Vine)
Russelia equisetiformis
Shasta Daisy (*Chrysanthemum* × *superbum*)
Schizolobium parahyba (yellow-flowering, thorny tree)
Tapioca Plant (*Manihot esculenta*)
Thevetia peruviana
Tulip Tree (*Spathodea campanulata*)
Umbrella Tree (*Schefflera actinophylla*) and Dwarf Umbrella (*S. arboricola*)
Wonga Vine (*Pandorea pandorana*)

Overleaf
Ixoras are shrubs from tropical Asia which flower for most of the year and are useful for adding colour to lightly shaded areas. This one is 'Coral Fire'.

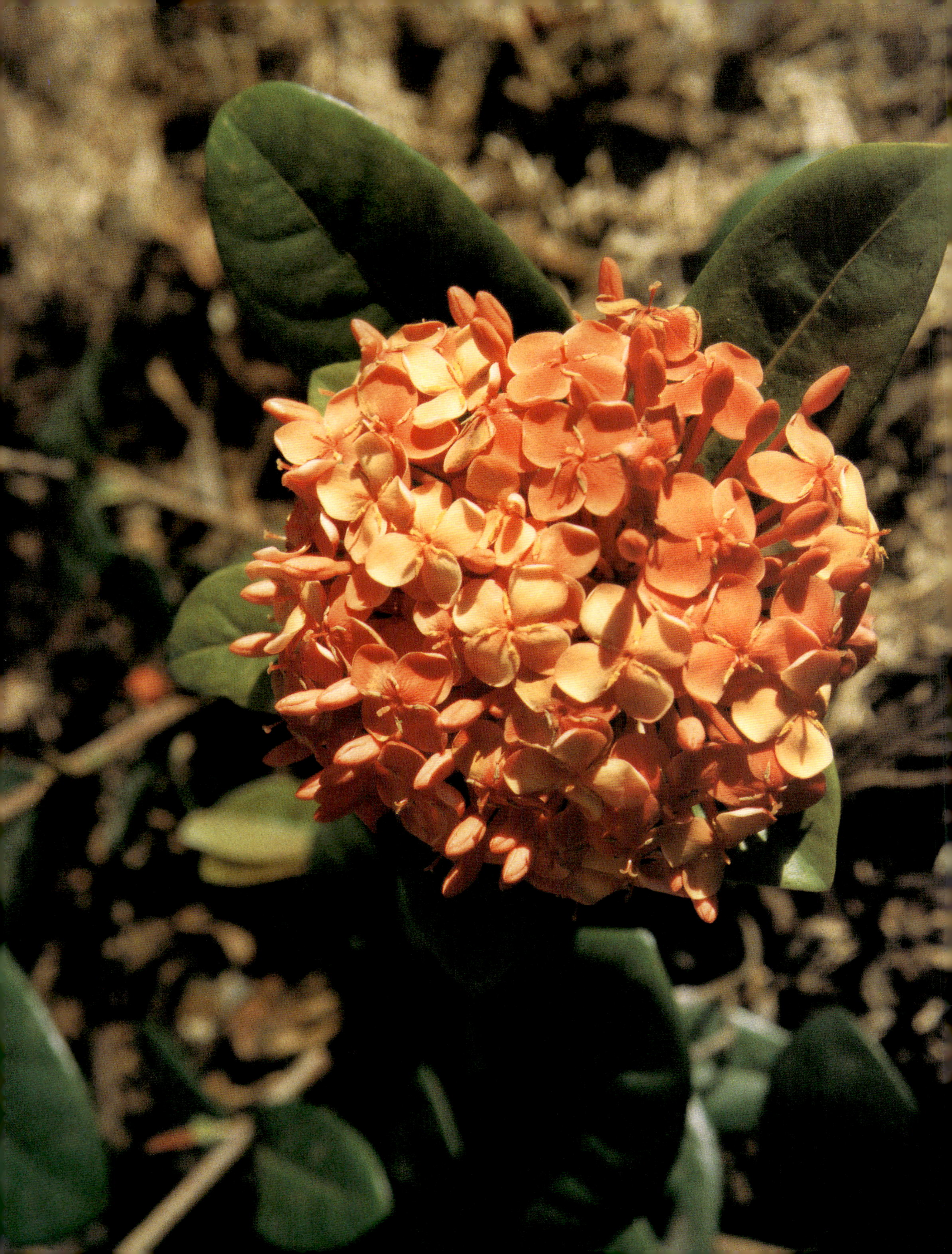

3
Garden design challenges

Planning for problem areas

NARROW SIDE AREAS

THE AVERAGE SUBURBAN HOUSE has a front garden, a backyard and a narrow area on either side of the house. These areas sometimes are all too easily neglected rather than put to good gardening use, or depending on size and the type of rooms adjacent to them they may be used to store boats, keep the garbage bin or build the garden shed. They do, however, offer opportunities to grow interesting plants which may not be available in the rest of the garden.

Side areas sometimes have to function as passageways. This doesn't mean they can't also be used as courtyards or patios. They may provide an exterior entrance to the back garden, or link the back and front garden, in which case they can be made to lead the eye intriguingly from one area to another. Whatever the overall garden theme, therefore, the side passageway should reflect it.

Such areas are often shaded over and used as ferneries, for which they are ideal. A narrow area on the northern side of the house is suitable for plants which need plenty of warmth and shelter from prevailing south-easterly or winter westerly winds, a rare palm from the true tropics, for example. In fact, in the sub-tropics, this area is a good place to grow very tropical plants which might not flourish elsewhere in the garden. It will get sun for most of the day, even if fenced. Or you may want to erect a shade over the area to grow some special plants, depending on which rooms adjoin them and how much light they need.

Side sections may be separated from the neighbouring gardens by screen plantings. These should be tall and not spreading in habit or they will require constant clipping. Fences (or walls) are better because they provide permanent privacy and protection and do not take up much horizontal space. They can be beautified with climbers, espaliered plants and hanging baskets. Some ephiphytes can also be grown on fences. Two things need to be remembered here; fenced or screened narrow side areas on the southern, eastern or western side of the house always receive shade, sometimes a lot of shade, for part of the day so plants must be selected accordingly. Rambling roses, bougainvilleas, spiny cacti and other thorny plants may well be unsuitable if the space is very narrow.

Side areas can make excellent herb, vegetable and cutflower gardens because they are easy to cultivate, particularly if the beds are built up. Those which get sun most of the day, for example on the northern side (much depends on width as to the amount of shade or otherwise any side area receives) can be used for plants with that requirement; other side areas can be used for plants which do well with either morning or afternoon sun. In a hot climate many annuals from cooler climates do better if they receive full sun for only part of the day.

In a hot climate the winds which are channelled through such narrow areas are not the sort of problem they are further south — indeed, they act as valuable breezeways to cool both plants and people and this might be taken into account when planting, so that the through-draught is not blocked.

Ground plan

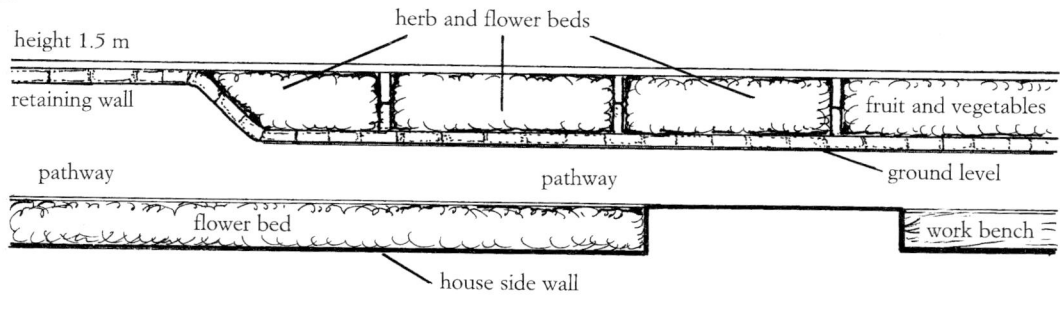

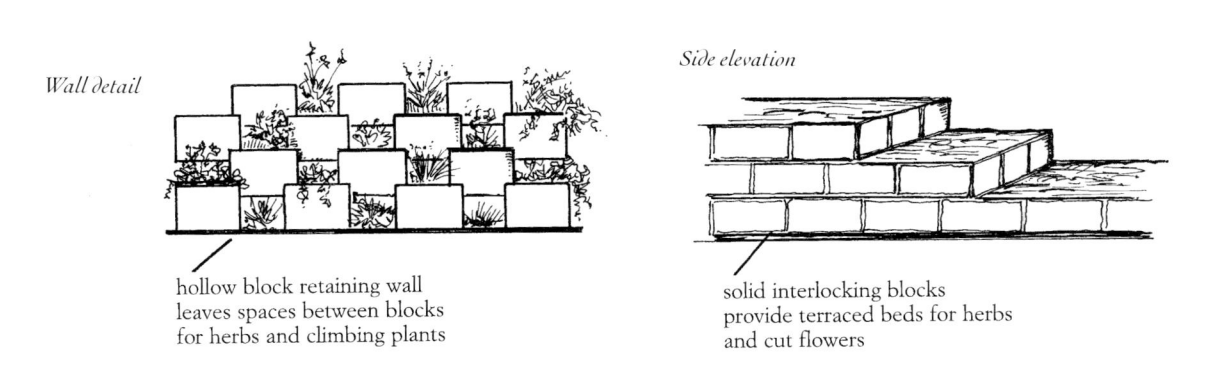

height 1.5 m — herb and flower beds
retaining wall — fruit and vegetables
pathway — pathway — ground level
flower bed — work bench
house side wall

Wall detail

hollow block retaining wall leaves spaces between blocks for herbs and climbing plants

Side elevation

solid interlocking blocks provide terraced beds for herbs and cut flowers

This sketch shows how a garden was designed for a narrow 2.5 m strip of garden on the northern side of a house which was further complicated by a sloping side boundary from a high point of 1.5 m down to ground level at the back of the garden. A retaining wall was built using linked, hollow concrete blocks spaced as shown. Herbs and plants grow and spill from within and between the blocks. This wall protected the steepest part of the embankment. At a height of one metre, it became a series of terraced beds supported by solid interlinked blocks. These beds are well drained and grow herbs and flowers with pawpaws and cherry tomatoes at ground level. A variety of types, shapes and colours of garden building blocks are available, providing a flexible and simple solution to many design problems.

STEEP BANKS

Banks are often looked upon as nuisances in the garden, yet they can be turned into features of great visual interest. If they are very steep, and close to the house, they may need stabilising by terracing with rocks, blocks, timber or even grow-bags filled with soil or potting mix. Less steep banks can be made more stable by using steel mesh, logs, weedmatting or chickenwire; this will also prevent erosion and offer initial plant support. Some particularly strong plants such as Singapore Daisy (*Wedelia trilobata*), honeysuckle, allamanda and prostrate grevilleas do an excellent job of bank stabilisation on their own.

Bare banks or those which are sparsely planted can become badly eroded in heavy rain. It helps to scoop out shallow drainage channels which divert the water on to adjacent lawns or shrubberies where it can do no harm. A thickly mulched and planted bank is unlikely to suffer severe erosion. Even terraced banks, though they are better able to absorb rainwater, can become scoured during tropical downpours.

Though any plant can be grown on a bank, those which are considered most suitable have tumbling, sprawling, spreading habits. Often unruly plants which might not suit other parts of the garden are the best choice for steep places. They should have strong, laterally spreading root systems to hold them firmly in place and the ability to survive in what is usually a thin layer of topsoil. Trees and large shrubs are usually too top-heavy to be grown successfully on banks; they look uncomfortable growing at an angle from the ground and are easily blown over in strong winds.

Plants for banks

Allamanda SPP. (yellow or beige flowers)
Acacia pravissima 'GOLDEN CARPET' (several other smaller-growing acacias are also suitable for banks)
BOUGAINVILLEA
Brachyscome multifida
Calliandra SPP. (prostrate forms)
Cerastium tomentosum (SNOW-IN-SUMMER, white flowers)
CONDAMINE COUCH
Cotoneaster horizontalis
Cuphea SPP. varieties (e.g. black and red, mauve or white flowers)
Ficus pumila (CREEPING FIG)
Gazania ringens (multicoloured flowers)
Grevilleas (prostrate varieties; various flower colours)
Hibbertia SPP.
HONEYSUCKLE (*Lonicera* SPP.)
IVY (*Hedera* SPP., shade or semi-shade)
Kunzea pomifera
Lantana montevidensis (mauve and other colours)
Marguerite daisies
Mesembryanthemum SPP. (multi-coloured flowers)
Portulaca SPP. (multicoloured flowers)
ROSEMARY (prostrate form; seaside sub-tropics only)
Russelia SPP. (orange-red flowers)
Shasta daisies
SINGAPORE DAISY (*Wedelia trilobata*, yellow flowers)
STAR JASMINE (*Trachelospermum jasminoides*, white flowers)

GULLIES

Probably the most practical and attractive thing to do with a gully is to turn it into a rainforest. If it is very small and narrow, use palms as the foundation planting. Otherwise, a selection of Australian rain-forest trees and shrubs will create a cool and shady area which will require no maintenance. Add pools and perhaps a small waterfall, particularly if the bottom of the gully is permanently damp. Suitable plant species are listed opposite, and see the chapter on pools, ponds and swimming pools, page 37.

Tecomaria capensis, which has red flowers in spring and summer, is a good hedge for the tropics and sub-tropics, growing equally well by the sea or adjacent mountain areas. The foliage is dense and easy to trim, perfect for a more formal garden design. For more on hedges, see pages 162–4. The pink flowers at centre are Lagerstroemia (PRIDE OF INDIA).

An interesting alternative is to turn the gully into a dry riverbed using gravel, stones and rocks over a weed-suppressing fabric. First, clear the area of weeds, then cover with thick polythene sheeting or geotextile fabric. A layer of coarse river sand can then be added, though this is not strictly necessary. The main surface of the riverbed can be of gravel or small stones, interspersed with larger rocks. The effect is particularly suited to native and dryland gardens.

DAMP SPOTS

Many plants need moisture around their roots permanently and these are ideal for badly-drained, permanently damp or boggy areas. The most imaginative way of dealing with a permanently poorly drained spot is to turn it into a pond or garden pool, planted with a selection of aquatic plants in the middle and bog plants around the edge, to convert a formerly ugly area into something of beauty.

STORMWATER RUNOFF

This can be a problem in monsoonal downpours, even on new suburbs where plenty of stormwater drainage is provided externally. Within the garden, stormwater runoff can cause considerable damage when it pours across sloping ground or off hard surfaces. Once problem areas have been identified, some kind of drainage will need to be installed, by yourself or a contractor.

Trees and palms for damp areas

ALEXANDRA PALM (*Archontophoenix alexandrae*)
Callistemon SPP. (most, particularly species such as *C. pachyphyllus* and *C.* 'HARKNESS' hybrid)
Casuarina glauca and *C. torulosa*
Ficus SPP. (e.g. *F. macrophylla*, MORETON BAY FIG)
Leptospermum brachyandrum and *L. laevigatum*
Licuala ramsayi (FAN PALM)
Livistona SPP. (CABBAGE TREE PALM)
Melicope elleryana
SWAMP CYPRESS (*Taxodium distichum*)
Tristaniopsis laurina
Waterhousea SPP.

Shrubs and smaller-growing plants for damp areas

Alocasia SPP.
ARROW BAMBOO (*Pseudosasa japonica*)
Bauera SPP.
Colocasia SPP.
CHRISTMAS BELLS (*Blandfordia* SPP.)
Cordyline SPP.
Cyperus involucratus
Lomandra longifolia (MATT RUSH)
Melaleuca SPP. such as *M. leucodendron* (PAPERBARK), *M. linariifolia* (SNOW-IN-SUMMER), *M. quinquinervia* (PAPERBARK TEA TREE) and *M. viridiflora*
Melastoma affine syn. *polyanthum* (NATIVE LASIANDRA)
NILE GRASS (*Cyperus papyrus*)
Physostegia virginiana (lily-like with pink and white bell flowers)
Rushes (*Restio* SPP. e.g. *R. tetraphyllus*)
STREAM LILY (*Helmholtzia acorifolia*)
SWAMP FOXTAIL (*Pennisetum alopecurioides*, a native grass not to be confused with the exotic pennisetum which is an invasive nuisance in some areas)
Tree ferns (*Cyathea* SPP.)

For groundcovers suitable for damp areas, see page 170.

Storm warning!

When a tropical cyclone comes roaring out of the sea with winds up to 200 km an hour then everything in its path, including gardens, will take a severe battering. Trees are uprooted, shrubs ripped from the ground, small plants torn to shreds. Fortunately, cyclones are occasional rather than common along the inhabited parts of our coastline. When they *do* come, however, they are very destructive to gardens and those who live in cyclone-prone areas should at least be aware of the dangers — and how to minimise them.

There are two schools of thought at work here. One is to establish a minimal garden consisting only of lawns and a few plants which are most able to stand up to strong winds. In the event of cyclone damage not much will be lost — and a similar minimum will be easy to re-establish.

The other is to cover the garden with as much vegetation as possible, so that the wind can be dissipated and deflected, while the sheer numbers of plants will serve to help protect each other. This school of thought is also based on the idea that the more plants there are, the more are likely to be left alive when the cyclone has passed. Historical evidence shows that this is sometimes the case; but cyclones are unpredictable and there are cases of entire, heavily vegetated gardens, as well as areas of natural forest, being totally stripped and reduced to mulch.

My own belief is that you cannot cultivate your garden, any more than you can live your life, without the acceptance of some risk. If you are the kind of gardener who gardens for the sheer pleasure of it then why limit your creativity for the sake of an occasional cyclone? Grow the kind of garden you want — but take sensible precautions during the cyclone season and consider the ideas outlined in this section.

WIND

Abnormally high winds have two effects on plants: either uprooting them or severely tearing, or stripping, their foliage. So two primary points need to be considered here:

1. Plants with deep or very widespread roots are less easily uprooted.

2. Plants with tough, small, narrow foliage stand up to wind better than those with large, soft leaves.

Trees with shallow roots and large canopies are particularly prone to toppling and this problem is accentuated when, as often happens, cyclones come at the end of a dry season when the ground has dried out and cracked, leaving roots without a sure grip. The sudden combination of strong wind against the canopy and a heavy deluge which loosens soil around already unstable roots can prove too much even for trees which are in their prime. Rainforest trees which are mostly shallow-rooted are particularly vulnerable under these conditions. Figs are even more vulnerable than most, because of their epiphytic nature. The sight of these forest giants on their sides, the great root ball exposed, is awesome.

Then again, many trees and other plants growing on sand dunes are also easily uprooted. This is less

Gardening in a Hot Climate

true of plants indigenous to that environment, which have found their own way of anchoring themselves firmly in a loose and unstable medium. In fact plants — especially trees — on low-fertility soils are often more strongly rooted than those on fertile soils, which encourage top growth of foliage rather than the wide-spreading of roots which don't have to forage far for food.

Plants which occur naturally on coastal dunes in cyclone-prone areas usually share the characteristics already described of small, tough, often narrow leaves which offer little resistance to the wind. Many Australian native plants have these characteristics, as well as some exotics. These plants should obviously be included in gardens in cyclone-prone areas.

Palms are the best example of trees which are particularly well-suited to withstanding strong winds. Their long, smooth, cylindrical trunks and small, fronded canopies offer little resistance. Sometimes they are uprooted, but they have a better chance than most of staying intact. This is why, after the severest cyclones, there are always a lot of coconut palms still standing. Even though their fronds may be stripped or broken off at the base, they are ready to start growing again.

It is advisable to establish salt and wind-tolerant plant species as screens to protect gardens, see page 47. Some of these plants have the ability to withstand very strong winds, others are less able. The screens will certainly offer some protection during the first onslaught. However, unlike coastal gales, cyclones come across the coast and then back again, with a slight lull in between. When the second onslaught comes, screens on the coastal side of the garden cannot, of course, offer any protection to the garden.

RAIN

Cyclonic winds are accompanied by deluges which cause rapid flooding and erosion. The sheer volume of water on hard surfaces such as roads and driveways can create problems beyond the capacity of otherwise perfectly satisfactory drainage. Banks and terraces can become cataracts. The rainfall problem is much less acute on sandy soils, though these can still erode very quickly if the water is pouring off a hard surface. Plants in non-sandy soils will not only be battered by the rain, they are also likely to be waterlogged for a long period. Combined with wind damage, the effect can be fatal.

STORMPROOFING YOUR GARDEN

Wise precautions

- Try to establish a new garden, and any new plants, well before the start of the cyclone season so their roots are firmly bound to the soil.
- Ensure the block is well-enough drained to handle cyclonic deluge. Look hard at vulnerable areas such as banks, terraces, driveway runoffs and narrow passageways between houses and retaining walls where water might not be able to get away. Make sure that water can be channelled away from vulnerable plants and flowerbeds. If your house is below roadway level, make sure the local authority has installed drainage to protect your house and garden from runoff during heavy rain.
- Select wind-resistant plant species or at least make sure these are well represented in your garden.
- Don't plant (and if necessary remove) trees with large canopies, particularly if they are shallow-rooted. Buttressed trees will almost always have shallow roots. Certainly such trees should not be close to the house or any built structure.
- Remember that low-growing, sprawling and horizontal shrubs are better able to withstand strong winds than tall, rounded types. Those with fairly thin, open foliage are better than those with a dense mass of leaves.
- Plant lots of palms (coastal types). A palm screen around the garden will help break up the force of the wind. And even if they are blown down, they are fast growing and easy to replace.
- Hedges and plant screens are better able to stand up to strong winds than timber fences and latticework, and should therefore be given preference. Of course, they are slower to replace if the cyclone is powerful enough to destroy them.
- Don't over-fertilise plants, particularly large shrubs and trees; instead encourage them to develop strong, spreading root systems by foraging for nutrition.
- Where wind exposure is a frequent problem it is difficult to establish taller-growing species without staking. It is worth remembering, however, that plants which are *not* staked quickly develop strong root systems to anchor themselves and these have an advantage during cyclones. The lesson is; if you *must* stake, remove the stakes as soon as plants seem able to cope by themselves — staking tends to encourage weak roots and stems.
- Sheds and shadehouses must be built to the cyclone rating standards for your area — stronger if you want them to be more secure. Aluminium sheds can become lethal weapons when they are flying through the air.
- Deeply mulch growing areas. This will protect plants from many of the problems associated with heavy rainfall and help control erosion.

When a cyclone is coming

- Take down and safely store hanging baskets.
- Put away all small, vulnerable objects in the garden. These might include container plants, birdbaths, bird feeders, wheelbarrows, unsecured garden seating — anything which can be picked up by the wind and turned into a weapon.
- If possible cut back heavy foliage on large shrubs or small trees so that less resistance is offered to the wind.
- Put a cover over the swimming pool to stop it overfilling and possibly causing flooding or erosion problems. This will also help keep the water uncontaminated with cyclone debris — swimming pools can be a useful source of water in the aftermath of severe cyclone damage.

Afterwards

- See whether any large trees are so damaged they need felling, or whether any damaged limbs and branches need lopping.
- Immediately replant uprooted plants — it may be possible to save them with quick action.
- Give all damaged and uprooted plants a thorough pruning back, getting rid of all old and tattered growth. This will encourage new growth and help the roots re-establish themselves. Leave some young growth if any still remains. Spray with a half-strength solution of a liquid fertiliser.
- Dig shallow channels where water needs to be drained away from waterlogged areas.
- Cyclones usually drag in enough rain to wash down plant foliage thoroughly. Sometimes, however, the strong winds that remain after the cyclone has passed or dissipated can carry salt spray into gardens well beyond the frontal beach zone. If this is the case and assuming water is available, hose down all plants
- Assess damage and determine whether better planning and plant selection will help the garden withstand future cyclones.

Fire protection

BUSH OR WILD FIRES CAN BE A PROBLEM even in areas with warm, wet summers such as the Australian tropical zone, because these areas also experience extended dry periods. Homes most at risk are those which back on to bushland or forest. Those in rainforest areas are less at risk because rainforest plants don't burn easily and a mature rainforest can stop a fire in its tracks. A severely logged forest, on the other hand, may not prove fire retardant, especially if it has been invaded by a more combustible alien species. Despite its apparently sparse growth, the vegetation of coastal dunes burns quite fiercely. Once a fire gets into peat swampland, it is very hard to put out and tends to keep flaring up again.

To the home gardener who fears fire damage, two kinds of plants are of interest: those that can survive fire and those which actively retard it. These are not always the same, unfortunately. On the contrary, many plants which have the ability to regenerate after fire are also extremely combustible, eucalypts being a case in point. And those which help retard fire may still be destroyed by it.

The first and obvious step in a fire-prone area is to keep the area around the house clean of combustible materials. This also means free of highly combustible trees and shrubs. The house surrounds can still be beautified by a lawn and low-growing, fleshy-leaved plants which retard fires. If there is room, a firebreak should be left between your boundary and the bush beyond. If you want to screen your garden you can do so with a barrier of fire-retardant trees. These should also have a shrub understorey because a shrub layer near the ground can reduce windspeed. At the same time, too impenetrable a layer of trees and shrubs directs the fire upwards and causes turbulence. Although all trees and shrubs burn, the plants listed on page 70 are resistant to easy burning and can help protect a house and vulnerable garden areas by blocking the spread of burning debris.

It is also worth remembering that:

- Thick-barked trees survive fires best but those with thinner, smooth bark are more fire-retardant.
- The most fire-retardant trees and shrubs are those which hold a lot of moisture, have a high salt content or are deciduous.
- A bare block is not necessarily a safety factor in a fire-prone area; instead a well-planted garden with fire-retarding vegetation will decrease the windspeed which drives bushfires. It also absorbs radiant heat and traps burning debris borne by the gusting wind. This may all help to save the house.

Diagram annotations:

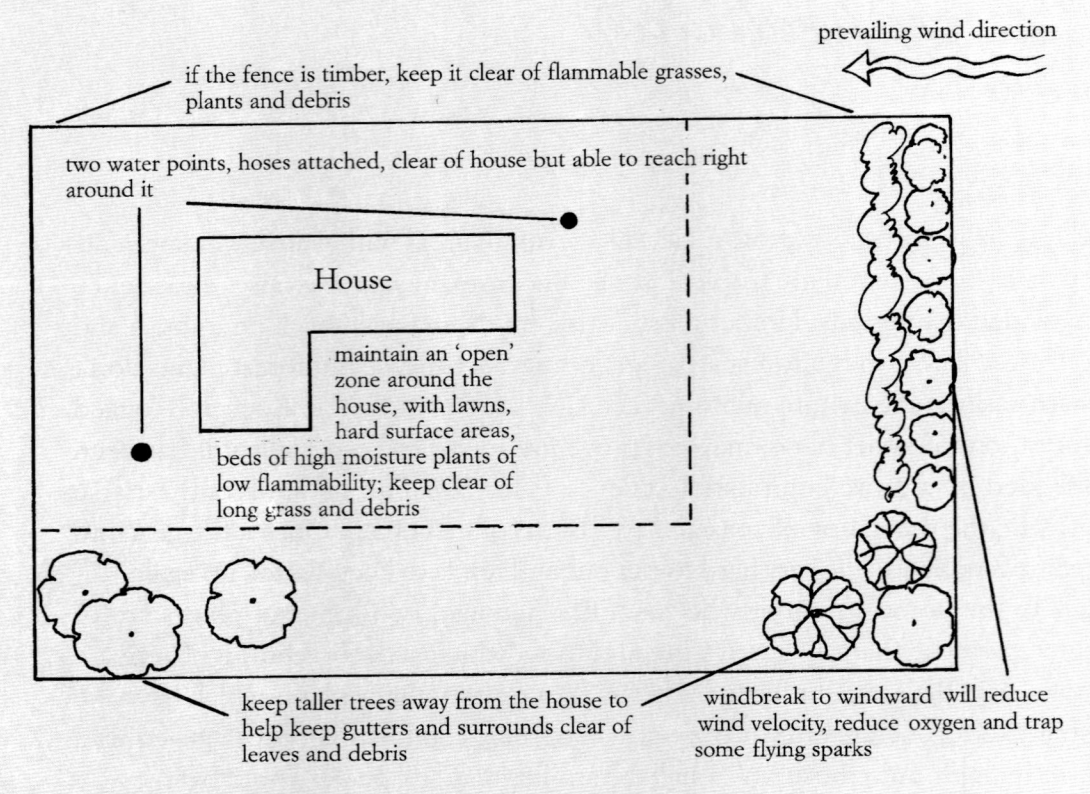

- prevailing wind direction
- if the fence is timber, keep it clear of flammable grasses, plants and debris
- two water points, hoses attached, clear of house but able to reach right around it
- House
- maintain an 'open' zone around the house, with lawns, hard surface areas, beds of high moisture plants of low flammability; keep clear of long grass and debris
- keep taller trees away from the house to help keep gutters and surrounds clear of leaves and debris
- windbreak to windward will reduce wind velocity, reduce oxygen and trap some flying sparks

Home owners in areas subject to bushfire hazard can design gardens to minimise fire risk

Fire-retardant trees

Fire-retardant species are low in oil and resin, high in moisture content, and have a smooth bark.

Acacia baileyana
   A. iteaphylla
   A. longifolia
Brachychiton populneum
   B. rupestris
CALLITRIS SPP.
CANARY ISLAND PINE (*Pinus canariensis*)
Eucalyptus cladocalyx (SUGAR GUM)
   E. leucoxylon
   E. maculata
FRANGIPANI
Hakea salicifolia
Hibiscus tiliaceus
LILLY PILLY (*Syzygium* SPP.)
Palms (most)
PEPPER TREE (*Schinus molle*)
Rainforest trees (many exotic and native Australian)
Schefflera actinophylla
Tamarix aphylla
Thevetia peruviana
WHITE CEDAR (*Melia azedarach*)

Fire-retardant shrubs

Atriplex nummularia
Coprosma repens
GOLDEN PRIVET (*Ligustrum aurea*)
Goodenia ovata
Grevillea SPP.
Macaranga tanarius
Murraya paniculata
Myoporum insulare
   M. viscosum
PLUMBAGO SPP.
Russelia SPP.
SALTBUSH (*Rhagodia* SPP.)
Tecomaria capensis

Fire-retardant understorey, lily-like and groundcover plants

Most plants with very large, fleshy leaves; long fleshy and straplike leaves; or small, shiny leaves, won't burn easily and will help retard fire.

Quick recovery

A few plants have the ability to recover or regenerate very quickly after fire. They include:

Banksias
Brachychiton diversifolius
CANARY ISLAND PINE (*Pinus canariensis*)
Eucalypts (most)
GRASS TREE (*Xanthorrhoea* SP.)
Melaleuca leucadendron (WEEPING PAPERBARK)
   M. quinquenervia (PAPERBARK)

4
Plant directory

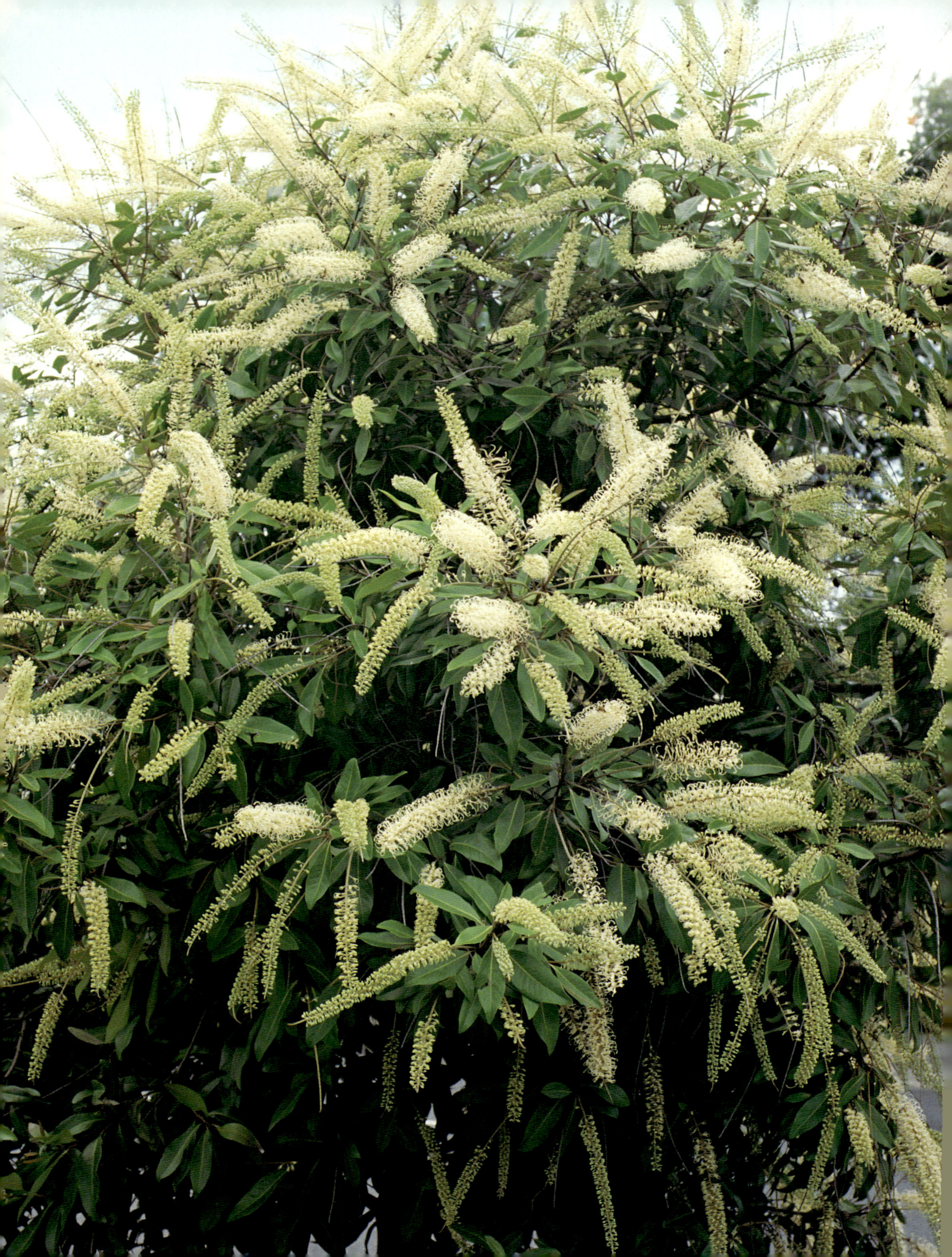

Trees

One great pleasure about living in a warm climate is the number of flowering trees which brighten the urban landscape. Even the least picturesque parts of a city can be glorified by a jacaranda or a poinciana in full bloom. The average suburban garden does not offer enough room to grow many trees but with good planning every garden ought to be able to grow at least one flowering tree which will also provide shade.

It all depends on the type of garden you wish to create — or re-create. If trees are important to you, then obviously you will plan to incorporate them into your lifestyle. For instance a large, spreading tree, which flowers splendidly in season, may be chosen as the centrepoint for your garden around which all else is designed. Or you may select a tree for its shade, rather than its flowering ability, and make this the focus of outdoor living activities.

Trees of the same type can be used as a backdrop, along a boundary where they don't interfere with the central garden space. If they are flowering trees, they will add a colour accent in season. Trees at the corners of the garden will soften the square or rectangular lines of so many of our suburban gardens and provide shady areas at different times of day. Even the smallest garden will have room for a conifer because of their neat foliage and generally un-exuberant branching: the smaller, columnar or horizontal types can be used to mark a front, back or side boundary, or to line a driveway.

What must not be forgotten is the sheer joy of growing a tree simply because it is beautiful. This is the most common reason for buying a tree and if that is the case it needs to be visible; perhaps framed by a window, or right at the front of the house where everyone can see it, or as a focal point of outdoor living in the back garden.

Where space for trees is limited, it's most important to make the right choice. If you have a new garden, choosing the trees you wish to plant is one of the first decisions you should make, and then you can go on to plan the garden around them. If you have an established or part-established garden, the choice is more difficult. Here the first question to ask yourself is: what is the tree for? For shade, for colour, perhaps also for fragrance? Once this question is answered, you have to select trees which meet your criteria *and* can fit into the garden without problems. For instance, trees with messy flower, fruit and leaf drop — and those with branch shedding habits — should not be planted around swimming pools, barbecue areas, or where they can be a nuisance to neighbours. While trees overhanging a house can create shade and have a softening effect, leaf and other tree litter cause gutter clutter.

It is, of course, possible to create a garden consisting mostly of trees. In this case, there will be a fairly closed canopy, perhaps of varying height, with a groundcover and understorey of shade-loving plants. In a warm climate, trees are one of the least expensive and most effective ways of providing much-needed shade. For this reason gardeners in the tropics, sub-tropics and hot inland areas, where light and warmth are less important than shade and

Buckinghamia celsissima (Ivory Curl Tree, see page 75) is one of the loveliest Australian trees in cultivation and is often used for avenue plantings in sub-tropical areas. Besides its lavish displays in summer of perfumed white flowers, this trouble-free tree produces flushes of glowing red new foliage.

coolness, should give more emphasis to trees in the garden than is the case in cooler climates. When the sun is blazing and the humidity high, the rustle of leaves close around the house, the filtering of light through foliage, the very patterns of it on the walls and paving, all help create a cool feeling.

The range of beautiful trees which can be grown in warm climates is large; the following list is merely a selection of the most popular garden performers which are easily obtainable. Height of trees at maturity is approximate only as this depends on many factors including soil, climate, available water, sun and individual habit.

For palms, see page 88; for hot-climate conifers, see page 83.

Acacia

The best acacias for gardens are shrubs because the tree forms are generally short-lived. They are still worth growing, either as quick cover which can be replaced later, or for their short-term beauty. Acacias are reliable flowerers, year after year, and are easy to grow in most conditions because they tolerate poor soils, require little care and are drought-hardy. When specimens of the same species are planted close together they make a spectacular massed golden show in season. Good native plant nurseries will generally have a range of acacias in stock and these may differ according to the season.

The following have been selected for their relative longevity, prolific flowering and general good garden performance in the tropics and sub-tropics. All have bright yellow or gold ball or rod-shaped flowers.

Acacia concurrens
HEIGHT To 4 m
HABIT Spreading
CONDITIONS Sun, good drainage, light soil
FLOWERING TIME Spring.

Acacia elata
HEIGHT To 10 m
HABIT Slightly weeping
CONDITIONS Sun, average soil
FLOWERING TIME Spring
OTHER POINTS Hardy.

Acacia fimbriata (BRISBANE WATTLE)
HEIGHT To 5 m
HABIT Weeping and bushy
CONDITIONS Sun. Average to very sandy soil
FLOWERING TIME Late winter and spring
OTHER POINTS Fragrant. Dwarf form available.

Acacia leucoclada SSP. *argentifolia* (GOLDEN SILVER FERN WATTLE)
HEIGHT To 7 m
HABIT Fairly bushy
CONDITIONS Sun. Average soils but lives longest and tolerates harsher conditions (such as frost) if on good soil
FLOWERING TIME Mid-winter to early spring
OTHER POINTS Silvery, fernlike foliage and perfumed flowers. Quite long-lived..

Acacia o'shanesii
HEIGHT To 5 m
HABIT Weeping
CONDITIONS Sun. Average to wet soils
OTHER POINTS Fern-like foliage.

AFRICAN TULIP TREE (*Spathodea campanulata*)
AFRICA
HEIGHT 12 m
HABIT Evergreen. Upright, not dense
FOLIAGE Large, pinnate leaves with light-green leaflets
FLOWERS Spectacular large, orange-scarlet blooms with upright petals which form a horizontally elongated tulip-shaped cup. Very showy
FLOWERING TIME Flowers for a very long period from late spring to early winter, differing slightly according to latitude. Flowering is longer in warmer, lowland areas
CONDITIONS Sun. Does best in a light, humus enriched, well-drained soil but will grow in heavier soils where it tends to be 'leggy' and below average height. Some light pruning in the early stages is advisable to curtail leggy habit. Frost tender when young but otherwise fairly hardy. Needs plenty of water but waterlogging will kill. This tree does not like strong winds when young, because the trunk at this stage tends to be long and branchless. Staking is advisable in exposed areas.

Alloxylon flammeum (TREE WARATAH, PINK SILKY OAK)
AUSTRALIA
HEIGHT To 25 m
HABIT Spreading to about 5 m, open canopy
FOLIAGE Lobed when young, changing to long, narrow, lanceolate leaves at maturity. Evergreen
FLOWERS Scarlet.
FLOWERING TIME Winter and spring
CONDITIONS Sun or light-shade. Rich well-drained soil preferred. Plenty of water when young
OTHER POINTS One of the more spectacular trees from the north Queensland rainforest. Similar species *Alloxylon wickhamii* is also a good garden specimen, with pinkish-red flowers and pink–mauve flushes of new growth. Trees grown from cuttings flower within about four years; those from seeds may take up to ten years.

Backhousia citriodora (LEMON-SCENTED MYRTLE, LEMON-SCENTED IRONWOOD)
AUSTRALIA
HEIGHT To 10 m
HABIT Fairly dense canopy, spreading to about 5 m
FOLIAGE Dark green, glossy and lanceolate with a strong lemon scent. Evergreen

FLOWERS White, with 4 or 5 petals. Profusely clustered
FLOWERING TIME Spring and summer
CONDITIONS Average soil, from light to medium-heavy. Good drainage.
OTHER POINTS A Queensland tree with two attractive close relatives, *B. anisata* (which is taller, with aniseed-scented flowers) and *B. myrtifolia* which has much longer leaves and subtly-scented flowers.

Barklya syringifolia (CROWN OF GOLD)
AUSTRALIA
HEIGHT To about 6 m*
HABIT Rounded form, bushy
FOLIAGE Glossy and heart-shaped. Evergreen
FLOWERS Dense racemes of golden blossom
FLOWERING TIME Early summer. Short but spectacular
CONDITIONS Does best in fairly rich but not heavy soil. Good drainage
OTHER POINTS Slow growing and can take ten years to flower from seed; cutting-grown specimens flower fastest.
* This tree or shrub can vary greatly in height and has been known to reach 20 m in the forest but is very slow growing. Height given is approximate for garden trees.

Bauhinia

Bauhinias are popular warm-climate street and garden trees because of their modest size, tolerance of climatic variance and attractive flowers. They come in several species and flowering forms. Some of the best known in cultivation are:

Bauhinia blakeana
HONG KONG
HEIGHT To 5 m
HABIT Fairly spreading and with open canopy
FOLIAGE Large, dull green, two-lobed like butterfly wings. Evergreen
FLOWERS Very large, orchid-like and deep, dull, red in colour like those of *B. rubra*
FLOWERING TIME Early to mid-summer and again in winter
CONDITIONS Does best in good, well-drained soil. Plenty of water when young
OTHER POINTS Very fast growing and early flowering.

Bauhinia variegata
INDIA
HEIGHT To 6 m
HABIT The spread is contained, with an open canopy.
FOLIAGE Large, dull green, two-lobed like butterfly wings. Briefly deciduous in late winter or (in the tropics) during cooler weather between monsoons.
FLOWERS Large, orchid-like, pink, mauve or white, depending on form
FLOWERING TIME Spring
CONDITIONS Sun. Average soil. Plenty of water when young
OTHER POINTS Needs thorough, regular pruning for good form and flowering. (See page 77.)

B. purpurea is similar, with purple flowers. *B. rubra* has deep, dull, red flowers.

Buckinghamia celsissima (IVORY CURL TREE)
AUSTRALIA
HEIGHT 6 m
HABIT Evergreen
FOLIAGE Very attractive, especially the lustrous red new growth. Leaves usually lobed on young trees
FLOWERS Terminal spikes of large white 'bottlebrush' flowers, very profuse, with curling stamens. Beautifully perfumed
FLOWERING TIME Summer
CONDITIONS Full sun. Very tolerant of most conditions though does best in light, well-composted soils with frequent watering when young. Pest free and requiring little or no pruning, it makes an excellent street tree. See page 72.

Callistemon SPP. (BOTTLEBRUSH)
AUSTRALIA
HEIGHT Variable, from small shrubs to small trees
HABIT Evergreen. Generally loosely columnar or weeping
FOLIAGE Narrow and pointed, leaf length varies depending on species
FLOWERS 'Bottlebrush' in form; white, cream, pink or red
FLOWERING TIME Seasonal flowering depends on species and variety, and sometimes also on local conditions. There are winter-flowering types, those whose flowering is limited to spring and early summer, those which flower throughout summer and others which produce flowers almost all year
CONDITIONS Sunny position for good flowering, though in the bush callistemons often grow as understorey plants in light shade on the edges of forests or along creek banks. Many species of callistemon are well-suited to both hot and humid or hot and dry conditions. Others thrive in poorly drained soils
OTHER POINTS The common name for this variable tree or shrub is 'bottlebrush', though this is also commonly applied to other plants with similarly shaped flowers. All species and varieties available from nurseries are good performers in the home garden, new cultivars are being produced every year and selection comes down to a question of personal preference (for colour, shape or size) and what is locally available. Like most Australian native plants, callistemons do best in the home garden if trimmed lightly but regularly so that they achieve a good form and don't become sparse and straggling. Regular, moderate fertilising promotes denser foliage growth. Mostly pest and disease free, though can be subject to borer attacks on stem tips.

Cassia

The large cassia family includes some very lovely trees which thrive in tropical and sub-tropical streets and gardens. Not all are readily available in Australia but collectors would find them well worth cultivating if some of the less well-known species could be obtained.

Cassia brewsteri (LEICHHARDT BEAN)
AUSTRALIA

HEIGHT 10–12 m
HABIT Semi-deciduous. Open crown
FOLIAGE Divided, dark green and shiny
FLOWERS Drooping sprays of yellow and orange-red flowers
FLOWERING TIME Spring
CONDITIONS Full sun. All but very heavy soils. Will stand light frost and moderate dry periods
OTHER POINTS This lovely Australian rainforest tree is hardier than most other cassias and appears to be quite resistant to pests and diseases. Interesting seed pods.

Cassia fistula (GOLDEN SHOWER)
INDIA AND SRI LANKA
HEIGHT 5–6 m
HABIT Deciduous. Open canopy
FOLIAGE Long, pinnate leaves. Rather sparse
FLOWERS Long, drooping racemes of scented yellow flowers
FLOWERING TIME Summer

CORAL TREE (Erythrina lysistemon) is one of the most commonly grown of this attractive genus. It is a small tree with a spreading, well-formed crown which is covered in bright red flowers during the cool season.

CONDITIONS Full sun. Good drainage. This cassia is generally said to prefer rich soils and certainly produces denser foliage if given good soil and regular feeding. However, it will grow quite well (and often somewhat smaller) in poorer soils including clay. Drought and frost tender
OTHER POINTS Fast growing. Bears long, interesting brown seed pods after flowering. Mostly pest and disease free. Do not prune.

Cassia javanica
MALAYSIA
HEIGHT 7–8 m
HABIT Evergreen. Spreading to about 6 m. Fairly flat canopy
FOLIAGE Long, light green, pinnate leaves
FLOWERS Densely packed, very florific, light pink in colour
FLOWERING TIME Spring and summer
CONDITIONS Full sun. Prefers a well-drained, rich soil but will grow in poorer soils. Drought and frost tender
OTHER POINTS A very beautiful and spectacular tree when in flower. Fairly fast growing. Not always easily available in Australia today, though many fine specimens can be found in long-established, hot-climate streets and gardens.

Cassia SP. 'PALUMA RANGE'
AUSTRALIA

When bauhinias begin to flower it is a reminder that the hot season is just around the corner. The exquisite white, pink, mauve, purple or mauvish–red flowers resemble large orchids. See page 75. This bauhinia is B. variegata, *sometimes called* HONG KONG ORCHID TREE.

HEIGHT 3–5 m
HABIT Evergreen. Bushy
FOLIAGE Neat, glossy, purplish-red new growth
FLOWERS Long racemes of bright yellow flowers borne 'inside' the tree canopy
FLOWERING TIME Summer
CONDITIONS Full sun for good flowering, though will flower reasonably in light shade. Does best in good soil with plenty of water but will grow well in poorer soils and can withstand dry periods even when quite young
OTHER POINTS This lovely Australian rainforest tree was first cultivated in the 1980s and has since proved an excellent street and garden tree.

Colvillea racemosa
EAST AFRICA
HEIGHT 7–8 m
HABIT Evergreen. Fairly spreading
FOLIAGE Large, divided, and fernlike
FLOWERS Dense sprays of gorgeous orange blossoms
FLOWERING TIME Either early summer or late summer–autumn, depending on form
CONDITIONS Tolerant of most soil conditions but does best in fairly rich, acid soil with plenty of water when young. Frost tender
OTHER POINTS This is a lovely, graceful, colourful tree which does not seem to suffer from disease or insect attack.

Dombeya natalensis syn. *D. tiliacea*
SOUTH AFRICA
HEIGHT 4 m
HABIT Evergreen or semi-deciduous. Bushy
FOLIAGE Dark green, soft, finely toothed and resembling the leaves of a grape vine
FLOWERS Large, cup-shaped white, fragrant
FLOWERING TIME Winter and spring
CONDITIONS A tough tree or large shrub which will stand most conditions except extreme cold and drought. Prune for shape
OTHER POINTS This is an attractive tree for difficult places in the garden as it will stand exposure and neglect. Fast growing.

Erythrina caffra (Coral Tree)
South Africa
Height 15 m
Habit Deciduous. Sparse canopy, fairly spreading
Foliage Leaves are made up of three rhomboid leaflets
Flowers Large, long-lasting, scarlet
Flowering time Winter and spring
Conditions Full sun. Withstands drought. Frost tender
Other points This decorative tree has spikes on the trunk which makes it not a good choice for street use, as does its tendency to 'fall apart' in heavily trafficked areas. The flowers on bare branches in spring make a spectacular show. Other, very similar erythrinas are also quite common in warmer areas of Australia. *E. crista-galli* is not drought resistant; *E. variegata* (syn. *sykesii* syn. *indica*) is hardier to frost though still frost tender when young. A variety *E. sykesii* 'Parcelli' is strikingly different to other 'tree' erythrinas, having large variegated leaves — it grows only in warm climates. *E. speciosa* is similar to the rest, with a denser canopy. *E. vespertilio* (Batswing Coral Tree) is an Australian native which can withstand long drought periods. (See pages 76 and 85.)

Eucalyptus

Australia is the home of the eucalypt or 'gumtree'. Of the several hundred species which grace our bushland, few are really suitable to any but the largest home gardens. Many are large trees which often have a habit of regularly dropping leaves, twigs, bark and even heavy branches, which makes them unpopular with tidy gardeners. On the other hand, they often have attractive flowers, aromatic foliage, decorative trunks and are excellent for attracting birds and bees to the garden. As eucalypts are found in all Australian climatic zones, there are many species suited to either dry or hot wet climates.

Gardeners who wish to grow eucalypts should first decide where they will go and what purpose they will serve, then seek advice from a nursery on what will suit; taking into account height, habit, flowering and other characteristics. Most eucalypts should not be planted around pools, nor close to houses and other buildings. Planted on the boundary, their untidy habits may annoy neighbours. But if the garden is large enough and particularly if you want to create a 'natural' landscape, one or more of these graceful Australians will be well worth planting.

In general descriptive terms, eucalypts are tall-growing with either straight stems or twisted, even bulbous trunks. Leaves are generally dull grey-green, narrow, often curved, or sometimes almost rounded in shape. Flowers are fluffy and can be coloured white, cream, pink, red, orange or yellow. Interesting seed capsules are common to many eucalypts. Some trees have bark 'stockings' at the base, others attractive reddish outer bark, or bark which is shed in strips or patches, leaving a smooth, shiny, very decorative surface beneath.

The following selection includes some of the smaller, ornamental eucalypts which are particularly suitable for all but very small hot-climate gardens. Like other Australian native trees and shrubs, many eucalypt varieties are now sold under trade names. Plants so labelled are generally suitable for the home garden but, if you are concerned about factors such as height and leaf or branch shedding, it is best to check the species name.

Eucalyptus caesia
Western Australia
Height 3–4 m
Habit Erect, with drooping canopy
Foliage Lanceolate, blue-grey
Flowers Large, pink or pinkish-red
Flowering time Winter and spring
Conditions Light, well-drained soil. Frost tender
Other points Sub-species *E. caesia magna* is a particularly good garden tree. Not suited to the tropics.

Eucalyptus ficifolia syn. *Corymbia* (Scarlet Flowering Gum)
Western Australia
Height 6 m
Habit Bushy crown
Foliage Bright green, slender
Flowers Masses of large flowers which, despite the name, can be almost any shade of white, pink, orange or red — as well as the vivid scarlet for which this tree is best known
Flowering time Late spring and summer
Conditions Full sun. Does best in coastal areas. Drought and frost tender.
Other points A delightful garden tree but grafted specimens are best if soil is not very well-drained.

Eucalyptus ptychocarpa (Swamp Bloodwood)
Northern Territory
Height Up to 4 m, depending on situation
Habit Erect
Foliage Dull green, broadly lanceolate
Flowers Large, vivid scarlet; some hybrids have orange flowers
Flowering time Spring and summer
Conditions Sun. Any soil. Needs moisture
Other points A very pretty, small eucalypt. May not flower early, or well, below about the Tropic of Capricorn.

Flame Tree (*Brachychiton acerifolius*)
Australia
Height 12 m (very approximate)
Habit Deciduous or semi-deciduous, conical
Foliage Large, lobed, maple-like leaves
Flowers Vivid red, bell-like in shape, profuse
Flowering time Early summer
Conditions Rich, light, deep, well-drained soil. Likes plenty of humus and moisture during establishment.
Other points One of the most spectacular Australian trees. Pest free. Very similar, but with a less reliable flowering habit, is the pink-flowered *Brachychiton discolor*.

Foambark (*Jagera pseudorhus*)
Australia
Height 10 m

HABIT Evergreen, dense, fairly spreading
FOLIAGE Very attractive light green, pinnate, fernlike leaves
FLOWERS Long sprays of tiny pink blossom
FLOWERING TIME Autumn to spring
CONDITIONS Sun or light shade. Any soil. Plenty of water. Will withstand light frosts
OTHER POINTS A pretty tree which also bears colourful red-to-brown fruits which contain hairs that can irritate the skin.

FRANGIPANI (*Plumeria* SPP.)
CENTRAL AMERICA AND MEXICO
HEIGHT Variable according to species and form but generally up to 5 m
HABIT Deciduous. Spreading and dense in summer, sparse during deciduous phase
FOLIAGE Large, leathery, elliptic leaves
FLOWERS Small, fragrant, five-petalled. Colours range from the common white with yellow centres through various shades of peach, pink and magenta
FLOWERING TIME Summer to autumn
CONDITIONS Grows fastest in rich, well-watered soils but is also very tolerant of poor soils and dry conditions
OTHER POINTS *P. rubra* is the most common species found in Australia, with several varieties available, though other species are present including the tall, evergreen *P. obtusa*. All frangipani stems are grey, coarse-fibred and brittle; the milky sap is poisonous but not palatable. It is easy to propagate by breaking off a piece of the stem, allowing it to callus by placing it in a dry medium such as sharp sand, then planting out and watering lightly but regularly until shoots appear. Regular watering should be continued until plant is well-established. (See page 80.)

Golden Penda (*Xanthostemon chrysanthus*)
AUSTRALIA
HEIGHT 4–5 m
HABIT Evergreen. Dense if pruned. Tree or large shrub
FOLIAGE Rather dull, with leathery, glossy, simple leaves
FLOWERS Bright gold and spectacular
FLOWERING TIME Spring and summer
CONDITIONS Full sun. Tolerant of most soils but prefers one which is light and well-drained, with plenty of humus. Can stand short periods of dry weather without watering but in general likes regular watering. Frost tender but grows quite well in cooler areas where it takes longer to flower. Flowering is improved by regular pruning
OTHER POINTS One of the loveliest Australian rainforest trees to be brought into cultivation. *Xanthostemon whiteii* has green flowers; *X. youngii* has red flowers.

Harpullia pendula (TULIPWOOD)
AUSTRALIA
HEIGHT 15 m (generally not this tall in home garden)
HABIT Evergreen. Dense-crowned and compact in cultivation
FOLIAGE Large, pinnate and glossy
FLOWERS Yellowish, insignificant
CONDITIONS Sun. Light to medium soils, though tolerant of most soil conditions except very heavy or very wet. Hardy but does not like severe frosts when young, nor long periods of drought
OTHER POINTS This is an excellent street and garden shade tree. Though the flowers are dull, the bright orange (sometimes yellow) seed capsules, which open to reveal shiny black seeds, give the tree plenty of colour throughout spring and early summer.

Jacaranda mimosifolia (JACARANDA)
BRAZIL
HEIGHT 10 m
HABIT Very spreading
FOLIAGE Soft and fernlike. Light green
FLOWERS Prolific, soft mauve flowers
FLOWERING TIME Spring
CONDITIONS Sun. Hardy. Jacarandas generally grow in areas with fairly high rainfall but have proved able to withstand drought periods. Although a warm climate tree which is commonly associated with coastal areas it performs particularly well in inland towns where temperatures range from quite cold (and frosty) to very hot
OTHER POINTS A jacaranda in full bloom is one of the glorious sights in many Australian towns. Young plants do best if protected from extreme cold and wind; as the plant has a leggy habit when young it needs staking against strong winds. One of the most beautiful trees found anywhere; although somewhat large for the average garden, it makes a fine feature tree which provides light shade in summer and allows plenty of light through in winter. The best-known is *J. mimosifolia* but other species, such as the attractive *J. semiserrata,* is available and there is a white-flowering form of *J. mimosifolia.* Relatively pest and disease free though can be attacked by stem borers.

Koelreuteria paniculata (GOLDEN RAIN TREE)
Because this is not the only tree commonly called 'Golden Rain' I have listed it by its taxonomical name, which is also well known.
CHINA
HEIGHT 6 m
HABIT Briefly deciduous in warm climates. Compact, with a rounded crown
FOLIAGE Attractive, with large compound leaves
FLOWERS Long sprays of yellow flowers
FLOWERING TIME Spring, sometimes also summer
CONDITIONS Performs well in a variety of climates and conditions, adapting its habits to suit. Moderate pruning improves form, particularly when young
OTHER POINTS Besides the flowers, another striking feature is the large, bladder-like shiny pinkish-red seed pod, produced in autumn. Pest and disease free.

Lagerstroemia SPP. (PRIDE OF INDIA, CREPE MYRTLE)
INDIA and MALAYSIA (some lagerstroemias also originate in China)
HEIGHT 8 m
HABIT Deciduous. Many erect branches
FOLIAGE Neat, elliptical leaves, not dense

FLOWERS Very prolific displays of crepe-textured blooms in various shade of pink and mauve
FLOWERING TIME Summer
CONDITIONS Full sun. Drought and frost tender. Does well in most soils. Pruning improves shape and flowering. Generally pest and disease free
OTHER POINTS Australians generally do not distinguish between the most commonly available lagerstroemia species *L. speciosa* and *L. indica*. They are very similar, though the former has larger leaves. A white-flowering form of *L. indica* is also available. This tree in youth can produce multiple trunks and is therefore sometimes described as a shrub. It is fast growing, trouble-free and adds a vivid splash of summer colour to many Australian sub-tropical and tropical gardens.

LEOPARD TREE OR LEOPARDWOOD (*Caesalpina ferrea*)
BRAZIL
HEIGHT 10 m

HABIT Briefly deciduous. Fairly spreading
FOLIAGE Fernlike and attractive, offering light shade cover
FLOWERS Clusters of small yellow flowers
FLOWERING TIME Summer to autumn
CONDITIONS Tolerates most soil conditions but though generally hardy is drought and frost tender when young.
OTHER POINTS A striking feature of this very attractive tree is the patterned bark. Pruning is advisable when young as trees are inclined to be 'leggy'.

*FRANGIPANI (*Plumeria* SPP., see page 79) is a true tropical which also grows well in sub-tropical and warm-temperate climates. Most species are deciduous and their bare branches add a dramatic note to the garden in the cooler months. In summer the tree is covered with fragrant blossom for a long period. White is the most common colour but deep red, pink and orange are also available.*

LILLY PILLY, see page 86.

Melicope elleryana syn. *Euodia* (PINK EUODIA)
AUSTRALIA
HEIGHT 10 m, though usually smaller in gardens, particularly in lower rainfall areas
HABIT Evergreen. Very open canopy
FOLIAGE Neat, smallish, glossy leaves
FLOWERS Pink and prolific
FLOWERING TIME Summer
CONDITIONS Plenty of water. Surface rooting so requires a position in lightly mulched soil
OTHER POINTS A pretty rainforest tree which looks best if thoroughly pruned after flowering to promote denser growth. A relative, *Evodiella muelleri* is a very good garden tree, and much smaller.

Metrosideros

Some confusion is caused by the name of this genus of trees and shrubs. The best-known of them come from New Zealand and varieties of the familiar *Metrosideros excelsa*, are known as 'New Zealand Christmas Tree'. This is an evergreen, hardy tree to about 15 m with unusual aerial roots and bright red bottlebrush flowers. Another popular garden tree is *M. kermadecensis*, a smaller tree than *M. excelsa*, with a rounder shape and shrubbier habit. Variegated forms are available. The New Zealand metrosideros perform well in gardens all over Australia and the new, small cultivars, some of which can be classified as shrubs, are very florific. Somewhat different in appearance is the Australian *Metrosideros queenslandica* (QUEENSLAND GOLDEN MYRTLE), a rainforest tree with handsome, glossy foliage, rounded form and clusters of golden-yellow flowers in summer. An excellent garden tree for warmer climates, though it is cold hardy to freezing for short periods (but young plants must be protected from frost). All the metrosideros like humus-enriched, well-drained soils which do not completely dry out. The New Zealand species prefer full sun while the Queensland tree will grow in full sun or light shade.

Michelia champaca (TROPICAL MAGNOLIA)
ASIA
HEIGHT 8 m
HABIT Evergreen. Conical
FOLIAGE Large, light green leaves
FLOWERS Yellow or pale orange and very fragrant
FLOWERING TIME Early summer to autumn
CONDITIONS Full sun. Does best in a light, humus-enriched, well-drained soil but will thrive in less than ideal soil conditions. Will stand low temperatures down to freezing but not severe frost. Water well during establishment
OTHER POINTS A trouble-free tree which adds fragrance to the garden during its long flowering period.

Pittosporum rhombifolium
AUSTRALIA
HEIGHT 4 m
HABIT Upright, with fairly sparse branching
FOLIAGE Tapered, medium-sized, mid-green leaves
FLOWERS Cream, perfumed
FLOWERING TIME Late winter–early spring
CONDITIONS Does best in a good soil with adequate seasonal rainfall
OTHER POINTS Striking orange berries in summer. Most other pittosporums are shrubs, see pages 104–5.

POINCIANA, FLAMBOYANT (*Delonix regia*)
MADAGASCAR
HEIGHT 6 m
HABIT Flat topped and spreading to about 15 m (more in some very large trees) at maturity. Briefly deciduous though some trees, in some years, do not lose their leaves, particularly in the warmest areas
FOLIAGE Long, bipinnate leaves
FLOWERS Orange–red to scarlet flowers
FLOWERING TIME Late spring and summer
CONDITIONS Does best at the coast in light soils but will grow further inland in warm areas with good rainfall. As long as it receives good monsoonal rain, the tree will withstand long, dry spells. Too much year-round watering promotes leaf growth at the expense of flowering. Roots are large and invasive though this does not prevent the poinciana from being a popular street tree. One of the world's most beautiful flowering trees, widely planted in many cities and towns which lie between the tropics of Cancer and Capricorn. Despite its provenance, this tree will take cold down to freezing point, if not prolonged, but young trees must be protected from frost and cold winds.
OTHER POINTS Though canopy is low and spreading, it is a fine tree for larger gardens or those which want one large feature tree to provide shade, shelter and spectacle. Long, dark seed pods add an interesting note. Although poincianas in Australia are subject to borer attack, borers and poincianas live a very long time together, generally without the host tree suffering much damage. Limbs which do show real damage can be lopped, though poincianas do not take kindly to unnecessary pruning. (See page 8.)

Radermachera sinica
CHINA
HEIGHT 10 m
HABIT Evergreen. Dense, with pendulous branches
FOLIAGE Shiny. Variegated forms
FLOWERS Insignificant
CONDITIONS Sun or light-shade. Any reasonable, well-drained, humus-enriched soil. Frost and drought tender.
OTHER POINTS An easy-to-grow tree which also makes a good indoor specimen. Variegated forms such as 'CRYSTAL DOLL' are excellent for creating foliage colour contrast in the garden.

Schotia brachypetala
SOUTH AFRICA
HEIGHT 8 m
HABIT Semi-deciduous. Spreading
FOLIAGE Pinnate, with small leaflets
FLOWERS Deep red, peaflower-shaped, florific in season

FLOWERING TIME Spring
CONDITIONS Sun. Does best in a deep, light, humus-enriched soil where it can make fast growth. Otherwise tolerant of poorer soils.
OTHER POINTS A very lovely tree when in flower and a good garden or street specimen. The flowers attract parrots and other nectar-eating birds and animals.

SILKY OAK (*Grevillea robusta*)
AUSTRALIA
HEIGHT About 20 m in cultivation
HABIT Semi-deciduous (loses leaves in colder regions and prolonged dry weather). Columnar, fairly sparse
FOLIAGE Stiff, fern-like, compound leaves
FLOWERS Large, showy, golden-bronze 'bottlebrushes'
FLOWERING TIME Spring
CONDITIONS Sun or shade, but flowers best in full sun. Tolerant of most soils. Frost and drought tolerant if given adequate water and protection when very young
OTHER POINTS A very hardy rainforest tree which will flower poorly and develop a spindly form in colder mountain regions. Though large for a garden, its upright habit and sparse shade make it quite suitable for bigger gardens and street planting where powerlines are not a problem. It thrives by the sea and in drier inland towns.

Tabebuia SPP. (TRUMPET TREE)
CENTRAL AMERICA
HEIGHT 10–15 m
HABIT Upright with a light canopy
FOLIAGE Deciduous. Compound and palmate, with small, neat, oblong or rounded leaflets, depending on type
FLOWERS Terminal clusters of trumpet-shaped blooms which are very showy
FLOWERING TIME Spring
CONDITIONS Sun. Prefers a light, humus-enriched soil which is well-drained. Protect from harsh weather. Frost and drought tender.
OTHER POINTS Tabebuias are medium-sized trees which add a grace note to any garden. *T. rosea* has pale to deep pink blooms which cover the tree in season and make an exquisite sight; *T. chrysantha* has yellow flowers, as does the similar *T. argentea* which also features silvery foliage, making a true spectacle in bright sunlight.

TAMARIND (*Tamarindus indica*)
INDIA
HEIGHT 15 m
HABIT Semi-deciduous. Spreading to about 6 m
FOLIAGE Long and pinnate, with many fern-like leaflets
FLOWERS Pale yellow with reddish veins, not particularly spectacular but lightly fragrant
FLOWERING TIME Summer
CONDITIONS Sun. Tolerant of most soil conditions; will not stand long periods of drought and needs frost protection when young.
OTHER POINTS Despite invasive roots this is an excellent shade or street tree.

Thevetia peruviana
TROPICAL AMERICA
HEIGHT To 5 m
HABIT Wide and spreading
FOLIAGE Long, slender, light green leaves
FLOWERS Yellow, tubular, flaring open
FLOWERING TIME Late spring and summer
CONDITIONS Any soil, from sandy to clay, but grows fastest in a good soil that is not too heavy. Sun. Frost tender
OTHER POINTS A pretty tree which is easy to grow. Often develops a multi-branched, shrubby form unless trained. Milky sap is poisonous.

Tipuana speciosa (TIPU TREE)
SOUTH AMERICA
HEIGHT 15 m
HABIT Semi-deciduous; inclined to shed leaves in cold or very dry weather. Large, rounded canopy
FOLIAGE Long, pinnate leaves
FLOWERS Racemes of yellow-to-orange flowers, very showy
FLOWERING TIME Spring
CONDITIONS Quite hardy, tolerating low temperatures if not prolonged. Frost tender when young. Does best in a light, humus enriched soil. Plenty of water during establishment
OTHER POINTS Decorative, fast-growing and trouble-free.

TUCKEROO (*Cupaniopsis anacardioides*)
AUSTRALIA
HEIGHT About 8 m
HABIT Evergreen
FOLIAGE Neat, shiny, upward-growing leaves with notched ends
FLOWERS Insignificant
CONDITIONS Sun. Hardy in most conditions. Regular watering and fertilising will hasten growth and promote a dense form
OTHER POINTS A tough tree which performs particularly well in difficult coastal conditions and can also withstand urban stress and pollution. Most spectacular feature is the yellow fruit which grows in thick clusters.

WHEEL-OF-FIRE TREE (*Stenocarpus sinuatus*)
AUSTRALIA
HEIGHT 10–15 m
HABIT Evergreen. Upright
FOLIAGE Leaves are up to about 30 cm long, entire but deeply lobed when young
FLOWERS Red and shaped rather like a wheel
FLOWERING TIME Late summer and autumn
CONDITIONS Sun or shade, though full sun will limit height for a garden tree and promote flowering. Though slow growing, will put on speed with regular but light applications of low-phosphorous fertiliser and water. Young trees are frost and drought tender.

WHITE CEDAR (*Melia azedarach*)
AUSTRALIA
HEIGHT About 12 m in cultivation, much taller in the forest
HABIT Deciduous. Fairly open canopy

FOLIAGE Rather attractive compound leaves with a slightly pendulous, lacy effect
FLOWERS Sprays of mauve, perfumed flowers
FLOWERING TIME Spring
CONDITIONS Best in full sun. Fast growing, particularly in light, humus-enriched soils but tolerant of most soils and conditions
OTHER POINTS A reliable garden tree although the attractive yellow-to-brown fruits, borne in autumn, are poisonous to humans and domestic animals. Can be subject to caterpillar attack in autumn but this rarely does long-term harm to the tree which in any case loses its foliage in winter.

HOT-CLIMATE CONIFERS

Conifers are often perceived by gardeners as strictly cold-climate trees, yet many of them either originate in warm climates or else adapt well to tropical and sub-tropical conditions. All conifers have handsome foliage, which is sufficiently dense to make an excellent windbreak or shelterbelt. Their compact form and neat habit make coniferous trees especially popular in small gardens where larger trees would be a nuisance. These virtues are enhanced by the fact that today's garden varieties come in all shapes and sizes: tall and slender, pyramid, rounded, dwarf. In fact there is a conifer shape to suit any position in the garden and colours range from gold, to blue-grey to many shades of light and dark green. Besides providing interesting texture and colour year round, conifers require no care once established.

Coniferous trees include the pines, cypresses, junipers, spruces, cryptomerias, thujas, callitris and araucarias. The following list includes exotic conifers only. Australian conifers of the genus Araucaria (Bunya, Hoop and Norfolk Pines) are generally too large for suburban gardens; *Callitris* species are included in the lists for hot and dry gardens, page 54, and trees for coastal gardens, page 46.

Pruning conifers

Conifers grown as specimens in the garden don't need to be pruned because they are bred to attain good form naturally. They should only be pruned where branches are in the way either of people, buildings or other plants. For this reason, it is better to plant coniferous trees where they are free to attain their natural size and shape; this is particularly true of those with a horizontal, spreading growth habit. On the other hand conifers grown as hedge plants will require some pruning. During the growing season, the top shoots and outer growth of a coniferous hedge can be regularly trimmed for height, shape and appearance as required. Main pruning should be done in early winter when no sap is rising; this should be limited to removing old wood and a general all-over tidy. Too-severe pruning of a coniferous hedge will in the short term expose the bare, brown centre which looks unattractive; in the long term it can cause them to die back.

Tall, pyramid shape

Araucaria cookii (COOK ISLAND PINE)
Cupressus glabra aurea 'GOLDEN ARIZONICA'
    C. torulosa (BHUTAN CYPRESS)
    C. torulosa 'ARCTIC GREEN'
Juniperus chinensis 'FEMINA'
    J. virginiana cupressifolia (HILLSPIRE JUNIPER)

Upright

Cupressus sempervirens var. *stricta* (PENCIL PINE)
Juniperus chinensis 'KAIZUKA' (HOLLYWOOD JUNIPER)
    J. chinensis 'ROBUSTA GREEN'
    J. virginiana
    J. virginiana 'SKYROCKET' (columnar)
Thuja occidentalis (BOOKLEAF PINE)

Spreading

Cupressus lambertiana 'HORIZONTALIS AUREA' (LAMBERT'S GOLDEN CYPRESS)
Juniperus horizontalis
    J. sabina 'BROADMOOR'
    J. sabina 'SCANDIA'

Dwarf

Cupressus torulosa nana (DWARF BHUTAN)
Thuja occidentalis compacta nana (GREEN BIOTA)
    T. occidentalis compacta nana aurea (GOLDEN BIOTA)
    T. orientalis 'MORGANII' (very dwarf form of GOLD BIOTA)

Globular

Thuja occidentalis compacta nana (GREEN BIOTA)
    T. occidentalis froebelli
    T. occidentalis 'LUTESCENS'

Groundcover

Juniperus conferta (JAPANESE SHORE PINE)
    J. horizontalis glauca (BLUE RUG)
    J. horizontalis 'PLUMOSA COMPACTA' 'ADVANCETOWN'
    J. horizontalis 'PRINCE OF WALES'
    J. procumbens 'NANA' (JAPANESE GARDEN JUNIPER)
    J. sabina 'TAMARISCIFOLIA' (TAM JUNIPER)
    J. virginiana prostrata

Golden

Chamaecyparis obtusa 'CRIPPSII'
Cupressus glabra aurea (GOLDEN ARIZONICA)
   C. lambertiana 'HORIZONTALIS AUREA' (LAMBERT'S GOLDEN CYPRESS)
Thuja occidentalis 'LUTESCENS'
   T. occidentalis beverleyensis
   T. orientalis compacta 'AUREA NANA'

Blue

Cupressus glabra 'BLUE STREAK'
Juniperus chinensis pfitzeriana
   J. c. pfitzeriana aurea (grey-green foliage with gold tips)
   J. c. pfitzeriana glauca
   J. horizontalis 'BAR HARBOUR'
   J. horizontalis glauca ('BLUE RUG')
   J. sabina 'BLUE DANUBE'

Grey or silver

Juniperus virginiana prostrata
Thuja occidentalis froebelli

Australian pines

The following, though not particularly similar in foliage to the exotic conifers, make excellent garden trees:
Podocarpus elatus (BROWN PINE)
Prumnopitys ladei (lovely foliage)

Trees with problem roots

Many trees have shallow, invasive root systems which can create problems when planted too close to houses, driveways, kerbing and underground services. Modern drainage systems will resist invasion by tree roots provided the pipes are not damaged, but any fracture or badly-fitting joint can be quickly penetrated as roots seek out water. In time, this may lead to a complete blockage. If you are not sure where your drains are, plans of private house drainage systems are available at the local council.

The following trees have particularly invasive root systems.

Allocasuarina SPP.
Brachychiton SPP.
Cinnamomum camphora (CAMPHOR LAUREL)
Erythrina SPP. (Coral Trees)
Eucalyptus SPP.
Ficus SPP. (figs)
Grevillea robusta (SILKY OAK)
Jacaranda mimosifolia
Lagerstroemia indica (CREPE MYRTLE, PRIDE OF INDIA)
LIQUIDAMBAR
Lophostemon confertus (BRUSH BOX)
MANGO
Melaleuca SPP.
Melia azedarach (WHITE CEDAR)
Melicope elleryana syn. *Euodia*
Pinus SPP.
Pongamia SPP.
POPLAR
Spathodea campanulata (AFRICAN TULIP TREE)
Schefflera actinophylla (UMBRELLA TREE)
Tipuana speciosa
WILLOW

Erythrina crista-galli is often used as a street tree because of its small size. It bears large sprays of medium to dark red flowers from summer right through the cool season. (See page 78.)

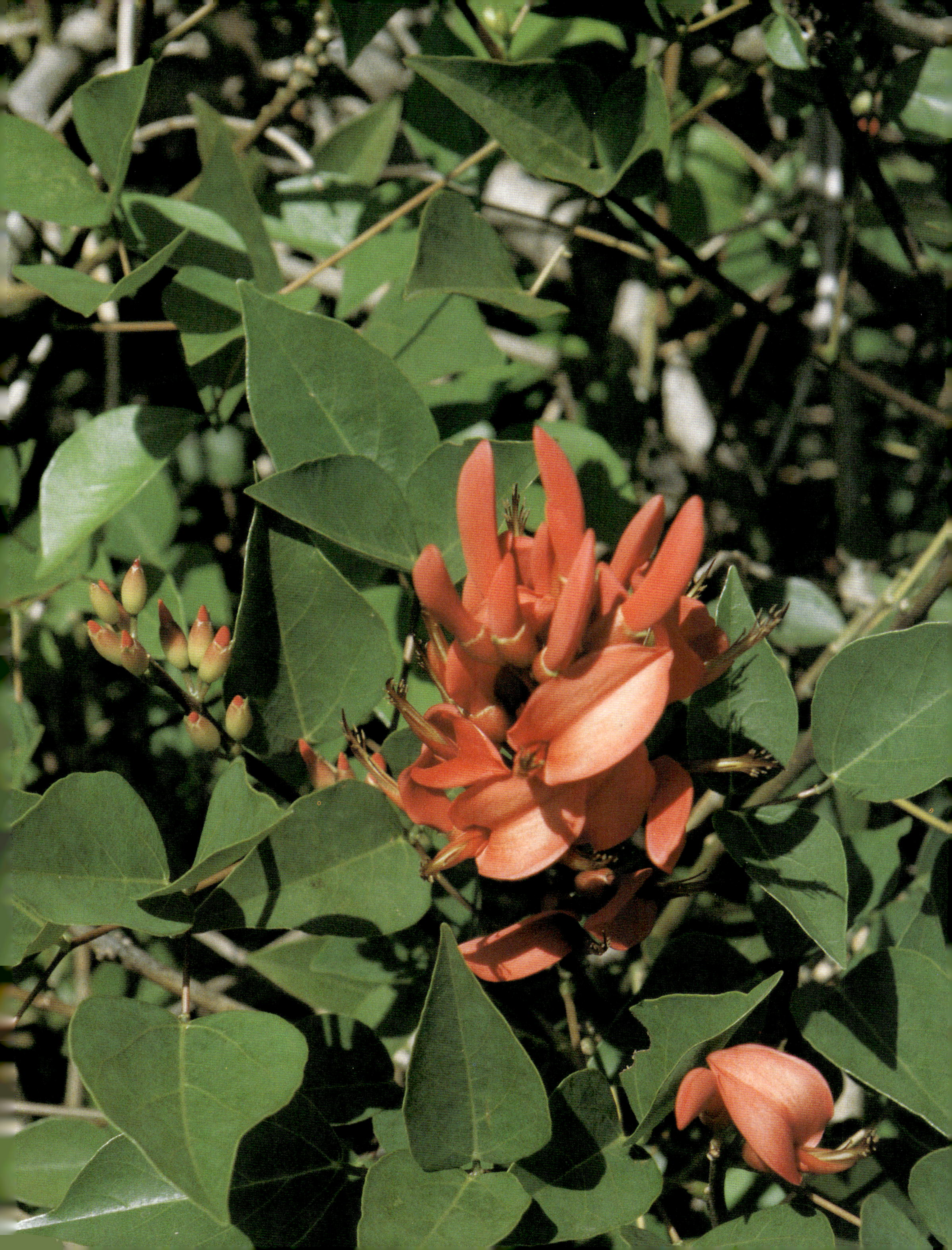

Lilly pillies

LILLY PILLY IS THE COMMON TERM for a wide range of trees and shrubs which used to be all lumped together as 'Eugenias'. Today some eugenias are still referred to as lilly pillies but the name is used mostly to describe species in the genera *Syzygium*, *Acmena* and *Waterhousea*. Most of those readily available to gardeners are Australian in origin, although the Brazilian Cherry (*Eugenia brasiliensis*), and *Syzygium jambos* are exotics.

Lilly pillies are among the best garden plants because they are very easy to grow and maintain, and lend themselves to a variety of uses. They have very decorative fluffy flowers and colourful, often edible fruits. The foliage is neat and glossy, with spectacular colour when new, ranging from pale pinks and apricots to bronze, copper, mauve and almost black, depending on species. This means that lilly pillies provide colour in the garden year-round.

It is no exaggeration to to say that there is a lilly pilly for almost every garden situation. They range from dwarf shrubs to rainforest giants, though even the latter will not grow so tall in a home garden. Most of those available in nurseries are a good garden size and can be used as feature trees, understorey shrubs, hedges, screens and border plants.

Lilly pillies are not too fussy about soil and, though they grow best in a fairly light but nutrient-rich, well-drained sandy loam, they can also handle heavier soils (such as some of the characteristic red mountain soils) and very sandy soils where nutrients are added (such as naturally occurring littoral rainforests). In the home garden they will grow without fertiliser and will withstand quite long, dry periods. However, they produce better flowers and foliage, and grow faster, if given a regular regime of watering and fertilising—controlled-release fertilisers are perfectly suitable.

Because lilly pillies are fast growing, they are popular in landscaping, and in establishing new home gardens. They are not usually spectacularly florific in nature; though some years shrubs will sport an extravagant growth for a short time which is quite stunning. In the garden, the use of flower-promoting fertilisers and regular light pruning *after* flowering will help promote more and better flowers.

Most lilly pillies will grow in any climate except the very coldest; however, in cooler regions it is as well to check the origin of the plant you are buying because some species are quite tropical in habit and their growth and flowering will be inhibited where the weather is cold.

The most common pest and disease problems which beset lilly pillies are the sooty mould caused by infestations of pink wax scale and pimple gall caused by psyllids. Treatments are found in the plant clinic section, page 226. Because they are bird-attracting plants, it is preferable not to spray them with harmful chemicals. Like most other plants, lilly pillies are sometimes subjected to attacks by swarms of caterpillars or beetles. The subsequent defoliation is rarely fatal to the plant (though it may be) but it is certainly unsightly. If detected in time, a thorough spraying with a garden hose, a dousing with a bleach solution or even smoke-pots placed under the tree should get rid of the pests — but beware of them heading straight for another victim in the garden!

Lilly pillies make good container plants, particularly the low-growing forms of *S. australe*. Forms with very neat, small foliage can be topiaried to a variety of shapes, which makes them very decorative for formal gardens, courtyards or in tubs either side of entrances. Most can be used indoors, where there is good light, though they will need regular spelling outdoors.

Popular lilly pillies for the home garden

Acmena smithii (NARROW-LEAVED LILLY PILLY)
HEIGHT About 3 m
FOLIAGE New growth is a glossy dark red
FLOWERS White flowers
FLOWERING TIME Summer
FRUITS Pink to mauve, sometimes white. Very decorative and long-lasting through to winter
OTHER POINTS A small garden tree which will tolerate damp or poor soils. Dwarf form available which is useful for tubs. Also a useful hedging plant for a variety of difficult situations. Prune well to encourage attractive fresh foliage growth. *A. hemilampra* has very shiny, laurel-like leaves and white fruits.

Syzygium erythrocalyx (RED BUD or JOHNSTONE RIVER APPLE)
HEIGHT 6 m
FOLIAGE Large, glossy, slightly ribbed leaves with dark red, shiny new growth
FLOWERS Very unusual lime-green flowers emerging from red buds on the trunk and branches
FLOWERING TIME Spring
FRUITS Large, red, edible
OTHER POINTS This is one of the most spectacular lilly pillies because of the unusual flowers and lovely new growth. However it is less hardy than most of its relatives, requiring both protection and reasonably constant humidity. An excellent plant for courtyards and sheltered spots in the garden, where it makes an interesting feature.

Syzygium francisii (WATER GUM)
HEIGHT 10 m
FOLIAGE Dark green and glossy with pinkish new growth
FLOWERS White, in dense clusters
FLOWERING TIME Summer
FRUITS Mauve

Syzygium leuhmannii (CHERRY SATINASH)
HEIGHT 15 m
FOLIAGE Neat, pointed, with lustrous purple new growth
FLOWERS White
FLOWERING TIME Summer
FRUITS Pinkish red
OTHER POINTS A compact tree, very easy to grow.

Syzygium oleosum (BLUE LILLY PILLY)
HEIGHT To 9 m
FOLIAGE Reddish-bronze new growth
FLOWERS White
FLOWERING TIME Late winter and spring
FRUITS Blue–mauve; spectacular
OTHER POINTS When grown in full sun and pruned regularly to encourage dense, ground-hugging growth, this is a useful plant for banks and to fill corners or other garden areas. Does well as a screening plant at the coast.

Syzygium wilsonii subsp. *wilsonii* (POWDER PUFF LILLY PILLY)
HEIGHT 1–2 metres
FOLIAGE Neat and glossy, with vivid pink new growth
FLOWERS Large and red
FLOWERING TIME Spring and summer
FRUITS White
OTHER POINTS The arched branches give this popular shrub a weeping habit. An excellent understorey plant because it likes light shade (and will do well in deeper shade). Water, mulch and fertilise regularly to promote good growth and flowering. Prune quite heavily after flowering to prevent a straggling habit and promote plentiful flowering. An excellent garden plant; dwarf form is particularly popular.

Lilly pillies with very colourful new foliage

Acmena smithii
    A. graveolens (and other acmenas)
Eugenia reinwardtiana
Syzygium australe
    S. erythrocalyx
    S. luehmanni
    S. oleosum
    S. wilsonii
    S. SP. 'LOCKERBIE SCRUB'
Waterhousea unipunctata (and other waterhouseas)

Other lilly pillies suitable for the home garden

Acmena brachyandra (RED APPLE)
    A. graveolens (CASSOWARY SATINASH)
Eugenia reinwardtiana (BEACH CHERRY)
Syzygium branderhorstii (LOCKERBIE SATINASH)
    S. cormiflorum (BUMPY SATINASH)
    S. crebrinerve (ROSE SATINASH)
    S. moorei (DUROBBY)
    S. paniculatum (MAGENTA CHERRY)
    S. wesa (WHITE EUNGELLA SATINASH)

Palms

PALMS ARE THE TREES people most readily associate with the tropics; indeed, it is hard to imagine a tropical garden which doesn't boast at least one of these graceful, often stately trees. Most palms grown in cultivation conform to the stereotype of a tall, slender trunk topped by several long fronds. Some, however, such as Lipstick Palm, are clumping in habit, with many slender stems, rather like bamboo; or else with thickly bunched fronds and short stems, like Golden Cane. Others, such as Sabals, or Palmettos, produce fan-like foliage. All are very decorative, in the garden or as pot plants in the house.

Palms are easy to grow and, once established, require little care. Some grow in sun, others need shade, some do well in coastal areas, others need protection from salt-laden winds. It is fair to say that just about all palms do well in the sub-tropics and tropics and a few will grow in considerably colder latitudes.

CULTIVATION

In general, palms require plenty of water during establishment and either reliable seasonal rainfall or ready access to available water thereafter. In nature many palms have to withstand quite long, dry periods; the exceptions are those which occur naturally in swamps or where underground water is always available, for example oases or creek beds. For the purposes of home gardening, palms should be considered as generally heavy users of water; though once mature they are efficient seekers and storers of soil moisture and in areas with good, seasonable rainfall can quite easily take care of themselves. Those palms which do well in arid areas are listed on pages 54 and 93.

Except for species prone to black spot in the cold season, palms benefit from regular sprinkling of the foliage. During the wet season this won't be necessary; when weather is dry for long periods, water the foliage as well as the base of the tree. This not only makes foliage more lush, it also helps plump out the trunk.

Palms are tough plants which will grow in most soils and are highly efficient miners of available nutrients, occurring naturally as they often do in areas where soil fertility is not particularly high. Nonetheless, most do best in the garden in light soils which have received some enrichment. Young palms will get a good start if planted in well-prepared beds to which organic fertilisers such as blood and bone, as well as compost, have been added. Thereafter, they can be fertilised in spring, mid-summer and early autumn with any balanced fertiliser. Plenty of nitrogen will promote healthy frond development and good foliage colour.

Good drainage is very important to palms. Because they are seen as water-loving plants, it is sometimes assumed that palms don't mind wet feet but, except for the few swamp species, this is incorrect. Root rot will set in, and the plant will die, if stagnant water remains around the roots. Where soil is not free-draining, palms should be planted on or just below the surface of the garden and soil mounded around the base, see page 216.

SILVER SAW PALMETTO (Acoelorrhaphe wrightii), sometimes known as Everglades Palm, resembles the Sabals and does well in tropical to warm temperate climate gardens. It withstands dry periods but grows slowly without water. It forms a large clump, reaching 3–4 metres in the home garden. See page 92.

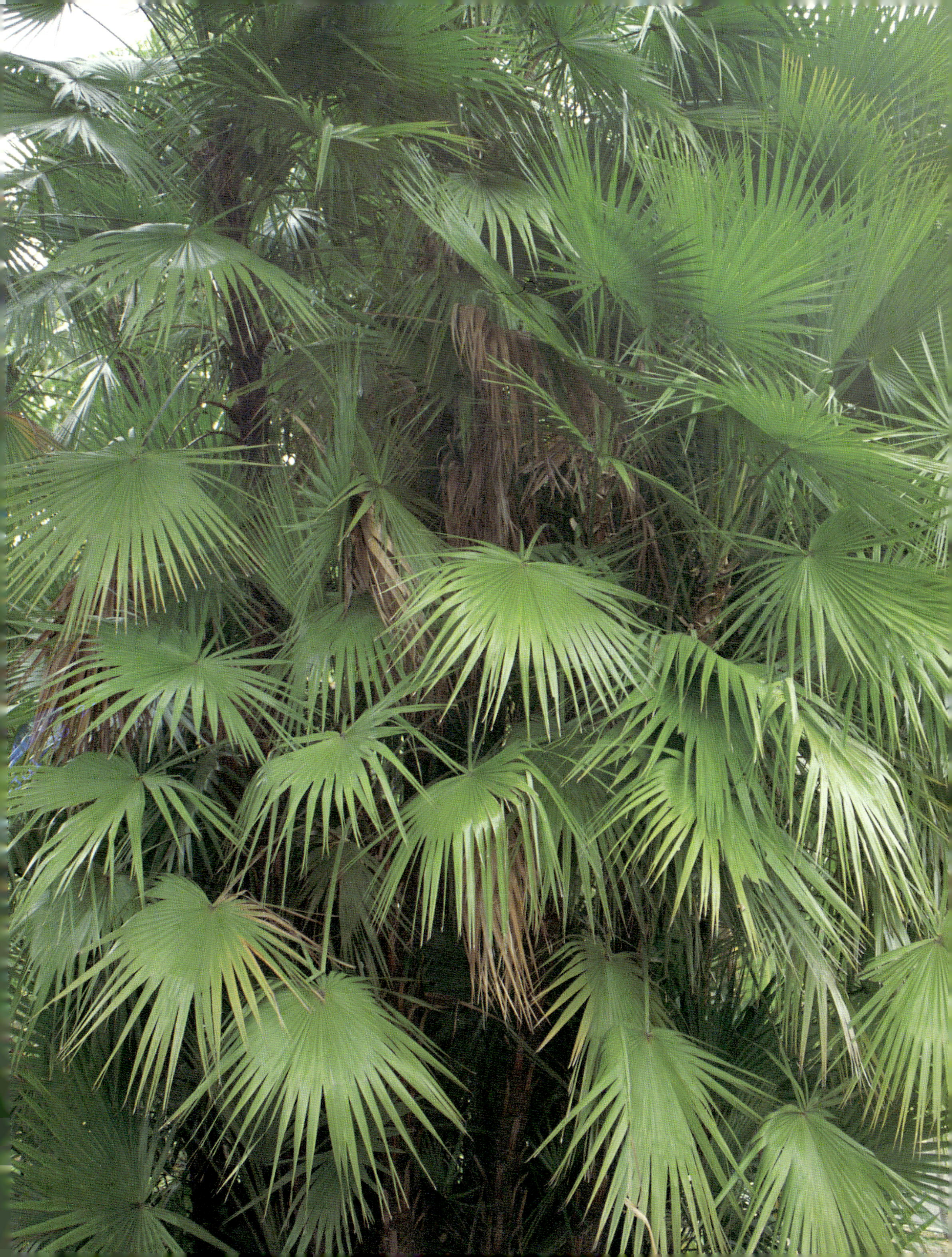

One of the best things about palms is that they require no maintenance once established, though it may be advisable to cut off and remove large, decaying fronds from species which are not self-cleaning. The following hints should help gardeners avoid some of the more common mistakes made in growing palms:

- Make sure adequate space is allowed for clumping palms. For example, Golden Cane palms grow into very large clumps indeed, yet young specimens are often established in brick or timber planter boxes which cannot contain the mature plant. This enforced enclosure of the plant's roots and stems may crack the boxes and also cause cracking in adjacent brickwork and paving. The same applies if clumping palms are grown in-ground in too confined a space.
- There is a frequent misapprehension among gardeners that all palms can be grown safely by the sea. Actually most palms occur naturally in forests far from the coast and those that do suffer badly, and even die, if exposed to salt-laden winds. Many of the more delicate palms, accustomed to the protection of the rainforest, also suffer badly from exposure to wind.
- Another common misapprehension is that palms are not messy. True, as a type they are among the tidiest of plants but some palms can drop large (sometimes prickly) fronds which might be a nuisance. Much more of a nuisance, however, are the fruits and flowers of certain palms which, though attractive, make a mess when dropped. Phoenix species and Alexandra Palms are two examples. Another is the Coconut Palm. It is rare that anyone is hit on the head by a coconut in the home garden but the risk does exist and should be recognised. It is not easy to remove nuisance fruits and nuts from tall trees, so those species which produce them should be planted where they cannot constitute a problem.
- The cultivation notes given here for palm trees are general for the Australian sub-tropics and tropics. However, palms that come from specialised habitats may have more particular needs. The best guide is to know where palms originate and re-create those conditions as much as possible in the garden. The origins of palms are included in the list.

PESTS AND DISEASES

Palms are occasionally subject to pests and diseases, though their natural resistance makes them relatively trouble-free and able to fight off attack or infestation.

GRASSHOPPERS have been known to defoliate or badly damage trees. Control with carbaryl, though vigilance and removing insects by hand is more environmentally friendly.

CATERPILLARS are another leaf-eating pest which can be controlled with carbaryl or maldison; remove by hand where possible, though caterpillars are often hard to see.

SCALE is an occasional problem, particularly in very humid weather. Control with half-strength white oil or diazinon.

BLACK SPOT can infest some clumping palms, particularly Golden Cane. It is generally a cold-season problem; control with triforine, and avoid spraying the foliage, particularly if watering in the evening.

GRUBS will attack palms, particularly young trees. Control with carbaryl or any other chemical recommended by your garden centre.

THRIPS can be a problem during the spring growing season and palms can become infected from infestations on nearby plants. Maldison is one control method; otherwise consult your garden centre for the latest, most effective and most environmentally sympathetic control.

MEALY BUG, though generally more of a problem with indoor plants, is very difficult to control outside. Frequent high-pressure hosing, sometimes combined with brushing down the base of fronds, is the most common treatment. Maldison or dimethoate are two possible chemical controls.

FUNGAL DISEASES, such as brown spots and patches often occur on palm fronds; they can be symptomatic of many conditions and don't usually constitute an ongoing problem. However, large numbers of spreading spots, allied with dead patches in the fronds, can indicate one of the fungal diseases which occasionally attack palms. Take action as early as possible by using a fungicide.

LANDSCAPING WITH PALMS

One of the greatest benefits of single-trunked palms in the garden is that they take up relatively little room, particularly at ground and mid-level. This makes them an ideal tree for small gardens or courtyards; conversely, multi-stemmed clumping types can quickly fill a gap.

Palms can be used in many ways. There is nothing to beat the stately effect of a row of palms on either side of a driveway. Unlike a hedge, no trimming is required; and there is still room, if desired, for a hedge alongside them to accentuate the driveway even further. A single palm makes a focal point in landscaping; a clump of the same or different species is a quick way of filling a large space and creating shade. Other effects created with palms include: planting either side of a doorway, gateway or other feature; planting in a row to demarcate one section of the garden from another; placing outside a window where the rustling of fronds in the wind creates a pleasing sound; turning a sunken area of garden into a small palmetum with multiple planting; establishing an area of lightly shaded greenery around a swimming pool or pond (use species which do not produce a profusion of flowers or squashy fruit); planting a selection of tall and low-growing species to create a different height effect; planting along the front, side or back boundary of a garden.

The following list is a selection of those palms which are generally considered the most popular and reliable in cultivation. Note that each year palms from all over the world are being introduced to mass cultivation and made available to gardeners; these may not all be carried by garden centres but should be available from palm specialists. To simplify frond description, I have used the different leaf shapes described by Queensland palm expert Jack Krempin in his book *Palms & Cycads Around the World* (Horwitz Grahame, Sydney, 1990): feather type (upright or drooping fronds with very narrow leaflets), fan type (roughly circular fronds, fan-like or resembling the palm of a hand, with pointed segments or 'fingers'), fishtail type (those with fronds which do not segment into 'hands' (fans) or fine leaflets but rather have segments or leaflets which appear bifurcated, truncated or cut at the end. Heights are based on natural maximums; about half to three-quarters of the height likely to be achieved in the garden.

ALEXANDRA PALM (*Archontophoenix alexandrae*)
QUEENSLAND SWAMPS AND RAINFORESTS
Feather type. Trunk to about 25 m and closely ringed. Green crownshaft (the smooth area between the top of the trunk and the frond bases). Produces a full, flared, skirtlike inflorescence of creamy-white flowers, followed by bright red fruits. Leaves have a silvery undersurface. Fast growing. A very common native palm for warm-climate gardens but *not* tolerant of coastal exposure. Shade. Water well. Good for permanently damp areas. *A. cunninghamiana* (BANGALOW or PICCABEEN PALM) is distinguished by green underleaf and yellowish crownshaft. Flowers are mauve. It is more cold tolerant.

CARPENTARIA PALM (*Carpentaria acuminata*)
NORTHERN TERRITORY RAINFORESTS AND ESTUARIES
Feather type. Trunk to about 15 m. Arching fronds are sparser than those of Queen and Royal palms. Short green crownshaft. Creamy inflorescence. Red fruits. Sun or shade, but best shaded when young. Good for permanently wet areas.

COCONUT PALM (*Cocos nucifera*)
PACIFIC AND INDIAN OCEAN
Feather type. Trunk to about 25 m. Large, edible fruits. This most famous of palms occurs naturally along tropical coastlines where it tolerates regular inundations of salt water. It also grows inland and on coastal mountain ranges, and does well in the sub-tropics, though in none of these locations will it fruit as well as it does in its natural environment. Dwarf varieties are available.

COTTON PALM (*Washingtonia robusta*)
MEXICO
Fan type, with rounded head of fronds which have orange stalks drooping at the tip. Thorny. Brown trunk to about 25 m. Creamy inflorescence, oval, dark-brown fruits. Full sun. Tolerates dry periods and seaside conditions. *W. filifera* (AMERICAN COTTON PALM, PETTICOAT PALM) is equally attractive and very tolerant of hot, dry conditions. It retains its old leaves, giving a skirt-like effect, hence one of its common names.

CUBAN ROYAL PALM (*Roystonea regia*)
CUBA
Feather type. Arched, fine-leaved fronds less 'fluffy' in appearance than those of Queen Palm. Trunk to about 25 m, tapering and swollen at top and base, giving this palm another common name of 'Bottle Palm'. Long, green crownshaft. Cream inflorescence. Black fruits. Tolerant of seaside conditions. Full sun. Other roystoneas or 'Royal' palms are also available and are similar in habit and appearance.

DWARF DATE PALM (*Phoenix roebelenii*)
INDIA, PARTS OF INDO-CHINA AND CHINA
Feather type. Moderately thick growth of downward-curving fronds. Thick trunk, very slow growing to about 10 m. Yellow inflorescence. Fruits black and oblong. Sun or light shade. Tolerates dry periods, but also tolerant of areas which are damp for long periods, and of seaside conditions. Other popular *Phoenix* species include *P. canariensis* (CANARY ISLAND DATE PALM), a very handsome, easy-to-grow species which is taller and more slender than *P. roebelenii*; and *P. reclinata* (SENEGAL DATE PALM). *P. dactylifera* is the edible date palm which only bears fruit in hot, dry, areas, which makes it very suitable for hot-climate gardens in inland areas of Australia.

FISHTAIL PALM (*Caryota rumphiana*)
AUSTRALIA, NEW GUINEA AND INDONESIA. Rainforests and adjacent open forest
Fishtail type. Frond segments have a slightly fluted appearance. Trunk to about 20 m. Pale greenish–white inflorescence. Red fruits. Full sun or light shade. *C. mitis* (CLUSTERING FISHTAIL PALM) is much shorter in size and has multiple trunks, making it a very attractive garden specimen which grows fast to fill in awkward spaces. Other caryotas, e.g. *C. urens*, are also available.

FOXTAIL PALM (*Wodyetia bifurcata*)
NORTH-EASTERN QUEENSLAND RAINFOREST AND WOODLAND
Fishtail type. Trunk to about 15 m and closely ringed. Green crownshaft with a whitish sheen. Arched fronds of close-set,

prolific, narrow leaflets give a brush-like effect. Green inflorescence. Oval red fruits. Full sun, but shelter from wind when young. Light soil. Can withstand dry spells, with occasional deep soakings. *Normanbya normanbya* (BLACK PALM) is very similar in appearance but is generally taller growing (to about 20 m without fronds) and has a very dark trunk. Leaflets have a more 'cut' appearance than those of wodyetia; fruits are pinkish-brown. It is a North Queensland rainforest palm which needs plenty of water.

GOLDEN CANE (*Chrysalidocarpus ludescens aurea*)
MADAGASCAR
Feather type. Clumping, with many stems. Purplish-black fruit. Full sun. Slightly tolerant of seaside conditions. Grows into wide, tall clumps.

Licuala ramsayi (FAN PALM)
NORTHERN QUEENSLAND, NEW GUINEA
Fan type with large, circular fronds with a pleated appearance. Trunk to about 6 m. Cream inflorescence, light red fruits. Tropical, but grows in the sub-tropics if given a warm, sheltered position. Shade. Tolerates permanently wet areas.

LIPSTICK PALM, SEALING WAX PALM
(*Cyrtostachys lacca* syn. *renda*)
MALAYSIA
Feather palm with clumping habit. Bright red crown shafts and frond stalks. Black fruits. Very tropical. Tolerates permanently wet conditions. A very striking and unusual palm. Light shade or morning sun.

Livistona SPP. (CABBAGE TREE and FAN PALMS)
Australian species of *Livistona* are commonly known as Cabbage Tree Palms, of which the most well known in cultivation is *L. australis*. Fan type, but with a feathery appearance from a distance. Fronds grow in a rounded head, hence the common name. Trunk at maturity may reach 20 m but this is a fairly slow-growing species and on young trees the fronds appear bushier and are close to the ground, so that medium height and mature specimens look like different species. Reddish–brown to black fruits. Tolerates sun or shade, dry periods and permanently wet areas, as well as seaside conditions. Other livistonas are also available. *L. chinensis* (CHINESE FAN PALM, from China) is a popular, low-growing palm with large, rounded, fan-like fronds, segmented at the margin. Trunk slow-growing to about 10 m maximum. Creamy inflorescence. Blue-grey fruits. *L. rotundifolia* is similar but grows larger, with larger fronds. Sun or shade.

PALMETTO (*Sabal* SPP.)
Palmetto is the popular name given in North and South America to a genus of fourteen fan-type palm species which grow well in Australia's warmer regions. They are slow growing, remaining for years with short trunks and thick foliage to ground level. At maturity trunks of taller species can reach 15–20 m. They are characterised by large, rounded fan-shaped fronds. Some, such as the 'true' palmetto, *S. palmetto*, are swamp-growers and tolerate permanent wet conditions. Others, such as *S. domingensis*, do well in dry, inland areas. They are all tough palms which tolerate a range of conditions including sun or shade and seaside exposure.

PARLOUR PALM (*Chamaedorea elegans*)
MEXICO AND CENTRAL AMERICA
Feather type with broad, pointed leaflets. Very slender trunk to about 2 m. Yellow inflorescence, black fruits. Shade. Plenty of water. This is a very popular indoor palm which also does well in gardens where conditions are warm and humid. Other chamaedoreas are also available; *C. elegans* has very narrow leaflets; *C. erumpens* has a decorative bamboo-like appearance; and *C. costaricana* is a tough garden plant which forms a clump.

PRINCESS PALM (*Dictyosperma album* var. *fufuraceum*)
MAURITIUS AND REUNION
Feather type. The many leaflets are divided at the apex into two points. Long, slender and smooth trunk. Very long, creamy-yellow inflorescence. Egg-shaped, purplish-black fruits.

QUEEN PALM (*Syagrus romanzoffianum*, syn. *Cocos plumosa*)
BRAZIL
Feather type. Fine-leaved fronds have a fluffy, plume-like appearance. Trunk to about 15 m and closely ringed. Cream inflorescence. Orange fruits. Very popular and easy to grow. Slightly tolerant of seaside conditions. Sun or shade.

Ravenea glauca
MADAGASCAR
Feather type. Small-growing, with trunk to about 6 m maximum, developing into a bottle shape with thickened base. Sun or shade; plenty of moisture. These handsome palms are still fairly new to cultivation but make excellent garden specimens. *R. glauca* is becoming popular because of its small size; other taller but equally good-looking raveneas are *R. moorei*, *R. hildebrandtii* and *R. robustior*.

Rhapis excelsa (LADY PALM)
SOUTHERN CHINA
Fan type, with long, slender leaflet 'fingers' fanning out from the centre of the frond. It is a small, clumping palm with very slender trunks to about 5 m. Cream inflorescence, white fruits. Shade, light shade or part shade. Fairly tolerant of wet areas. Though best known as an indoor palm, it does well outdoors in warm, humid conditions. Various cultivars are available including variegated forms. *R. humilis* (SLENDER LADY PALM) is similar but more compact, has thinner stems and female plants do not produce flowers.

SILVER SAW PALMETTO, EVERGLADES PALM (*Acoelorrhaphe wrightii*)
FLORIDA, CENTRAL AMERICA, CARIBBEAN
A truly excellent clumping palm for the tropics, sub-tropics and coastal warm-temperate areas. Large fan-shaped leaves are silvery underneath and grow on multiple stems. Cream-coloured inflorescence and small black fruits. Height to about 3–4 metres in the home garden.

SOLITAIRE PALM (*Ptychosperma elegans*)
EASTERN QUEENSLAND
Feather type but with broad leaflets, abruptly truncated at the ends. Ringed, slender trunk to about 10 m. Green crownshaft. White inflorescence. Red fruits. Shade; will also grow in full sun but needs some shading when young. As the name implies, a very elegant palm. *P. macarthurii* (far north Queensland and Papua New Guinea) is a clumping palm with very handsome fronds and is popular with gardeners. Other ptychosperma are also available.

SUGAR PALM (*Arenga pinnata*)
EAST INDIES RAINFORESTS
Feather type. Large, arching fronds with many dense leaflets. Trunk to about 12 m. Inflorescence produces a sweet, edible sap. Yellow to brown fruits. Full sun. Other arengas are available, some of which are sufficiently handsome and unusual to warrant a place in the garden.

WALKING STICK PALM (*Linospadix monostachya*)
NORTHERN NSW AND QUEENSLAND RAINFORESTS
Fishtail type. Slender trunk to about 3 m. Cream inflorescence. Red fruits. Shade. Suitable for indoor or outdoor growing; needs plenty of moisture.

Palm look-alikes

These species resemble palms and are often mistaken for them. They help to add a tropical touch to the garden.

Dracaena draco (DRAGON TREE)
CANARY ISLANDS
A large (eventually to about 6 m), multi-branched giant of the *Dracaena* genus with rounded heads of spiky fronds, borne at the top of the branches. Very slow-growing. Can withstand dry periods but needs plenty of water during establishment. Full sun. *D. marginata* is a popular pot plant which is also grown outdoors in warm, humid climates.

Nolina recurvata syn. *Beaucarnea recurvata* (PONY TAIL PALM)
MEXICO
A curious, multi-branched (often multi-stemmed) tree or clumping plant which produces long, grasslike, drooping leaves bunched at the tops of branches. Slow-growing. Tolerates dry periods. Full sun.

Pandanus SPP. (SCREW PALM)
AUSTRALIA
A plant of swamps and seashores, depending on species. Multi-branched trees to about 5 m with long, thick, drooping, grey-green leaves and fruits which resemble pineapples. Very popular in cultivation. Very tolerant of seaside conditions.

TRAVELLERS' PALM (*Ravenala madagascariensis*)
MADAGASCAR
A member of the banana family which is popularly thought of as a palm. Long-established as a feature in sub-tropical and tropical gardens, this plant grows to about 6 m and can be classified as clumping. The stalks grow upright from the trunk in a perfect fan shape, topped by large, banana-like, glossy leaves. When young, the 'fans' rise up from the ground; as the tree matures it develops a long, palm-like trunk. Can withstand long dry periods.

Palms for dry, inland areas

Bismarckia nobilis
Borassus flabellifer
Brahea SPP.
Butia capitata (JELLY PALM)
Copernicia glabrescens
Date Palms (*Phoenix* SPP.)
FOXTAIL PALM (*Wodyetia bifurcata*)
Hyphaene petersiana (DOUM PALM)
Sabal uresana (SONORAN PALMETTO)
Thrinax radiata (FLORIDA THATCH PALM)
Washingtonia filifera (AMERICAN COTTON PALM)

Palms for shady gardens

ALEXANDRA PALM (*Archontophoenix alexandrae*)
Calamus SPP. (LAWYER PALMS)
Howea forsterana
Laccospadix australasica
Licuala ramsayi (FAN PALM)
Linospadix monostachys (WALKING STICK PALM)
Normanbya normanbya (BLACK PALM)
PALMETTO (*Sabal palmetto*)
QUEEN PALM (*Syagrus romanzoffianum*)
Rhapis SPP. (lady palms)
SOLITAIRE PALM (*Ptychosperma elegans*)

Palms for wet spots

ALEXANDRA PALM (*Archontophoenix alexandrae*)
CUBAN ROYAL PALM (*Roystonea regia*
Licuala ramsayi (FAN PALM)
LIPSTICK PALM (*Cyrtostachys lacca*)
Livistona SPP. (Cabbage Tree Palms)
Normanbya normanbya (BLACK PALM)
PALMETTO (*Sabal palmetto*)
SOLITAIRE PALM (*Ptychosperma elegans*)

Shrubs

SHRUBS ARE THE MOST IMPORTANT FEATURE in almost any garden; and this is particularly true in hot climates where they make up the main garden vegetation in place of the annuals and many of the perennials commonly grown in cooler regions. Some of the world's most beautiful flowering shrubs originate in hot climates, giving gardeners an exciting choice. There are shrubs for all situations; sun, shade, damp spots, dry and rocky ridges, rich soils, poor soils. They can be used as individual flowering specimens or for hedges, shrubberies, under-tree plantings, screens, buffers, windbreaks and around swimming pools. Shrubs can be as large as a small tree or less than half a metre high. They can be massed for colour or strategically planted to provide fragrance. Many beautiful gardens do without trees, or flowering annuals, but it is very rare to see a garden without a few shrubs.

Householders who want to minimise garden work in a hot climate should consider gardens created entirely from shrubs. With careful selection, shrubs are far less labour-intensive than other plants. Many very beautiful easy-care hot climate gardens consist only of shrubs and lawn; even easier-care gardens consist of shrubs and no-mow groundcovers in place of the lawn.

When planning a garden, the placement of shrubs should come second to decisions about where the trees should go—if the garden is too small for trees then shrubs become the dominant plant feature. Apart from their individual aesthetic value shrubs provide the backdrop against which smaller plants can show their colours. When the garden plan is formulated, hedges, screens, understorey plantings and other shrub uses as mentioned above should be sketched in and selection made. After that, individual shrubs can be planted from time to time as required or desired.

With established gardens it is easy to see where improvements can be made by adding, say, a flowering or perfumed shrub to a particular corner, or massed shrubs to create a colourful effect. Often the gardener sees a desirable shrub in a magazine, or buys one on impulse from a garden centre. With all except very large shrubs it is easy to fit a newcomer or two into the established garden.

SHRUBBERIES

A shrubbery, by definition, is a dense planting of different shrubs, resembling a natural thicket. When creating a shrubbery it is important to put larger shrubs at the rear and to ensure that all plants get sufficient sunlight, with none but shade-tolerant species becoming overshadowed by their neighbours. Shrubberies are an attractive way of creating boundaries, ensuring privacy, buffering noise and pollution and providing shelter for birds and other wildlife. If established entirely or predominantly with native species, they bring the bush to the backyard.

Shrubs are distinguished from trees generally by their multi-stemmed growth habit. For the purposes of the following list we have also distinguished them from clumping, fleshy-leaved or non-flowering foliage plants which are listed elsewhere in the book.

FLOWERING SHRUBS

NOTE 'Resistant' is a qualified ability to tolerate the conditions specified in each case; 'hardy' means easily able to do so.

Abelia × grandiflora
ITALY
HEIGHT 2 m
HABIT Long, arching branches
FOLIAGE Evergreen. Neat, small, simple leaves with bronze tinge
FLOWERS Small, dainty, bell-shaped, white with purplish markings
FLOWERING TIME Summer and autumn
CONDITIONS Tolerant of most soil and climate conditions except the very coldest. Frost and drought resistant. Sun or shade
OTHER POINTS Besides the commonly available hybrid A. × grandiflora, other abelias grown in Australian gardens include cultivars of A. floribunda, A. schumannii and A. chinensis (China).

Adenium obesum
NORTH AFRICA
HEIGHT 2 m
HABIT Evergreen or briefly deciduous. Thick stem, sparse branches
FOLIAGE Oblate, thick
FLOWERS Clusters of vivid pink-to-red flowers
FLOWERING TIME Winter, spring
CONDITIONS Sun. Light, well-drained soil. Drought and frost hardy. Do not over-water, particularly in the winter flowering period
OTHER POINTS A good tub specimen for courtyards.

Allamanda neriifolia
SOUTH AMERICA
HEIGHT 1½ m
HABIT Evergreen. Sprawling but can be controlled into a manageable shrub
FOLIAGE Single, shiny leaves with well-marked veins
FLOWERS Trumpet-shaped yellow blooms with an orange tinge
FLOWERING TIME Summer
CONDITIONS Sun. Well-drained, humus-enriched soil. Water well in summer
OTHER POINTS A. neriifolia is the most naturally 'shrublike' of the allamandas, the others being best used as climbers.

Aphelandra SPP.
CENTRAL AMERICA
HEIGHT Variable, according to type, but all under ½ m
HABIT Evergreen. Upright
FOLIAGE Large, glossy leaves. The popular Zebra Plant has variegated leaves with white veins
FLOWERS Tall spikes of showy flowerheads which are either bright yellow, orange or orange-and-pink depending on species and variety
FLOWERING TIME Summer, autumn
CONDITIONS Part-shade or shade. Need winter protection where temperatures drop below 10°C. Humus-enriched soil preferred. Feed and water regularly in summer. Prune after flowering in late summer or early spring.
OTHER POINTS Several species of aphelandra grow in Australia, including A. squarrosa, A. aurantiaca, A. sinclaireana though not all are readily available. Best known is A. squarrosa 'Louisae', the Zebra Plant.

Azalea
JAPAN
The azaleas which do best in a warm climate are species and cultivars of Azalea indica which have been bred for the garden over many years and remain one of the most popular garden plants, even though they require quite a lot of care. Other types of azalea which do well in climates with relatively high winter temperatures are kurumes and cultivars of A. macrantha. As azaleas are generally sold under their varietal names, these distinctions mean little to all but the most knowledgeable gardeners. However, it is worth remembering that kurume azaleas are generally smaller growing, with neat, small leaves and flowers, which makes them very suitable for rockeries and low border plantings.
HEIGHT 2 m maximum for the taller A. indica, with many species and varieties smaller than that. Read the label or consult nursery staff if height is important
HABIT Evergreen. Generally fairly compact, especially smaller-growing varieties
FOLIAGE Small, neat, dark-green, oval-shaped, tightly held to branches
FLOWERS Variable in size, from dainty to 6 cm across, some larger. Single and double. Continuous cross-breeding has resulted in azalea flowers in a vast range of exciting colours: reds, whites, all the shades of pink and mauve, yellow, apricot and orange
FLOWERING TIME Spring and autumn
CONDITIONS Light, well-drained, humus-enriched, acid soils are essential for healthy azaleas. Their surface roots need to be able to roam free of a heavy soil cover and the pH range should be from 5–6. Azaleas soon show (by poor growth and leaf yellowing) if soil conditions are unsuitable; light mulching helps to acidify soil and the pH can also be lowered by applying some form of sulphur dressing which can be easily applied to the soil and watered in. For good flowering, morning sun is required. Hot afternoon sun on western-facing flowerbeds will spoil blooms unless the plants are in light shade. Azaleas will require plenty of water in very hot weather but this should not be sprinkled over flowers and foliage; water under the foliage using a slow-running hose, or using trickle or drip irrigation. Azaleas are prone to fungal diseases and these are accentuated by humidity; for this

reason they do better in a sub tropical or hot, dry climate (where irrigation is available), than in the tropics where year-round humidity means constant spraying and vigilance. Azaleas are vulnerable to root rot, gall, petal blight, red spider mite, mildew, thrips, lace bug and leaf miner. Because of their vulnerability, sprays especially formulated for azalea problems are available in garden centres. Special azalea fertilisers are also available. Shelter is an important factor as azaleas don't care for exposure, which damages blooms
OTHER POINTS As they flower for long periods in spring and autumn, azaleas are the ideal shrub for massed colour displays. Gardeners should not be put off by the problems outlined above; vigilance and a sound regime of care, particularly during the flowering periods is worth the effort because these are such rewarding plants to grow. The main thing to remember is that azaleas are unpredictable — although their 'ideal' conditions are generally believed to be hill regions with good soil, fairly high rainfall, moderate temperatures, not too much humidity and not too much aridity, I have seen azaleas flourishing in coastal gardens on sand dunes and in Rockhampton, Queensland, where summer temperatures are high, drought is common and soil is poor.

Baeckea virgata (miniature form)
AUSTRALIA
HEIGHT 3 m
HABIT Evergreen. Erect, open
FOLIAGE Small leaves, willow-like appearance
FLOWERS Small, white, profuse
FLOWERING TIME Summer
CONDITIONS Sun. Light, moist soil. Appears to be pest and disease free
OTHER POINTS A good plant for filling damp spots in the garden. Other species of baeckia are available and there are also pink and mauve-flowering forms.

Barleria cristata (PHILIPPINE VIOLET)
INDIA
HEIGHT 1 m
HABIT Evergreen. Erect, with many branches
FOLIAGE Soft, slightly hairy
FLOWERS Five-petalled, trumpet-shaped mauve blooms
Flowering time Summer
CONDITIONS Light shade better than full sun. Very tropical and does not like prolonged cold weather. Rich, acid soil, as for azaleas. Plenty of water in hot weather
OTHER POINTS Makes a good hedge or border plant where climate is warm and humid most of the year.

Bauhinia galpinii
SOUTH AFRICA
HEIGHT 2½ m
HABIT Briefly deciduous. Sprawling
FOLIAGE Leaves with double lobes
FLOWERS Orange-red, paddle-shaped, large
FLOWERING TIME Summer and autumn
CONDITIONS Sun. Tolerant of most conditions including light frosts once established. Drought tolerant. Most soils
OTHER POINTS A tough, trouble-free plant which needs hard pruning after flowering to prevent straggling.

Bouvardia longiflora (syn. *humboldtii*)
CENTRAL AMERICA
HEIGHT 1 m
HABIT Evergreen. Very slender, rather weak branches
FOLIAGE Small and spear-shaped
FLOWERS Long, white tubes which open into four petals somewhat resembling propellers. Fragrant
FLOWERING TIME Autumn to spring
CONDITIONS Full sun. Humus-enriched, well-drained soil. Shelter from exposure. Water well in summer
OTHER POINTS This plant is grown mainly for its delightful perfume and has to be pruned hard after flowering to prevent straggling. Rather tropical in habit, it will take short spells of cold below 10°C.

Brunfelsia pauciflora (YESTERDAY-TODAY-AND-TOMORROW)
SOUTH AMERICA
HEIGHT Variable, according to type, but not over 3 m
HABIT Evergreen, slightly spreading
FOLIAGE Long and pointed, tough
FLOWERS Five-lobed, changing colour from mauve to pale bluish mauve to white over several days, giving a three-coloured effect and earning this lovely plant its common name. Very fragrant
FLOWERING TIME Spring, summer.
CONDITIONS Sun or light shade. Not fussy about soils though does best where soil is rich and well-drained. Plenty of water in summer. Fairly tough but cannot tolerate drought or frost
OTHER POINTS A pretty plant with a superb perfume. Definitely one for the fragrant garden. Equally attractive is *B. americana* which comes in shades of yellow and produces a strong night fragrance.

Calliandra haematocephala (POWDER PUFF)
SOUTH AMERICA
HEIGHT 3 m
HABIT Evergreen, with long, twining stems
FOLIAGE Pinnate, with small, oval leaflets
FLOWERS Large, red, showy 'powder puffs'
FLOWERING TIME Autumn and winter
CONDITIONS Full sun. Light soil. Plenty of water in summer
OTHER POINTS An easy, reliable, colourful plant to grow. A white form is sometimes available. Other, very attractive calliandra species include the pink-and-white flowering *C. surinamensis* and *C. schultzei*. Red-flowering *C. tweedii* 'HORIZONTALIS' is a popular groundcover.

Azaleas are popular garden plants in most parts of the world. Despite their Japanese origins, they do well in hot climates if given adequate care. This variety is 'MORTII'.

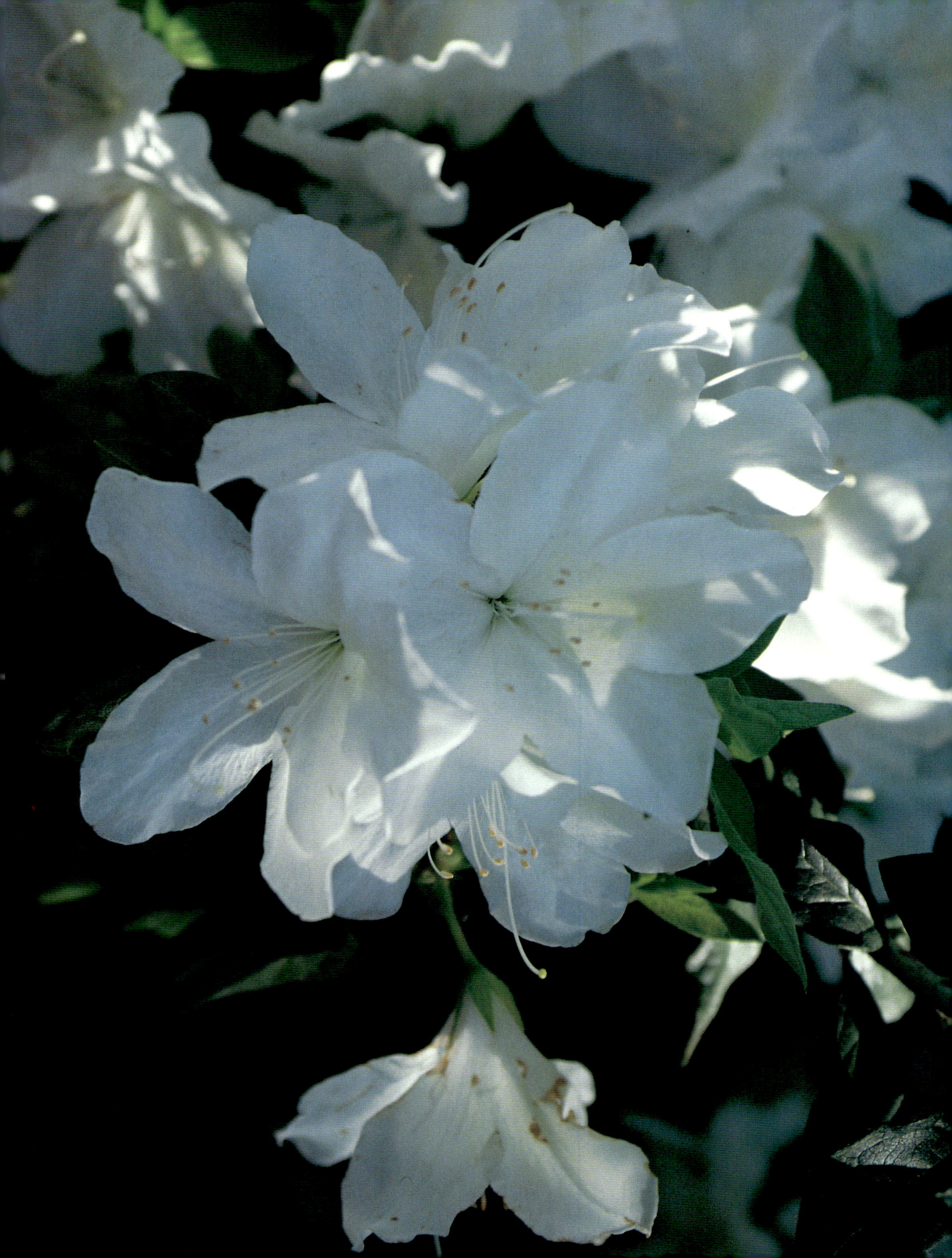

Callistemon (Bottlebrush)

AUSTRALIA

Many species and varieties of callistemon are medium or small shrubs which grow well in most situations. There are callistemons which grow in sun, light shade, mountain slopes, hot and dry areas, wet and humid places, in city streets and by the sea. Therefore this plant is very popular with home gardeners and landscapers. So many attractive callistemon cultivars are now available it would be impossible to list them here and do justice to the variety. They do, however, have certain features in common. Leaves are small, narrow, pointed, dull green, often with pinkish new growth, borne on branches which may be erect or weeping. Flowers are 'bottlebrush' shaped, varying slightly in density and form. Size is very variable. Colours are white, greenish-white, cream, shades of pink, shades of red and purplish-red. Flowering time can be from spring to autumn, depending on type, with early summer being the most florific period. Flowers on a healthy bush can be borne so prolifically they almost cover the foliage

CONDITIONS Most callistemons are hardy in a range of conditions though on average they do best with light, sandy soil, regular watering during establishment and protection from frost when young. However, some species are more drought and frost tolerant than others, generally depending on origin, so it is best to check the plant label when buying, or else inquire at the local garden centre. Callistemons are fast growing and generally trouble-free though they become unkempt and woody if not pruned after flowering and given a regime of light fertilising. In dry periods they do best with a good soaking every two or three weeks, to maintain foliage quality. Whatever the type of garden, beauty and reliability has earned the callistemon a place in it.

Camellia

CHINA AND JAPAN

Although they are more suited to cooler climates, many of today's camellia cultivars do well in the sub-tropics, and some even grow in the tropics, provided they are protected from excessive heat as much as possible, and provided that you select suitable varieties. Pinks and pale reds appear to hold their flowers longer and varieties of *C. sasanqua*, which are drought and frost tender, do better in warm climates than *C. japonica*, the other commonly available camellia species. Foliage of *C. sasanqua* is smaller than that of *C. japonica*; the neat, lanceolate, glossy leaves are on longish stems which tend to arch when young but can be pruned after flowering to maintain a compact shape. Japonicas have a naturally compact, upright form and both are very handsome shrubs even when not in flower. Flowers come in a range of whites, pinks and reds, double or single. In hot climates they don't last long but can be picked for indoor show.

CONDITIONS Like azaleas, camellias like a well-drained, humus-enriched soil which is slightly acid. They need protection from strong winds and temperature extremes and do best planted in light shade or where they don't get full morning sun. They are less prone to pests than azaleas but can be infested by red spider mites, scale, mealy bug, aphids and thrips. Diseases include root rot and a condition called 'balling' in which buds swell and outer petals become exposed, though the flower does not open. Well-balanced nutrition generally helps to prevent this problem, though it is inherent in some varieties. Root rot can be a problem during summer monsoons; the only cure is to dispose of the plant.

Cestrum nocturnum (NIGHT JASMINE)
SOUTH AMERICA
HEIGHT 1.5–2 m
HABIT Evergreen, sprawling
FOLIAGE Medium-sized, pointed leaves on arching branches
FLOWERS Small, greenish-white, tubular, opening to five petals. Very fragrant at night
FLOWERING TIME Spring to autumn
CONDITIONS Prefers a humus-enriched, well-drained soil though it grows in most soil types. Sun or light shade but needs protection from hot or cold winds. Frost tender when very young, it will withstand subsequent light frosts and temperatures down to freezing if not prolonged. Plenty of water in summer and fertilise regularly during growing period
OTHER POINTS This cestrum's very strong and sweet nocturnal fragrance adds romance to the garden. It is also easy to grow, as are other available cestrums such as Red Cestrum and Purple Cestrum (*C. elegans* cultivars); both vigorous growers with flower colours to match the names. Flowers are born very prolifically in summer.

Clerodendrum ugandense (BLUE BUTTERFLY BUSH)
EAST AFRICA
HEIGHT 2 m
HABIT Evergreen, spreading
FOLIAGE Medium-sized single leaves on long canes
FLOWERS Dainty, delicately suspended flowers with four pale blue petals surrounding a darker, mauve-blue 'slipper' petal
FLOWERING TIME Summer
CONDITIONS Sun or light shade Good, humus-enriched soil. Plenty of water, particularly in summer. Frost and drought tender. Prune after flowering
OTHER POINTS A very pretty plant which requires minimum care. Other available clerodendrums include *C. philippinum* (CASHMERE BOUQUET) and the red-flowering *C. paniculatum* syn. *fragrans* (PAGODA FLOWER).

Crotalaria agatiflora (CANARY BIRD BUSH)
AUSTRALIA
HEIGHT 2 m
HABIT Evergreen, erect
FOLIAGE Soft, pale leaves made up of three leaflets and resembling the laburnum, hence the plants synonymous name of *C. laburnifolia*
FLOWERS The yellow flowers are also laburnum-like at first; when barely open they look like birds in flight, which gives the plant its common name. At maturity, they are pea-shaped like all the crotalarias and other flowers in the Fabaceae family

FLOWERING TIME Any time throughout the year
CONDITIONS Light, well-drained soils. Sunny but protected position. Prune after flowering. Fertilise and water moderately. Frost tender.
OTHER POINTS A fast-growing shrub for quick cover and a touch of bright yellow in the garden.

CROWN OF THORNS (*Euphorbia milii*)
MADAGASCAR
HEIGHT To 1 m, generally shorter
HABIT Evergreen, compact, sparse
FOLIAGE A very few, young leaves which don't last
FLOWERS Small and scarlet
FLOWERING TIME All year round (except winter in cooler climates)
CONDITIONS Full sun. Light, sandy soils low in nutrients. Drought resistant but needs occasional soakings during long, dry periods. Can withstand light frosts.
OTHER POINTS This plant has many stout thorns on the stems and branches, instead of leaves, so it makes an excellent hedge against wildlife and other intruders. Otherwise a good backrop plant for rockeries.

Cuphea hyssopifolia
MEXICO
HEIGHT 1/2 m
HABIT Evergreen, bushy
FOLIAGE Neat, small, heather-like leaves
FLOWERS A profusion of small, starry flowers, white or mauve
FLOWERING TIME Almost all year in improved varieties
CONDITIONS Full sun or light shade. Light, humus-enriched soil which does not dry out. Water well. Otherwise hardy and easy to grow
OTHER POINTS One of the best-known cupheas is the dwarf 'MAD HATTER' which graces many garden beds, pots, hanging baskets and rockeries. This grows only 25 cm high and is often labelled for sale with its varietal name only. Another popular cuphea is *C. ignea* (MEXICAN CIGAR FLOWER), which has small, tubular, red flowers with red and black tips. This is also a good bedding, border or rockery plant.

DREJERELLA, SHRIMP PLANT (*Justicia guttata*, syn. *jrejerella*, *Beloperone guttata*)
MEXICO
HEIGHT Usually just over 1/2 m
HABIT Evergreen, spreading
FOLIAGE Small, single leaves with deeply-etched veins
FLOWERS Like bougainvillea, the colourful 'flowers' are actually large bracts of an unusual brownish-pink, very prolific and borne in small sprays
FLOWERING TIME Spring to autumn and even longer in the tropics
CONDITIONS Semi-shade, though will take full sun. Rich, well-drained soil. Frost tender when young, though will take cold below 10°C.
OTHER POINTS Rather an untidy plant which benefits from constant tip-pruning to promote bushiness. Unusual flowers and reliability make it worth growing.

Eupatorium megalophyllum (MIST FLOWER)
SOUTH AMERICA
HEIGHT 2 m
HABIT Evergreen, sprawling
FOLIAGE Large, soft leaves with a rough surface and deeply etched veins
FLOWERS Lilac-coloured 'cushions' at centre, surrounded by a fluffy edging of stamens. Prolific and very pretty
FLOWERING TIME Spring
CONDITIONS Sun or light shade. Humus-enriched, well-drained soil. Water well in summer. Need protection from cold winds and frost; very much a warm-climate plant
OTHER POINTS Though not a particularly attractive plant when not in flower, the spectacular spring show makes this a good shrub and its otherwise dull appearance is not too obvious when set amongst other shrubs.

Feijoa sellowiana (PINEAPPLE GUAVA)
SOUTH AMERICA
HEIGHT 1 1/2 m
HABIT Evergreen, erect, dense
FOLIAGE Greyish–green, oval
FLOWERS Bright red, edged with white
FLOWERING TIME Spring and early summer
CONDITIONS Full sun, humus-enriched soil. Plenty of water in summer. Frost and drought tender
OTHER CONDITIONS The unusual, very pretty flowers make this well-formed shrub worth growing. The fruit is delicious eaten fresh or as jam.

Fuchsia
SOUTH AMERICA, MEXICO, PACIFIC REGION
Fuchsias will grow in the sub-tropics and even in the tropics, particularly in mountain areas or near the coast, if they are given warmth (but not strong heat or direct sunlight), humidity and protection from exposure. They like wet, warm summers and can survive cool winters if protected from frost. Soil should be neutral to slightly acid (about pH 6–6.5), with excellent drainage. Improve it with plenty of humus and lighten heavy soils with coarse sand. Add nutrition with applications of a controlled-release fertilser in late winter and early autumn; an annual application of organic manure and or compost to the base of the plant will help keep up both nutrition and soil structure. Fuchsias available in nurseries are usually cultivars of *F. boliviana*, *F. arborescens* and *F. magellanica* × *gracilis* hybrids. All are upright-growing, to about 2 m, though *F. arborescens* can grow much taller, throwing out long, straggling, arched branches. Most fuchsias purchased from garden centres, however, are not that tall and tend to straggle if not gently pruned. Fuchsia flowers are exquisite, shaped like little purses in a vast range of combined reds, pinks, mauves and creams. If you can find a semi-shaded, very sheltered, cool place in your garden, and supply year-round moisture, try one of the tougher types suited to a hot climate. Otherwise, try them in hanging baskets where ideal conditions can more easily be simulated. Cultivars of *F. procumbens* make excellent hanging basket plants. They are subject to aphids and scale, so treat accordingly.

Galphimia glauca (Rain of Gold)
Tropical America
Height 2 m
Habit Evergreen, upright, sparse
Foliage Greyish-green, not dense
Flowers Long spikes of bright golden yellow flowers which are very long lasting and quite spectacular
Flowering time Summer
Conditions Full sun. Humus-enriched, well-drained soil with plenty of year-round moisture. Dislikes cold
Other points The unusual red branches and long flowering period make this a useful plant for adding colour to the garden.

Gardenia jasminoides (syn. *grandiflora*)
India and China
Height ½–3 m depending on type
Habit Evergreen, bushy and fairly upright
Foliage Dark green and glossy, very handsome
Flowers Gorgeous, large, white or creamy-white blooms
Flowering time Spring and summer; longer in tropics
Conditions Sun or light shade. Warmth and humidity all year round, though will withstand temperatures under 10°C for short periods. Humus-enriched, well-drained, acid soil. Water regularly. Requires shelter from harsh elements
Other points The gardenia flower has long been associated with romance and adds lustre to any garden. However it is not a plant for the lazy gardener because of the amount of care required in feeding, watering and protecting it from scale, aphids, thrips and mealy bugs. For those who want the gardenia's beauty without too much work, dwarf varieties may be the answer. Sweet-smelling Australian native species are also available.

Geraldton Wax (*Chamaelaucium uncinatum*)
Australia
Height To about 2 m depending on variety
Habit Evergreen. Open. Straggling
Foliage Very small, narrow, dull green
Flowers Prolific. Pink, mauve-pink, white
Flowering time Spring and early summer, depending on area
Conditions Full sun. This plant is very fussy as to soil, requiring a light alkaline gravel. Tolerates low temperatures and long dry periods provided annual rainfall is sufficient to provide an occasional good soak
Other points Geraldton Wax does not usually like coastal soils or humidity; it is more a plant for warm inland areas.

Gordonia axillaris
China
Height 4 m
Habit Evergreen, spreading
Foliage Tough, glossy, dark-green leaves
Flowers Large, with frilled white petals around a central cluster of golden stamens
Flowering time Autumn, winter
Conditions Sun or light-shade. Frost and drought tender. Humus-enriched acid soil
Other points A hot-climate shrub which is very decorative and can take cold below 10°C for short periods. Does well by the sea, though not on an exposed frontage.

Grevillea
Australia
Like callistemons, leptospermums and melaleucas, grevilleas are a native shrub or tree with so many types from which to choose that it is pointless to list them here. More than the other three, however, grevilleas have been the subject of extensive selective breeding to produce the wide range of cultivars available to us today. Grevillea breeding pioneer David Gordon of Queensland has given his family's name to many popular cultivars from which still other fine varieties have been bred. Another Queenslander, Merv Hodge, has done a great deal of valuable work to improve grevillea forms including grafting on to more versatile stock. For, despite their floral beauty and attractive foliage, grevilleas are often 'fussy' about soil conditions and are subject to death from root rot. Work continues to produce resistant varieties and some fine specimens can be purchased which have been grafted on to *G. robusta* rootstock, enabling them to be grown as handsome standards in a range of conditions. Foliage is variable, either very fine and rather fernlike or thicker and lobed. Flowers are large, long, often spidery, in a range of gorgeous colours.
Flowering time Depends on species
Conditions Today's cultivars do best in light, slightly acid, mulched soil, preferably mounded for perfect drainage. Regular light dressings of a low-phosphorous fertiliser should be given. Water regularly, particularly in summer, but do not over-water and do not allow to become waterlogged. Most grevilleas are quite cold-hardy down to freezing and below and will tolerate dry conditions. Some of the rainforest species, such as *G. baileyana*, do well in humid conditions. If the reasonable conditions as outlined are met, these shrubs are easy and fast to grow; there is a grevillea suited to every garden.

Heliotrope, Cherry Pie (*Heliotropum arborescens*)
Peru
Height To 1 m
Habit Evergreen, bushy
Foliage Dull, with deeply-etched veins and a rough surface
Flowers Mauve, very sweet-smelling
Flowering time Spring to autumn
Conditions Full sun. Humus-enriched, well-drained soil. Frost tender but otherwise quite cold-hardy. Drought tender
Other points The main reason for growing this plant is its delightful fragrance. Needs tip-pruning to prevent a ragged appearance. Suitable for borders or as an individual specimen in the garden; as the foliage is not particularly attractive it might be better suited to the herb or cutflower garden.

A gordonia (see opposite page) soaks up the sun in a seaside garden. This is a very large shrub, to the height of a small tree, which makes an excellent screen. Though they grow welll on the coast, gordonias flower best in adjacent highland areas.

Holmskioldia sanguinea (CHINESE HAT)
INDIA
HEIGHT To 3 m
HABIT Evergreen, sprawling
FOLIAGE Roundish, pointed or heart-shaped single leaves
FLOWERS A round calyx from which a long tube and stamens depend, looking rather like a little cap. Colours are orange, red or yellow
FLOWERING TIME Spring and autumn
CONDITIONS Sun. Any well-drained soils. Drought and frost tender. Water well in summer. Prune lightly in winter
OTHER POINTS A pretty plant despite its straggly nature and relatively short flowering periods which do at least add colour to the spring and autumn garden. New cultivars are much more compact and longer flowering.

Hydrangea macrophylla
CHINA AND JAPAN
HEIGHT Variable, according to type, rarely over 3 m
HABIT Semi-deciduous according to climate; in warmer climates plants remain evergreen
FOLIAGE Large, dark-green, handsome leaves; dense
FLOWERS Huge heads of flowers in shades and mixtures of palest to darkest pinks, blues and mauves, often with a creamy shading; so prolific they cover the plant in season. Colours can be governed by soil pH; acid soils produce blue flowers, alkaline soils produce pink flowers so you can acidify or sweeten the soil chemically to create the desired colour
FLOWERING TIME Summer
CONDITIONS Hydrangeas perform well in the sub-tropics if given part or light shade, a rich soil, plenty of additional fertiliser and a lot of water in summer

OTHER POINTS Cultivars of *H. macrophylla* come in all shapes and sizes, with differing flower forms. All make a spectacular summer show and are one of the best ways of getting fast colour into the garden. It is generally trouble-free. Remove dead flowers systematically, particularly once flowering is over.

Ixora SPP.
TROPICAL ASIA
HEIGHT Average 1½ m
HABIT Evergreen, upright
FOLIAGE Narrow, tapering, glossy
FLOWERS Large, showy heads or orange, red or pink flowers
FLOWERING TIME Early summer through autumn; longer in the tropics
CONDITIONS Sun or light shade. Light, humus-enriched, well-drained soil. Plenty of water in summer. Frost and drought tender.
OTHER POINTS One of the most typically 'tropical' flowers. Several cultivars of *I. chinensis* (PRINCE OF ORANGE) and *I. coccinea* (JUNGLE FLAME) are available from garden centres. All have spectacular, long-lasting flowers.

Justicia carnea
SOUTH AMERICA
HEIGHT 1½ m
HABIT Evergreen. Erect and self-contained
FOLIAGE Large, rough-surfaced leaves
FLOWERS Tall spikes of white, yellow, orange, pink or red flowers; quite showy
FLOWERING TIME Spasmodically through summer and autumn
CONDITIONS Part or full shade. Needs protection from harsh elements and is frost and drought tender. Humus-enriched, acid soil. Spring pruning promotes neat foliage
OTHER POINTS One of the few plants which flower well in shade.

Lantana montevidensis
SOUTH AMERICA
HEIGHT 30 cm
HABIT Evergreen, dense and bushy
FOLIAGE Small, soft-green leaves
FLOWERS Small, colourful flowerheads in white, mauve–pink and mauve, borne profusely
FLOWERING TIME Spring to autumn; longer in hotter climates
CONDITIONS Rich soils with plenty of moisture, though will grow in poorer, sandy soils also. Full sun. Very tough.
OTHER POINTS Popular low-growing plants used extensively in landscaping. Dwarf varieties make effective low border or rockery plants. *L. camara* has become a notorious problem plant in many areas where it smothers natural bushland; ornamental cultivars of it are said to be sterile but there is some concern that they may be cross-pollinating with their wild progenitor. Check with your garden centre when buying this plant to make sure it is suited to your area.

Leptospermum SPP. (TEA TREE)
AUSTRALIA
Like melaleucas, with which they share their common name, leptospermums are an Australian bushland plant which do equally well in 'native' or mixed gardens because of their general hardiness and adaptability. They make excellent informal hedges and screens but also look good as specimen plants, alone or in a shrubbery. There are now many attractive cultivars available from garden centres. Heights and habits vary according to type but in general leptospermums have fine, neat foliage and range in height from 0.5 m–3 m. Flowers can be white, pink or red, very dainty and prolific during the spring season (some also flower in late summer–autumn), when they can cover a bush, giving rise to varietal and common names such as 'SNOW FLURRY' and 'SNOW IN SUMMER'. Cultivars of *L. petersonii* (LEMON-SCENTED TEA TREE) have a citrus fragrance.
CONDITIONS Leptospermums are very easy to grow in full sun in most soils. A regular but very light fertilising is recommended for quality foliage. Watering requirements are not great in all but very arid areas but some additional watering after establishment, during dry periods, will help maintain foliage quality. In other words, leptospermums need a little bit of care but should not be spoiled. Some types can be subject to mealy bug and scale but generally these shrubs are trouble-free. They are also attractive to birds and butterflies.

LILLY PILLIES
Many 'Lilly pillies' of the genera *Syzygium*, *Acmena*, *Eugenia* and *Waterhousea* are shrubs rather than trees. In either case, their looks and habits are the same. See page 86.

LITTLE BOY BLUE (*Otacanthus caeruleus*)
BRAZIL
HEIGHT ½ m
HABIT Evergreen, quite compact
FOLIAGE Soft, bright green, attractive
FLOWERS Delicate, vivid blue flowers with a long vase life
FLOWERING TIME Early summer to winter, longer in warmer areas
CONDITIONS Full sun or light shade. Medium, well-drained soil. Plenty of moisture, with generous watering in dry periods. Frost tender. Prune hard in spring
OTHER POINTS A very pretty and popular plant which can be close-planted as a small hedge or massed for a colour display that lasts for most of the year.

Malpighia coccigera (SINGAPORE HOLLY)
WEST INDIES
HEIGHT 1½ m
HABIT Evergreen, multi-stemmed
FOLIAGE Shiny, spiky, holly-like leaves
FLOWERS Small, pale pink with frilly petals
FLOWERING TIME Summer
CONDITIONS Full sun or light shade. Medium, well-drained soil. Plenty of moisture. Drought and frost tender, though can tolerate cold below 10°C
OTHER POINTS Slow growing. Makes a good hedge.

Malvaviscus arboreus (TURK'S HAT)
MEXICO
HEIGHT To 3 m

HABIT Fairly spreading but rounded in form
FOLIAGE Toothed, pointed leaves. Quite dense
FLOWERS Bright red, resembling an unopened hibiscus
FLOWERING TIME Summer
OTHER POINTS An easy-to-grow plant which is not fussy about conditions. Does best in a light, humus-enriched soil with plenty of water in summer. Frost tender but otherwise withstands cold below 10°C. Pale pink and cream forms available.

Medinilla magnifica
SOUTH-EAST ASIA
HEIGHT 1½ m
HABIT Evergreen. Strong, upright stems. Not dense
FOLIAGE Large, thick leaves with pale veins
FLOWERS Large, pendant, pink. Very showy
FLOWERING TIME Summer
CONDITIONS Light shade. Shelter. Grows best in a very light, open, rich humus that is kept moist. Water and feed well. This is a very tropical plant that can only be grown outdoors where temperatures do not fall below about 18°C and even then it needs a warm, moist, protected spot. Can be grown in a bush house with winter heat.
OTHER POINTS Not an easy plant to grow in any circumstances but the beauty of its flowers is worth the effort for dedicated gardeners.

Megaskepasma erythroclamyx (BRAZILIAN RED CLOAK)
SOUTH AMERICA
HEIGHT 3 m
HABIT Evergreen, upright
FOLIAGE Large, handsome leaves with marked veins
FLOWERS Tall spikes of dark pink flowers
FLOWERING TIME Late summer or autumn
CONDITIONS Shade or light shade, though will grow in full sun also. Light, open, rich, moist humus. Water and feed well.
OTHER POINTS Like justicia and pachystachys, which it superficially resembles, this is another plant which adds colour to shady places. However, megaskepasma is more tropical than the other two and requires higher year-round temperatures, though will grow in the sub-tropics if given a warm, sheltered spot.

Melaleuca SPP. (TEA TREE)
AUSTRALIA
These evergreen natives range from the large trees with papery trunks which grace many Australian swamps, to smaller trees and shrubs. Though mostly suited to bush gardens, some are suitable specimens for general garden use, particularly smaller-growing types from which cultivars have been selected. Most popular of these are probably the varieties 'REVOLUTION GREEN' and 'REVOLUTION GOLD', both cultivars of *M. bracteata*. Melaleucas sold in nurseries for the home garden are generally hardy and tolerant of poor soils. Others are useful screening plants and there are species which will thrive in waterlogged soil. Flowers can be white, cream, red, mauve or yellow, depending on type. Sometimes flowering can be profuse and at such times these rather dull trees (dull, that is, when transplanted from their natural habitat to the home garden) are transformed by a mass of small blossoms. Some melaleucas produce flowers rich in nectar which attract birds, bats, possums and other wildlife and fill the night air with a heavy honey fragrance.

Melastoma affine (PINK LASIANDRA)
AUSTRALIA
HEIGHT 2 m
HABIT Evergreen, spreading
FOLIAGE Fairly large, hairy leaves with deeply etched veins, resembling those of tibouchina
FLOWERS Large, six-petalled, pinkish–mauve flowers. Very decorative
FLOWERING TIME Summer to autumn, longer in hotter climates
CONDITIONS Sun or light shade, will grow well in full shade but will not flower so well. Light, open, humus-enriched soil topped with sprinkling of leaf litter or bark. Feed occasionally but very lightly. Fast growing. Do not over-water
OTHER POINTS A pretty native plant from warm and humid coastal areas of New South Wales and Queensland. Other native and exotic species of melastoma are also available. Berries are also decorative.

Metrosideros SPP.
See 'Trees', page 81.

Michelia figo (PORT WINE MAGNOLIA)
CHINA
HEIGHT 6 m
HABIT Evergreen, compact
FOLIAGE Neat, tough, mid-green leaves
FLOWERS Tulip-shaped cups in an unusual deep, dull red with a winey fragrance
FLOWERING TIME Spring
CONDITIONS Full sun. Quite hardy and will stand light frosts and dry periods; however, regular watering improves foliage quality and hastens growth in this rather slow-growing shrub. Will grow in quite heavy soils. Add humus or mulch well
OTHER POINTS This is a popular plant which performs well in the sub-tropics as well as further south.

Murraya paniculata (MOCK ORANGE)
MALAYSIA
HEIGHT 2½ m
HABIT Evergreen, dense
FOLIAGE Handsome compound leaves with small, dark green leaflets
FLOWERS Clusters of sweet-smelling, small, creamy-white flowers resembling orange blossom
FLOWERING TIME Spring to autumn
CONDITIONS Full sun, or light shade in very hot areas. Rich, well-drained and well-mulched soil. Quite hardy but growth is slow in areas with fairly cold winters. Will tolerate light frosts and dry periods. Excellent hedge plant. Prune well after flowering
OTHER POINTS This plant is so pretty, so fragrant and so easy to grow that it deserves a place in any garden.

Mussaenda erythrophylla
EQUATORIAL AFRICA
HEIGHT 2½ m
HABIT Evergreen, sprawling, quite dense
FOLIAGE Large, light green, rounded leaves on slender canes
FLOWERS Pretty, white or yellow, too tiny to be significant in themselves but attached to large, colourful bracts in shades of pink, white and salmon which make this a very colourful plant
FLOWERING TIME Summer through autumn and longer in tropical climates
CONDITIONS Full sun. Will thrive in poor soils but produces a lusher foliage in light, humus-enriched, open and well-drained soils. Water well but feed only very lightly or flowering will be poor. Frost tender
OTHER POINTS Hardier, and with a more sprawling growth habit, is the very similar *M. frondosa*. Other mussaendas, including varieties of *M. philippica* (from the Philippines, as the name implies) are sometimes available. Some have red, white, cream or pale pink bracts. Prune hard after flowering finishes.

OLEANDER (*Nerium oleander*)
MEDITERRANEAN
HEIGHT Variable up to about 4 m
HABIT Evergreen, open, multi-stemmed, spreading
FOLIAGE Trifoliate with narrow, tough, pointed, dull green individual leaves
FLOWERS Double or single blooms in many shades of white, pink, apricot, orange, yellow and red, according to type
FLOWERING TIME Spring through autumn
CONDITIONS Almost any except very cold regions
OTHER POINTS Despite their Mediterranean origin, oleanders flourish in the tropics and sub-tropics and are often thought of as 'typically tropical'. They are tough under all conditions and flower beautifully for much of the year. Despite their open growth habit they make good hedges or screens if judiciously pruned for control and are particularly useful along main roads or beachfronts because they are not adversely affected by exhaust fumes and salt spray. Their only drawback is that all parts of the plant are highly poisonous; parents with young children may consider them a risk but as the plant is unpalatable, the chance of a child actually being fatally poisoned is rare indeed.

Orthosiphon aristatus (CAT'S WHISKERS)
AUSTRALIA
HEIGHT 1 m
HABIT Upright, spreading
FOLIAGE Neat, pointed, serrated leaves on purplish stems
FLOWERS White or pale mauve, depending on form
FLOWERING TIME Most of the year
CONDITIONS Sun or light shade. Prefers a light, humus-enriched, well-drained soil which is not allowed to dry out. Water well in summer. Fertilise regularly and prune hard after flowering. Frost tender
OTHER POINTS This is a useful plant because it grows anywhere in the garden, including 'difficult' spots in full sun or damp, shady places. *O. stramineus* is very similar but with white flowers only.

Pachystachys lutea (GOLDEN CANDLES)
SOUTH AMERICA
HEIGHT To 1 m
HABIT Evergreen, erect, fairly spreading. Fast-growing
FOLIAGE Medium-sized, dark-green leaves with deeply etched veins
FLOWERS Tall spikes of yellow flowers
FLOWERING TIME Spring through autumn, longer in hot climates
CONDITIONS Light shade. Fairly open, humus-enriched soil which is not allowed to dry out. Plenty of water and fertiliser. Prune after flowering
OTHER POINTS A pretty, long-flowering plant which adds colour to shady areas. The very similar *P. coccinea* has red flowers.

Pentas lanceolata
TROPICAL AFRICA
HEIGHT To 1 m maximum
HABIT Evergreen, compact
FOLIAGE Small, soft, pointed leaves with deeply etched veins
FLOWERS Terminal clusters of small mauve, pink, white, red or bi-coloured individual flowers
FLOWERING TIME Spring to autumn, longer in warmer climates
CONDITIONS Sun. Not fussy about soil, but prefers one which is humus-enriched and well-drained. Frost tender. Can withstand long dry periods but should be watered well in summer if water is available to maintain foliage quality. Prune after final flowering. Subject to aphids and, rarely, to scale infestation.
OTHER POINTS An easy-to-grow plant which requires little maintenance and adds colour to the garden most of the year.

Pittosporum SPP.
AUSTRALIA, NEW ZEALAND AND ASIA
Of the several shrub-sized pittosporums available in Australia, two are indigenous. *Pittosporum undulatum* (SWEET PITTOSPORUM) has handsome, glossy, wavy-edged leaves, small sweet-smelling spring flowers and a profusion of vivid orange berries. *P. revolutum* (BRISBANE LAUREL) has very dark leaves and yellow flowers. Both are fast-growing, prefer humus-enriched soils, need plenty of summer moisture (though will withstand winter–spring drought periods) and are resistant to light frosts. They make attractive garden plants. *P. undulatum* has been declared a nuisance in some areas but is still a useful plant where it can be kept from invading nearby bushland. Height is variable, according to conditions; in the garden *P. undulatum* can reach about 8 m and *P. revolutum* no more than 3 m. The exotic pittosporums include attractive cultivars of *P. eugenioides*, *P. tenuifolium* and *P. crassifolium*. All have handsome, in some cases variegated, foliage and attractive, often fragrant flowers.
CONDITIONS Heights vary according to type but all are small, compact shrubs with good form. All do best in full sun with humus-enriched soils and plenty of water at establishment. Frost hardy. They thrive in warm climates without protection unless placed in areas exposed to strong, salt-laden or hot/cold western winds. In such cases, protection of young

Cat's Whiskers (Orthosiphon aristatus, *see opposite page*) *is a versatile Australian rainforest shrub which flowers well in the shade. It is a useful landscaping plant for difficult areas such as banks and gullies.*

trees is required. Most pittosporums can be planted in light shade as well as sun, but full sun is needed to develop good flowering and the leaf colour in variegated types. All pittosporums are good, reliable specimens for home garden growing. Only problems are sooty mould and, sometimes, white scale, both of which can infest certain varieties, including the Australian pittosporums.

Plumbago auriculata (syn. *capensis*)
SOUTH AFRICA

HEIGHT 3 m
HABIT Evergreen, spreading, suckering, fast-growing
FOLIAGE Small, neat, dense
FLOWERS Dainty five-petalled, pale blue, mauve-blue or white flowers. Prolific
FLOWERING TIME Summer and winter
CONDITIONS Sun. Not fussy about soil but does best in a good soil. Withstands light frost and drought but grows faster in warmer, higher rainfall areas. Fertilise during establishment period. Prune for shape
OTHER POINTS Though generally grown as a warm-climate hedge, plumbago makes an attractive single specimen plant in the garden, particularly the newer varieties which tend to be more compact, with brighter flowers. Very easy to grow almost anywhere, and trouble-free. Suckers can be invasive.

POINSETTIA (*Euphorbia pulcherrima*)
MEXICO
HEIGHT About 0.5 m
HABIT Evergreen, spreading
FOLIAGE Quite large, close-packed, with slight lobing
FLOWERS Insignificant, but this plant gets it beauty from the large, showy bracts (or modified leaves) which can be single, double or even denser than double in the case of some contemporary cultivars. Best known colour is vivid scarlet but pink, salmon, cream and yellow forms are also popular
CONDITIONS Not fussy as to soil conditions but is drought and frost tender
OTHER POINTS Hot-climate gardeners are lucky enough to be able to grow these popular indoor plants outdoors, where they can be massed for a red and creamy–white colour contrast if desired. They also make excellent small hedges. Alone, their spreading, dense habit and year round colour makes them a desirable single specimen in any garden. Tall growing (to about 2 m) poinsettias make excellent screening plants; the Ecke cultivars are the best choice.

Raphiolepis indica (INDIAN HAWTHORN)
SUB-TROPICAL ASIA
HEIGHT 2 m
HABIT Evergreen, spreading
FOLIAGE Small, glossy leaves with pinkish-red or pale green new growth on long, arching branches
FLOWERS Small, five-petalled, profuse, white flushed with pink
FLOWERING TIME Winter through summer
CONDITIONS Sun. Not fussy about soil provided it is fairly well-drained. Frost hardy. Needs plenty of water at establishment. Scale can be a problem
OTHER POINTS One of the few shrubs which combine toughness, beauty of flower and foliage. Grows almost anywhere except very low rainfall areas, with no trouble. Another popular raphiolepis species is *R. umbellata* (YEDDA HAWTHORN), as well as *R. × delacouri* which is a hybrid cross of *R. indica* and *R. umbellata*.

Rondeletia amoena
CENTRAL AMERICA
HEIGHT To about 2.5 m, depending on type
HABIT Evergreen, spreading, fast-growing
FOLIAGE Broad, oval in shape.
FLOWERS Terminal clusters of pink flowers
FLOWERING TIME Most profuse in spring but flowers through summer and autumn, longer in warmer climates
CONDITIONS Sun. Frost and drought tender; will withstand cold below 10°C for very short periods only. Well-drained, humus-enriched soil. Water well in spring and summer. Can suffer from scale. Prune after flowering. Fertilise during main growth period
OTHER POINTS A pretty plant which requires little care. *R. odorata* has fragrant salmon-coloured flowers with conspicuous yellow centres and is more tropical than *R. amoena*. Other rondeletia species are also grown in Australia but are not always readily available. (See page 109.)

Ruellia macrantha
BRAZIL
HEIGHT 1½ m
HABIT Evergreen, compact
FOLIAGE Stiff and lightly covered in hair
FLOWERS Tubular, pinkish–mauve flowers growing from stem. Very decorative
FLOWERING TIME Winter and spring
CONDITIONS Light shade in tropics; in sub-tropics plant so that several hours of winter sun are available each day or flowering will be poor. Frost and drought tender. Prune after flowering
OTHER POINTS These lovely flowering shrubs do need a bit of care outside the tropics. In sub-tropics they are probably best grown in tubs which can be moved to take advantage of light shade in summer and full sun in winter.

Russelia equisetiformis syn. *juncea*
MEXICO
HEIGHT Between ½ m and 1 m
HABIT Spreading. Fast-growing
FOLIAGE The leaves are so small and sparse on the long, arching, bushy green stems that they hardly matter to the gardener
FLOWERS Small, long, thin red tubes
FLOWERING TIME Spring and summer
CONDITIONS Sun. Any well-drained soil will do, particularly light and sandy soils, but humus-enrichment will hasten growth. Too rich a soil, too much water and too much fertiliser discourage flower growth so moderation is the key.
OTHER POINTS This plant is excellent for banks because it looks at its best when allowed to cascade. It is very popular with landscapers in warm climates and is often used in balcony planter boxes in large buildings. When used in this way, or in the home garden, russelia needs full sun to flower. When not flowering, it is unattractive. Prune for control, but lightly, or flowering will be inhibited.

Streptosolen jamesonii (BROWALLIA, MARMALADE BUSH)
SOUTH AMERICA
HEIGHT 2 m
HABIT Evergreen, spreading. Fast-growing
FOLIAGE Very small, neat, dense, pointed, mid-green leaves with deeply etched veins
FLOWERS Very florific clusters of small orange and yellow flowers
FLOWERING TIME Spring to autumn, longer in warmer climates
CONDITIONS Sun. Frost tender but able to withstand long dry periods in winter and spring provided it gets adequate summer water. Prefers a humus-enriched, well-drained soil. Prune lightly for control only
OTHER POINTS Adds a touch of vivid colour to the garden for most of the year. Usually reliable but not long-lived. Dwarf forms available including the popular 'GINGER MEGGS' which many people now think of as the common name for this plant.

Tibouchina SPP.
SOUTH AMERICA
HEIGHT Variable — largest up to 12 m
HABIT Upright but loosely branched
FOLIAGE Single, velvety leaves with deeply etched parallel veins
FLOWERS Quite large, prolific and deep purple or pink
FLOWERING TIME Spring, autumn and sometimes early or late summer
CONDITIONS Sun. Light or heavy soils. Frost and drought tender
OTHER POINTS The spectacular, purple-flowering tibouchina (formerly known as lasiandra) is a common sight in hot-climate gardens. Cultivars of *T. lepidota* such as 'ALSTONVILLE', developed in Australia, are particularly well-adapted to local conditions and can be encouraged to grow as small trees rather than shrubs. True shrub forms of *T. granulosa* are smaller growing; cultivar 'JULES' grows less than 1 m. A taller growing shrub species is *T. urvilleana*. All tibouchinas are fast growing and easy to maintain. Pink-flowering cultivar 'KATHLEEN' is also spectacular.

Viburnum tinus
MEDITERRANEAN
HEIGHT 3 m
HABIT Evergreen, upright
FOLIAGE Small, neat, handsome
FLOWERS Clusters of pink-tinged, small, white blossoms
FLOWERING TIME Winter and spring
CONDITIONS Very hardy in almost all conditions. Very susceptible to thrips
OTHER POINTS Although viburnums grow and flower better in cooler climates, *V. tinus* is so versatile it will grow anywhere and makes a useful plant for low-maintenance gardens in the sub-tropics, where it can add winter colour to the garden. *V. odoratissimum*, which has fragrant flowers and attractive red fruit also grows well in the sub-tropics and has very handsome foliage.

Westringia fruticosa (syn. *rosmarinifolius*)
AUSTRALIA
HEIGHT 2 m
HABIT Evergreen, fast-growing
FOLIAGE Silvery grey-green, thin, small, pointed leaves resembling those of rosemary
FLOWERS Small, lavender blue or white
CONDITIONS Any
OTHER POINTS This is a truly versatile plant which will grow almost anywhere, from coast to mountains and dry, inland areas. Though drought resistant, it will grow where summer rainfall is quite heavy. It prefers light soils (it grows well on sand dunes provided some light nourishment is given, or humus added) but thrives in heavier soils also. It is frost hardy yet flourishes in warmth and humidity. It does best in full sun but grows in light shade (where it will flower less well). And it needs no care, being pest and disease free. An excellent hedge or single specimen plant. Also excellent for landscaping in areas where there is heavy people traffic, such as around schools and other public buildings.

SHRUBS AT A GLANCE

Small flowering shrubs — to 1 m

Agapetes serpens (red flowers)
AZALEA (small-growing varieties)
Barleria SPP.
Bouvardia SPP.
Callistemon 'CAPTAIN COOK'
　　C. 'LITTLE JOHN'
Calothamnus villosus (red flowers)
Cuphea SPP. (dwarf varieties)
Duranta 'SHEENA'S GOLD'
Euphorbia milii
Grevillea 'NED KELLY'
HELIOTROPE
Hypericum patulum (yellow flowers)
Lantana montevidensis
Nandina domestica 'NANA'
Otacanthus (Little Boy Blue)
Orthosiphon SPP.
Pachystachys lutea
Pentas SPP.
Russelia SPP.
Serissa foetida
Syzygium SPP. (dwarf varieties)

Larger flowering shrubs — from 1 m

Abelia SPP.
Adenium SPP.
AZALEA
Bauhinia galpinii
Brunfelsia SPP.
Callistemon SPP.
Camellia SPP.
Cestrum SPP.
Chamaelaucium SPP.
Clerodendrum ugandense
Eupatorium SPP.
Euphorbia characias
　　E. pulcherrima
　　E. wulfenii
Galphimia SPP.
Gardenia SPP.
Grevillea SPP.
Holmskioldia SPP.
Hydrangea SPP.
Ixora SPP.
Malvaviscus SPP.
Megaskepasma SPP.
Michelia SPP.
Murraya SPP.
Mussaenda SPP.
Nerium SPP.
Raphiolepis SPP.
Rondeletia SPP.
Streptosolen SPP.
Syzygium SPP (larger varieties)
Tibouchina SPP.
Westringia SPP.

Flowering shrubs for shade

Most require light shade only; those which can grow in deeper shade are marked with an *

Abelia SPP.
Abutilon SPP.
Acalypha SPP.
Ardisia SPP.
AZALEA
Bauera rubioides (pink flowers)
Brunfelsia SPP.
Camellia SPP.
Cestrum SPP.
Clerodendrum ugandense
Drejerella syn. *Justicia* SPP.
Eupatorium SPP.
Euphorbia pulcherrima
Gardenia SPP.
Fuchsia SPP.
Hydrangea SPP.
Ixora SPP.
Justicia SPP.*
Kerria japonica (yellow flowers)
Malpighia SPP.
Melastoma SPP.
Megaskepasma SPP.
Metrosideros queenslandica
Pachystachys lutea and *P. coccinea*
Syzygium SPP.

Fast-growing flowering shrubs

Abelia SPP.
Acacia SPP. (shrub types)
Bauhinia galpinii
Calliandra SPP.
Callistemon SPP.
Cassia spp. (shrub types)
Cestrum SPP.
Chamaelaucium SPP.
Crotolaria SPP.
Euphorbia milii
　　E. pulcherrima
Grevillea SPP.
Hydrangea SPP.
Ixora SPP.
Lantana SPP.
Malvaviscus SPP.
Megaskepasma SPP.
Murraya SPP.
Nerium SPP.
Ochna serrulata (yellow flowers)
Pachystachys SPP.
Pentas SPP.
Plumbago SPP.
Russelia SPP.
Streptosolen SPP.
Tibouchina SPP.
Westringia SPP.

Rondeletia amoena (page 106) flowers prolifically throughout spring and summer; the hotter the climate, the longer it flowers. This easy care shrub makes an excellent hedge or specimen plant.

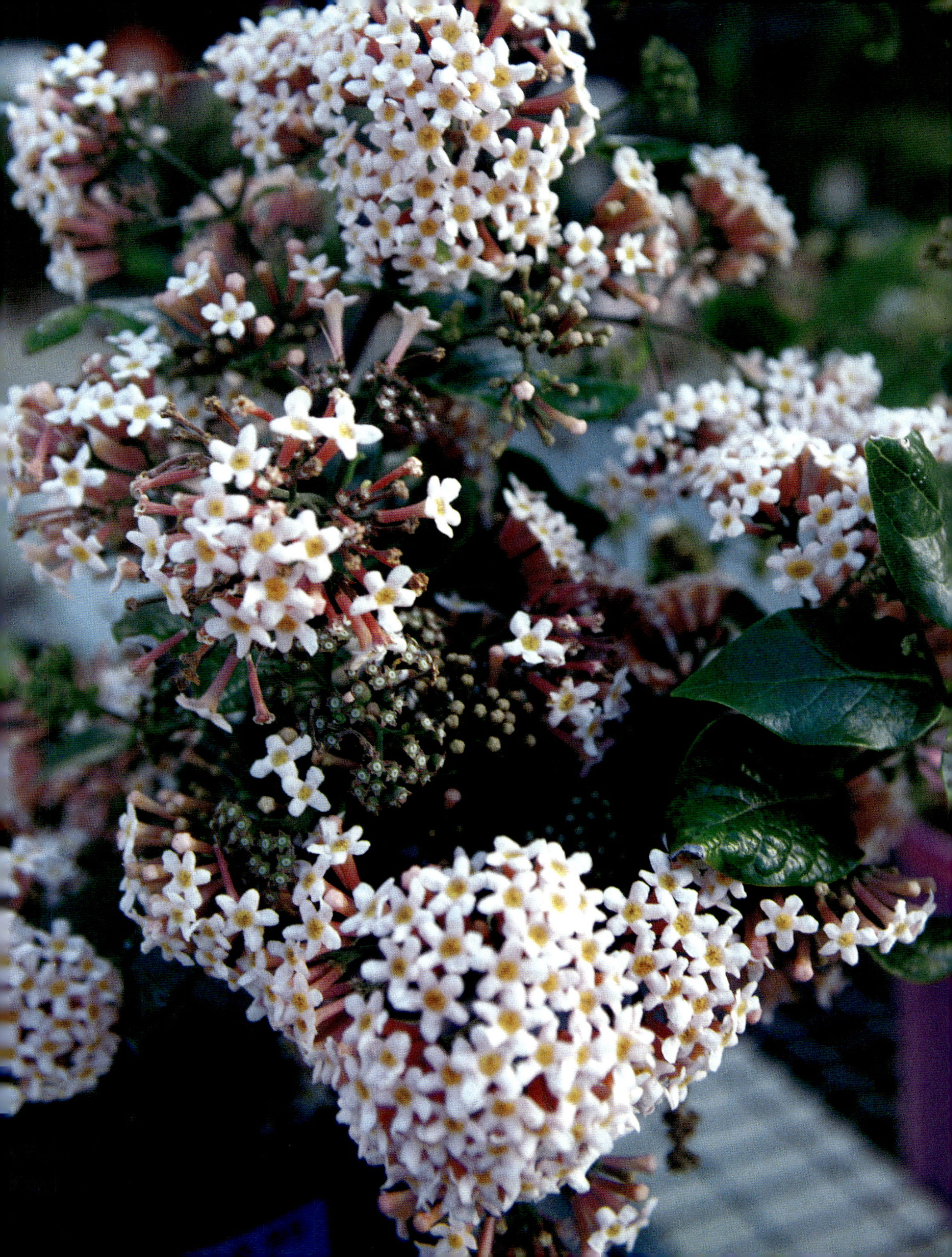

Hibiscus

THE HIBISCUS IS generally considered to be the most tropical of flowers; whether worn behind the ear, woven into a garland or used as a table decoration, these colourful, wide-open flowers make us think of palm trees and South Sea islands. Yet though today's hibiscus shrub is frequently grown in tropical seaside regions, it actually does best in the sub-tropics. Indeed, as far as Australia is concerned, at least one expert has demarcated coastal northern New South Wales for having the ideal year-round climate for growing hibiscus. Where winters are cool and dry, summers warm but cooled by sea breezes, and there is little risk of frost, this popular plant will produce blooms for most of the year. However, if grown within about 50 km of the coastline, the hibiscus will do well in the tropical regions and further south with adequate care and protection (though they may not flower so freely).

The hibiscus hybridises easily and because of this, amateur and professional breeders have over many decades produced a bewildering number of named cultivars. The range and combination of colours is vast, so gardeners are best advised to find a nursery or garden centre with a wide selection of hibiscus on offer. You may wish to restrict yourself to certain flower colours to suit your overall garden plan, or you may allow yourself to be seduced by whatever colour catches the eye.

Hibiscus require a free-draining, light, humus enriched soil with a pH level of about 6.2. To achieve and maintain the right soil tilth, add organic mulch continuously. This is important because the plant's delicate feeder roots need a rich, protected zone where they can roam freely, undisturbed by digging or other harsh interference. Ideally the mulch should be fairly open in construction, such as hay, straw, nut shells, wood chips or sugarcane trash. Add some nutrient-rich organic matter such as compost and/or manure.

Although hibiscus require good drainage they also need plenty of water. Except when there has been heavy rain, they should be given a thorough soaking at least once a week, more frequently during dry, hot, windy conditions. Much less water is required during the brief, winter non-growing season. The best guide, during the summer growing season, is to water whenever well-drained soil shows signs of completely drying out.

Good flowering requires generous applications of fertiliser throughout the growing season. The regime should start in spring and shrubs should be given three-weekly applications of a fertiliser which is higher in potash than in nitrogen, to promote flowering. A suggested NPK ratio is Nitrogen 12, Phosphorus 5 and Potassium 14, in doses of two teaspoons for shrubs up to 1 m, increased progressively to two small handfuls for shrubs over 2 m high. Or follow the recommendations on the packet. Apply the fertiliser around the base of the plant where the soil has been moistened, then water in thoroughly. Don't be tempted to over-fertilise as this can harm the plant; it is usual to stop feeding hibiscus during winter except in areas where year-round blooming occurs. In other words, as long as plants are flowering they need feeding, though a seasonal reduction in flowering should be matched by a corresponding reduction in the amount of fertiliser applied.

Annual pruning promotes good flowering. In warmer areas this can be done in late winter through to early spring, in cooler areas it should be done when all risk of cold weather is past and there is plenty of sap in the branches. Remove about one third of the branches, cutting back to the thick, base areas of branches and leaving the shrub sufficiently open to allow flowers to develop and discouraging the dense foliage growth which provides a haven for insect pests.

The main problem with growing hibiscus is posed by the many insect pests which suck the sap, chew the leaves, devour the buds, deform flowers and foliage and otherwise harm your precious plants. The two most notable pests are the Hibiscus Flower Beetle (*Macroura concolor*) and the Erinose mite (*Eriophyes hibisci*), both of which are very destructive. Hibiscus beetles are small and black, penetrating into developing flower buds. They are most active in summer and can be controlled to some extent by spraying. The Australian Hibiscus Society also recommends removing all buds from affected bushes and placing them in a plastic bag for disposal in the rubbish bin. This breaks the cycle which starts when the beetles lay eggs in the blooms. When repeated three or four times each week during summer, this non-chemical control method is extremely effective though it is time-consuming.

Erinose mites are tiny creatures almost invisible to the human eye. More visible is the yellowish to red-brown velvety growth on leaves and the blisters on the upper surface. Foliage also tends to become curled and twisted. Overall damage to the plant can be severe. Suggested control methods such as monthly spraying may provide some protection but may also create a worse problem by destroying the predator mites which prey on the common pest red spider.

Other pests which prey on hibiscus include caterpillars, harlequin beetles, aphids, grasshoppers, mites and snails. For treatments, see the Plant Clinic, page 226, or ask your nursery and garden centre staff.

Hibiscus may also be susceptible to fungal diseases which lead to dieback or leaf-yellowing, though these occur only rarely. Once the problem has been identified, it can be treated with a fungicide. Yellowing of old leaves, particularly those near the base of the plant, occurs naturally with old age. Another cause of leaf yellowing may be lack of fertiliser. This may also cause bud drop.

Despite their carefree appearance, hibiscus shrubs require quite a lot of work. Those true fanciers who are prepared to put in the time, effort and vigilance required will find it well worthwhile because they will be rewarded with plants which produce a mass of exquisite, varied blooms for many months of the year. As I have already suggested, if you want to grow a selection of these plants, it may be best to establish special areas for them in the garden. Otherwise, the less-dedicated home gardener would be best to plant just one or two good-flowering specimens, preferably those which have already demonstrated some resistance to insect attack, and give them the care required. Whatever you do, *don't* buy hibiscus because you like the look of them and stick them in the garden without bothering to cultivate and protect them properly — not only will you end up with a disappointing plant, you will attract insect pests to the garden which may attack other plants.

OVERLEAF
*This magnificent flower (*TOP*) is Hibiscus 'CROWN OF WARRINGAH' which is a good choice for hot-climate gardeners everywhere. Generally considered as the most typically tropical of all flowering plants, the hibiscus is in fact a sub-tropical plant which does best where the humidity is not too high. Another firm favourite is* Hibiscus 'GOLD COAST' (BOTTOM)*, a double-flowered variety. The range of hibiscus flower colours is so large today that they can be planted to suit every kind of colour scheme.*

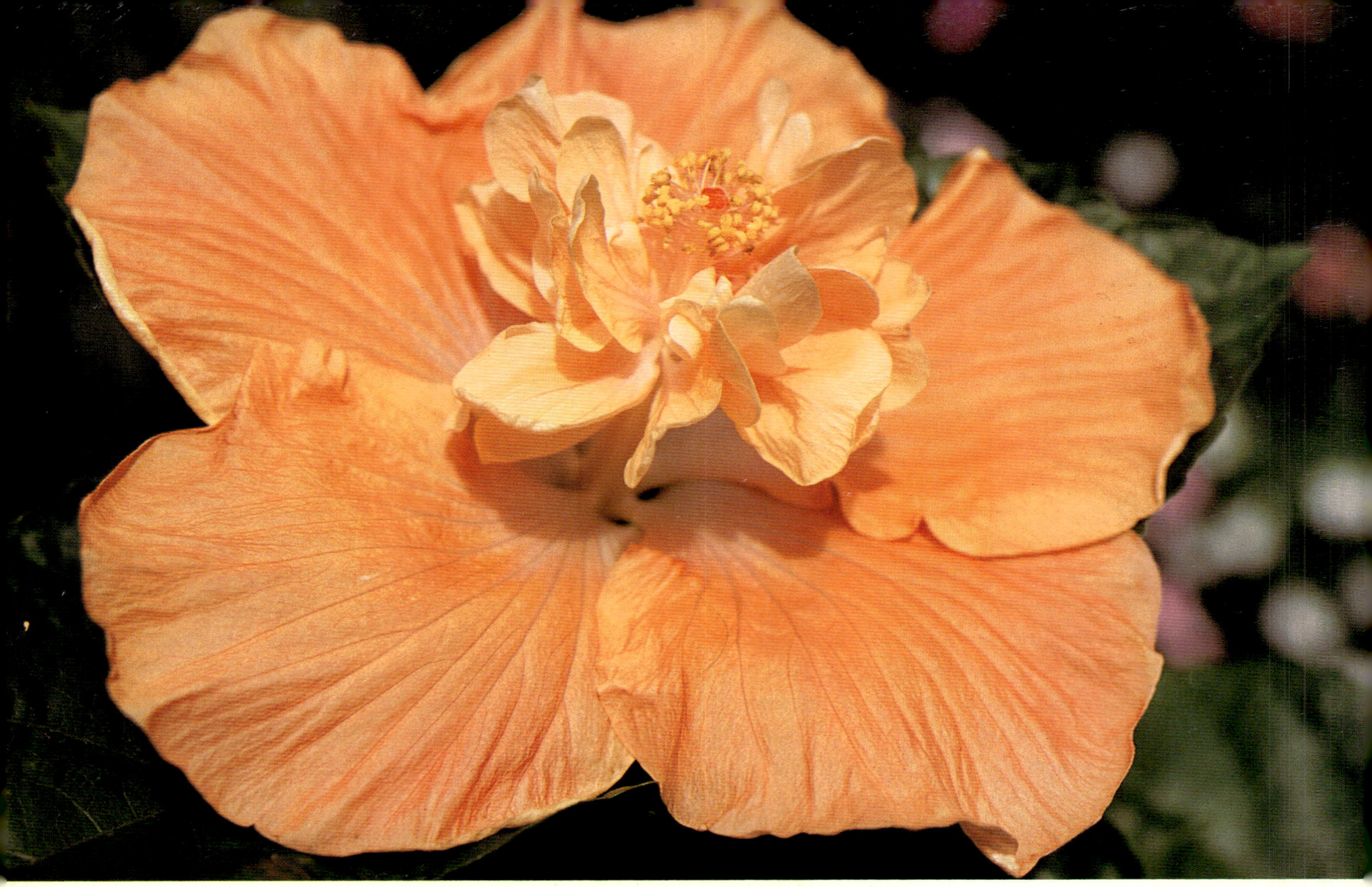

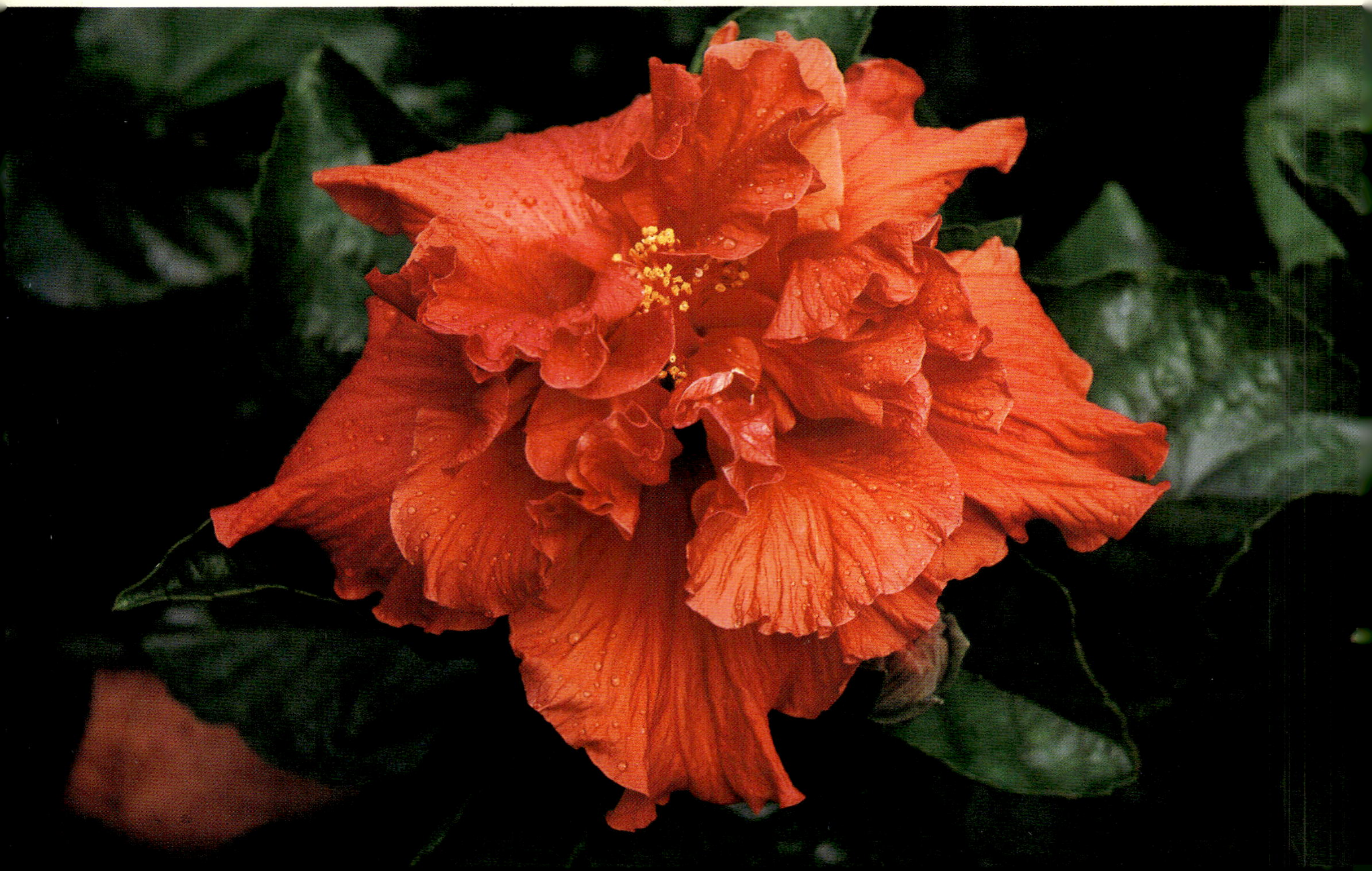

Vireyas

VIREYAS ARE COMMONLY KNOWN AS TROPICAL RHODODENDRONS but as with so many of our favourite so-called 'tropical' plants, the name can be misleading. Although they are native to Indonesia, the Philippines, Malaysia, Papua New Guinea and nearby areas (including one species in Australia), they occur at high elevations up to 3000 m or more above sea level. This means that, while they are not cold-climate plants and hate frost, they nonetheless need to be well understood if you are to grow them at sea level in hot climate areas.

Though their form resembles that of any flowering shrub, their natural habit is semi-epiphytic. In the garden, they must have excellent drainage and a very loose, free medium in which to grow. If you wish to grow vireyas in beds, these must be built between 30 to 45 cm above the regular soil (which must first be broken up to prevent an impervious pan forming).

Fill vireya beds with an organic mix of ingredients such as peatmoss, leafmould, pine bark, sand or vermiculite. These can be mixed with existing soil in any sort of combination which gives a rich but very open organically enriched blend. Sawdust and lawn clippings are unsuitable. Add gypsum to ensure an adequate calcium content; lime in any form is inappropriate because vireyas like a slightly acid soil (between pH 5 and 6). If your soil is not acid enough, it will need to be made so with a dressing of chelated sulphur or some similar acidifying product. Mulching is essential. Some growers have found that an easier alternative to digging over heavy soil is to plant vireyas in a wide, shallow hole filled with cymbidium mix and well mulched after planting.

The plants should be placed with their roots only just under the surface so that they grow semi-epiphytically on top of the soil. Again, the addition of cymbidium orchid mix will help get the plant off to a good start. Putting rocks and pieces of timber around the plant can also be helpful, to help support it and provide a 'natural' growing environment. Certainly young plants will need staking or supporting in some way until their roots have taken hold.

Away from their natural habitat, where monsoonal deluges can saturate the soil around their roots for long periods, vireyas do best in pots and hanging baskets where the right soil and drainage conditions can be guaranteed. Use a very open mix; that formulated for cymbidium orchids is fine, or a high quality, non-compacting potting mix based mainly on composted pine bark. If this tends to compact, loosen it up with coarse sand or perlite.

While the smaller-growing varieties look very attractive in hanging baskets, the larger vireyas will need to be in non-suspended containers. These must be kept clear of the ground, on benches which allow free drainage.

Vireyas like a sheltered position where there is morning sun and afternoon shade — an easterly or north-easterly aspect is best, shaded from the west by trees. They will also do well enough under the light shade of trees, or under 30–50 per cent shadecloth.

PREVIOUS PAGE
Vireyas or tropical rhododendrons are easy to grow if they are given the right care and conditions. Their remarkable beauty, astonishing diversity and ready adaption to shadehouse conditions makes them popular with collectors. This one is rightly named 'SHOW STOPPER'.

Many gardeners prefer to keep their vireyas under cover in a shadehouse, where several varieties can be shown off to perfection, as is done with orchids.

Vireyas need humidity but the soil in which they grow should not be over-watered. A reasonable watering regime is twice a week in summer, once a week in the cooler season, either by sprinkling or dunking. In very hot, dry weather it may be necessary to water the soil three times a week. In their natural environment vireyas get a rainshower just about every day, but the water never collects around their roots. These conditions can be simulated in the shadehouse by lightly sprinkling the foliage of suspended plants and those on well-drained benches every day, without significantly wetting the soil.

In the garden, less watering is needed but they should not be allowed to dry out completely.

Vireyas are not overly hungry plants and moderate feeding only is required. An easy regime is to apply a controlled-release fertiliser with something extra, such as a teaspoonful of Osmocote Plus in spring, and blood and bone at the recommended rate in autumn. Liquid fertiliser is also suitable but apply in weak dressings every couple of weeks while the plant is young. Good flowering and strong growth is promoted by an annual dressing of sulphate of potash in slow-release form. Fowl manure is not recommended for vireyas.

Vireyas tend to straggle, particularly when grown in the ground. They should be trained into a compact, bush form from an early age by regular tip-pruning or, as some professional growers recommend, taking out every second new growth. If plants become very leggy they can be cut back hard, still leaving some leaves on each stem. As vireya flowers are long-lasting in the vase they make excellent cutflowers; regular picking of the flowers is a good way of keeping the plant in good shape.

Although vireyas are rather demanding plants, if given reasonable care they can be grown quite comfortably in the home garden, particularly those in mountain areas just back from the coast. Vireyas come in all sizes, from dainty miniatures to those with flowerheads several centimetres across. Some varieties, mainly the whites and pinks, are delicately perfumed. The one Australian representative is *Rhododendron lochae*, which has small red flowers and is found growing naturally on the tops of mountains in far north Queensland.

Climbers

PLANTS WHICH CLIMB, TWINE AND SCRAMBLE ADD an upwardly-mobile dimension to gardens. Climbing plants can effectively bind a garden together, their free-and-easy ways linking the diverse elements of trees, shrubs, garden beds, groundcover and hard landscaping into a harmonious whole.

There are climbers suited to every purpose in the garden. They can be grown up and over pergolas, trellises, walls, banks, fences and trees. They can be used to provide shade and shelter for more delicate plants, hide unsightly objects, screen different sections of the garden from one another, and make otherwise dull vertical surfaces into part of the garden by covering them with foliage and flowers. Some hot-climate climbers prefer sun, others need shade, and most do well in semi-shade. Some have rampant growth habits which make them unsuitable for small gardens; others are sufficiently delicate in habit to make ideal courtyard plants. Most are evergreen but some are briefly deciduous, allowing winter sun to penetrate if that is what you need in your garden.

Many climbing plants are actually shrubs, or else woody herbaceous plants, which grow upwards and outwards by means of tendrils, suction pads, twining stems, aerial roots or thorns which serve as hooks. You need to understand the different climbing methods of each plant so that you can provide the appropriate support. Delicate-stemmed twiners such as sweet peas will require light but closely meshed support; whereas the long, strong, thorn-studded arching canes of bougainvilleas will need sturdy supports which can be widely spaced. There is no end to the effects which can be achieved with climbing plants. The different coloured forms of dipladenia, for example, can be planted to provide striking contrast, either twined together or planted apart, such as on alternate verandah or house support posts. A similar effect can be achieved with different coloured forms of pandorea. Bougainvillea, too, comes in many different colours which can be used to create contrast: a particularly striking effect is achieved when some bougainvilleas are grown as climbers and others as standards.

A colour-themed garden, or section of garden, can only be enhanced by using climbing plants; the plant lists below include all flower colours. Generally climbers are fast-growing which means that you can quickly achieve that effect you want. Climbing plants will help achieve year-round colour because each season sees several hot-climate climbers in flower.

Climbing plants have the same care requirements as shrubs. A few, such as bougainvillea and hardenbergia, will tolerate poor soils and some neglect but most require heavy feeding to encourage growth. As a general rule good quality, humus-enriched, mulched soils are best because climbers depend on healthy root development for their vigour. Water the root area regularly, particularly in dry periods, and apply fertiliser frequently. Foliar

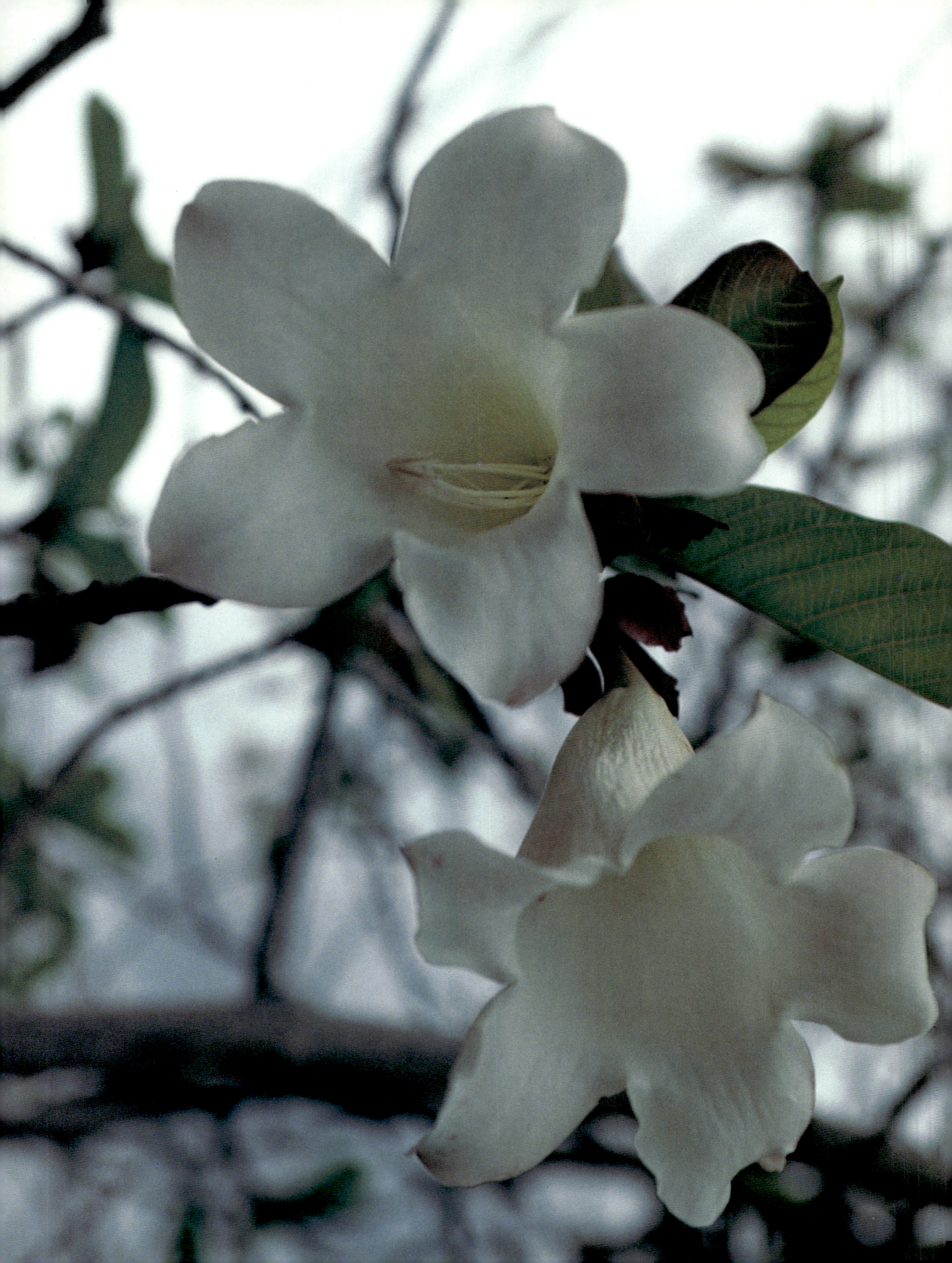

fertilisers are particularly good for encouraging young plants and are easy to spray on large, established climbers although the over-use of nitrogen-rich foliar fertilisers will encourage foliage growth at the expense of flowers. If you want prolific flowering, it is better to apply a well-balanced fertiliser to the base of the plant during the flowering season.

Some climbers benefit from pruning, usually in the cool season after flowering has finished. This allows them to develop strong new growth and flower well in the following season. Tip-pruning encourages bushy growth in young climbers and also helps to control too-vigorous growth. As with hedges, most climbers need regular pruning of new shoots throughout the growing season to maintain appearance and suppress too-rampant growth.

String, wire, wooden slats, lattice, mesh or some other form of support is needed to help the tendrils of young plants on their way. Climbers which use thorns to get ahead also need something to cling to. Twiners and plants with long canes can be given their head for a while before being twisted around supports such as trellises and pergolas. Climbers with aerial roots merely need a rough surface and those plants which climb by means of suction pads are content with almost any surface except smooth metal or plastic. Many 'shrubby' or ground-creeping climbers such as allamanda, pyrostegia and honeysuckle will find their way across the ground and up the sides of fences, garden sheds or other structures which you may want covered.

When selecting climbers, first decide how they are to be used. Plants with drooping flowers such as *Thunbergia mysorensis*, aristolochia and wisteria will only be seen to best advantage over trellises from which the flowers can be suspended. They are less appropriate for growing up the side of the house, or where hanging flowers would be a nuisance. However, the flowers of most climbers grow outwards and often upwards to face the sun; they, too, must be planted in a position where they can be seen to advantage. Climbers such as solandra and dipladenia

Beaumontia grandiflora (page 118), with its huge white flowers, is a spectacular though somewhat sparse-leaved climber which looks particularly attractive if allowed to make its way up a large tree.

have spectacular flowers but their relatively sparse foliage make them inappropriate for overhead use where you require heavy shade.

Because so many climbers grow more vigorously in hot climates, they often require more careful positioning in the garden than other plants. Rampant growers like honeysuckle, *Pandorea jasminoides* and some bougainvilleas should not be planted in small spaces where they will soon become a nuisance. If you want your climbers to drape themselves over trees or shrubs, take particular care when making your selection; climbers which are very vigorous in habit will eventually throttle the tree or smother the canopy so thickly that they inhibit photosynthesis. Rampant climbing plants may create a dramatic effect but they can also kill supporting trees and shrubs. The same caution needs to be taken in choosing appropriate climbers to cover hard structures; many a garden shed and trellis has collapsed under the weight of a vigorous climber in full maturity.

Three popular climbers which are too rampant for use in hot climate gardens, and spread so readily into surrounding bushland that they have become declared nuisances in some areas, are *Ipomea purpurea*, *Thunbergia grandiflora* and *Thunbergia alata*.

The following climbing plants have been selected as being readily available and particularly suited to gardening in a hot climate. With the exception of bougainvillea and pyrostegia, which will tolerate light frosts once established, they are all frost tender.

Allamanda cathartica
SOUTH AMERICA
HABIT Twiner. Evergreen, vigorous and fast-growing
FOLIAGE Dark-green, glossy
FLOWERS Large, bell-shaped yellow flowers in clusters of 5–7. Variety 'JAMAICAN SUNSET' has pale mauvish–buff-coloured flowers.
FLOWERING TIME Summer
OTHER POINTS A very tough garden performer which likes sun and plenty of water. Needs fairly strong support. Relatively pest and disease free but may be infected by thrips, scale and red spider mites. *A. nerifolia* has smaller flowers and tolerates cooler (but still frost free) conditions; *A. violaceae* has dark pinkish-violet flowers and is often grown as a shrub.

Antigonon leptopus (CORAL VINE)
MEXICO
HABIT Tendrils. Fairly vigorous and fast-growing. Briefly deciduous

FOLIAGE Mid-green, crinkly
FLOWERS Salmon pink, red or white. Showy
FLOWERING TIME Spring and late summer
OTHER POINTS Grows in full sun but does best in semi-shade. Do not allow soil to dry out completely. Subject to thrips, red spider mites and scale.

Aristolochia elegans (DUTCHMAN'S PIPE)
SOUTH AMERICA
HABIT Twiner. Evergreen, vigorous, fairly fast-growing
FOLIAGE Heart-shaped and dense
FLOWERS Hanging clusters of pipe-shaped, mauvish–brown, purple-splotched flowers
FLOWERING TIME Summer
OTHER POINTS Best in semi-shade. Attractive, basket-shaped seeds are produced after flowering.

Beaumontia grandiflora (HERALD'S TRUMPET)
INDIA
HABIT Sturdy-branching twiner. Evergreen
FOLIAGE Large and glossy; rather sparse
FLOWERS Very large, white, trumpet-shaped, fragrant flowers
FLOWERING TIME Summer
OTHER POINTS Best in semi-shade, such as growing up a large tree. Tip-pruning will promote foliage growth; prune also after flowering to stop it growing straggly. Best in true tropics but will do well enough in sub-tropics if protected from too much exposure in winter. (See page 116.)

Bougainvillea SPP.
See page 122.

Cissus antarctica (KANGAROO VINE)
AUSTRALIA
HABIT Tendrils. Evergreen, vigorous
FOLIAGE Green, toothed, glossy
FLOWERS Insignificant, but black, grape-like fruits are interesting.
OTHER POINTS A rainforest plant grown for its foliage. A reliable garden and indoor performer, best in shade or semi-shade. Other cissus species available.

Clerodendrum splendens
TROPICAL AFRICA
HABIT Twiner. Evergreen, fast-growing
FOLIAGE Large, pointed
FLOWERS Red, in showy clusters
FLOWERING TIME Summer and autumn
OTHER POINTS A long-flowering vine which makes a spectacular show and grows easily. *Clerodendrum thomsonae* (BLEEDING HEART VINE) has white and crimson flowers and is ideal for protected spots where there is no room for a more vigorous climber. *C. nutans* is an even daintier climber, to about 1.5 m, with creamy–white tubular flowers. Clerodendrums do best in shade or semi-shade with protection from cold.

Dipladenia sanderi (CHILEAN JASMINE)
BRAZIL

HABIT Twiner. Evergreen, fast-growing
FOLIAGE Oval and glossy. Not dense
FLOWERS Pink, pale pink, red or white flowers, depending on form
FLOWERING TIME Most of the year
OTHER POINTS Very attractive climber which provides garden colour for most of the year. Today's well-bred varieties have good flower quality and thicker foliage than their predecessors. Good drainage is essential. Can be grown as a shrub. This dipladenia is more correctly known as *Mandevilla sanderi* but as most garden centres still stock it under the former name, that is the one we have used here.

Faradaya splendida (POTATO VINE)
AUSTRALIA
HABIT Twining. Evergreen, vigorous
FOLIAGE Heart-shaped, light green
FLOWERS White. Similar to those of beaumontia but smaller and very fragrant
FLOWERING TIME Variable; usually in summer
OTHER POINTS Similar to the beaumontia but less straggling in habit. Large, white, oval fruits are edible but not particularly palatable. A good vine for growing over trees, trellises or pagodas. Not readily obtainable except from native plant or specialist rainforest nurseries.

Ficus pumila
CHINA AND JAPAN
HABIT Aerial roots. Clinging. Fast-growing
FOLIAGE Very small, neat, dense, often tinged gold or red
FLOWERS No
OTHER POINTS A clinging creeper which provides good coverage of brick, stone or timber walls. Can become too heavy for a fence or otherwise lightweight support. Needs regular clipping. Sun or shade. (See page 21.)

Hardenbergia violacea (PURPLE CORAL PEA)
AUSTRALIA
HABIT Twiner and scrambler. Evergreen, easily controlled
FOLIAGE Long, leathery, prominently veined
FLOWERS Spikes of mauve, pink, white or purple pea-shaped flowers
FLOWERING TIME Spring and intermittently throughout the year
OTHER POINTS A dainty, non-rampant climber, ideal for small spaces. Tolerates drought and most soil conditions.

Hoya carnosa
SOUTH CHINA
HABIT Aerial roots. Evergreen, vigorous, fairly fast-growing
FOLIAGE Oval and waxy
FLOWERS In rounded clusters of small, waxy white-to-pale pink, fragrant flowers with red centres
FLOWERING TIME Summer–autumn
OTHER POINTS A very decorative, easy-to-grow climber. Shade or part-shade. *H. australis* is a Queensland native with white flowers which does better in full sun. *H. macgilvrai* with huge red flowers is a must for hot, humid gardens.

Ipomea horsfalliae (CARDINAL CREEPER)
WEST INDIES
HABIT Twiner. Evergreen
FOLIAGE Green and bronze-purple
FLOWERS Tubular, magenta flowers with a waxy texture and contrasting white stamens
FLOWERING TIME Spring, sometimes autumn
OTHER POINTS While *Ipomea purpurea* (MORNING GLORY) has acquired a deservedly bad reputation for its rampant growth habit, and is a weed in many parts of New South Wales and Queensland, the lovely CARDINAL CREEPER deserves to be more popular. The variety 'BRIGGSII' is the best performer and does well in the tropics and sub-tropics, though it dislikes cold. Prune new growth for overall control but too severe cutting of old growth will prevent flowering.

Jasminium SPP.
Many types of jasmine are available from different parts of the world; what they have in common is evergreen foliage and sprays of small, star-shaped white, pink or yellow flowers which are usually very fragrant. Jasmines do well in a range of climates except the very cold and flowers are generally borne for long periods through spring, summer and autumn. They are vigorous growers but easily contained. The long canes need to be trained around supports. Some species sucker freely, others such as *J. polyanthum* (PINK JASMINE) need frequent deadheading and trimming to get rid of unsightly dead flowers and foliage. Jasmines are generally marketed under their common name; common species include *J. polyanthum*, *J. nitidum*, *J. sambac* (ARABIAN JASMINE) and *J. grandiflorum*. Mostly pest and disease free.

Lonicera SPP. (HONEYSUCKLE)
Like jasmine, honeysuckles originate in several temperate parts of the world but do well in the sub-tropics, with some species being grown in the tropics also. They are all tough, easy-to-grow plants with dense foliage and delicate, scented flowers which are white, yellow or pink, often in combination. Best known to gardeners are varieties of *L. japonica*. *L. hildebrandiana* is a large-flowering species which does best in tropical areas. Mostly pest and disease free.

MANDEVILLA
SOUTH AMERICA
HABIT Twining. Evergreen, quite vigorous
FOLIAGE Dark-green and heart-shaped
FLOWERS Large, trumpet-shaped, pink, yellow or white.
FLOWERING TIME Summer and autumn
OTHER POINTS There has in the past been some confusion, both between mandevilla species and between mandevillas and the closely related, very similar dipladenias, with considerable argument as to whether they are in fact separate genera. Today, they are marketed as different plants, any of which serve very nicely in the garden. The most obvious difference between mandevillas and dipladenias is in the leaf shape, and mandevillas tend to be slower growing, and have slightly denser foliage than dipladenias. The best-known mandevilla is *Mandevilla × amabilis* 'ALICE DU PONT' which has pink flowers borne for most of the year. Does well enough in semi-shade but needs sun for good flowering.

Pandorea jasminoides
AUSTRALIA
HABIT Twiner. Evergreen, very vigorous, rampant if not controlled
FOLIAGE Compound, with several neat, oval leaflets
FLOWERS Clusters of large, bell-shaped, pink, white or mauve flowers
FLOWERING TIME Summer
OTHER POINTS This very tough, decorative but rampant climber is suitable only for strong supports where there is plenty of room to spread. *P. pandorana* (WONGA VINE) is a less rampant but still vigorous grower, more suitable for smaller spaces. It has clusters of small, delicate, bell-flowers which can be creamy with mauve and brown markings, pure white or golden yellow. *P. pandorana* tolerates cool conditions better than *P. jasminoides*. Sun or semi-shade.

Passiflora SPP. (PASSION FLOWER)
Although most passiflora originate in the tropics, many species are surprisingly cold-tolerant. These evergreen twiners are usually fast-growing and vigorous. The flowers are beautiful, in a range of colours from vivid scarlet to bright blue to orange and white. *Passiflora caerulea* (BLUE PASSION FLOWER) does well in temperate climates; *P. coccinea* (red flowers) is limited to warm temperate to tropical climates. Other, less common species are sometimes available, such as *P. mollissima* which is a cool-climate plant. Australian native species are also sometimes available from rainforest nurseries. *P. edulis*, the edible passionfruit, also makes an attractive ornamental vine. Sun or semi-shade.

Petrea volubilis (PURPLE WREATH)
CENTRAL AMERICA
HABIT Twiner. Semi-deciduous, slow-growing, easily-controlled
FOLIAGE Rough-surfaced and somewhat sparse
FLOWERS Very delicate, with violet-like centres and long, blue-mauve sepals
FLOWERING TIME Late winter through summer
OTHER POINTS A lovely creeper whose controlled habit makes it suitable for small spaces and courtyards. Sun or semi-shade.

Pyrostegia venusta (ORANGE TRUMPET VINE)
BRAZIL
HABIT Twiner. Evergreen and vigorous
FOLIAGE Compound, with three attractive leaflets; quite dense
FLOWERS Thick clusters of small, tubular orange flowers from autumn through spring, longer flowering in warmer areas.
OTHER POINTS A tough, seasoned performer which gives a welcome dash of bright colour to the winter landscape. Gives good cover but is quite easy to control. Fairly drought-hardy. Sun.

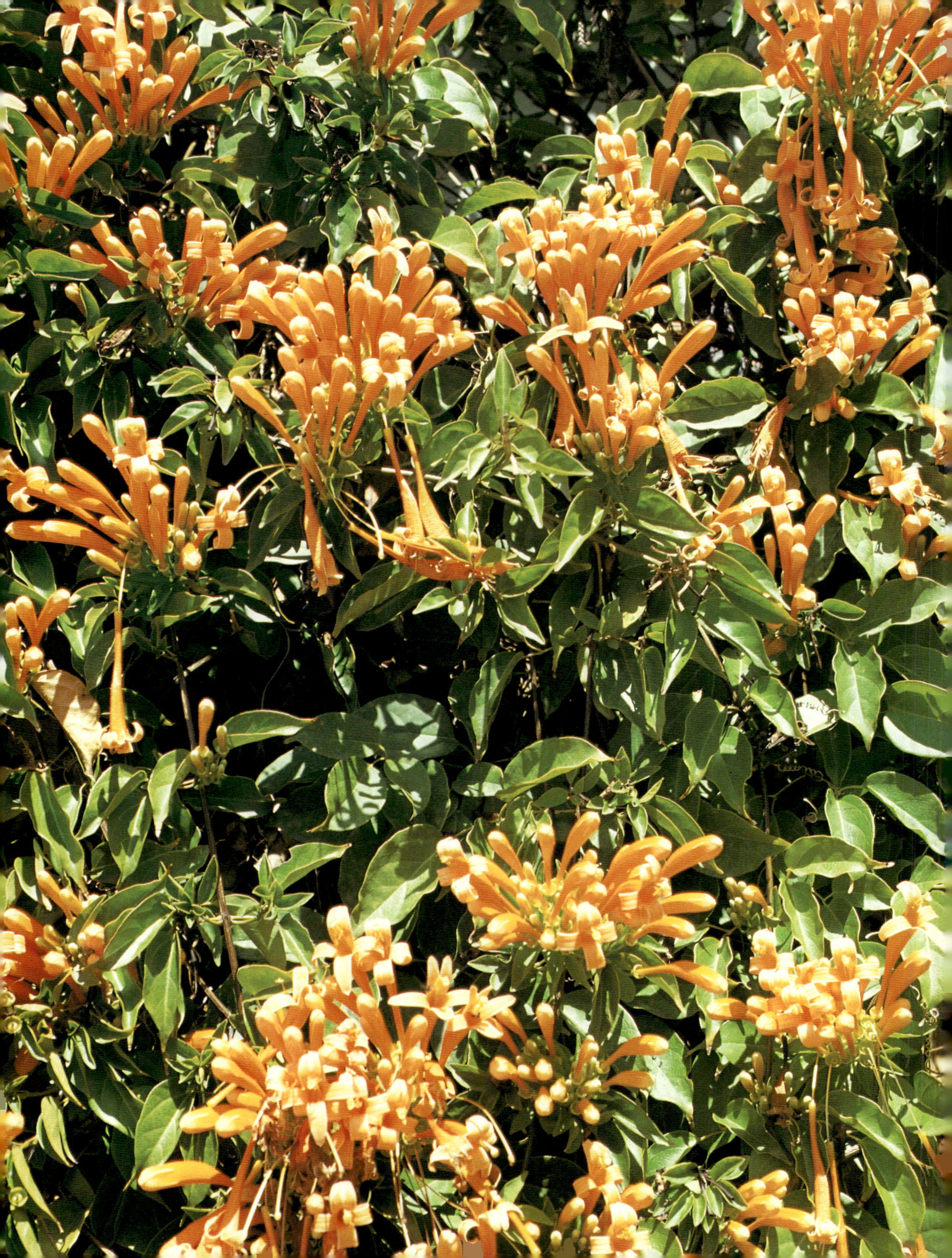

*Pyrostegia venusta (*Orange Trumpet Vine, *see page 119) in full flower. This flamboyant climbing plant can be used to cover fences and pergolas quickly, and gives a glow to the garden throughout the cool season.*

Quisqualis indica (Rangoon Creeper)
Malaysia
Habit Twiner, with thorns. Evergreen
Foliage Oval, dense
Flowers Clusters of long, tubular flowers in shades of pink, orange and and red
Flowering time Summer and autumn
Other points A very tropical creeper which needs plenty of warmth, food and moisture. Sun or semi-shade.

Solandra maxima (Golden Cup)
Mexico
Habit Twiner. Semi-deciduous in sub-tropics. Easily controlled
Foliage Long, large, smooth-surfaced
Flowers Large, yellow, cup-shaped flowers up to 12 cm across
Flowering time Spring and early summer
Other points One of the most spectacular tropical vines. The long canes need careful training over supports but the plant is not rampant. Good pergola climber though foliage is too sparse to provide heavy shade. Sun.

Solanum jasminoides (White Potato Vine)
Brazil
Habit Twiner. Evergreen, vigorous, fast-growing but not rampant
Foliage Upper leaves simple and entire, lower leaves with three leaflets. Neat
Flowers Clusters of star-shaped, white flowers with yellow centres, faintly tinged with blue
Flowering time Spring to autumn, sometimes all year
Other points A very popular scrambler whose self-controlled growth habit makes it trouble-free in the garden. Does well in temperate climates but in areas with cool winters it can be deciduous.

Stephanotis floribunda
Madagascar
Habit Twiner. Evergreen
Foliage Leathery, dark-green and glossy
Flowers Clusters of small, white, fragrant flowers with tubular corollas opening wide to five petals
Flowering time Late spring and summer
Other points Can be subject to red spider mites, thrips, scale and mealy bug. Sun or semi-shade.

Tecomanthe hillii (Fraser Island Creeper)
Australia
Habit Twiner. Evergreen, rather slow-growing
Foliage Serrated, prominently veined, dark-green and glossy
Flowers Trumpet-shaped, pink, with pale throats
Flowering time Spring

Other points A good climber for small spaces in semi-shade.

Thunbergia mysorensis
India
Habit Twiner. Evergreen and easily-controlled
Foliage Small, neat, pointed
Flowers Very showy, drooping, tapered clusters of yellow, tubular flowers with red or purplish-brown lobes
Flowering time Spring to autumn
Other points One of the most spectacular tropical creepers and probably the best thunbergia for Australia's hotter areas because it does not run out of control as *T. alata* and *T. grandiflora* are inclined to do. *T. coccinea* and *T. laurifolia* are also attractive thunbergias for the hot-climate garden and can be easily controlled.

Other climbing plants suitable for hot-climate gardens

Bauhinia corymbosa
Campsis grandiflora syn. *chinensis*
Clytostoma spp.
Combretum spp.
Kennedia rubicunda
Manettia bicolor
Philodendron spp.
Podranea rosea
Pothos spp.
Sweet Pea (*Lathyrus odorata*)
Wisteria spp.

Popular climbers from cooler climates such as sweet pea and wisteria will grow in the sub-tropics with some care. Choose a cool position for wisteria where there is some shade to help ensure a cool root run. Sweet pea, grown as an annual, will flower in late winter and early spring and, though blooms don't last as well as they do in cooler climates, they make a good show and add both colour and fragrance to the garden at a time when most other climbing plants are not in flower.

Climbing roses

Some varieties of climbing roses do well in sub-tropical climates though their blooms do not last well in hot, humid summer weather. Early-flowering varieties give a good spring show and white forms produce longer-lasting blooms. Banksia roses do particularly well in sub-tropical mountain areas. Climbing roses like sun but can be prone to the fungal diseases associated with humidity, so plant them where fresh air can circulate freely and avoid wetting the foliage.

Bougainvilleas

BOUGAINVILLEAS ARE ONE OF THE GLORIES of hot-climate gardening and probably the most commonly grown climber in those parts of the world which fall between the tropics of Cancer and Capricorn. Despite their origins in tropical South America, bougainvilleas also do very well in drier, cooler Mediterranean climates. These lovely climbing shrubs are everything a plant should be: colourful, reliable, tough, unfussy about conditions, versatile, virtually pest and disease free, long living and easy to grow.

Bougainvilleas were first introduced into cultivation in the late 1800s, following their discovery by a Frenchman in Brazil. The three species in cultivation are *Bougainvillea spectabilis*, *B. glabra* and *B. peruviana*. *B. spectabilis* has rose, orange-red or purple bracts; *B. glabra* has white, mauve or purple flowers; *B. peruviana* has pink to pale magenta bracts. It is the colourful bracts which give bougainvilleas their visual appeal; the white flowers are tiny, though still visible.

The three major hybrid groups are *B. × buttiana* (*glabra × peruviana*), *B. × spectoperuviana* (*spectabilis × peruviana*) and *B. × spectoglabra* (*spectabilis × glabra*). From these three groups, and the three original species, come all the bougainvilleas which we grow in our gardens today. Bougainvilleas hybridise freely and also produce sports (branches which differ significantly, perhaps in leaf or flower form, from the parent plant). In this way, many new hybrids are born and some are sufficiently worthwhile to become named varieties.

Today's bougainvilleas come in a vast range of different colours including white, red, magenta, purple, mauve, pink, orange and gold. Some have bi-coloured or double bracts and there are also varieties with variegated foliage. Bract sizes and shapes can also differ, though this is of interest mainly to botanists, plant breeders and collectors. To the average gardener the main point about bougainvilleas is that their colour range and versatility make it possible to fit them into any garden scheme. They are, quite simply, one of the best plants to grow in a hot climate.

There is still some confusion as to the correct names of bougainvillea cultivars and some are still sold under a wrong name, which can make it difficult to find a particular variety. While old favourites such as 'KLONG FIRE' and 'THAI GOLD' are still popular, new bougainvilleas cultivars in all colours and under a variety of names are being introduced all the time. The four points which most concern gardeners are colour, form (e.g. doubles or singles), number of thorns and whether or not it is a rampant grower. These characteristics should all appear on the plant label; if they do not, ask the retailer. Of course, if you are taking cuttings from someone else's plant, you will be able to judge these characteristics for yourself.

Bougainvilleas climb by means of arching canes, armed with thorns. These need to be trained over supports such as trellises or pergolas. The canes are twined around and, where necessary, tied with soft material such as string, plastic twine, rags or stockings. If ties start to cut into stems they should be loosened or removed. Although climbing bougainvilleas should not be severely pruned, they should be pruned lightly after the flowering period is over to control rampant growth and encourage bushiness. You should also remove stray canes and water shoots if they are unsightly or a nuisance; this will help strengthen the main climbing stems. Because bougainvillea flowers develop at the end of branches, too-frequent pruning in spring and summer will prevent good flowering.

Most bougainvilleas are very vigorous growers, needing a lot of space as well as strong supports to grow freely. Where space is limited, or you want to grow bougainvillea over a light support, choose one of the lighter, smaller-growing types.

Bougainvilleas are very adaptable and will grow well in any kind of soil including those which are sandy or rocky and infertile where they often flower spectacularly, particularly if fed well. Nonetheless, bougainvilleas perform best and live longest if planted in friable, compost-enriched, fertile soil, in a sunny position, and are watered well and fed regularly.

Once established, you won't need to water during the wet season, but during dry periods, particularly during the growing season, an occasional deep soaking will keep the plant in good condition. How often depends on conditions; the best guide is to water thoroughly when the soil just below the surface is dry. This may be once a week when conditions are very dry, perhaps twice a week if strong, hot winds are causing the plant to dry out. Bougainvilleas show stress very quickly; if the leaves look lifeless, water is urgently needed. A heavy soil will retain sub-surface moisture longer than a light soil; where bougainvilleas are planted in sand, such as near the beach, they will need frequent watering. Little watering is required in winter because bougainvilleas dislike wet feet — and also wet leaves, which tend to drop when conditions are cold and rainy. For this reason, too, it is advisable to water only the base of the plant, though in very hot, dry, weather, leaves can be sprayed to reduce water loss. The best time of day for watering is first thing in the morning; if the only time you can water is in the evening, then try to avoid wetting foliage and bracts.

Bougainvilleas need regular feeding during the growing season with any suitable, balanced fertiliser applied to the base of the plant. Foliar fertilisers are excellent for giving young plants a head start; however they usually have a high nitrogen content which may promote foliage growth at the expense of flowering. A good mulch will provide ongoing nutrition and help retain moisture; but keep the mulch well clear of the plant stem and, if weather is very cold and damp for a long period, scrape it away from the base to allow the soil to dry out.

Plant out potted bougainvilleas as you would any other shrub or climber. Where drainage is good, the base of the plant should be level with the soil surface, with the roots firmly packed in just below. Where drainage is poor, plant into a mound raised a few centimetres above the soil surface so that the roots cannot become waterlogged. Mature bougainvilleas can be easily transplanted, provided you take care, see page 216.

It is quite easy to raise your own plants from cuttings. Bougainvillea cuttings usually strike readily, but take enough to allow for a few failures. Within 10–12 weeks, roots and leaf shoots should be well-developed and ready for planting out. Both hardwood and softwood (semi-ripe) cuttings can be taken. Take hardwood cuttings between 15–20 cm long in late winter, before spring growth begins. Dip them in a rooting hormone powder and place in a mixture of sand and peatmoss. This can be in a trench in open ground, in a plastic pot or a well-drained wooden box. Protect the cuttings from too much exposure to the elements.

Semi-ripe cuttings are taken in spring from the previous season's growth, when new buds are appearing. They should be about the thickness of a pencil and the same length as hardwood cuttings. Semi-ripe cuttings need to be protected in a greenhouse, bush-house or sheltered spot on the verandah. In areas with sub-tropical or Mediterranean climates, don't repot until the cold season has finished.

Bougainvilleas are remarkably free of pests and diseases. Leaf spot, a fungal problem, can occur during prolonged hot, humid spells but is mainly limited to the tropics. The leaves are marked by tiny round, red-brown spots surrounded by a pale green patch; these develop into darker patches and in severe cases the plant can lose its leaves. Remove affected leaves and burn them to avoid spread of infection. The best control method is to spray with a fungicide such as mancozeb. Wet foliage increases the problem so watering the leaves in the evening is inadvisable, though in the wet season and regions where the problem occurs, overnight rainfall is usual, providing ideal conditions for fungal development. Leaf spot is not a common problem in Australia. Two other pests of bougainvillea are aphids and mites; severe infestation is rare but, if it occurs, maldison is a recommended treatment, used as instructed on the packet.

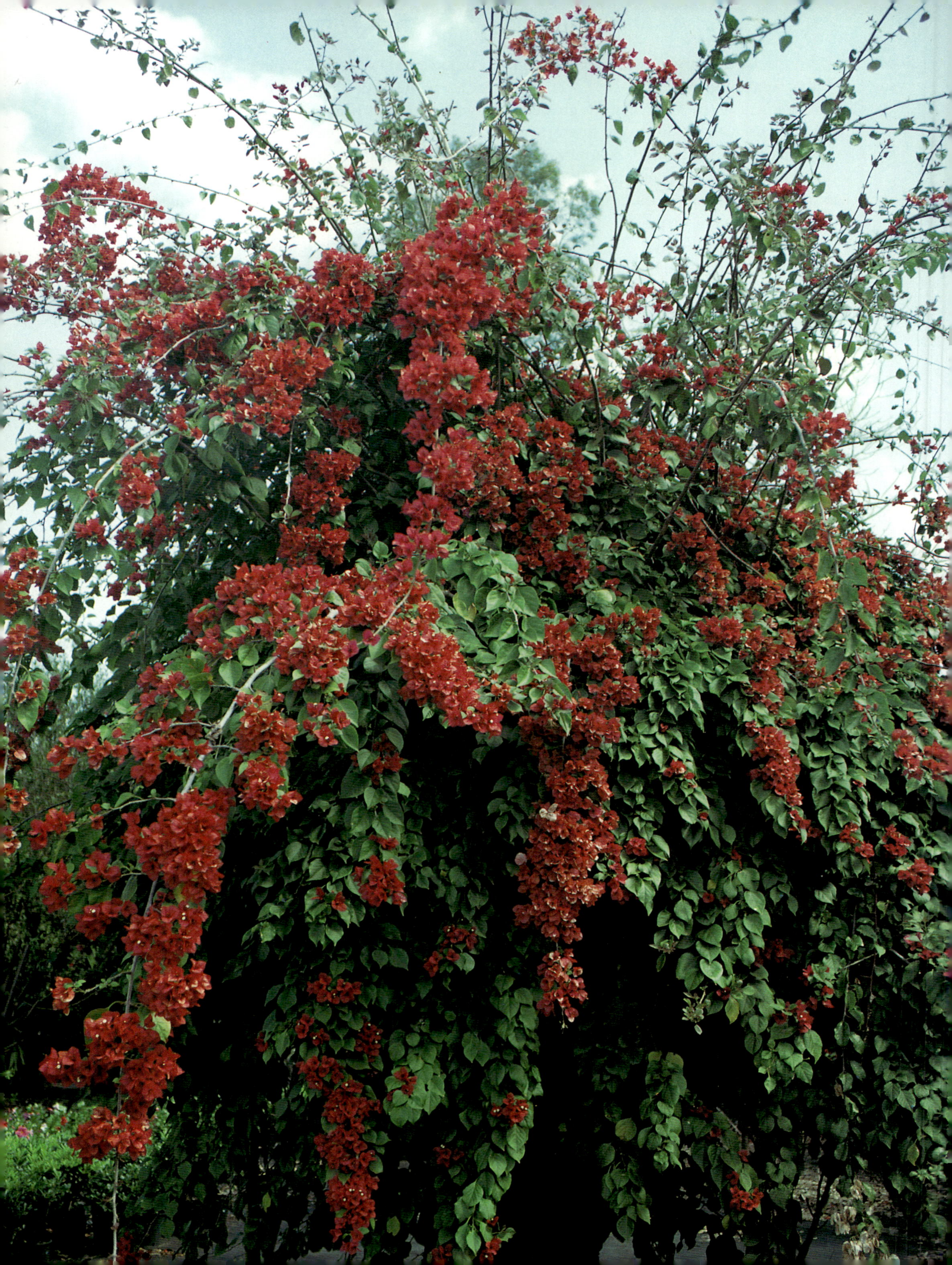

Bougainvillea is a splendid sight in any garden, although some older varieties are too vigorous for confined areas. Many of today's popular cultivars are less rampant and more compact in their growth habit and make ideal plants to cover pergolas and other supports, or to trail through the branches of mature trees. They can also be grown as shrubs or standards. This one is an old variety, 'Turley's Special'.

Standards

Bougainvilleas are rarely thought of as suitable plants for formal gardens, yet they look most dignified when grown as standards, either in ground or in tubs. To do this, choose a strong, well-developed plant of about 200 mm pot size, with a couple of water shoots. The idea is to train the plant to stand alone, either on one stem or with several stems grown close together (or even entwined for an attractive effect). Place a stake next to the plant and tie one long shoot to it, held firmly (but not too tightly). This (and any other upright-trained shoots) will become the main stem or 'trunk'. Keep the trunk free of all extraneous growth such as leaves and thorns; remove any shoots promptly. The only growth permitted is the development of branches at the top of the shoot.

To form a canopy, keep the strongest shoots and tip-prune when they reach 10 cm in length. As shoots develop further twine them back on themselves or, better still, around a framework fastened to the top of the stake. Prune to the required shape and size: globular shapes are the most common but square, triangular and other more ambitious forms can be attempted. Regular light pruning is essential, with the standard being given a good pruning after flowering to get rid of unwanted growth. The overall effect of a mature, well-kept bougainvillea standard in full flower can be quite stunning.

Bushes and hedges

For those who prefer an informal effect, and who don't want to take the time and trouble to grow a standard, bougainvilleas can be grown in bush form. Select those cultivars which have a naturally shrubby habit, then all that is required is occasional but regular pruning of the leader(s) to develop a strong trunk. After this, trim the laterals regularly to prevent them climbing (if there is anything nearby to which they can cling) or straggling. In this way, a bush is formed which can easily be maintained.

Several of these 'bushes' can be grown at 1–2 m intervals to form a hedge. In a hot-climate garden a well-maintained bougainvillea hedge, perhaps in more than one colour, or several shades of one colour, is a truly spectacular sight. Cultivars of *B. spectabilis* and *B. glabra* can be trained into neat, formal hedges, while other types can be used for an informal effect. Bougainvillea hedges do need quite a bit of maintenance; they must be regularly fed and watered, and top and side growth pruned. Growth is so vigorous that many new lateral canes are constantly being produced which should be removed at the base. Set against this need for constant pruning is the fact that bougainvilleas are fast-growing and the long canes can be tied to or twined around each other to create a thick hedge within a remarkably short space of time.

Containers

Bougainvilleas are good tub performers provided they are planted in fairly large containers to accommodate their vigorous root systems. They can be trained as climbers, standards or shrubs; they can be allowed to trail and tumble downwards to create a very attractive effect. A pruning regime depends on the form required, whether the plant is a climber, standard or trailing bush.

Choose a fairly loose, permeable, good quality potting mix, perhaps with extra peatmoss added, and a layer of sharp sand at the base of the container if pot stability is important. You will need to top up the mix about twice a year.

If the mix contains no fertiliser, this will need to be added from the start: controlled-release fertilisers are ideal. If the mix already contains fertiliser, this should be enough to sustain the plant until the next growing season, when new fertiliser should be added. Foliar fertilisers are also easy apply to container-grown plants in the early stages, but select one formulated to encourage flowering. Because bougainvilleas are grown in large containers they need large amounts of potting mix. Although proprietary mixes are not particularly expensive, some people may prefer to mix their own, see the recipe on page 223.

The flower garden

PERENNIALS

PERENNIALS ARE SOFT-STEMMED PLANTS which live and flower for more than two years. They can be used for bedding, as individual specimens, border or rockery plants. There are so many available perennial plants which are suited for sub-tropical and tropical climates that it is impossible to mention them all here. What I have done is to describe those plants which will perform most reliably, are attractive and most commonly available, followed by a list of some other suggestions which may be worth growing.

Generally, the average gardener will always do better to concentrate on the plants which are easy to grow in a hot climate — after all, the choice is very wide, as the plant lists in this book show. It is possible to grow a wider range of cool-climate perennials in the sub-tropics than appears in these listings, but these plants need expert gardening care and the provision of special conditions; for example very good soil, prevailing cool breezes, protection from hot winds and shade from hot overhead sun. In other words, they will thrive only in gardens where cooler, southern conditions can be simulated as much as possible. Such conditions are easier to simulate on the slopes of the mountain ranges which lie behind the warmer coastal areas. For most gardeners, the best advice is to plant those plants which will thrive in your climate.

NOTE 'Resistant' is a qualified ability to tolerate the conditions specified in each case; 'hardy' means easily able to do so.
ST— Sub-tropics only
T — Tropics only

Acanthus mollis (OYSTER PLANT)
SOUTHERN EUROPE
HEIGHT 1.5 m
FOLIAGE Large, glossy leaves with deeply incised margins
FLOWERS Tall spikes of mauve-white flowers
FLOWERING TIME Spring and early summer
CONDITIONS Sun. Humus-enriched soil. Water sparingly. Feeding is not necessary in good, mulched soil
OTHER POINTS An attractive plant which is best at the back of a bed. It is not very interesting when not in flower so needs to be established where other plants can disguise it during the non-flowering period.

AFRICAN VIOLET (*Saintpaulia* SPP.) T
AFRICA
HEIGHT Under 20 cm
FOLIAGE Small, neat, rounded rosettes of brittle, soft-textured leaves
FLOWERS Very variable in form and colour, with a wide range of gorgeous colours — whites, pinks, mauves and bi-coloured flowers available
FLOWERING TIME Summer
CONDITIONS Part-shade. Very warm, protected position in enclosed area or under trees/shrubs. Soil should be light but rich, open, well-composted. Water well and feed regularly for good flowering
OTHER POINTS This popular indoor plant can be grown outdoors in the tropics, provided it is used as a bedding plant in the flowering season. In the sub-tropics plants can be placed outside in pots in a very protected, lightly shaded position during summer.

Angelonia angustifolia (GRANNY'S BONNET)
TROPICAL AMERICA
HEIGHT About 75 cm
FOLIAGE Pointed, sticky and hairy
FLOWERS Mauve, purple, white, blue or pink on long spikes
FLOWERING TIME Summer
CONDITIONS Light shade. Rich soil. Sheltered position
OTHER POINTS One of the best perennials (sometimes classified as a small shrub) for hot-climate gardens.

Begonia SPP.
SOUTH AMERICA
Some begonias are grown as annuals and others as

perennials; some are deciduous, others evergreen; some will grow only in the tropics, others also in the sub-tropics. When buying begonia seeds, or plants from a nursery, it is important to establish that they are suited to outdoor growing in *your* garden. As a general guide, the tuberous and semperflorens types of bedding begonias are grown as summer annuals while Rex, 'ANGELWING', winter-flowering and shrub-type begonias are grown as perennials. Shrub-type and 'ANGELWING' can be grown in the sub-tropics; some of the more truly tropical begonias can be grown outdoors in the sub-tropics if provided with year-round warmth and high humidity. The plants are so lovely that, if you think you have the right sort of garden in the sub-tropics, it is worth experimenting with a few to see if you can grow them.

CONDITIONS All begonias need a warm, very protected, sunny or part-shaded position. Water well and often, though water left on foliage can encourage fungal diseases. Frost and drought tender. Feed regularly; liquid manure is excellent.

FOLIAGE AND FLOWERS Begonia foliage varies greatly according to species, with many types having succulent stems and leaves. Flowers can be single and simple, or like miniature roses and gardenias; they are always exquisite and the colour range is vast. Flowering time depends on type; some begonias even flower in winter. (See page 147 for Rex begonias.)

Bergenia ciliata
ASIA
HEIGHT To 20 cm
FOLIAGE Rounded, slightly succulent, hairy leaves
FLOWERS Small, bell-shaped, white flowers with four petals
FLOWERING TIME Spring
CONDITIONS Sun or shade. Well-drained soil. Frost and drought resistant
OTHER POINTS This bergenia is the best for a warm climate, though it will not thrive in the tropic zone. In the sub-tropics it is very hardy in all conditions.

Centranthus ruber (RED SPUR VALERIAN) ST
MEDITERRANEAN
HEIGHT 30 cm
FOLIAGE Large, pointed, fleshy leaves
FLOWERS Small and star-like; red, pink or white
CONDITIONS Sun or part-shade. Medium, alkaline soil. Can stand exposure. Frost and drought resistant
OTHER POINTS Despite its Mediterranean origin this plant does well in the sub-tropics although it dislikes extreme humidity. Soil should be sweetened with dolomite.

Chrysanthemum frutescens (*see* Daisies)

Dahlia SPP. (perennial)
MEXICO
HEIGHT Variable, according to type, larger types to 1.5 m maximum
FOLIAGE Deeply lobed, dull green leaves
FLOWERS Large, multi-petalled flowerheads which can be single, double, or pom-pom
FLOWERING TIME Perennial dahlias flower in autumn, adding a welcome touch of colour to the garden at that time

OTHER POINTS Although dahlias readily perform as perennials in a warm climate, they are mostly grown as annuals, particularly in the tropics where they soon wilt in the heat and humidity of full summer.

Daisies

The common flower name 'daisy' generally relates to plants in the family Asteraceae (Compositae) which originate all over the world, including Australia. Put simply, the flowers feature many petals (or florets) sprouting like rays from the circular yellow pollen centre, or 'cushion'. Though most are white or yellow, some are pink, mauve and blue and the breeding of daisy plants such as chrysanthemums and asters has considerably broadened the colour range. Height is very variable, from low-growing groundcovers such as the erigerons to the very tallest chrysanthemums.

The following range of daisies includes those most commonly grown in hot climates. Although most originate in cooler and drier regions they do surprisingly well in hot, humid areas, though they do not generally thrive in the tropics.

Most members of this family require little care, except for the large hybrids of aster and chrysanthemum which must be fed and watered regularly for good performance and quality flowering. Most of these perennials can also be grown as annuals.

Aster SPP. (MICHAELMAS DAISY) Dull green, long, pointed leaves. Large flowerheads in a range of colours; summer or autumn, depending on type. Requires sun or part-shade, well-drained soil, feed and water regularly. Frost resistant. Does not thrive in extreme heat and humidity which cause flowers to drop. Subject to powdery mildew.

Brachyscome SPP. These Australian plants do best in light, sandy to medium soils with excellent drainage, although *B. basaltica* grows in moist soils. No care is required, once planted. Many species and cultivars available. Blue, pink, white or mauve flowers. Most are spring and summer flowering but some species flower intermittently or continuously throughout the year. SWAN RIVER DAISY (*B. iberidifolia*) is grown as an annual.

Erigeron SPP. Small, white, blue and mauve flowering forms. Likes medium, well-drained soil and a sunny position. Best where winters are warm and dry. Many species and cultivars available. Most species are spring and summer flowering but some flower intermittently or continuously throughout the year.

Gazania SPP. Quite large yellow, orange, red and white flower colours with a yellow centre, some with a black ring. Very decorative and long flowering through summer and autumn. Best in full sun and light, sandy soil but not fussy. Very light annual dressings of fertiliser will promote flowering. Water only during long, dry periods.

MARGUERITE (*Chrysanthemum frutescens*) Tall (up to 1 m) with large white, pink or yellow flowers. Prefers sunny position and rich, well-drained soil. Feed lightly during flowering season and water well during dry periods. Flowers in late winter and spring.

Osteospermum SPP. (VELDT DAISY) Grows to about 0.5 m in the garden, with a shrub-like habit and narrow leaves. Daisy flowers are large and white, white with a dark blue centre, pink, yellow or mauve, depending on species. A very pretty flower which grows well in hot climates. Needs full sun and a well-drained soil, withstands drought and light frosts.

PAPER DAISIES or EVERLASTINGS (*Bracteantha* SPP. and *Chrysocephalum* SPP. syn. *Helichrysum* SPP.) Perennial and annual types. Bright yellow or white papery-textured flowers which last for a long time when dried. Well-drained soil and full sun. Most dislike humidity and prolonged wet weather but can still be grown in hot climates. Even if some plants are lost during monsoon weather, they are easy to grow again. Cultivars of *B. bracteatum* are the best known in cultivation. Most paper daisies species flower in spring and summer but some will flower intermittently or almost constantly throughout the year.

Rudbeckia SPP. (CONEFLOWER) Perennial and annual. Tall to 1 m maximum with serrated leaves and yellow flowers with black or purple conical centres. Very attractive. Sun or shade, any soil including moist. A very hardy plant for all gardens. Little care required.

SHASTA DAISY (*Chrysanthemum × superbum*) Quite tall (some varieties grow to 0.5 m) perennial with white flowers. Similar to marguerite only usually with more florets on the flowerhead. Flowers in late summer–autumn. Likes heavy soils and a sunny position. Water well in dry periods.

Wedelia trilobata (SINGAPORE DAISY) This has been a popular plant in tropical landscaping and for quick, vigorous cover in home gardens. It is, however, very invasive, smothers other garden plants if unchecked, and needs constant cutting back. In some areas it has been declared an environmental nuisance. Flowers are bright yellow. Grows on any soil. Requires water in dry periods. Grows in sun or part-shade.

Dianthera nodosa 'PRETTY IN PINK'
SOUTH-EAST ASIA
HEIGHT Up to 1 m
HABIT Spreading to about 1 m at maturity
FOLIAGE Quite dense
FLOWERS Small, pink, claw-like flowers borne along the top side of branches. Somewhat resemble those of up-turned kangaroo paw flowers. Continuous throughout year.
CONDITIONS Sun or shade, any soil, but plants grown in good soil and full sun tend to perform better and be more compact. Fast-growing in favourable conditions. Prune lightly in late winter and give a moderate feed of controlled-release fertiliser for good spring growth and prolific flowering.

GERANIUM (*Pelargonium* SPP.)
Pelargonium is the more botanically correct name for these popular garden plants but most of us still prefer to call them 'geraniums' so we shall stick to that name here. Geraniums are marvellous plants, combining attractive flowers and foliage with easy habits. And many of them are fragrant also.

Geraniums of the 'zonal' or common garden type typically have fairly large, soft leaves on the end of longish stalks. The leaves are roundish with irregular margins, often with a dark shading. Flowers are small, bunched and attractive, single or double, in a range of colours from white through many shades of pink, mauve, orange, scarlet and crimson, often bi-coloured. Flowering takes place mostly in summer but some will flower at other times or intermittently or continuously throughout the year. They are versatile plants which have been considerably hybridised (except for one or two Australian indigenous species such as *P. australe*).
CONDITIONS They do best in a light, fibrous, humus-enriched, slightly alkaline and well-drained soil but in the garden are not particularly fussy about soil conditions and will grow almost anywhere with good drainage. They prefer full sun but will grow in light shade, or on a side of the house which is shaded for part of the day. They also grow very well in tubs, planters and window boxes while the trailing, ivy-leaved types are excellent hanging basket plants.

While geraniums, like any plants, do best if fed, watered and occasionally pruned, they will thrive on very little attention. They are certainly one of the easiest and most reliable garden plants for warm climates; the laziest gardener can hardly go wrong growing geraniums. Even if excessive heat and humidity sets them back, they can readily be replanted and will fill a bed with remarkable speed.

The very many scented-leaf geraniums are a fine way to add fragrance to the garden; some have leaves like soft velvet though flowers are generally smaller and less colourful than those of zonal species. The other type of geranium commonly available is the taller-growing Regal type, which has large, trumpet-shaped flowers.

Freesia SPP. ST
SOUTH AFRICA
HEIGHT Below 30 cm (some varieties slightly taller)
FOLIAGE Rosettes of narrow, pointed leaves, insignificant compared with flowers
FLOWERS Long, funnel-shaped, very attractive and fragrant flowers in a wide range of colours
FLOWERING TIME Late winter and spring
CONDITIONS Despite their delicate appearance freesias will grow well in most soils, provided they are well-drained. Plant first bulbs in autumn and lightly mulch ground. Water lightly but regularly during winter. Composting and/or fertilising during the growth period will improve flowering. Otherwise they need little care
OTHER POINTS Freesias are one of the few cool-climate bulb plants which do well in the sub-tropics and, though their

---

Some kalanchoes are trade-named 'Winter Wonders' because they provide easy-care colour during the cooler months. In hot climates these versatile succulents can be used in place of cool-climate bedding plants. Very moderate water requirements make kalanchoes a good choice for low rainfall areas. See page 130.

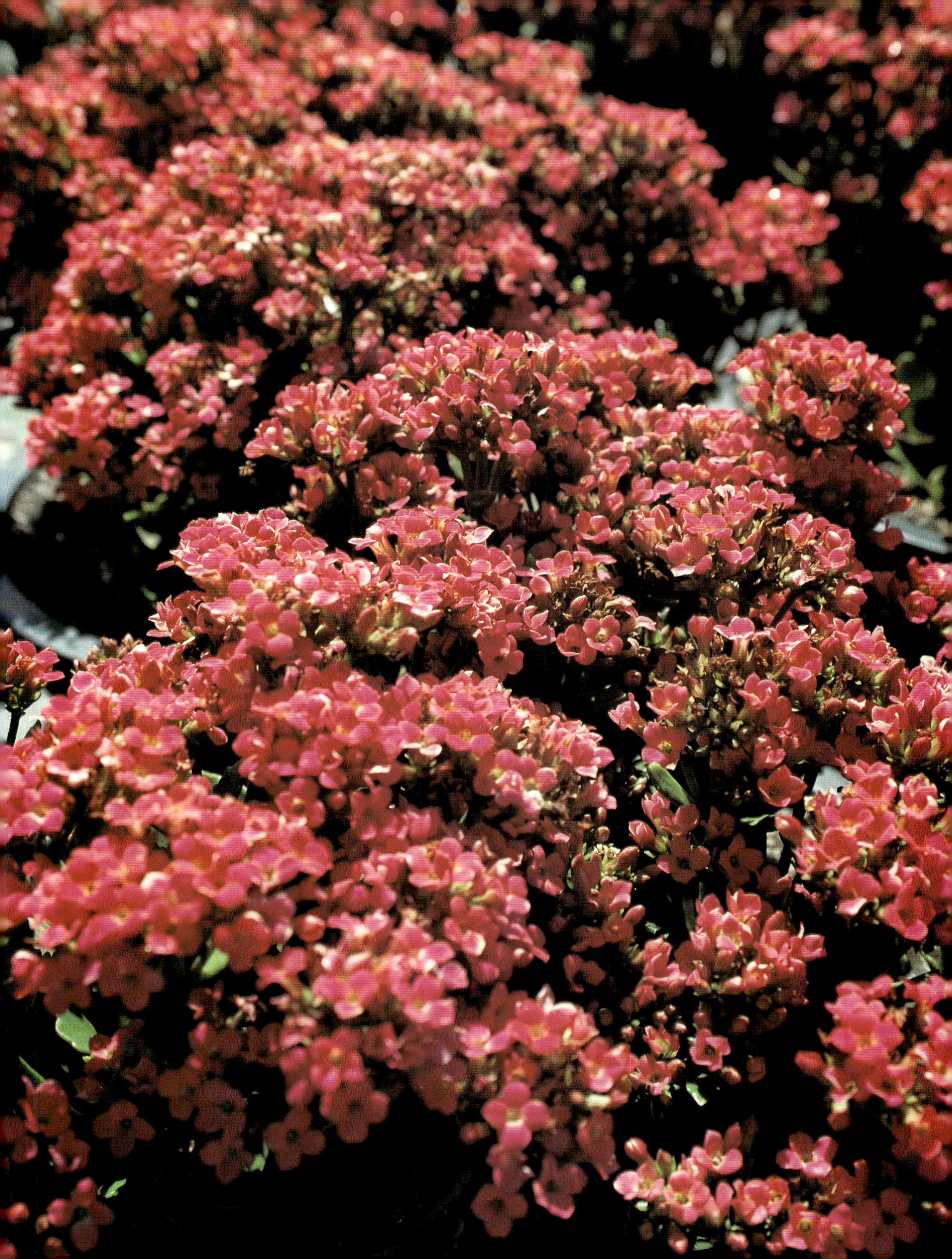

flowering period is brief, they are worth the small effort involved in planting the first bulbs. Once established they should give you reliable flowering for a couple of years before vigour is lost and bulbs should be replaced.

Gerbera SPP.
SOUTHERN AFRICA
HEIGHT 1 m (top average for most garden varieties; dwarf varieties are much smaller)
FLOWERS Large flowerheads with many florets, raised on a long stalk. Seemingly endless range of flower colours and colour combinations
FLOWERING TIME Early summer through autumn, longer with some varieties and in warmer areas
CONDITIONS Sun or part-shade in very hot areas. Light, sandy, humus-enriched, well-drained soil. Minimum care but water and fertilise moderately during growing period
OTHER POINTS In recent years the Australian-bred Bauer cultivars have changed the once rather dull gerbera into an exciting flower of infinite variety. Today's gerbera has a spectacularly large flowerhead, with florets doubled and redoubled, in an equally spectacular range of paintbox colours. A beauty in the garden and in the vase. Gerberas can suffer from powdery mildew in hot and humid periods; they are also subject to red spider mite, thrips and leaf spots.

Gingers

I have used this term rather loosely to group all those plants which, like the true Ginger (*Zingiber* spp.) have in common tuberous rhizomes, big leaves and attractive flowers. Alpinia, hedychium and zingiber are all in the Zingiberaceae family and are alike in habit and growth requirements, as well as appearance.

Alpinia SPP. Long, narrow, shiny leaves; striped white in some varieties. Spikes of pinkish white or white flowers with red bracts; Australian *A. caerulea* has scented white flowers followed by striking blue berries. Usually flowers in summer but can do so at any time. A good filler plant for the tropical garden which likes part-shade, a humus-enriched, well-drained soil and high humidity. Frost tender.

Hedychium SPP. These gingers come from India and Nepal and are less tropical in their requirements than alpinias, though still frost tender. They have similar leaves and the flowers are more attractive, and more fragrant, though they don't last long on the spike. Full sun and a rich soil which is not allowed to dry out. Water regularly, particularly during dry periods. Flower colours are white, pink or red, depending on species.

Zingiber SPP. As with some alpinias it is the bracts rather than the petals which make ginger flowers attractive; in *Z. zerumbet* they change from green to red, encasing white or yellow petals. The leaves are long, bright green, handsome and stem-clasping. Requirements are part-shade, high humidity, a humus-enriched soil and plenty of water. Frost tender.

Heliconia SPP. T
TROPICAL AMERICA AND THE CARIBBEAN
HEIGHT Variable according to type; up to 2 m or more, though garden ornamental varieties generally smaller than those grown for cutflowers
FOLIAGE Large leaves, rather like banana foliage
FLOWERS Truly spectacular large (sometimes up to 1 m) hanging or upright spathes of boat-shaped flowers in a variety of pinks, reds and yellows set off by green bracts
FLOWERING TIME Mostly summer. Restricted when temperature is below 15°C.
OTHER POINTS These very frost-tender plants are truly tropical in habit, though some species will grow in sheltered gardens in the sub-tropics, where foliage will die back drastically in cold winters.

Impatiens SPP. (BUSY LIZZIE)
ASIA AND PAPUA NEW GUINEA
HEIGHT Up to 0.5 m, usually less, depending on type
FOLIAGE Pale, oval leaves on succulent stems
FLOWERS Very pretty single or double flowers in a wide range of colours including bi-coloured
FLOWERING TIME Spring to summer, with slight variation according to type
CONDITIONS Light shade. Light, humus-enriched soil is best but any well-drained soil will do. Plenty of water and regular light dressings of a liquid fertiliser during summer
OTHER POINTS This is one of the best flowers for hot, humid climates, where it is usually grown as a perennial. Several species and cultivars are available; some are able to stand more cold, or more direct sun, than others. If these factors are important to you, it is best to check with the garden centre when buying.

Kalanchoe SPP.
AFRICA
HEIGHT 30 cm to about 80 cm, depending on type
FOLIAGE Succulent, on branching stems
FLOWERS Showy, florific clusters of small, bell-like, yellow, orange, pink and/or red flowers
FLOWERING TIME Some kalanchoes flower in spring and summer, others in winter, and those that do are often commonly called 'Winter Wonders'
CONDITIONS They grow in full sun on any well-drained soil and require little care, only moderate watering in dry periods and an application of controlled-release fertiliser in spring. Will tolerate cold below 10°C but some species are frost-tender.

Kniphofia SPP. (RED HOT POKER)
SOUTH AFRICA
HEIGHT Usually from just under 0.5 m to 1.5 m, depending on variety
FOLIAGE Clumps of long, reed-like leaves growing from the base
FLOWERS Large vivid red or red and yellow flowerspikes borne on long stems
FLOWERING TIME Summer
CONDITIONS Full sun. Humus-enriched, well-drained soil.

Quite hardy, able to withstand light frosts and long dry periods, but drought will adversely affect foliage quality and flowering
OTHER POINTS Massed displays of red hot pokers are a splendid sight, and they are very easy to grow.

Liriope spicata ST
JAPAN AND CHINA
HEIGHT 25 cm
FOLIAGE Long, narrow, dark-green, strap-like leaves
FLOWERS Densely covered spikes of mauve or white bell-shaped flowers
FLOWERING TIME Late summer
CONDITIONS Sun or part-shade. Humus-enriched, well-drained soil. Frost hardy. Requires little care
OTHER POINTS Rather a dull plant for most of the year but lovely when in flower and foliage makes an acceptable filler. Does well in the sub-tropics.

Lobelia SPP.
AFRICA, USA, MEXICO AND AUSTRALIA
HEIGHT Variable, according to type but generally below 30 cm, though the CARDINAL FLOWER (*L. cardinalis*) grows to 1 m. Most species and cultivars of lobelia grow well in the sub-tropics, including the Australian *L. alata*, and one or two will grow in the tropics. In general they like sun or part-shade and a moist but well-drained soil. Some types are also grown as annuals. Flower colours are red, blue, pink, white and mauve; some are bi-coloured. All are very dainty. Whatever is stocked in your local garden centre is likely to be the kind most suited to your area.

Lychnis chalcedonica (MALTESE CROSS) ST
EUROPE
HEIGHT 0.5 cm
FOLIAGE Basal rosette
FLOWERS Heads of small pink or red flowers, each with four petals which together form a Maltese cross shape, on a long, sticky stem
FLOWERING TIME Spring and summer
CONDITIONS Frost resistant. Needs water in dry periods. Sun or part-shade. Any soil
OTHER POINTS At its best in a massed display.

Mesembryanthemum SPP. syn. *Dorotheanthus*
SOUTH-WEST AFRICA
HEIGHT Ground-hugging
FOLIAGE Succulent
FLOWERS Single heads with masses of florets around a yellow centre. The vivid colours include white, yellow, orange, pink, purple and red
FLOWERING TIME Summer and most of the year
CONDITIONS Sun. Light, sandy, well-drained soil
OTHER POINTS An ideal groundcover for hot, dry areas. Does well in the sub-tropics and even the tropics provided it is in an open, sunny area where humidity is dispersed. Requires no watering in areas of average to high annual rainfall.

Mirabilis jalapa (FOUR O'CLOCK PLANT)
TROPICAL AMERICA
HEIGHT 0.5 m
FOLIAGE Mid-green, oval leaves
FLOWERS Tubular red, white, yellow or pink. They remain closed until late afternoon, hence the plant's common name
FLOWERING TIME Summer to autumn
CONDITIONS Sun. Sheltered position. Humus-enriched, well-drained soil. Will withstand light frosts. Needs water during dry periods
OTHER POINTS An attractive curiosity.

TUBEROSE (*Polianthes tuberosa*)
CENTRAL AMERICA
HEIGHT 1 m maximum, usually smaller
FOLIAGE Long, reed-like, pale green leaves
FLOWERS Spikes of fragrant, funnel-shaped white flowers. Single and double forms available
FLOWERING TIME Summer
CONDITIONS Sun. Shelter. Well-drained soil. Plenty of water and fertiliser during growing period, responds well to liquid manure or seaweed extract fertilisers which can be watered in. Can withstand light frosts but not extended cold periods. Leaves die down during winter dormancy when no watering should take place
OTHER POINTS A very pretty plant which is easy to grow. Lift clumps and divide bulbs in spring; new growth will take place from bulbs growing from the 'mother' which can be discarded annually.

POLYANTHUS (*Primula* SPP.) ST
EUROPE AND ASIA
HEIGHT To 20 cm
FOLIAGE Oval, crumpled, sometimes slightly hairy leaves
FLOWERS Dainty, open flowers with yellow centres in colours ranging from white and blue to yellow, orange, pink and red
FLOWERING TIME Mostly summer, though some flower in late winter and spring
CONDITIONS Light shade, or where garden is in shade for part of the day. Well-drained, humus-enriched neutral soil, sweetened with dolomite
OTHER POINTS Polyanthus are the warm-climate hybrids adapted from parent primulas. They have larger heads and will take summer heat if protected from all-day sunshine. Water and feed well during the growing period.

Salvia involucrata
MEXICO
HEIGHT About 1 m or below
FOLIAGE Bushy. Longish (about 7 cm) pointed, mid-green leaves
FLOWERS Deep pink, on spikes
FLOWERING TIME Late summer and autumn
CONDITIONS Full sun. Any soils. Can withstand drought. Frost tender
OTHER POINTS Apart from the common red-flowered salvia which is grown as an annual, other salvias are also available. They include *S. coccinea*, *S. argentea* and the shrub *S. aurea*; as well as the edible sage (*Salvia officinalis*), see page 190.

Strelitzia reginae (BIRD OF PARADISE)
SOUTH AFRICA
HEIGHT 1m or more
FOLIAGE Large, upward-growing and stiff, with a greyish look
FLOWERS Large purple and orange flowers, with petals and sepals arranged to resemble the crested head of a long-billed bird, which is why it is also known as CRANE FLOWER
FLOWERING TIME Spring and summer
CONDITIONS Sun. Prefers a sandy, well-drained soil. Water moderately in summer; otherwise can withstand dry periods, though foliage quality and flowering will suffer. Fertilise lightly in spring. Can withstand light frosts but otherwise is a hot-climate plant
OTHER POINTS A striking plant which does well in hot and cooler southern climates; it can be very slow growing where winter temperatures are regularly below 10°C. (See page 52.)

Streptocarpus SPP. T
SOUTH AFRICA
HEIGHT About 25 cm
FOLIAGE Small, oval and softly hairy rosettes
FLOWERS Delicate, funnel-shaped, lilac-coloured flowers
FLOWERING TIME Summer
CONDITIONS Light shade, protected position. Light, well-drained soil. High humidity. Tender below 10°C and low temperatures will retard flowering or kill the plant
OTHER POINTS *S. rexii* has long, crumpled leaves and there is a range of cultivars with different-coloured flowers including vivid reds and blues.

Verbena SPP.
Most verbenas in cultivation come originally from North or South America

HEIGHT Variable according to type but those commonly in cultivation usually below 1 m
FOLIAGE Variable according to type but common varieties usually have neat, small, dullish-green leaves with deeply toothed margins
FLOWERS Common garden varieties are dainty, not dissimilar to polyanthus; white, pink, mauve, purple and shades of red, usually with white centres
FLOWERING TIME Spring and summer
CONDITIONS Sun. Well-drained, humus-enriched soil, dressed lightly with dolomite. Will tolerate light frosts. Water lightly but regularly in dry periods.
OTHER POINTS A pretty little bedding flower which is adaptable to most climates, including the tropics, though it may suffer during periods of extreme high temperatures and humidity. Humidity can encourage powdery mildew.

Viola odorata ST
EUROPE
HEIGHT Ground-hugging
FOLIAGE Tiny, heart-shaped leaves with slightly toothed margins
FLOWERS Violet or white, borne on the ends of fine stems. Dainty
FLOWERING TIME Late winter and spring
CONDITIONS Light or full shade. Humus-enriched soil. Frost hardy but drought tender
OTHER POINTS This cool-climate plant grows quite well in the sub-tropics provided it is protected from hot sun. The Australian violet (*Viola hederacea*) is quite similar in appearance but with more flattened flowerheads and entire leaf margins. It does best in light shade and grows more readily in the tropics and sub-tropics.

Other attractive and interesting perennials

Achillea SPP.
Aubretia SPP. ST
Chrysanthemum SPP. (esp. cultivars of *C. frutescens*)
Columnea × *banksii*
Dianthus SPP.
Echium fastuosum
Eremurus SPP.
Erodium manescavii
Gaillardia SPP.
Gladiolus SPP.
Helianthus SPP. (SUNFLOWER)
Kohleria digitaliflora
Liriope muscari ST
Mimulus SPP. ST
Nicotiana alata
Oxypetalum caeruleum
Phlox SPP. perennial
Polygala virgata
Stokesia laevis
Tritonia SPP.
Xeronema SPP.

Truly tropical perennials

Aeschynanthus SPP.
Alsobia SPP.
Chirita SPP.
Dimorphotheca SPP.
Eucharis SPP.
Globba wingitii
Smithiantha SPP.
Tetranema SPP.

ANNUALS

ANNUALS ARE PLANTS WHICH COMPLETE THEIR LIFE CYCLES in only one year or season. Most garden-grown annuals originate in cool climates. The constant sun and humidity in hot climates which encourages vigorous, rapid growth tends to overwhelm some of the more delicate annuals so growing annuals demands a lot of the hot climate gardener. They need to grow in beds with well-prepared soil; they have to be thoroughly weeded, fed frequently during the growing season and watered often.

IN THE TROPICS AND SUB-TROPICS annuals are grown for flowering in the cooler periods of late winter and spring. This is also the dry season, which means providing them with water from the tap. Weeds grow more vigorously in a hot climate and plant-devouring insects are many. Fertiliser breaks down faster than it does in cool climates and needs to be more frequently applied. Soils are rarely the perfect-tilth loams required to grow healthy annuals, and must be extensively worked. And by early summer, sometimes earlier, the humidity is sufficient to encourage fungal diseases. All in all, it is a lot easier in hot climates to give colour to the garden by the judicious use of tropical and sub-tropical shrubs and perennials.

Yet the appeal of annuals endures; partly because these plants are embedded as firmly in our folklore as they are in our gardens, partly because they are attractive plants. Dedicated hot-climate gardeners are prepared to give the necessary time and care for the reward of a few glorious weeks' flowering. And it is fair to say that today there are more aids available to improve soil easily and protect plants in hot climates, as well as more cultivars suited to hot-climate growing. This all helps to make the growing of annuals a better proposition than it used to be and, in response to this, garden centres now stock a seasonal range of bedding annual seedlings, as well as seeds, and can provide the advice needed to help grow these plants successfully in the home garden.

The following list covers those annuals considered best suited for hot-climate growing, with a brief summary of special cultivation needs. Certain cultivation factors apply to all annuals. They need a rich soil which has been worked to a depth of about 0.5 m and has a fine-crumbed surface, suitable for small and delicate plants. The soil will need to be sweetened with lime for most annuals, particularly as sub-tropical and tropical soils tend to be acid. Beds are best raised to provide good drainage in the event of heavy tropical rains. Plants will need to be fed every couple of weeks, preferably with a liquid fertiliser applied at a time of day when it cannot cause leaf burn. The hotter the climate, the better it is to use the fertiliser at a weaker strength and apply it once a week. Little and often is the rule.

Unless it is raining, you will need to water seedlings daily, often twice daily if it is very dry, and then either daily or every two days during the flowering period. Weeding must be thorough and frequent; delicate plants cannot compete with vigorous weeds. Usually, if the flower garden is to be kept looking good, insects pests and fungal diseases need to be controlled by spraying or dusting. Position is important; most of the annuals which are usually grown in full sun in cooler climates will benefit from light shade, or at least shade for part of the day, in a hot climate.

In addition to all this, annuals require careful planning so that the garden is not left with empty flowerbeds. This means trying to grow some annuals all through the year, even during the hottest time. Some hot-climate gardeners are content to leave beds fallow from late summer until it is time to plant the next crop, which means bare beds until late winter at the earliest. This may not matter if one section of the garden, perhaps screened from obvious view, is set aside for annual growing. An alternative is to grow vegetables in the beds during the hot period. Yet another method which has gained popularity is planting summer/autumn flowering perennials in beds and putting pots of winter–spring–summer flowering annuals among them; the pots to be removed when the annual spell is over.

Approximate time to flowering (FT) from the planting or emergence of seedlings is included in the lists of annuals. This will generally be a couple of days faster than the time given on the packet or label (if any). Other information, such as the distance which seedlings or seeds should be planted from one another, and the depth of planting, is given on the seed packet or punnet label.

Seed for most annuals in a hot climate should be sown direct or into seed beds in late autumn or early winter, unless other instructions are given on the packets. Seedlings are available from garden centres at appropriate times for planting out.

FT — time to flowering from seedling stage

Annuals

Ageratum SPP. (FLOSS FLOWER)
Feather pink, blue or white flowers. Remove spent flowerheads. Plant any time of year. (FT) 10 weeks.

ALYSSUM (*Lobularia maritima*)
Small, prolific mauve or white flowers. Good rockery or edging plant. Plant late summer or late winter. (FT) 6 weeks. Can be grown as a perennial.

Amaranthus SPP. Tall plant (1 m) with colourful red or multi-coloured twisted foliage and attractive, usually red, flowers. Full sun. Mulch and feed well. Sow late winter/spring.

Anthemis SPP.
Small white daisy flowers. (FT) About 12 weeks. See Daisies, page 127, for general information on daisies.

Antirrhinum SPP. (SNAPDRAGON)
Flowers with curiously rounded petal formation and upper and lower 'lips' in shades of white, yellow, pink and red. Remove spent flowerheads. Subject to rust and other fungal diseases. Sow from late summer to spring. (FT) 14 weeks.

BEDDING BEGONIA (*Begonia semperflorens*)
Small, waxy, white, pink or red flowers and succulent foliage. Sow winter/spring. (FT) 14 weeks.

Calendula SPP. (POT MARIGOLD)
Single or double daisy-like flowers in white, cream, yellow, orange and orange-red. Sow in winter. (FT) 7 weeks.

Celosia SPP.
Feathery flowers in a range of colours from yellow to red. Very easy to grow. Sow spring and summer. (FT) 10 weeks.

Clarkia SPP. syn. *Godetia*
Single, double or semi-double flowers in shades of white, pink and red. Does well in poor, sandy but well-drained soils. Sow in winter. (FT) 10 weeks.

Cleome spinosa (SPIDER FLOWER)
White, mauve or pink spidery flowers. Very good in a hot climate. Subject to aphids. Sow late winter–autumn. (FT) 10 weeks.

Cosmos SPP.
Large white, pink, mauve or yellow sparsely petalled daisy-like flowerheads. Very tough. Sow winter/spring. (FT) 10 weeks.

Dahlia SPP.
Dahlias are often grown as annuals, particularly the smaller-growing, summer-flowering types. Sow (seed-grown types) winter/spring. (FT) 14 weeks.

Dianthus SPP. (SWEET WILLIAM, PINK)
Dainty, rounded flowers born in profusion, often with fringed petals, in a wide range of colours and bi-colours. Sow autumn to late spring. (FT) about 16 weeks. Can be grown as a perennial.

Gaillardia SPP.
Yellow, pink or red rather daisy-like flowers, some bi-coloured. Sow late summer to late spring. (FT) 12 weeks.

Lobelia SPP.
Dainty, vivid blue flowers; some cultivars have white, pink or red flowers. Needs protection from weather extremes, including frost. Can be grown as a perennial. Sow late summer/autumn. (FT) about 10 weeks.

LUPIN (*Lupinus* SPP.)
Spikes of white, blue, yellow and pink flowers, several shades on same stem. Full sun. Frost tender. Sow late summer to late winter. (FT) about 20 weeks average.

MARIGOLD (*Tagetes* SPP.)
African and French marigolds have yellow, gold and bronze-brown, many-petalled, rounded or pom-pom flowerheads in a variety of sizes. Very tough and reliable in any well-drained soil. Full sun. Remove spent flowerheads. Sow or plant out seedlings any month of the year when there is no frost danger. (FT) 6–8 weeks.

NASTURTIUM (*Tropaeolum majus*)
Yellow, gold red trumpet-shaped flowers, very prolific. Hardy in most soils and conditions. Sow spring to early autumn or later. (FT) 8 weeks.

PANSY (*Viola* SPP.)
Prettily-formed flowers, some with velvety dark patches which makes them look like little faces peering up from the foliage. Best in afternoon shade. Sow summer to early winter. (FT) 14 weeks.

Petunia SPP.
Probably the most popular annual for hot climates because it grows so easily and flowers so prolifically. In sub-tropics petunias will grow for most of the year and will thrive well into summer in the tropics; longer if conditions are not too hot and humid. Perennial varieties may not be very long-lived in hot climates where humidity is high. Flowers are trumpet-shaped, large, in shades of white, mauve, blue, purple, pink and red. Can grow in fairly poor soils and should not be over-fed or watered. Sow autumn to late spring. (FT) 10 weeks.

Portulaca grandiflora (Sun Plant)
Large flowers with six petals arranged in a cup shape; white, pink, red or yellow. Does best on poor soils in full sun, or flowers won't open. Minimum watering. Sow winter to late spring. (FT) 5 weeks.

Salvia spp.
The most familiar salvia, *S. splendens*, has spikes of vivid scarlet flowers borne for long periods. Several red-flowering varieties are available and there is also a blue or white salvia (*S. farinacea*). A very easy way of adding brilliant colour to the garden for much of the year in a hot-climate where it will usually grow as a biennial quite well. Pineapple Sage (*S. elegans*) is a perennial or shrub, with spikes of small, red flowers and pineapple-scented leaves which can be used in cooking or cool drinks. Sow all year. (FT) 10 weeks.

Statice (*Limonium* spp.)
Mauve, pink, yellow or white papery flowers which can be used as 'everlasting' fillers in floral arrangements. Can be grown as a perennial. Sow autumn/winter/early spring. (FT) 18 weeks.

Sunflower (*Helianthus* spp.)
These tall-growing plants with their huge, yellow faces are rather untidy for the home garden but nonetheless make a bold show in late summer and autumn, particularly as a background plant. Unlike smaller-growing plants they are not too fussy about soil but do need good drainage. Fertilise monthly. The best garden types are grown as annuals but they can also be grown as perennials; with the clumps cut back, then lifted and divided every couple of years. (FT) 18 weeks.

Sweet Pea (*Lathyrus odorata*)
A plant which climbs by means of tendrils. Though at their best in cooler climates, sweet peas can be grown in late winter and spring in the sub-tropics. The very fragrant, pea-shaped flowers are in pastel shades of white, pink, blue and mauve. Except for dwarf varieties, sweet peas are usually grown on trellises, generally with netting, string or twigs at the base to provide support for the first tendrils. In hot climates the seed should be sown in raised beds which have been very well worked and prepared with dolomite and a low-nitrogen fertiliser or well-made compost. Water sparingly except in very dry weather until plants are well-established, then they will need more water. Sow late summer–autumn. (FT) 12–14 weeks.

Zinnia spp.
This rivals petunia and marigold as the most popular hot-climate annual, being very tough in most conditions. Multi-petalled flowerheads in a range of brilliant colours. Sow year round. (FT) 10 weeks. Sometimes grows as a perennial.

LILIES AND LILY-LIKE PLANTS

This term 'lily' has been used rather loosely here to describe a range of plants which produce their flowers on the end of long, tube-like stems growing from bulbs, corms or rhizomes underground. They generally have fleshy and stem-clasping or sword-like or strap-like leaves. I have divided plants into over or under 1 m, with occasional qualifications. Because the foliage tends to be similar, I have not described it except where it is in any way special. All are good cutflowers. Most of the plants have a winter dry-season dormancy period; often the foliage dies back. Plants should not be watered during this period. Clumps should be divided every one or two years, in spring or autumn, and the individual bulbs or sections replanted to make new plants or clumps.

Agapanthus spp. (African Lily, Lily of the Nile)
Height Over 1 m, dwarf forms available
Flowers Blue, mauve-blue or white, tubular, in rounded clusters
Flowering time Spring and summer
Conditions Full sun. Any soil. Drought and frost resistant
Other points This is a marvellous plant as a single specimen or massed for landscaping effect. Because it is so easy to grow it is often treated with contempt by gardeners, yet it is still one of the loveliest plants around.

Alocasia macrorrhiza (Cunjevoi Lily)
Australia
Height 3 m
Flowers Large, greenish-white flowers, like those of an Arum Lily, with a strong fragrance
Flowering time Summer
Conditions Shade. Humus-enriched, moist soil. Frost tender, though will usually recover from a light frost
Other points Not a prolific flowerer but the fragrant spathes are lovely when they do appear, intermittently

Dietes bicolor is a versatile landscaping plant which tolerates a wide range of difficult conditions. In the home garden they will thrive just about anywhere, rewarding minimum care with generous flowering in spring and summer. See page 138.

throughout summer. Surprisingly, although alocasias will grow in boggy ground by streams, they will also withstand long dry periods quite well. Feed once a year by topping up compost, leafmould or similar organic matter.

Alstroemeria aurea (syn. *aurantiaca*. PERUVIAN LILY)
CHILE
HEIGHT 1 m
FLOWERS Large, orchid-like flowers; yellow, orange or pink. Very showy
FLOWERING TIME Summer
CONDITIONS Sun. Shelter from strong winds. Humus-enriched, light, well-drained soil. Frost hardy

OTHER POINTS Several species and cultivars of alstroemeria, besides *A. aurea*, are available. All have very beautiful flowers.

Aristea SPP.
SOUTH AFRICA
HEIGHT Under 1 m
FLOWERS Loose racemes of deep blue flowers
FLOWERING TIME Summer. Long-flowering
CONDITIONS Sun. Any well-drained soil. Do not over water. Can withstand light frosts
OTHER POINTS An attractive but not common garden plant. Leaves are very long, strong and sword-like.

The DAY LILY (Hemerocallis sp., see pages 139–40) can be grown as a bedding plant for massed display, as a single exquisite specimen, or naturalised in woodland areas where they do very nicely without too much care. Each flower only lasts a day, but another soon takes its place; today's varieties will keep flowering for many months. This one is 'ROYAL SARACEN'.

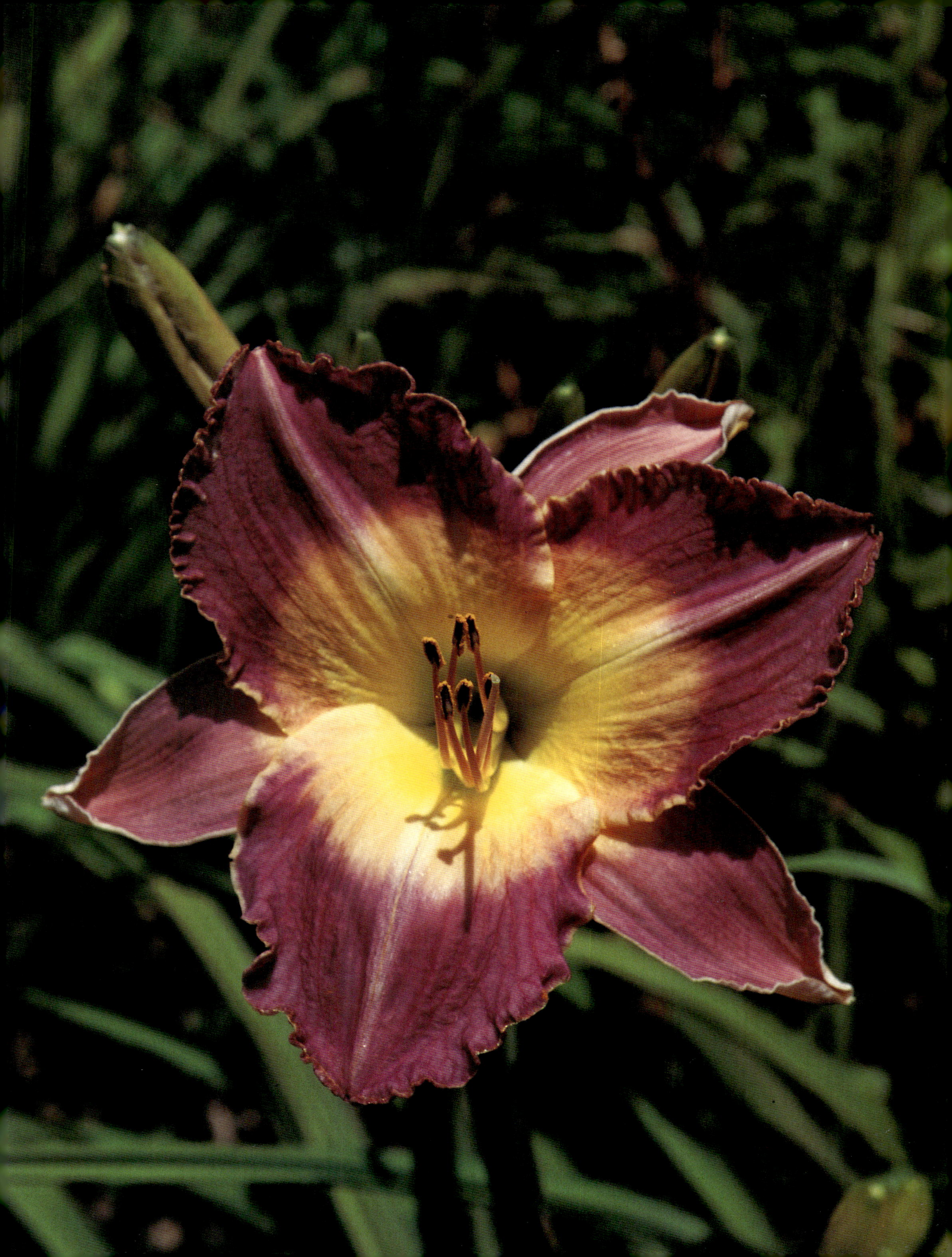

Canna SPP.
SOUTH AMERICA AND CARIBBEAN
HEIGHT Over 1 m
FLOWERS Terminal heads of large, showy flowers with big, soft petals in a wide range of yellow, orange, pink and scarlet
FLOWERING TIME Summer. Long-flowering
CONDITIONS Any soil, any position, sun or light shade, withstands light frosts which will burn off the plant but rarely kill it. Water well for best performance and feed in spring and late summer
OTHER POINTS Cannas are just about unbeatable for massed displays of colour in beds, or around ponds, or under trees, or to fill with colour any difficult part of the garden, including low-lying, swampy areas. Yet despite their love of water, cannas can go for surprisingly long periods without it, though foliage quality will suffer. A tough plant for the lazy gardener.

Clivia miniata
SOUTH AFRICA
HEIGHT Below 1 m
FLOWERS Beautifully-shaped trumpet flowers with six bright orange or orange-scarlet flowers
FLOWERING TIME Late winter and spring
CONDITIONS Shade. Humus-enriched, well-drained soil. Frost tender and dislikes cold below 10°C so in sub-tropics needs a year-round warm and sheltered position. In cooler, more exposed parts of sub-tropical latitudes plants can be taken outdoors in pots in summer and removed to a warmer spot in winter.
OTHER POINTS This is a strong-growing plant in the right conditions and provides rich colour in shady areas. Leaves are straplike, shiny, dark-green and handsome.

Crinum SPP. (SPIDER LILY)
Crinums come from all over the world, including Australia. Those in cultivation are generally between 0.5 m and 1 m in height and have similar cultural requirements, though their hardiness depends on origin. Most dislike cold below 10°C and some, for example *C. asiaticum*, are more tropical than that; all are frost tender. Flowers can be pink, white or red and vary according to type; *C. asiaticum* has very delicate white flowers with long, slender petals while the hybrid *C. × powellii* flowers are more robust, with a slight droop. Those of *C. moorei*, from South Africa have pink flowers grouped on a strong stem, rather like day lilies. The very tropical Australian *C. pedunculatum* has greenish-white, scented flowers resembling those of *C. asiaticum*. The leaves of some species have a red or mauve colouring. All spider lilies do best in full sun or light shade, in a protected position, in well-drained soil.

Curcuma australasica (CAPE YORK LILY)
AUSTRALIA
HEIGHT To 1 m
FLOWERS Long spikes of pink flowers
FLOWERING TIME Summer
CONDITIONS Shade. Protected position. Light to medium soil covered with light mulch or leaf litter. Plenty of water in summer. Not too tropical for the sub-tropics, provided adequate protection from exposure is given, and will even withstand light frosts
OTHER POINTS Still rare in cultivation, this lovely plant is well worth a place in a shady garden.

Day lilies, see page 139.

Dianella SPP. (FLAX LILY)
AUSTRALIA
HEIGHT 1 m or under
FLOWERS Small, dainty white, blue or mauve-blue flowers with notable yellow stamens
FLOWERING TIME Spring or summer, depending on type
CONDITIONS Sun or light shade. Well-drained, slightly acid soil. Drought and frost tolerant; the Australian species will grow well in hot climates
OTHER POINTS Several species are available, including the very decorative New Zealand *D. intermedia* which has mauve-white flowers in spring, followed by blue berries.

Dietes SPP.
SOUTH AFRICA
HEIGHT To 1 m
FLOWERS *D. bicolor* has pale yellow flowers with brown markings near the centre, *D. grandiflora* has white and mauve flowers with yellow markings near the centre, *D. vegata* has white flowers
FLOWERING TIME Spring and summer
CONDITIONS Sun, shade or part-shade. Humus-enriched, well-drained soil. Thrives in moist soil, yet can withstand long dry periods
OTHER POINTS Easy to grow in a range of conditions.

Doryanthes excelsa (GYMEA LILY)
AUSTRALIA
HEIGHT To about 4 m
FLOWERS Large, round head of red flowers on an immensely tall stem
FLOWERING TIME Spring and summer
CONDITIONS Sun or light shade. Humus-enriched, well-drained soil. Withstands light frosts and drought
OTHER POINTS The tallest of the lily-like plants and something of a novelty. Only flowers intermittently but makes an interesting specimen amongst other colourful plants in the same bed, or as a backdrop to smaller plants.

Hippeastrum SPP.
SOUTH AMERICA AND WEST INDIES
HEIGHT Under 1 m
FLOWERS Large flowers on sturdy stems, the fairly stiff-petalled blooms come in a wide range of colours, including a popular red and white candystripe. Very showy; generally larger than day lilies
FLOWERING TIME Summer or autumn, depending on type
CONDITIONS Less hardy than day lilies, though will withstand light frosts and cold below 10°C for short periods. Water well in summer only. Fertilise in early summer.
OTHER POINTS One of the most stunning of the lily-like plants.

Hymenocallis spp. (Spider Lily)
South and Central America
Height Under 1 m
Flowers Thin-petalled, fragrant, spidery flowers in white or pale yellow
Flowering time Spring or summer, depending on type
Conditions Grow in a protected, well-drained spot in sun or shade. Frost-tender below 10°C.
Other points Best in a sheltered spot; the delicate flowers make a fine narcissus-like show. Very pretty, fragrant plants which are often considered the hot-climate equivalent of daffodils.

Lomandra longifolia
Australia
Height Under 1 m
Flowers Spikes of fragrant, cream-coloured flowers
Flowering time Spring and early summer
Conditions Sun or shade. Any well-drained soil. Drought and frost resistant; very tough
Other points The flowers are not spectacular but this is a useful garden filler plant, being very easy to grow in all conditions. The long, reed-like leaves make it an attractive waterside plant.

Lycoris spp. (Spider Lily)
Asia
Height Under 1 m
Flowers Large, showy heads of flowers which, like others in this schedule commonly known as 'Spider Lilies', have recurved petals and a 'spidery appearance'. Colours are white, yellow or pink
Flowering time Late summer or autumn
Conditions Sun. Well-drained soil. Unlike other lily-type plants, lycoris have an early summer dormancy period and thus require watering throughout winter for good growth in the following season. Feed regularly during late summer growing period; liquid fertilisers such as seaweed extract give good results.

Nerine spp.
South Africa
Height Under 1 m
Flowers Delicate, thin petals with wavy margins, either white, pink or red in colour
Flowering time Autumn; some varieties start blooming in late summer
Conditions Sun. Sandy, well-drained soil. Can withstand light frosts and cold below 10°C for short periods. Drought tender
Other points A lovely way of providing the garden with autumn colour.

Watsonia spp.
South Africa
Height Under 1 m
Flowers The best garden varieties have fairly large, funnel-shaped pink flowers, thick on the spike and looking rather like gladioli at first glance. Very showy
Flowering time Spring
Conditions Sun. Light, humus-enriched, well-drained soil. Will withstand very light frosts but does best where temperatures don't drop below about 5°C in winter.

Zantedeschia spp. (Arum Lily)
South Africa
Height 1 m
Flowers Large, cornet-shaped white, waxy, with yellow pollen spike
Flowering time Spring and summer
Conditions Sun or light shade. Any humus-enriched soil, including boggy areas. Likes plenty of water during growing period but, conversely, can withstand long, dry periods
Other points Cultivars are now available with yellow, pink and even green flowers. They are very beautiful, but the traditional white Arum Lily still retains a stately beauty and is very adaptable to a range of conditions.

Zephyranthes spp. (Rain Lily)
Tropical America
Height Under 1 m
Flowers Dainty flowers with six waxy petals; white, pink or yellow
Flowering time Summer and/or autumn, depending on species
Conditions Semi-shade. Open, well-drained soil which is not allowed to dry out. Water well during growing period and fertilise lightly with a liquid feed. Can withstand light frosts but dislikes long periods of cold below 10°C.

Day Lilies

Day lilies (*Hemerocallis* sp.) originate in the cold regions of east Asia and yet flourish in the sub-tropics and tropics where they can take the place of traditional cool-climate garden plants such as daffodils and bluebells. They have fairly stalwart stems carrying gorgeous flowerheads in a breath-taking range of colours. Some have delicately frilled petals. Older varieties grow up to 1 m but there is a trend towards more compact, smaller-growing plants. Day lilies bear their flowers in 'scapes' which open only for one day, but are quickly replaced by others. Today's varieties are very long-flowering, some of them up to eight months a year.

Day lilies are remarkably tough plants. They grow in sun or light shade, in any soil and will withstand dry periods and neglect. However, they flower best when given a fairly open but humus-rich soil and plenty of water in summer. They should be fertilised regularly in summer with any well-balanced fertliser, though plant foods high in potash will produce better flowers. At least once a year a dressing with organic manures and/or compost will maintain a good soil structure and fertility.

These plants reward minimum care with generous flowering and have a place in any hot-climate garden. As they flower in shade (dark-coloured varieties hold their hue better in the light shade of overhanging trees), they look pretty scattered through a grassy woodland area, giving a very natural effect. Or they can be massed in beds, to spectacular effect. The range of sublime colours makes this an excellent plant for creating colour themes in the garden. Though they stand the heat well, they are also frost hardy.

Other lily-type plants suitable for the hot-climate garden

ST — sub-tropics only
Babiana SPP. ST
Costus SPP.
Cyrtanthus SPP.
Eucharis SPP.
Habranthus SPP.
Haemanthus SPP.
Helmholtzia SPP.
Lilium SPP.
Marica gracilis
Ornithogalum SPP.

ROSES

Roses grow very well in a hot climate provided they are given plenty of fertiliser, water and prompt treatment for the fungal disease black spot, which is quite as nasty as it sounds.

ROSES NEED a medium soil, neither too heavy nor too light and sandy, so if your soil is one or the other it will need to be improved. This is best done by digging in plenty of compost and animal manure, and if soil is very poor bringing in some good soil from elsewhere. Roses grow well on the red, fairly heavy soils found in some areas along the coast and in nearby mountains; the kind that are used for vegetable growing. The bed or planting area should be thoroughly dug over and all clods broken up, until the soil attains a fine tilth.

Good drainage is particularly essential in areas seasonally prone to monsoonal deluges. Unless the soil is naturally very well-drained, it is best to put in raised beds. Roses need to be spaced well clear of each other in a sunny position to reduce the danger of black spot.

Bare-root roses are available in large quantities in the cooler months; container-grown roses can be planted out year-round. At planting, dig well-rotted animal manure and some bone meal, with a handful of blood and bone, around the base of the plant. Roses are sold as grafted plants so you'll need to make sure that the graft union (the slightly ridged mark towards the bottom of the stem, where the rose variety has been planted on to a rootstock) is left about 5 cm clear of the soil when planting.

Fertilise newly planted roses about two weeks after planting. Any fertiliser will do; there are special rose fertilisers available but, though excellent, they are not necessary. Controlled-release fertilisers are very good but organic fertilisers and/or compost will need to be added from time to time also, to maintain good soil structure. There is one very important point to remember when fertilising roses in a hot climate. The instructions on the fertiliser packet are for plants grown in cooler climates and it is necessary to increase the rate in a hot climate where plants feed more greedily and the fertiliser breaks down and loses value more quickly. Controlled-release fertilisers like Osmocote and Nutricote are excellent for roses because they are so easy to use and they make their nutrients available over a period of time. But just because the little pellets are still visible on the soil surface does not mean that they still contain viable nutrients. A reasonable feeding regime is to apply a complete fertiliser every three months throughout the year, and dig well-rotted animal manure and compost into the bed each spring.

Just as roses need to be fed more frequently in a hot climate, so also they need more water. If flowers are small and poor, and the foliage likewise, they are probably not being watered often enough. Frequency depends on soil and weather but as a general rule they will need a good soak with a hose or dripper two or three times a week in the hot season and once a week at other times.

It is not necessary to prune roses, except to remove spent and straggling growth or to train them into a desirable shape. Dedicated gardeners may like to give their plants a very light trimming after each flower flush — about once every 4–6 weeks. This will keep bushes in trim and promote further flowering. Certainly the plants look better if given an occasional trim, but traditional hard pruning is pointless unless, as occasionally happens, a sick, very old or neglected plant needs to be cut back by way of therapy.

Black spot is the curse of roses. Spray them with a Triforine-based product once every two weeks; this will also help control rust. Downy Mildew, the other common problem, can be controlled by spraying Fongarid on the foliage and pouring a cupful around the roots. Organic gardeners will find it very hard to control these problems in roses without chemical means; however planting marigolds and garlic in the rose bed is said to be helpful. Insects on roses can be controlled in the same way as with any other plant — see the Plant Clinic, page 226.

Roses make excellent container plants and this does, at least, ensure they have good drainage. Container-grown roses should be fertilised every two months and repotted every three to four years. If you can follow the advice carefully, there is no reason why you should not grow roses as well (if not better) than in any cooler climate garden. Some people grow them successfully even in the tropics and in hot climates they are likely to flower most of the year. Of course, roses require quite a bit of work so are not for the low-maintenance garden, nor do they belong in a tropical theme setting. Yet many of us like to grow at least one or two for their beauty, perfume and cutflower quality. Pick them early at the bud stage, just before opening, so that you get the most out of them in the vase.

Despite their beauty, roses are not ideal plants for the main garden because they are prickly and the bushes themselves too open, sparse and rather ugly (when not in bloom). For these reasons, and because of the care needed, they are best grown in a section of their own, or in a cutflower garden. It is not a good idea to scatter them among other plants.

Roses come in all shapes and sizes; bushes of hybrid teas and floribundas, standards, miniatures (particularly lovely in pots) and climbers. Some roses are better suited to hot-climate growing than others; for example those with more layers of petals hold better in the heat and humidity, while others have shown at least a certain resistance to fungal disease. It is a fair bet that such varieties will be the most readily available from retailers. The sheer number of cultivars available is bewildering. 'PEACE' is an old favourite though it is not a great cutflower; the white 'ICEBERG' is gorgeous and reasonably resistant to fungal diseases; 'DOUBLE DELIGHT' with its combination of ivory and nasturtium red petals is one of the most sought-after roses ever released; 'DOROTHY PERKINS' remains a popular climbing rose; while the dainty, climbing Banksia rose is thornless and therefore a good choice for training up patio supports or along verandahs. Besides these popular roses we also offer a few tried-and-true favourites for your guidance. They are all hybrid teas or floribundas which have been selected for their cutflower ability but are also good garden performers.

Perfumed

'Mr Lincoln' (red) (one of the most resistant to fungal disease)
'Cardinal' (red)
'Kentucky Derby' (red)
'Royal Highness' (pale pink)
'Carla' (pale pink)
'Mabella' (yellow)
'Friesia' (yellow)
'Princess of Monaco' (two-tone ivory and cerise)
'John F. Kennedy' (white)
'Blue Moon' (lilac)

Non-perfumed (or with faint fragrance)

'Gabriella' (red)
'Samantha' (red)
'Rondelay' (red)
'Sylvia' (pink)
'Sonia' (salmon pink)
'Kordes Golden Times' (yellow)
'Mercedes' (orange)
'La Minuette' (two-tone ivory with pink flush)
'Champagner' (creamy white)

THE ROCKERY

In a hot climate with heavy monsoonal rain a rockery is particularly suited to growing plants which require excellent drainage; cactus species do best in rockeries in a hot climate and so do most herbs.

Rockery plants

(Flower and foliage colour is given with some plants.)

Achillea clavennae (white)
ALYSSUM (*Lobularia maritima*, white, mauve)
Anigozanthos SPP. (KANGAROO PAW, small-growers, yellow, red and orange)
Astartea 'WINTER PINK'
Baeckea virgata miniature (white)
Callistemon 'LITTLE JOHN' (red)
Canna iridiflora (orange-pink)
Celosia cristata (red and yellow)
Correa 'DUSKY BELLS' (pink)
Crinum moorei (pink)
Crowea SPP. (pink)
Cuphea SPP. (*C. ignea* red and white, *C. hyssopifolia* mauve, white)
Dampiera linearis (blue)
Dianella tasmanica (blue flowers and berries)
Dianthus SPP. (pink, red, white etc.)
Dietes grandiflora and *D. bicolor* (white, pale yellow)
Echeveria SPP.
Erigeron karvinskianus (white)
Erodium reichardii (pink)
Euphorbia millii (CROWN OF THORNS) (orange-red)
Geraniums (*Pelargonium* SPP.)
Gunnera magellanica (bronze-green foliage)
Hibbertia obtusifolia (yellow)
Hymenocallis × *marostephana* (greenish-white)
Lantana montevidensis (mauve)
Leptospermum 'PINK CASCADE'
Lobelia SPP. (blue)
Orthanopsis cheirifolia (yellow)
Oxalis lobata (yellow) and *O. depressa* (pink)
PAPER DAISIES or EVERLASTINGS (*Bracteantha* SPP. and *Chrysocephalum* SPP. syn. *Helichrysum* SPP. yellow, white)
Pratia pedunculata (blue)
Ranunculus 'FLORA PLENO' (yellow)
Scaevola SPP. (blue)
Sedum SPP.
Sempervivum SPP.
Senecio SPP.
Zantedeschia aethiopica varieties
Zauscheria SPP. (orange-red)

Orchids

AMONG THE MOST POPULAR PLANTS for shadehouse growing are orchids. Along with their glamorous reputation, orchids are reputed to be difficult to grow. This is quite untrue; orchids are no more difficult to grow than any other worthwhile plant; only if you plan to breed them do you require a lot of specialised knowledge.

For the purpose of home gardening, orchids can be divided into two main kinds, ground (terrestrial) orchids and those that grow epiphytically in trees, using the trees as support and getting much of their nourishment from water-borne decaying matter

Terrestrial orchids include:
Cymbidiums
Epidendrums (Crucifix Orchids)
Paphiopedilums (Slipper Orchids)
Phaius

Epiphytic orchids include:
Cattleyas
Dendrobiums
Lycaste
Oncidiums
Odontoglossum
Phalaenopsis
Vandas

Not all orchids come from hot climates. Most cymbidiums, for example, originate in areas with cool temperatures; some can be grown in the sub-tropics but they will not flourish in tropical heat and humidity. Vandas, by contrast, grow well outside in the tropics but need more warmth and humidity year-round if grown in the sub-tropics. If you buy your orchids from a local outlet, perhaps an orchid specialist, then you will be able to select those appropriate to your area. Serious collectors and breeders will select from a wider range and create the necessary conditions for good growth.

ORCHIDS CAN BE GROWN OUTSIDE, on or under trees, if they are sheltered. Here they can do very well and need little care because they can feed and water themselves—provided they are suited to the climate. Because of their floral beauty, however, most people like to grow them in bush or shadehouses where they can be collected together, cared for and even taken into the house for short spells. The shadehouse should be covered with no more than 50 per cent shadecloth; the bush house must permit an equivalent light level.

Ground orchids such as calanthes should be planted on or around the boles and roots (if exposed) of trees. If grown in a pot in the shadehouse, use a good quality soil mixed with compost or plenty of leafmould to make it more open. Though terrestrial by nature, they don't like their roots restricted. Cymbidiums can also be grown in the ground outside; though in fact they should be placed lightly but firmly in an open growing medium of gravel, very coarse sand or crushed stone and leafmould.

It is possible to simulate the terrestrial orchid's

natural environment by placing them on branches, stumps and the crooks of trees, where they will need little attention. In a shadehouse, terrestrial orchids are best grown off the ground in hanging pots or baskets, or on pieces of timber or treefern fibre, so that the air can circulate freely around them. Special orchid pots with lots of holes are available. All terrestrial orchids need an open mix which sustains and supports, rather than feeds them. The easiest thing for the home gardener to do is buy one of the special mixes formulated for different types of orchids, such as cymbidiums and cattleyas. Otherwise, home-made mixes can be prepared using combinations of ingredients such as sphagnum moss, pine bark, wood shavings, coarse sand and charcoal. For cattleyas a simple mix of pine bark and charcoal, in equal amounts, is satisfactory, while cymbidiums, which like a slightly heavier mix, do well in pine bark and coarse sand. Add a small amount of fowl manure, blood and bone and complete fertiliser to provide organic nutrition, and leafmould. Dendrobiums are quite fussy and require very little growing medium. A commercially formulated mix is the safest bet if you are growing them in a shadehouse.

A KING ORCHID (Dendrobium speciosum) in full flower in its natural habitat is one of the most splendid sights of the Australian bush. In the home garden they are easy to grow on trees (as here) where they make an eye-catching display, or on tree stumps or rocks. In the wild they are often found on rocks and cliff faces, giving these plants their other common name of ROCK ORCHID. At right, tropical impatiens and cool-climate petunias go together beautifully while a huge cymbidium orchid dominates the foreground.

CARE

When gardeners have problems with orchids it is usually because they over-water them. In the garden, they should rarely be watered because seasonal rainwater is usually adequate. If grown in shadehouses they should be given occasional, thorough drenchings and the mix allowed almost to dry out in between. As a general rule, ground orchids need more watering than epiphytes and watering too little is better than watering too much.

There are many ways of fertilising orchids. One easy method for home gardeners is to give plants a dressing of controlled-release fertiliser during spring. Fertilisers with plenty of phosphorus and potash are necessary for healthy, good-flowering plants. Occasional sprays of liquid fertiliser at half strength will boost the nutrition level during hot summers when fertiliser breakdown is most rapid. The bigger they get, the better they flower! But when orchids grow too big for comfort in their containers they can be easily divided at the roots and the separate sections repotted. A light misting for a few days afterwards will give vulnerable repotted plants sufficient moisture until new growth appears and they can be watered in the usual way. Don't put orchids into too large a pot.

Orchids are sadly susceptible to many pests and diseases, especially under shadehouse conditions. Red spider mites, aphid, mealy bugs, scale, thrips, orchid beetle and fungus diseases can all be problems, see the plant clinic, page 226. Orchid beetles are rather like ladybirds, coloured orange with black spots, and can be controlled by spraying with carbaryl. Hygiene, good ventilation and vigilance in the shadehouse will help keep problems at bay. Sterilise pots and any tool used for separating the roots. Orchids are often most vulnerable just after repotting and it is a good idea to spray with a copper-oxychloride fungicide at this time.

Cattleyas are probably the home gardener's first choice in a hot climate because they are easy to grow, have spectacular flowers, and are readily available in a great range of colours. Slipper orchids are another favourite; though they are ground orchids in nature they do best in the home garden when grown in shallow pots off the ground. Dendrobiums include the spectacular KING ORCHID (*D. speciosum*), illustrated above, which grows both in trees and on rocks and stumps; and the delicate COOKTOWN ORCHID (*D. bigibbum*) which is the Queensland state flower.

Tropical Treats — Orchids

Foliage and Fillers

WHILE SOME SHRUBS ARE GROWN FOR their flowers, others are grown for their handsome, evergreen foliage. These are the plants which 'fill up' the garden and give it interest year-round. In a hot climate, plenty of greenery creates coolness; areas of light and heavy shade offer relief from the constant sunshine. This greenery is provided by a selection of woody-limbed shrubs grown for their attractive foliage, as well as fleshy-leaved, low-growing plants which in cooler climates are grown indoors but in warmer climates help give the garden a lush and 'tropical' atmosphere.

Many foliage shrubs and most fleshy-leaved plants need plenty of water year-round, particularly where winters are dry (though winter watering needs to be approximately half of the amount provided during summer dry periods). Those plants suited to tropical and sub-tropical climates generally require slightly acid, light, fibrous, humus-enriched soils which should never be allowed to dry out completely.

To maintain foliage quality, generous and regular feeding with nitrogen-rich fertilisers is best. If controlled-release or other chemical fertilisers are used, composting once a year is advisable. Mulching is also important, with the mulch kept well away from the plant stem. While adding well-made compost to all garden soils is recommended, a good mulching of the surface once a year with organic materials will be sufficient on all but very poor, light soils, to maintain a healthy soil; chemical fertilisers can then be used without the need to add compost as well.

The following evergreen foliage plants which can be used to 'fill' the garden include clumping and grass-like plants and, of course, ferns. Most of the soft or fleshy-leaved plants such as aglaeonemas, rex begonias, caladiums and calatheas grow from tubers or rhizomes and can be readily propagated by separation and replanting of the segments — usually in spring.

Other plants grown for their foliage are, of course, the conifers which are dealt with in the chapter on trees, see pages 83–4.

Acalypha SPP.
SOUTH PACIFIC
HEIGHT Variable, according to type, to about 3 m
FOLIAGE Large, handsome, striking leaves in a range of bright colours
CONDITIONS Sun or semi-shade. Warm and sheltered position. Tender below 15°C. Humus-enriched soil. Plenty of water in summer. Prune for shape
OTHER POINTS There are many cultivars of several *Acalypha* species available in Australia, including the indigenous *A. nemorosa*. Best-known is probably the FIJIAN FIREBUSH (*A. wilkesiana*) which has gorgeous pink-edged, bronze leaves. Acalyphas are easy to grow for colour in the garden year-round. They make excellent hedges, though old leaves need regular pruning.

Aglaeonema SPP.
TROPICAL ASIA
HEIGHT Variable, depending on type, from 30 cm to 1 m
FOLIAGE Large, thick leaves in shades of dull green, splotched with grey-green or pale green. Leaf shape varies according to type; oval, almost oblong or lance-like
CONDITIONS Sun or part-shade, with sufficient sunlight to develop leaf colour. Humus-enriched, well-drained soil. Moderate watering, mostly in summer. Tender below 15°C
OTHER POINTS The subtle colours of the large leaves offset the more vivid caladiums and calatheas. (See page 152.)

Alternanthera SPP.
SOUTH AMERICA
HEIGHT Variable according to type; to 0.5 m maximum
FOLIAGE Neat, elongated, sometimes ruffle-edged, very colourful leaves in many shades of red, purple, orange and yellow
CONDITIONS Sun or part-shade. Warm and sheltered pos-

ition. Humus-enriched soil which is not allowed to dry out. Plenty of water in summer. Tender below 15°C

OTHER POINTS Alternanthera is really a bedding perennial but has been included here because it is grown for its very colourful foliage. While *A. denticulata* is upright and very spreading, *A. ficodea* 'AMOENA' (PARROT LEAF) is very low growing, forming a dense mat, which makes it a useful groundcover in part-shaded areas.

Begonia SPP. REX GROUP
SOUTH AMERICA
HEIGHT To about 0.5 m maximum
FOLIAGE Patterned leaves in various shades of green, with pink, red or silver markings
CONDITIONS Part shade. Warm and sheltered position. Light, open, humus-enriched, well-drained soil. Tender below 15°C. Subject to fungal diseases
OTHER POINTS Rex begonias are grown for the beauty of their foliage but, though they thrive on humidity, this also encourages the fungal diseases to which they are prone. For this reason, drip or trickle irrigation is best. Plants watered from above in the evening and left with water on the leaves overnight are most likely to develop disease problems.

Caladium SPP.
TROPICAL AMERICA
HEIGHT 0.5 m
FOLIAGE Large, patterned, arrowhead-shaped leaves perched on long stems. Colours are pink and green or mottled green and cream–white
CONDITIONS Part-shade or shade. Warm, sheltered position. Open, humus-enriched, slightly acid soil which is not allowed to dry out. Tender to below 18°C
OTHER POINTS The foliage adds year-round colour to the garden. Cultivars of *C.* × *hortulanum* (ANGELS' WINGS) are particularly attractive.

Calathea SPP.
SOUTH AMERICA
HEIGHT Variable, depending on type, to 1 m
FOLIAGE Large, broad, fleshy leaves with interesting patterns
CONDITIONS Part-shade or shade. Warm and sheltered, humid position. Requires open, humus-enriched, mulched, slightly acid soil which is not allowed to dry out. Plenty of water. Tender below 5°C
OTHER POINTS These are very handsome plants. Best known varieties are *C. zebrina* (ZEBRA PLANT) which has soft leaves striped with dark and pale green and *C. makoyana* (PEACOCK PLANT) which has sumptuously patterned green and pale green leaf surfaces, patterned red and pink underneath.

Coleus SPP.
TROPICAL ASIA AND AFRICA
HEIGHT Variable, depending on type, from 30 cm to 1 m
FOLIAGE Soft, serrated, pointed leaves on soft, juicy stems. Leaf colour varies according to type but is generally vividly patterned in shades of red, rust, yellow and green
CONDITIONS Sun or part shade. Warm, protected position. Any soil, but colour development is better in light, humus-enriched, lightly mulched soil. Feed and water regularly. Frost tender but can tolerate cold below 10°C for short periods
OTHER POINTS Coleus is grown as a perennial in the tropics and sub-tropics where it is a very common filler plant for adding quick colour to the garden. Easy and fast to grow. Easily propagated by tip cuttings and stem segments.

Coprosma repens (MIRROR PLANT)
NEW ZEALAND
HEIGHT To about 2 m
FOLIAGE Tough, very glossy leaves, either deep green or attractively variegated
CONDITIONS Very tough in all conditions and requires no care except, perhaps, an occasional watering during very dry periods
OTHER POINTS This is a New Zealand plant which does well just about anywhere the soil is well-drained. It grows on sand dunes, withstands salt-laden winds and copes well with car exhaust fumes and other forms of pollution. Other New Zealand and Australian coprosmas are also available, including ground-hugging forms. Most are able to withstand light frosts. Several of the New Zealand varieties have variegated foliage.

Cordyline SPP.
AUSTRALIA, NEW ZEALAND AND THE PACIFIC
HEIGHT Variable, according to species
FOLIAGE Long, stiff, often variegated leaves which grow upwards from the erect stem then either protrude outwards and upwards, or droop like palm leaves, depending on type
CONDITIONS Part or full shade. Needs humus-enriched, well-drained, fairly open soil which is not allowed to become completely dry. Water well in summer but most cordylines can withstand dry periods. Fertilise to maintain leaf quality. Frost tender
OTHER POINTS *C. terminalis* has plain green or pink-red marked leaves and is tender below 15°C. Australia is the home of several handsome cordylines which do well in shady parts of the garden. They include *C. rubra*, *C. petiolaris*, *C. stricta* and *C. australis*. All except the latter also have attractive flowers. *C. marginata*, from Madagascar, has striking greyish leaves, edged with purple. Other cordylines come in a range of rich, varied reds and pinks. (See page 149.)

CROTON (*Codiaeum variegatum*)
MALAYSIA
HEIGHT 2 m
FOLIAGE Stiff, glossy leaves in a variety of colours, often with wavy margins
CONDITIONS Sun or part-shade, with sufficient light to allow colour development in leaves. Needs humus-enriched, acid, well-drained soil which is never allowed to dry out completely. Warm, protected position. Tender below 10°C. Feed and water regularly in summer with a high-nitrogen fertiliser. Tip prune to promote bushiness, otherwise plants tend to become leggy
OTHER POINTS These are very common garden plants in the tropics and sub-tropics because of their colourful year-round

Rex begonias (see page 147) have hairy leaves which should be kept free of water as much as possible. Although best known as pot plants for patios, verandahs and well-lit indoor positions, they also do well in the garden if given light shade, a permanently warm position and protection from exposure.

foliage. Subject to mites, thrips, scale and mealybug (when indoors).

Dieffenbachia SPP. (DUMB CANE)
TROPICAL AMERICA
HEIGHT Variable; usually from 1–2 m
FOLIAGE Large, oval, variegated leaves with pointed tips
CONDITIONS Part-shade with enough light to allow development of leaf colour. Open, humus-enriched, well-drained soil. Water and feed regularly. Tender below 15°C.
OTHER POINTS Like syngoniums, spathyphyllums and anthuriums these well-known indoor plants can be grown outdoors in the tropics. In the sub-tropics, unless a very warm and sheltered spot with year-round humidity can be created, it is best to keep them outside in pots during summer and move them indoors or into a warm sheltered spot in winter. Sap is poisonous. Subject to red spider mite and scale; mealy bug can be a problem when grown indoors. Prune in late spring or early summer by cutting back to 15 cm.

Dizygotheca elegantissima (FALSE ARALIA)
PACIFIC ISLANDS
HEIGHT 1 m
FOLIAGE Long, lightly mottled, coarsely-toothed leaves
CONDITIONS Part-shade. Humus-enriched, well-drained soil. Water regularly but moderately in summer, less in winter. Tender below 15°C
OTHER POINTS An open shrub whose unusual leaves make it a distinctive garden plant which is easy to grow in a hot, humid climate.

Cordylines (see page 147) add year-round colour to shady areas and the many variations range from green, pink and palest cream through to a deep ruby red. Many species have attractive flowers and commonly available Australian types also have colourful berries. This one is called 'CARBINE'.

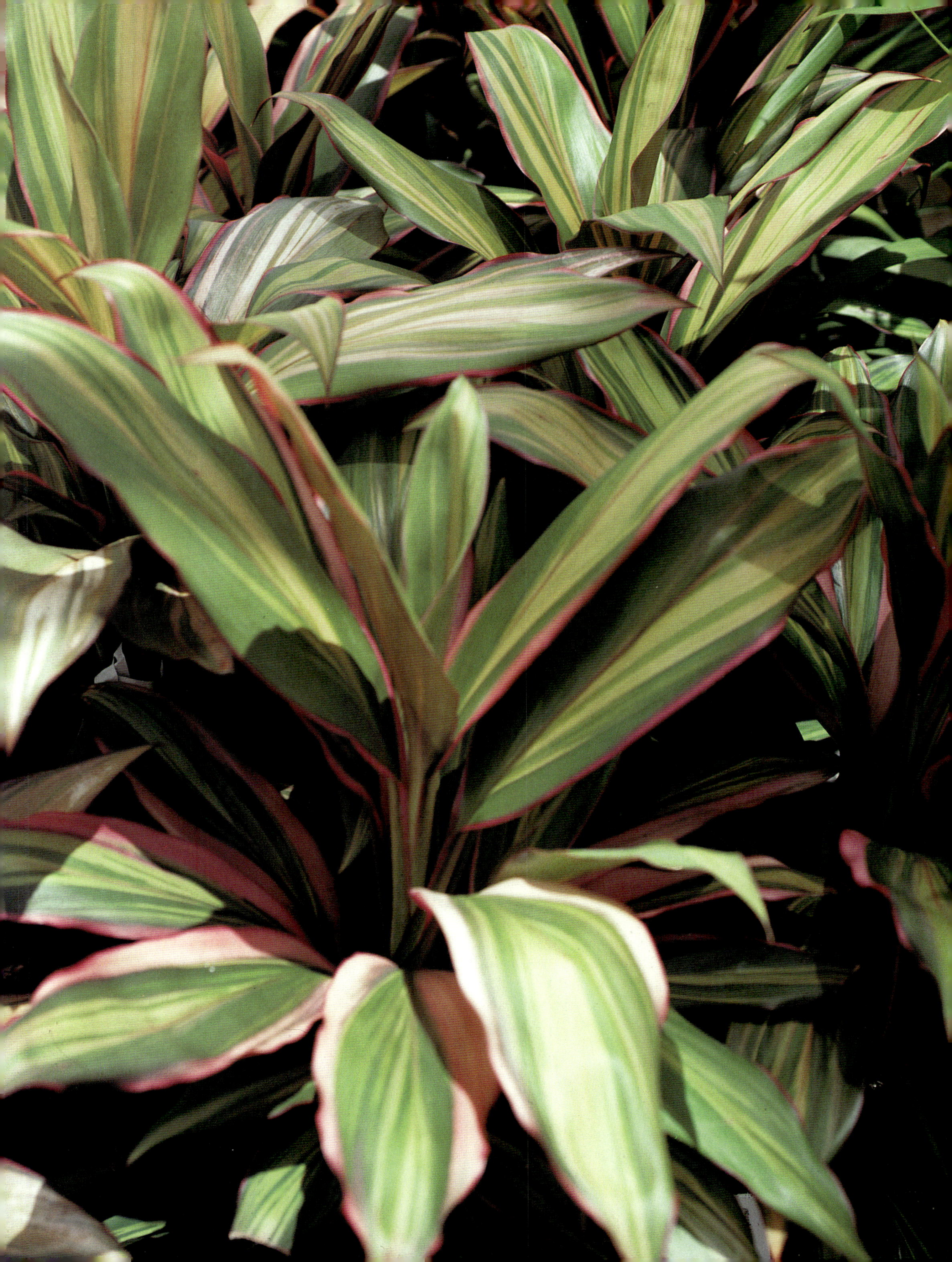

Dracaena SPP.
AFRICA
HEIGHT Variable, according to type. Ornamental pot varieties remain under 1 m, garden plants can reach 3 m
FOLIAGE Long, thin, straplike leaves with stripes or coloured margins
CONDITIONS Sun or part-shade. Well-drained soil. Water moderately. Generally tender below 10°C
OTHER POINTS These very popular indoor plants also do well in the garden. *D. fragrans* can reach 4 m outside and has shiny green leaves and tiny, fragrant flowers. *D. marginata* is even larger and has long, bare stems bearing dense clusters of leaves with red or purple-red margins.

Duranta 'SHEENA'S GOLD'
SOUTH AMERICA
HEIGHT 1 m
FOLIAGE Neat, dense, glossy golden-green leaves
CONDITIONS Sun for best colour but will grow in part-shade. Humus-enriched, well-drained soil. Tolerates cold below 10°C for short periods
OTHER POINTS A fast-growing plant with sumptuous foliage which makes a good hedge, border or specimen plant. The larger *Duranta repens*, also grown in warm climates, has spreading, bush green foliage, mauve flowers and striking yellow berries. Other durantas are also available, without striking foliage but with blue flowers and yellow berries.

Euonymus SPP.
MANY PARTS OF THE WORLD
HEIGHT Variable according to type, from groundcovering to about 4 m
FOLIAGE Gold and green, yellow and green or white and green; very handsome
CONDITIONS Sun or light shade. Good soil. Plenty of moisture
OTHER POINTS This is really a cool-climate plant which does well in hotter areas if well-watered. *E. fortunei* appears more heat-hardy than *E. japonicus*. Both are frost hardy. Some types make good hedges.

Fatsia japonica (ARALIA)
JAPAN
HEIGHT 3 m
FOLIAGE Large, glossy, palm-like leaves on long stems
CONDITIONS Sun or shade. Humus-enriched, well-drained soil. Frost hardy. Feed and water regularly
OTHER POINTS A tough, reliable foliage plant. Although a cool-climate plant it adapts well to hot, humid areas where it can fill difficult spots which might be too cold, exposed or otherwise unsuitable for more tender, delicate plants.

Hosta SPP.
JAPAN
HEIGHT Below 1.5 m
FOLIAGE Large, broad, usually rounded or oval leaves, pointed at the tips. Sometimes with a ruffled or quilted effect. Shades of green or with attractive variegations
CONDITIONS Part-shade or shade. Sheltered position. Rich, fairly open soil which is not allowed to dry out. Frost and drought tender
OTHER POINTS These are some of the loveliest foliage plants and perfect for planting around a swimming pool or other water feature as they are tidy and easy to manage.

Iresine SPP.
SOUTH AMERICA
HEIGHT 1 m
FOLIAGE *I. herbstii* has bushy, stiff, leaves which are broad at base, coming to a point, with yellow or red veins and red stems. *I. lindenii* has spectacular, pointed, dark red and mauve-red leaves.
CONDITIONS Part-shade. Humus-enriched, loamy, well-drained soil. Plenty of water during summer. Tip-prune to maintain bushy, compact growth. Tender below 10°C
OTHER POINTS A very striking plant which is quite easy to grow.

Maranta SPP.
TROPICAL AMERICA
HEIGHT Under 0.5 m
FOLIAGE Large, fleshy, broadly oblong leaves with a satiny or velvety texture, depending on species
CONDITIONS Shade or part-shade. Sheltered, warm, humid position. Needs fertile, humus-enriched, well-drained soil which is not allowed to dry out. Fertilise at least twice during summer. Tender below 10°C
OTHER POINTS These striking plants from the jungle are very similar to calatheas and give a very tropical touch to any garden.

Melaleuca 'REVOLUTION GOLD' and 'REVOLUTION GREEN'
These have been mentioned in detail on page 103. The bright gold or green colours of these selectively bred melaleucas make them ideal shrubs for the garden which relies on foliage instead of, or as well as, flowers to provide year-round colour.

Monstera deliciosa (FRUIT SALAD PLANT)
CENTRAL AMERICA
HEIGHT As a shrub, about 1 m but can climb or scramble much higher
FOLIAGE Large, glossy, indented leaves with 'windows'
CONDITIONS Semi-shade or shade, though can take direct sun for part of the day. Light, open, humus-enriched soil is best but grows in most soil conditions. Frost tender but tolerates cold below 10°C. Grows best with plenty of water and fertiliser but can withstand dry periods and grows adequately with no feeding in good soils
OTHER POINTS A reliable plant to fill shady and otherwise difficult garden areas but does tend to become rampant in hot, humid climates. Bears a long, pointed, edible fruit. *M. friedrichsthali* is more delicate in appearance and habit.

Nandina domestica (SACRED BAMBOO)
CHINA AND JAPAN
HEIGHT 2 m
FOLIAGE Compound leaves with long stems and thin, mid-green leaflets drawn out to a fine point. Foliage has a slight resemblance to bamboo and turns red in winter in cooler areas
CONDITIONS Sun or part-shade. Humus-enriched, well-

drained soil. Frost hardy and will tolerate long dry periods, though grows fastest when regularly watered
OTHER POINTS A deservedly popular filler plant which bears attractive red berries, suitable for flower arrangements. Very easy to grow in most conditions. Dwarf form 'Nana' takes up less space and makes a good low border plant.

Phormium SPP. (NEW ZEALAND FLAX)
NEW ZEALAND
HEIGHT Variable, from 1–3 m depending on type
FOLIAGE Long, thin, pointed leaves in a range of bold colours depending on species and variety
CONDITIONS Sun. Well-drained soil. Plenty of water. Frost hardy
OTHER POINTS These very decorative foliage plants can be used to create dramatic, low-level landscaping effects in the garden. Very easy to grow.

Pisonia SPP.
AUSTRALIA
HEIGHT As a tall shrub, to about 5 m. Tree forms, or shrubs allowed to develop into single-trunked tree specimens, grow twice that height
FOLIAGE Large, shiny, light green or strongly variegated leaves
CONDITIONS Sun or part-shade. Any well-drained soil, though will grow fastest in rich soil. Water well while young. Will tolerate light frosts and dry periods, once established
OTHER POINTS The variegated forms are decorative. A tough, reliable shrub or tree for foundation plantings.

Pseuderanthemum SPP.
SOUTH-EAST ASIA
HEIGHT 1 m
FOLIAGE Large, shiny, purplish leaves
CONDITIONS Part-shade. Open, humus-enriched, well-drained soil. Water and feed regularly. Tender below 15°C
OTHER POINTS Quite an attractive filler plant for lightly shaded areas in the tropical garden.

Schleffera arboricola (MINIATURE UMBRELLA TREE)
SOUTH-EAST ASIA
HEIGHT To about 4 m
FOLIAGE Large, palm-like leaves. Very striking yellow and green form
CONDITIONS Sun or part-shade. Light, humus-enriched, well-drained soil. Feed and water regularly to maintain foliage quality. Tender below 15°C
OTHER POINTS Like its bigger Australian cousin the UMBRELLA TREE (*Schefflera actinophylla*), this tropical shrub or small tree performs as well in the hot climate garden as it does in the pot. Variegated forms are very popular.

Syngonium SPP.
TROPICAL AMERICA
HEIGHT Variable; non-climbing types generally to about 1 m
FOLIAGE Large, arrowhead-shaped leaves, either glossy green or variegated in several colours
CONDITIONS Semi-shade or shade. Warm, sheltered, humid position. Needs light, fibrous, open, humus-enriched, well-drained soil which is not allowed to dry out. Feed and water well. Tender below 15°C
OTHER POINTS These very tropical plants are more familiar indoors but will grow in hot, humid areas without much annual temperature variation. Most syngoniums are root climbers; however some make excellent groundcovers if they are discouraged from climbing and trimmed accordingly.

Xanthorrhoea (GRASS TREE)
AUSTRALIA
HEIGHT Trunk from 0.5 to 1 m in very large, old specimens
FOLIAGE Long, slender, stiff, grass-like leaves which stick out from the thick, dark, trunk like a ballerina's tutu. Tall pollen spikes can grow up to 2 m above trunk
CONDITIONS Full sun or part-shade. Peaty, sandy or rocky soil. Water daily for first three months after planting. After that, no watering beyond natural rainfall required. Do not feed. Tolerates extreme heat, humidity, dryness or cold down to –10°C
OTHER POINTS Unusual, very slow-growing, ancient plants which make interesting garden specimens in warm climates. Trouble-free once established. As I suggested on page 58, buy only from licensed operators or grow from seed.

More foliage plants

Here is a list of other foliage plants which can be used to good effect in the garden. All require the same conditions but some, like anthurium and xanthosoma, are very tropical in habit and cannot be grown outdoors where temperatures drop below 15°C. Aucuba, *Cleyera japonica* and rhamnus are all cold-hardy and easy to grow outdoors in the sub-tropics.

Anthurium SPP.
Aspidistra elatior
Aucuba japonica
Chlorophytum comosum
Cleyera japonica
Ctenanthe SPP.
Elaeagnus SPP.

Elettaria SPP.
Pilea cadierei (very tropical)
Plectranthus SPP.
Polyscias SPP. (shrub types)
Rhamnus SPP.
Sanchezia nobilis
Xanthosoma SPP.

Ground-hugging foliage plants

Ajuga SPP.
Coprosma × *kirkii* 'Variegata'
Episcia SPP.
Fittonia SPP.
Gunnera magellanica (peaty soil)
Pellionia SPP.
Peperomia SPP.
Syngonium SPP.

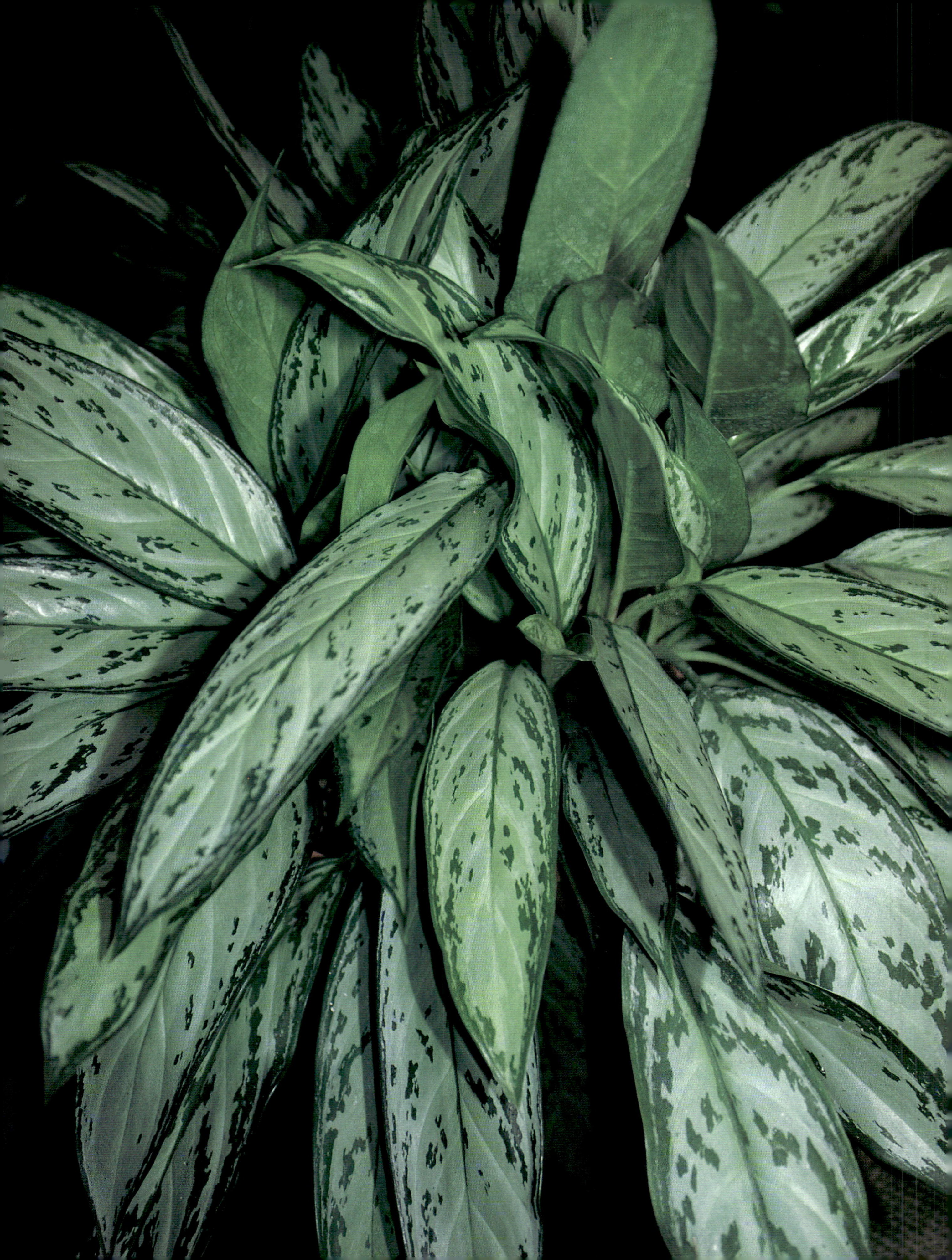

FERNS

Ferns are gentle-looking plants which add a soft touch to the garden landscape. Because they mostly grow in shade, they make useful understorey plants in shrubberies and around the base of trees. They are also easy-to-manage plants for courtyards and other small, sheltered areas. They grow well in tubs, hanging baskets and planters.

There are many different types of ferns, from those like asplenium with single, straplike fronds to those such as Asparagus Fern with very fine, much-divided foliage. The majority of ferns have a simple, pinnate form with pairs of fronds growing opposite (or alternate) from the stipe or leaf stem. All ferns grow from rhizomes underground and many of the more easy-to-handle garden types can be readily propagated by rhizome division. In nature, ferns propagate themselves by means of spores, in a complicated sexual cycle.

THE TYPICAL FERN HABITAT is sheltered, moist and shaded. However some ferns grow in less hospitable places, sprouting from rocks or tree trunks where there are sufficient nutrients to maintain life. This tells us that while ferns often grow in rich soils, they should not be over-fed and that, while they like plenty of moisture, only a few of them can tolerate waterlogged conditions. In fact, once established, all but a few rare and particularly fussy ferns are very easy to grow.

Ferns are generally not too fussy about soils, though they thrive on plenty of organic matter. Although most ferns occur naturally on acid soils, a few such as pteris prefer some alkalinity. In the garden it is best to give soil a light cover of humus or compost once a year to add organic bulk, and a few nutrients which will facilitate healthy fern growth. A light leafmulch is also desirable, but do not mulch heavily. They need plenty of water, though most Australian ferns can withstand dry periods if well watered at other times. Although a few ferns are frost hardy, most, particularly those originating in warm climates, are frost tender and it is safer to treat all the ferns in your garden that way. As ferns are usually planted under taller plants, frost is not likely to be a problem, even where light frosts do occur.

Aglaeonemas (see page 146) have a subdued elegance which makes them very popular as indoor plants. In hot climates they can be grown outdoors in light shade. They look particularly handsome around the edge of pools.

Some of the more commonly grown ferns

Adiantum SPP. (MAIDENHAIR FERNS)
Delicate pinules (leaflets) create a lacy effect. Several species and varieties available. Very decorative and easy to grow.

Allantodia australis (AUSTRAL LADY FERN)
Robust and bracken-like.

Blechnum cartilagneum (GRISTLE FERN)
Rather coarse, strong growing, attractive pink new growth. Other blechnums of similar appearance also available.

Christella dentata
Erect, pinnate leaves. Grows just about anywhere without good soil or much water.

Culcita SPP. (SOFT BRACKEN)
Large, divided fronds rather like a small bracken. Fast-growing.

Cyrtomium falcatum (FISHTAIL FERN)
Unusual large, rounded, shiny pinules with fine teeth.

Davallia SPP. (Hare's foot ferns)
Very tough, fine foliage. Easy to grow. Several species.

Dennstaedtia davallioides (LACY GROUND FERN)
A large fern with exquisite lacy foliage. Needs plenty of water.

Doodia SPP. (Rasp ferns)
Small, simply pinnate ferns with a rough texture. Pinkish–red new growth which can look spectacular after rain.

Dryopteris SPP.
Elegant ferns with arched stems and feathery foliage.

Lycopodium SPP. (Tassel ferns)
Not a true fern but similar in habit. Most are epiphytic in habit so can be grown on trees, from where they hang down long, glossy fronds. Spectacular.

Lygodium SPP.
Rather bare-stemmed ferns with interesting lobed leaflets.

Microlepia SPP.
Creeping ferns with large, pointed leaves divided into many small leaflets.

Microsorum SPP.
Creeping ferns which can climb or cover the ground. Requires high humidity so does best near water.

Nephrolepis SPP.
Tall, upright, pinnate fronds.

Onoclea SPP.
Soft, deciduous, fine foliage. Flushed pink new growth.

Pellaea falcata (SICKLE FERN)
Simple, upright, pinnate leaves. Fast growing. Water well in summer.

Phlebodium SPP.
Large, handsome, strongly-toothed leaflets with a pale glaze. Underleaf spore-cases (sprangia) are orange-yellow.

Pityrogramma SPP.
Very handsome ferns with angled pinnules and lobed leaflets with a whitish coating underneath.

Polypodium SPP.
Fronds either simply pinnate with patterned leaflets or with a finer foliage to give a lacy effect.

Polystichum SPP.
Soft, dainty foliage. Very handsome.

Pteris SPP. (Brake ferns)
Tough ferns which can feature either variegated fronds or handsome red new growth. Likes a humus-rich soil which is slightly alkaline.

Pyrrosia rupestris (ROCK FELT FERN)
A ground-hugging fern with tiny rounded fronds with a felt-like undersurface. Good for rockeries and hanging baskets.

Selaginella SPP.
Not a true fern but rather like a large moss, with bright green frondlets. Prostrate and trailing, needs plenty of water.

Large ferns

Cyathea SPP. (Tree ferns)
Very large ferns with tall, single trunks which look like trees at maturity. Several species are found in Australia. The brown trunks are covered in scales; the huge fronds have leaflets joined at the base, with entire margins. Difficult to transplant but easy to grow in sheltered, shady areas where water is plentiful. Most common species in cultivation are *C. australis* (ROUGH TREE FERN) and *C. cooperi*. Very handsome garden specimens but they must be given sufficient room; *C. australis* and *C. cooperi* can grow to 12 m in the forest and, though they are unlikely to grow this large in the home garden, they are likely to achieve at least half that height in time. Best in humus-enriched soils with plenty of moisture. Shade or part-shade, though will grow in full sun if plenty of water available. Young plants can be badly damaged by frost and heavy frost will damage the fronds on older plants.

Dicksonia antarctica (SOFT TREE FERN)
Very similar to cyathea but trunk is covered in soft, rust-brown hairs instad of scales. Also, the pinnules (leaflets) are slightly segmented at the margins. Conditions as cyatheas.

Osmunda regalis (ROYAL FERN)
A 2–m high 'flowering' fern with large leaflets and attractive, rust-coloured 'flower' spikes, which contain spores.

Todea barbara (KING FERN)
Trunk up to 1 m, carrying long branches of finely segmented leaflets. Very handsome.

STAGHORNS AND ELKHORNS

Epiphytes are plants which are physically supported by another plant but are not parasites. They grow on tree branches, in the forks of trees, on stumps and sometimes on rocks. The best-known epiphytes are probably the platyceriums (staghorns and elkhorns). The bird's nest ferns (*Asplenium* spp.) also grow epiphytically. Other epiphytes include orchids, bromeliads and vireya rhododendrons.

They are included here in the foliage plant section because they are grown for this purpose; either outdoors in trees or on posts, or in a bush-house. Staghorns and elkhorns have large, rounded bases and long leaves, divided into segments. They can be fastened to trees (except those which shed bark), tree branch sections, tree fern trunk sections, sections of compressed fibre, fence posts, patio uprights and other mountings. Ties can be of plastic-coated galvanised wire or panthose; though as platyceriums grow very large the support must be strong. Be careful that the tie does not penetrate the rhizome, which extends well into the peaty material behind the fronds.

If epiphytes such as staghorns and elkhorns are in the shade of trees, they will get their nourishment from tree litter, dead insects and rain-water containing nutritious matter. Otherwise they should be fed with an occasional handful of chopped leafmould or compost. A small amount of slow-release fertiliser or organic fertiliser such as blood and bone, with a teaspoonful of dolomite, is enough nutrition for plants that are not growing on trees.

ORNAMENTAL GRASSES

There is more to grass than the low-growing green stuff that makes up a lawn. Many of the tall growing grasses make interesting features in the garden, particularly where large, bushy plants are inappropriate. Ornamental grasses also look fine around swimming pools or ponds. They require only minimum care, benefiting from medium to good soils, regular watering and some feeding to maintain foliage quality. Here is a selection of those suitable for gracing the garden in hot climates.

Arundo donax (long, reed-like, variegated leaves)
Carex SPP. (ornamental tufted sedges)
Cortaderia SPP. (including *C. selloana*, PAMPAS GRASS)
Cymbopogon SPP. (*C. citratus* (LEMON GRASS) and *C. Nardus* (CITRONELLA GRASS), both lemon-scented, used in cooking
Cyperus SPP. (ornamental sedges, often with striped leaves)
Dietes bicolor (a flowering, reed-like plant)
Glyceria SPP. (similar to *Arundo donax*)
Koeleria SPP. (soft-textured, ornamental grass)
Lepidosperma SPP. (long, tough, reed-like leaves. Good for around ponds and natural waterways)
Ophiopogon SPP. (MONDO GRASS, including 'mini' and striking dark-leaved forms. Small, tightly-clumped grasses with shiny leaves)
Restio tetraphyllus (feathery branches)
Zea mays (long, coarse, variegated leaves, very decorative)

BAMBOO

The plants commonly known as 'bamboo' include not only the genus Bambusa but several other genera, with a whole swag of different species and a few selectively bred varieties. This can make choosing a bamboo for the home garden complicated, though most nurseries only carry a selection of the more obviously ornamental types. If you want a wider range, you will need to contact a specialist bamboo nursery.

Despite their attractive appearance, bamboos have gained an unfair reputation for rampant growth, but this is being overcome by the increasing availability of species suitable for the home garden. First of all, it is necessary to know that bamboos come in two basic types, clumping and running. Clumping bamboos, which make up the majority of the hot-climate types, are the best choice for all but the largest home gardens. Unlike the running types, which are responsible for bamboo's bad name, clumping types do not rampage out of control and invade the rest of the garden. However, several of the smaller-growing running types are very decorative and quite manageable, even in small gardens.

BAMBOOS ARE FOUND in many parts of the world, including Australia. Though generally associated with the tropics, many types originate in much cooler areas such as Japan, where the use of bamboo wood has long been an art form. Even so, bamboos give a distinctly tropical 'feel' to any garden both because of their appearance and the sound as the breezes rustle their leaves.

There are all sizes of bamboo, from the dwarf Sasa types which start at 30 cm to veritable giants which are used as windbreaks. They are remarkably fast growing, with the larger-growing types reaching up to 10 m or more in three or four years. The woody, hollow stems — or culms to give them their correct name — are ridged at nodular intervals and can be green or striped green and yellow, cream or beige.

Leaves are long and narrow, sometimes sheathed, in shades of green, striped with cream or white.

Bamboos will thrive in a range of soil conditions, from sandy soils to clay, but they perform best when given a well-drained, humus-enriched soil which is not allowed to dry out. Feeding will hasten growth.

Bamboos for the home garden include:

Bambusa multiplex varieties (clumping type)
Bambusa vulgaris varieties (clumping type)
Chimonobambusa marmorea variegated (running type)
Phyllostachys nigra (BLACK BAMBOO) (running type)
Pseudosasa amabilis (TEA STICK BAMBOO) (running type)
 P. japonica 'TSUTSUMINIA' (running type)
Shinobambusa tootsik (TEMPLE BAMBOO) (running type)

CYCADS, ZAMIAS AND BOWENIAS

Cycads often resemble palms in appearance. They are often grouped with them in gardening books but I feel that for the purposes of this book palms belong more with trees and cycads belong here because they are grown for foliage and to fill large spaces in the garden at low-to-mid level.

Cycads are very old plants; so old in fact that they have even been marketed as 'the food of dinosaurs'. Whether or not this claim is strictly true, those plants which appear under the collective name of cycadales are both attractive and interesting, so much so that, once prized mainly by collectors, they have gradually become popular with gardeners everywhere. One of the reasons is their slow, contained growth habit.

DESPITE THIS GROWING POPULARITY, cycads have acquired a reputation for being poisonous. It is true that the outer coating of some cycad seeds contains toxins harmful to humans if ingested; yet the seeds in this condition are hardly palatable and in any case were used by Australian Aborigines as food (but only after suitable and lengthy treatment). New fronds also contain toxins, though this disappears as the fronds mature. Pollen of at least one cycad has also been blamed for a disease of the nervous system occurring on some Pacific Islands, though no cases have been reported in Australia and the risk of exposure is so slight as to be negligible.

Cycads are either male or female (dioecious) and only male plants produce pollen, on elongated cones. Females also produce cones; the decorative cones of cycad species add to their attractions.

I have selected four genera as being of interest to hot-climate gardeners; among them are several plants which are very familiar and some which are not so well known.

Bowenia SPP.
These are rather rare Australian cycads with fernlike foliage, now available in cultivation. The two species are *Bowenia serrulata* (BYFIELD FERN) and *B. spectabilis* (ZAMIA FERN). They do well in the garden if given a protected, shady spot which doesn't dry out completely. Though *B. serrulata*, in particular, is able to withstand long dry periods, regular watering is advisable. Fertilise as with any foliage plant or fern, but do not over-feed.

Cycas SPP.
These attractive plants have palm-like trunks and foliage. Some, such as the Northern Territory's *Cycas angulata*, grow more than 3 m tall. All are very long-living. Once established in the gardens, cycas are slow-growing but do not require any care. They do well in full sun or shade and thrive on poor soils; though composting for humus enrichment will hasten growth. Most can withstand long dry periods without harm, though foliage quality is improved by regular watering. Do not over-water. All cycads make excellent pot plants.

C. armstrongii A Northern Territory and Western Australian species with light to mid-green fronds.

C. circinalis (FERN PALM) Originating in India and parts of South-East Asia, this handsome species somewhat resembles a giant fern because of its dark-green fronds with their many very fine leaflets.

C. media (AUSTRALIAN NUT PALM) A Queensland species which grows to about 3 m and has long, palm-like, mid-green fronds. *C. cairnsiana* is similar, with narrower fronds.

Platyceriums (Staghorns and Elkhorns, see page 154) are epiphytes which in nature need trees or rocks to provide support. As they can grow very large, the support has to be strong, a point which needs to be understood by home gardeners. Here a fine platycerium specimen has been artificially fastened to a tree, yet it looks very natural in this rainforest garden setting.

C. neocaldedonica (BREAD PALM) An Indonesian and New Caledonian species which may also be indigenous to Northern Australia. It has open fronds and is very palm-like in appearance.

C. revoluta (SAGO PALM) The best-known cycad, originating in Japan's sub-tropical Ryukyu Islands and long a popular plant in that country and elsewhere. It has very handsome dark-green, thick, shiny fronds which grow outwards in a basket-shape from the base. The central cones, when they appear, are very striking.

C. rumphii This is a large-growing species from Asia and the Pacific, very similar in appearance to *C. media* but with very narrow leaflets.

These are just a few of the better-known cycas species available to gardeners. Many others are being brought into cultivation and there are many interesting Australian species worth growing. They include *C. angulata*, *C. basaltica*, *C. calcicola*, *C. kennedyana*, *C. lane-poolei*, *C. normanbeyana* and some interesting forms of established species such as 'MARYBOROUGH BLUE'.

Lepidozamia SPP.
These are 'typical' cycads in that they have long, palm-like fronds and form long trunks. *Lepidozamia peroffskyana* has a 'fluffy' appearance which distinguishes it from *L. hopei* and most other cycads. The trunk can reach 6 m tall. *L. hopei* reaches a similar height. Its leaflets are broader and sparser in appearance than those of *L. peroffskyana*. Both make handsome garden or pot plants and, as they occur naturally in rainforests, require shade or semi-shade.

Macrozamia SPP.
Australian macrozamias bear a superficial resemblance to lepidozamias and cycas, except that in most species the trunk remains underground and only the large, palm-like fronds can be seen. Most macrozamias do best in the shade but a few, such as the popular *Macrozamia moorei*, can be grown in full sun. All are good pot plants. These are just some of the 17 macrozamias found in Australia, most of which are not freely available in cultivation.

M. communis syn. *spiralis* (BURRAWANG) A mostly subterranean trunk topped by many upright fronds, up to 2 m in length. The several large and striking cones are a feature of this plant, as they are of most zamias.

M. lucida Plenty of thick, spreading fronds.

M. miquelli This is a particularly attractive species with long, bluish-green, arching fronds. It makes a fine garden specimen. The female cones are very large, the pineapple-like outer segments bordered with red lines.

M. moorei The best known of the macrozamias and the largest found in cultivation. It has a thick trunk which can grow (though very slowly) up to 8 m height. Fronds reach up to 1.8 m in length and are wide-spreading. A slow-growing but very handsome species which is often mistaken for a palm. Grows happily in full sun.

Bromeliads

BROMELIADS ARE POPULAR HOUSEPLANTS ALL OVER THE WORLD; in hot climates they are very easy to grow outdoors, provided they are given shade and a coarse, open growing medium. In their natural habitat they are epiphytes, growing on trees, stumps or the loose debris of the rainforest floor. Some species are actually desert plants, but they still need shade and the same type of growing conditions as their forest cousins.

Bromeliads often owe their attraction to vivid leaf colour but they also have unusual flowers; in some species these have a hard, plastic-like texture quite unike that found on any other plant. There is something unearthly about them, which is what fascinates collectors. What is more, each plant produces only one flower. After this, it produces an offset which flowers in its own right and can be removed to form another plant (usually when they are about half the size of the parent plant). Parent plants can produce more than one offset, which makes bromeliads easy to propagate. And even though the parent plant won't actually flower again, it still looks attractive.

THE BEST PLACE TO GROW bromeliads is in the shade of a home garden rainforest. They go very well with palms and treeferns, adding a touch of vivid red or yellow to the greenery.

Here they can be attached to trees with soft cloth ties or plastic-covered wire, their roots bound in orchid mix. Or they can be placed on (rather than in) the ground, in a loose soil, with their roots lightly covered. The litter from taller plants will protect their roots and help provide nourishment.

CARE

Some of the more common bromeliads have a basket-like central rosette which collects and stores rainwater. During dry weather they need additional water; as they are not likely to be growing in isolation, they should obtain this from whatever system is used to water the rest of the plants around them.

It isn't usually necessary to feed bromeliads; in fact it is safest to keep all chemicals well away from them as they are sensitive. A little organic fertiliser such as well-rotted manure or blood and bone can be fed to them occasionally if their environment is particularly deficient in nutrients.

Bromeliads are easy pot plants because they need only reasonable watering — about twice a week in the hot season and once a week the rest of the year. Use a light, coarse, orchid potting mix and a fairly shallow pot. Additional nutrition can be given easily in the form of a controlled-release fertiliser used at a quarter the usual recommended rate. This usually only needs to be applied once a year, in spring, but a further dose can be given in mid-summer if the plant doesn't appear to be thriving. An occasional quarter strength dose of the liquid fertiliser formulated for orchids may be a better regime than the second application of controlled-release fertiliser.

Bromeliads have striking foliage, generally with a red heart which is believed to attract insects that then become trapped in water, held in the centre of the plant, thus becoming part of a nutritious 'soup'. Because this plant is so adept at feeding itself, it needs no help from the home gardener. Bromeliads also produce unusual but very striking flowers. This variety is 'VICTORIA'.

5
Walls'n'floors

Hedges and screens

HEDGES

GARDEN HEDGES MAKE JUST AS MUCH SENSE in a hot climate as they do in cooler regions where, in the northern hemisphere at least, they are very much part of a longstanding garden tradition. Wherever hedges are planted they act as screens for privacy and to hide unsightly objects, protect against wind and unwelcome visitors (animal or human), or divide one section of the garden from another. A hedged driveway makes a handsome entrance to any home. And there is no more natural or attractive way of marking the barrier between your garden and the neighbours, or the street outside, than a hedge.

In hot climates, hedges provide additional greenery and coolness. Tropical and sub-tropical shrubs and trees usually grow much faster than their cool-climate equivalents and many have gorgeous flowers which make a hedge into a spectacle rather than just a green screen.

Other good points about hedges are:

- ❖ 'Green' consciousness-raising has led to people seeing hedges as a more natural barrier/divider than fences, adding valuable oxygenising and visually attractive plantlife to the urban landscape.
- ❖ Hedges are useful buffers against noise and visual pollution. For example, a hedge can be grown taller than a fence and has more horizontal substance, yet it has a neater appearance than a mixed barrier planting.
- ❖ The advent of the electric hedge trimmer makes hedges far easier to maintain than in days gone by.
- ❖ There are far more shrubs suited to hedging available than there used to be, especially for hot-climate gardens — probably the largest range of hedging plants in the world. No longer are types of hedges restricted to the traditional, formal, boxes and privets, which only do really well in cool areas with reliable rainfall.
- ❖ Hedges make useful and increasingly necessary wildlife corridors, providing haven and safe passage for birds and small creatures.

In theory, a hedge can be created from any type of shrub (and some trees) planted close together in a row so as eventually to form a continuous wall of foliage. In practice, some shrubs are more suitable than others. The best hedging plants are those with small, neat, dense foliage which is retained close to the ground. For easy maintenance they should be steady, reliable but not-too-rampant growers which do not readily shed foliage. And, as hedges form an important part of garden structure, the chosen species needs to be long-lived. It goes without saying that hedge plants should not have nasty habits such as parts which poison, sting, prickle or stab. (Thorny plants can make an effective barrier against animal and human intruders and are sometimes grown as a hedge for this reason, though check your public liability if this is near a regular thoroughfare.) Bougainvillea and Crown of Thorns are good examples of hedges which are lovely to look at but not to touch.

Hedges can also consist of two or even three different plants though these should be compatible in texture, colour and height. A non-flowering type may be interspersed with one which flowers, giving a colourful panelled effect when in bloom. Attractive, tiered hedges can be created by using three or more plants of different heights — the result is a very effective layered, sculptured look. A non-flowering hedge can provide a backdrop to a lower, flowering type, or a pale-coloured floral display can be used to set off a smaller hedge with more vivid flowers in the foreground; a variety of interesting effects can be created in this way, the only rule being to plant the lower hedge on the sunward side.

The following plants are suggested as suitable for a range of hot-climate garden purposes.

T — recommended for tropics only
ST — recommended for sub-tropics only

Formal hedges

These must present a solid, tidy, permanent appearance and therefore must be created from long-lived plants with neat, dense foliage and a naturally good form. Small-leaved azaleas (which appear also on the flowering list) can be used for this purpose in the sub-tropics; in Japanese-style gardens they are clipped to prevent flowering.

Azaleas
Conifers (see next column)
GOLDEN PRIVET (*Ligustrum ovalifolium* 'Aureum')
Lilly pillies (small-leaved types such as selected forms of *Syzygium australe*, *S. luehmannii* and the dwarf form of *S. wilsonii*)
Murraya paniculata

Informal

Informal hedges are those which look good with only minimal trimming. They are generally less dense and compact in growth habit than shrubs used for formal hedging.
Abelia SPP.
Abutilon SPP. (This is a decorative plant for a very informal hedge; foliage is not very dense and needs plenty of tip-pruning when young to promote bushiness.)
Acalypha wilkesiana
Azalea (single-flowering types are regaining popularity as hedge plants) ST
Baeckea virgata
Bamboo
   Bambusa multiplex varieties (clumping type)
   Bambusa vulgaris varieties (clumping)
   Chimonobambusa marmorea variegated (running type)
   Phyllostachys nigra (BLACK BAMBOO, running)
   Pseudosasa amabilis (TONKIN CANE, running)
   Pseudosasa japonica var. *tsutsuminia* (running)
   Shinobambusa tootsik (TEMPLE BAMBOO, running)
Buckinghamia celsissima
Coprosma repens (syn. *baueri*) all forms
Duranta repens (e.g. 'SHEENA'S GOLD' and 'AUSSIE 2000')
Escallonia macrantha (and other *Escallonia* SPP.) ST
Lonicera nitida (needs support to start)
Melaleuca 'REVOLUTION GREEN' and 'REVOLUTION GOLD'
Metrosidero excelsa and *M. kermadecensis*
Plumbago auriculata
Raphiolepis indica and *R. × delacouri*
Rondeletia amoena
SACRED BAMBOO (*Nandina domestica*)
Viburnum odoratissimum and *V. tinus*
Westringia fruticosa

Conifers as hedges

Many coniferous trees make excellent hedges. Don't prune too drastically or new growth will not be made and you will expose the old, brown, growth at the centre and base. Over-pruning can cause dieback in coniferous hedges; the best method is to trim top shoots and outer growth lightly as required, with a more thorough pruning of old wood in early winter when no sap is rising. Those forms with tops which are very pointed or rounded are unsuitable as the effect would be uneven (though possibly novel!). Types which have some horizontal spread and can be readily trimmed across the top for an even effect are best. Those conifers which are particularly suitable are: BOOKLEAF and dwarf BOOKLEAF pines (*Thuja orientalis*), *Thuja occidentalis*, *Cupressus macrocarpa* (a very tough hedge), BHUTAN CYPRESS (*Cupressus torulosa*) and its dwarf form, *Chamaecyparis lawsoniana*, and the taller-growing horizontal cypress types such as *Cupressus glabra aurea*.

Colourful foliage

Hedges don't have to be green. Dramatic effects can be created in landscaping by planting hedges with foliage which is colourful for all or part of the year. One of the most spectacular hot-climate hedging plants is POINSETTIA (*Euphorbia pulcherrima*) with its large, vibrant red or cream bracts.

Gold/yellow

Cupressus macrocarpa 'AUREA' ST
Duranta 'SHEENA'S GOLD' and 'AUSSIE 2000'
Euonymus fortunei and *E. japonicus*
GOLDEN PRIVET (*Ligustrum ovalifolium* 'AUREUM')
Melaleuca 'REVOLUTION GOLD'
Metrosideros kermadecensis gold and variegated forms
POINSETTIA (*Euphorbia pulcherrima*)
Thuja orientalis gold forms

Red

Acalypha wilkesiana (coppery-red and orange)
Alternanthera dentata
Berberis 'RUBY GLOW' (ST; colour not as vivid in warm climates)
Lilly pillies, austromyrtus and other Australian native shrubs with red new growth. Outstanding is the dwarf syzygium 'BLAZE' which has vivid red colour throughout the year.

Blue, grey or silver

Chamaecyparis 'BOULEVARD'
LAVENDER (*Lavandula* SPP.) ST (French lavender best tolerates humidity)
Westringia fruticosa
WORMWOOD (*Artemisia absinthium*)

Hedges which will grow in shade

Abelia SPP.	*Nandina domestica*
Azaleas	*Raphiolepis indica*
Bauera rubioides	*Viburnum tinus*
Coprosma repens	
Ixora chinensis and	
I. coccinea	

CARE AND CULTIVATION

The main challenge with developing a good hedge, quickly, is to ensure that plants remain at the same height, density and state of health. Height uniformity is maintained by trimming, density by tip-pruning; adding plenty of nitrogen-rich fertiliser will help promote bushiness and foliage colour. Unhealthy plants which lag behind the rest and do not respond quickly to remedial treatment should be promptly replaced.

Spacing depends on the type of plant but planting too close is usually better than planting too far apart. As a general guide, plants used for hedges should be spaced one quarter of the average width of a free-standing specimen apart; for example, a free-standing plant width of 2.5 m will require a spacing of 60 cm. Hedge shrubs need heavier feeding and watering than single specimens because they are in closer competition with one another.

Although the fast rate of plant growth in a hot climate means hedges can be established very quickly, it also means they need fairly constant pruning to keep them in shape. Novice gardeners usually need advice on pruning hedges, mainly because they are inclined either to leave pruning for the first year or so in favour of height, or else are too severe. A middle way is desirable. It is better to sacrifice height in order to develop a well-formed, bushy hedge, so light pruning only should be done in the first year or two. After that, prune regularly for size and shape.

The degree of pruning depends on the type of hedge. Formal hedges obviously require meticulous and frequent pruning, while rampant-growing plants in informal hedges will need to be controlled. Cut back flowering hedges after flowering is over; the method depends on the shrub's requirements. Some hedges such as GOLDEN PRIVET and plumbago should be cut back hard to about 30 cm high after planting and pruned hard for the first two years.

SCREENS

Screens differ from hedges in that they do not necessarily have to be pruned to shape. They act as a buffer zone between one area or another, block out undesirable sight or sound, and even keep traffic fumes at bay on a busy street.

The usual requirements for screening plants is that they be reasonably tall, tough, fast-growing, dense enough to do the job, and with foliage to ground level. Delicate plants, those which cannot stand exposure and those with high water or other cultivation requirements are obviously unsuitable. The idea with a foliage screen is that, once established, it will look after itself.

Screens can consist of a single plant species but it is generally better if several plants are used. Not only does this tend to look bushlike and natural, it also means that plants of different heights and densities will provide more efficient screening. This is particularly true of noise and pollution buffers, which need to be thick rather than high. A variety of plants also means that even if some do not do so well, the risk of losing the screen is minimised.

Plants for screens

Acacias (select long-lived species such as *A. aulococarpa*, *A. floribunda*, *A. harpophylla*, *A. melanoxylon*)
Acalypha SPP.
  A. wilkesiana
Bamboo (those with non-rampant root systems only should be used in small gardens; a clumping bamboo with a phenomenal growth rate is *B. oldhamii* which can grow to 18 m)

Casuarinas and allocasuarinas	*Melaleuca* SPP.
	Nerium oleander
Coprosma repens	*Pittosporum* SPP.
Glochidion ferdinandi	*Rondeletia amoena*
(CHEESE TREE)	Sugarcane
Leptospermum laevigatum	*Syzygium* SPP.

Fast-growing species

Acalypha	*Pittosporum*
Austromyrtus	*Plumbago*
BOUGAINVILLEA	POINSETTIA
Brunfelsia	*Streptosolen* SPP. syn.
Callistemon	*Browallia*
Hibiscus	*Syzygium*
HONEYSUCKLE	*Viburnum*
Melaleuca 'REVOLUTION GREEN' and 'REVOLUTION GOLD'	*Westringia*

Lawns and groundcovers

LAWNS

IN MOST GARDENS A LAWN IS THE MAJOR FEATURE around which all other features are established. A lawn is the simplest yet most dramatic way of 'setting off' a house; it also provides an attractively surfaced area of multi-use open space. When the weather is warm, an expanse of soft, green lawn has a cool, refreshing effect. To sit outside on the grass in the evening, when the heat of the sun begins to fade, is one of the delights of living in the tropics or sub-tropics.

Having said that, maintaining your lawn in good condition can be hard work in a hot climate. The grass grows fast — and so do the weeds. Even in areas with heavy seasonal rainfall, the evaporation rate is so high that frequent watering is needed. The sun fades the colour of all but the most persistent grasses. Above all, the work required in weeding, fertilising and mowing can seem much harder in the sweltering heat of a humid summer.

Is it worth it? Obviously gardeners think it is, judging by the number of fine lawns which can be seen around our suburbs. In this chapter, I try to show gardeners how to create and maintain the best lawns with minimum effort.

The secret is good preparation to ensure that a top quality lawn is established in the first place. This means hard work up front, and a fair bit of maintenance thereafter, but the results are worth it because if a lawn is worth growing, then it is worth growing well. The alternative is an area of patchy, weed-ridden, troublesome grass which drags down the appearance of the house and the rest of the garden.

The following steps are those which need to be taken when establishing a lawn. Any one of them (except planting!) may be omitted according to individual circumstances or inclination; the result may be an acceptable lawn, but an unsatisfactory long-term result is more likely.

If it looks like too much hard work, consider employing a contractor to do it for you. Money spent now will save time, trouble and more money later on.

DRAINAGE

Water which is unable to drain freely will swamp grass roots and, as it stagnates, possibly infect them with disease. The result is an unhealthy or dying lawn. The problem is most common on clay soils. The most drastic solution is to lay agricultural pipes to provide drainage, but because this is costly and beyond the scope of the average gardener it should only be considered by those keen gardeners to whom any trouble and expense is worthwhile. Less drastically, gypsum can be used (at the rate recommended on the packet) to improve the porosity of the clay, then a good quality loam topsoil laid over it to a depth of about 10 cm. If the clay is not too solid, the surface can be lightly but thoroughly dug over and mixed with the imported soil if desired. Or a layer of ash or coarse sand can be laid between the clay surface and the imported topsoil. This combination should provide adequate drainage clear of grass roots.

Much depends on the topography; a sloping lawn will drain more freely than one established on flat ground; the greater the degree of slope, the more freely the lawn will drain. In such cases, a working over of the topsoil with imported soil or sand, or merely the addition of a layer of good topsoil, will be enough.

Very light, sandy soils are also a problem when establishing a lawn, because they are too free-draining for grass roots to take up enough water and will dry out fast, particularly in hot periods when evaporation is high. To improve moisture retention, imported topsoil or compost should be worked into the soil to a depth of about 10 cm.

SOIL BASE AND LEVELLING

The soil base will depend on the natural soil and its drainage. It is not uncommon for turf to be laid directly on to very heavy or very sandy soils with little or no preparation, and for an apparently satisfactory lawn to result. In the former case, unless the ground is sloping, problems caused by poor drainage are likely to result. In the latter case, the lawn will require prodigious amounts of water to stay alive. In both cases, exceptionally large amounts of fertiliser will have to be applied for continued growth. A good lawn requires an underlying soil which is loamy, with a fine tilth. Unless you already have this kind of soil already, you will need to bring it in.

Break up any large clods and level the surface. A lawn does not have to be absolutely flat; indeed a sloping lawn can add interest to the garden and, as has already been stated, is better drained. But the soil surface needs to be reasonably level, with any bumps or dips evened out. You can hire a roller or use a large rake, a heavy piece of timber attached to ropes or chains, and dragged over the ground, or any other method you can devise, even tramping over the ground and firming it with your feet. The advantage of a roller is that it consolidates the soil into a condition firm enough for seed germination or good root development of turves.

The prepared soil may appear to be free of weeds but seeds may be in the ground, or may blow or creep in from elsewhere. To prevent future problems, a thorough spraying of existing weeds with an appropriate control, and/or treatment with a pre-emergent weedicide is recommended at this stage. If this results in a lot of dead weeds, remove them. Compost added to the topsoil will ensure nutrition over a prolonged period; the compost should be a fine humus, free of coarse material. Most soils in our tropical and sub-tropical populated areas, such as the seacoasts and adjacent mountains, tend to be acid. You will need to raise the pH level above 5.5 by digging dolomite into the soil. After about a month, apply a lawn starter fertiliser and give a final rake over, preparatory to planting.

PLANTING

'Planting' is not exactly the correct word to use for establishing a lawn, because grass is 'planted' by sowing seed, turfing or sprigging. Before you begin check that the soil base is free of any late-emerging weeds.

Seed should be sown in mid–late autumn so that the new lawn does not have to battle against summer heat and monsoon rainfall. Choose a windless day and broadcast seed evenly by mixing it with fine sand. Try to work to a grid pattern; up and down one way, then the same crossways, so that the seed is evenly spread across the soil base. Rake it lightly and water in gently by hand or with sprinklers. The area should be watered once a day until a green fuzz of new shoots appears, more frequently if weather is very hot, dry and windy.

The lawn seed mixes available from your garden centre should be appropriate to your area but check the packet or ask for advice. These will be warm season types; an admixture of grasses, probably with green or blue couch predominant. They will be marketed under different brand names, with some very fast-growing varieties now available. Some contain 'extras' such as the naturally occurring beneficial fungus Endophyte which produces an insect-repelling toxin.

Turfing requires less work than seeding, particularly if it is laid by a contractor. If you are doing it yourself, you can lay it at any time of year but pick a cool time of day, preferably early morning. The range of turf is limited; the supplier will be able to advise on what is most suited to your needs. The turf will be delivered in rolls; keep them moist if you can't lay it immediately and then unroll carefully. Lay the turf as you would carpet, making sure there are no gaps between the strips and cutting the rolls if necessary so that the crossways joins don't match in one uninterrupted line. Water well after laying and continue watering once or twice a day, depending on weather conditions, for about a week.

Don't be too eager to mow the newly laid lawn.

Unless growth is unusually lush during the cooler dry season, mowing can be left until late spring; this is also the time when the fertiliser regime should begin.

Sprigging is the more time-consuming method of planting a lawn. You can take sprigs from other lawns or from buying a few turves and breaking them up into small sprigs. Only stoloniferous grasses, which spread by surface runners, can be successfully established this way. Sprigging should be done early in the growing season, spring to early summer, when the runners can quickly establish themselves.

The soil bed should be prepared as I have described and the sprigs planted about 30 cm apart. Plant each sprig by laying it flat and covering most of the runner, except the green tip, with soil, then firming in by hand. Water well for the first week and fertilise every six weeks.

In some areas, professional lawn sprigging services are available. One such service uses sands from coastal back-dunes, which contain quite a lot of organic matter, as an undersurface. The sand is less coarse than river sand, has more body and produces a better lawn. The sprigging technique produces a very flat, even surface with full coverage within six weeks. Cost is about half that of turfing.

Types of lawn

Buffalo grass
A very tough, coarse, close-growing grass which requires regular mowing or it becomes unsightly. A good grass for areas with poor soil and the colour does not fade in strong sunlight.

Carpet grass
This is the best performer in the tropics and does well in the sub-tropics too. There are two kinds, broad and narrow-leaved, though both types have much broader blades and a more open growth habit than the couch grasses. Carpet grass needs year-round warmth so grows less vigorously in the sub-tropical winter. It requires plenty of water. Because it has a coarse appearance, carpet grass is best used on large lawn areas. Its main disadvantage is its open growth habit which allows weeds to invade. A good grass if you want a tough, reliable performer which won't require too much maintenance.

Couch
The best warm-season grasses for hot climates are varieties of the common green couch or Queensland blue couch, or mixes in which these predominate. Green couch runners spread quickly and it is a dense-growing, tough grass which smothers weeds if well cared for and tolerates both hot sun and dry periods, once established. Queensland blue couch is similar but has a finer leaf with a bluish tinge. This grass is less suited to the tropics than green couch, though it is better able to withstand dry periods.

Cough grass
A low water-use grass which is hardy and handles heavy traffic. Goes brown in winter. Sun only.

Dawson grass
A tropical lawn grass which does well in sub-tropical areas also and is very tough and adaptable, with a fine, dense texture. Colour is blue-green and holds well even on poor soils. Dawson is a stoloniferous (long runner) grass but is not invasive like kikuyu. It is resistant to drought and thus needs less watering than other lawn grasses, less fertiliser, and the grass is not troubled by insects or disease. It comes in a seed pack especially designed for easy spreading; 500 g covers 250 m^2 so it is economical to establish.

Kikuyu grass
This is an aggressive, highly invasive, coarse grass which grows well in the cooler, mountain areas of the tropics and sub-tropics. It requires little maintenance but cannot be cut very low or the exposed grass stalks turn pale. Though resistant to frost it will brown off.

Shadegro
This is one of the better grasses designed to grow in shade. Shadegro is a tufted grass which makes a dense, persistent short lawn even under heavy shade conditions. It is naturally short and dense in habit, becoming more so with heavy traffic, and requires mowing only about twice a year. Grows on all soils.

Sweet smother
A good grass for shady areas in the sub-tropics

Smartgrass
This grass has been especially developed for hot, dry areas and consists of tall fescues, sometimes treated to ensure greenness in all conditions. It contains Endophyte.

Two other popular lawn grasses are WINTERGREEN and GREENLEES PARK.

Blends

Most grass seed purchased at garden centres consists of blends of improved turf grasses such as Kentucky bluegrass, perennial ryegrass, fescues and chewings. These do not have to be mown as often as couch, make a thick and cushiony lawn, but need plenty of water. They are sold under names such as Sun and Shade, or Mowless.

LAWN CARE

Lawns need a lot of mowing during the summer months and an occasional light trim in the cool season. It is a common mistake to mow lawns too short; this exposes grass roots to burning by direct sunlight and opens the way to disease. Instead, just skim the surface as often as is needed to keep the lawn neat and tidy. Grass clippings should be collected in the catcher and either used as compost, mulch for shrubberies and beds, or otherwise disposed of. Never mow when the grass is wet; this is bad for both the lawn and the mower.

Lawns need a lot of water in a hot climate. As with all plants, a deep soaking with the sprinklers once or twice a week in dry weather, to encourage deep root development, is better than a light daily sprinkling. In hot, dry weather and when the lawn is established on very light soil, such as coastal sand dunes, watering at least twice a week will be necessary. Sprinklers are the easiest way to water a lawn but a more water-conserving method is to flood the lawn thoroughly with a garden hose once or twice a week.

To remain green and growing, a lawn needs to be fed regularly. Several brands of fertiliser especially formulated for lawns are available, with the high-nitrogen content required for healthy lawn growth. Particularly recommended are organic granules made from chicken litter which are easy to handle and have a controlled-release action that feeds the lawn and improves the soil for months.

As fertiliser breaks down quickly in hot climates, regular and frequent applications are required. The best regime is to use a complete lawn food at the beginning and end of the growing season, and a nitrogen-rich fertiliser every six weeks in between. Many lawn specific fertilisers contain sulphate of ammonia which helps repel broad-leaf weeds.

A healthy lawn which is well-watered and fertilised is less likely to be invaded by weeds than one which is neglected. Lawn weeds grow vigorously in a hot climate and will invade even the best tended lawns. All can be controlled by using a proprietary brand weedkiller; check the packet to see that the contents are suitable to your particular weed problem as treatments for broad-leaf and other types of weeds can differ. General herbicides such as glyphosate (marketed as Round-up, Zero, etc.), will certainly kill weeds but cannot be sprayed because they will also kill the grass. Instead apply to each weed by hand with a sponge (wearing gloves!) or a weeding wand. Using a specific weedicide in lawns is the better method.

IMPROVING AN EXISTING LAWN

If your lawn is far from perfect, you can replace it by digging it up or, more easily, spraying it with a herbicide such as glyphosate and then removing the dead grass. Then follow the steps outlined here. If you don't want to take such a drastic step, improvements can still be made to the existing lawn, provided there isn't a major problem such as very poor drainage.

First, assess whether there are any disease problems and treat accordingly. Then get rid of weeds. The next step is to top-dress the lawn by applying a light but sufficient cover of sandy loam, filling in any holes, smoothing down any mounds and allowing grass tips just to protrude above the new soil. This can be done at any time of year but it is best in late spring or early summer, before the main growing period and seasonal rainfall. If you know that the underlying soil is very poor and thin, mix a light compost through the loam to add soil bulk. After top-dressing, apply a complete lawn fertiliser and water well for the next week. If lawn grass has become very thin, it can be thickened by re-seeding or sprigging. This is not a bad idea anyway with old lawns as the new, improved seed mixes produce better quality lawns.

A combination of fast germinating grass seeds, fertiliser and recycled paper mulch, such as Easy-Grass, is useful for filling in bare patches, reseeding or rejuvenating a lawn. It is very easy to apply and grows within two weeks.

LAWN ALTERNATIVES

Lawn alternatives should be considered

- ❖ When the underlying surface is rock, shale or very heavy clay and you don't wish, or cannot afford, to overlay it with sufficient topsoil to grow a lawn.
- ❖ When gardens are developed on coastal sand dunes. Trying to maintain a lawn on sand is very consuming of time, water and fertiliser. Water run-off into nearby swamps and bushland can overdose and often kill the natural vegetation with a too-rich supply of nutrients. In these areas it is more environmentally sympathetic to develop a garden which does not require large amounts of fertiliser.
- ❖ When gardens are on very steep hillsides.
- ❖ When you don't want the work involved in mowing and otherwise maintaining a lawn.

Groundcover plants

Groundcovers are spreading plants which creep over the surface of the ground, such as condamine couch; very low-growing or prostrate shrubs or herbaceous plants which can be planted close together for a groundcovering effect, such as ajuga; or shrubs with a low, horizontally spreading growth habit such as *Juniperus horizontalis*. The first category can include plants generally thought of as climbers, such as jasmines, honeysuckles, ivies and *Ficus pumila*. In fact many low-growing types of plant can be used to cover the ground; these include hostas, ferns and almost any very small shrub or herbaceous plant. The following lists are limited to plants which are commonly considered as essentially groundcovering in habit and are, for the most part, planted for that purpose. Most can be easily walked over and these are designated in the lists as 'ground-hugging'. Exceptions include the prostrate junipers and some grevilleas. These should be placed where low, dense, coverage is required but where people do not need to walk.

Groundcovers which make good lawn alternatives

CONDAMINE COUCH (*Phyla nodiflora*, syn. *lippia*)
A good lawn alternative for coastal areas and those with dry, sandy soils. Can be mown. White or pink flowers.

DRYARNA
A tough, fast-growing native grass which makes an excellent lawn. Tolerates both drought and waterlogging.

KANGAROO GRASS (*Themeda triandra*)
Popular, ornamental landscaping grass which forms large tussocks if not mown and tolerates some shade. Good for filling in difficult areas.

MONDO and MINI MONDO GRASS (*Ophiopogon japonicus*)
Dark green leaves, 'cushiony' appearance. Very handsome landscaping plant, black form is unusual.

SEASIDE DAISY (*Erigeron karvinskianus*)
Very good for coastal gardens. White flowers.

WALLABY GRASS (*Danthonia* SPP.)
A drought-tolerant species for sun or semi-shade which does well on poor soils. Can be mown or left to reach its full height of 15 cm; should not be cut to less than 2 cm. Low-wear situations only.

WEEPING GRASS (*Microleana stipoides*)
A dark-green native grass which makes an excellent lawn that thrives in shade. Compact growth, requiring low maintenance.

Zoysia SPP. (*Z. japonica*, *Z. tenuifolia*, *Z. mattrella*)
Grass-type plant, can be mown.

Groundcovers for sunny spots

GH — ground-hugging

Ajuga reptans (CARPET BUGLE)
Colourful foliage, mauve or blue flowers. Dense. Good for borders. GH

Artemisia schmidtiana 'NANA'
Very pretty, silvery, fern-like foliage. Good for banks. GH

Chrysocephalum apiculatum 'RAMOSISSIMUM FORM' syn. *Helichrysum ramosissimum*
Dense, suckering plant with gold flowers. Other low-growing daisies also make good groundcovers and do well in dry areas.

Coprosma × *kirkii* 'VARIEGATA'
Handsome, glossy foliage. Good for seaside conditions. GH

Erigeron SPP.
Lower-growing species of these daisy-type plants make excellent groundcovers and most do well in dry areas. Various species and cultivars available with white, gold, yellow or pink flowers.

Gazania ringens
Spreading plant with many flowers in a variety of colours. Very tough performer and tolerates dry or seaside conditions. A very popular groundcover.

Geranium 'JOHNSON'S BLUE'
This one of several creeping geraniums which make good groundcovers. Blue flowers.

Goodenia hederacea
Trailing Australian plant with yellow flowers. Other groundcover goodenias include *G. rotundifolia* and the prostrate form of *G. ovata*. All good for dry areas.

Grevillea SPP
There are many excellent, fast-growing grevilleas which are ground-hugging or prostrate in habit. They include *G. curviloba*, *G. lanigera* 'MT TAMBORITHA', *G. juniperina* hybrids and cultivars. All produce plenty of attractive flowers.

Hardenbergia violacea
Trailing and dense native plant with blue flowers. Tolerates dry conditions. GH

Juniperus SPP. (JUNIPER)
There are several low-growing, spreading junipers which can be used as groundcovers. They look very attractive and are tolerant of most conditions. Those which do well in hot climates are listed on pages 83–4.

Lantana montevidensis
A low-growing shrub with trailing stems and mauve-blue or white flowers throughout the year. Very tough in most conditions. Good for banks.

Liriope spicata
Spreading, grass-like plant with mauve flowers. Frost hardy. GH

Mesembryanthemum SPP.
Succulent plants with large, colourful flowers in a variety of colours. Best on coast, where sea breezes dispel humidity, or in drier areas.

Myoporum parvifolium (BOOBIALLA)
Very dense, ground-hugging plant with white flowers all year

Nierembergia repens
A dense-growing plant with tiny, open-faced white flowers in spring and summer. Very tough in difficult situations such as paving cracks because it requires little soil.

Oenothera SPP. (EVENING PRIMROSE)
Not really a plant for the tropics but grows well in the sub-tropics. Pink flowers. Other suitable oenothera species are *O. pallida* (white flowers) and *O. caespitosa* (yellow flowers). All are frost hardy and do best in seaside or drier inland areas.

Portulaca SPP. (SUN PLANT)
Very tough succulents which tolerate any conditions except overwatering. Long-flowering in a range of vivid hues. Good for banks. Marketed under various varietal names, usually with the word 'sun' attached; e.g. Sundance, Sunnyside and Sun Jewells.

Pultenea pedunculata (BUSH PEA, PYALONG GOLD)
Creeping Australian groundcover with soft foliage and bright yellow flowers. *P. spinosa* is similar. Both need excellent drainage and are good in dry areas.

Scaevola SPP. (FAN FLOWERS)
Compact, spreading, Australian ground-hugging plants with blue, pink, white or mauve flowers

SWAMP FOXTAIL (*Pennisetum alopecuroides*)
A native tussock grass with large, ornamental, purplish-brown flowerheads. Thrives in most soils and tolerates some waterlogging.

Tradescantia fluminensis (WANDERING JEW)
A very popular tropical and sub-tropical groundcover with purple-tinged green leaves. Very vigorous. Good for banks and withstands most conditions except cold. Several forms available. Another popular tradescantia is *T. zebrina* which has leaves striped white, pink, red and green. Very decorative and vigorous. These are good plants for quickly covering large areas but can become rather rampant and may need control.

Wedelia trilobata (SINGAPORE DAISY)
One of the most popular groundcovers for hot climates. Produces fast-growing runners topped with yellow, daisy-like flowers. Tough in most conditions but tends to be rampant. Widely used in landscaping. GH

Groundcovers for shady spots

Dampiera hederacea
Trailing perennial. Blue flowers. Frost hardy.

Hibbertia SPP. (GUINEA FLOWER)
Hibbertia scandens, *H. serpyllifolia*, *H. stellaris*, *H. ovata* and other hibbertias are Australian plants which do well in most conditions. They make excellent groundcovers and some are also used as climbers. Yellow flowers.

Pilea nummulariifolia (CREEPING CHARLIE)
A creeping foliage plant with small, crinkled, mint-like leaves. Quite tropical. *P. cadierei* (ALUMINIUM PLANT) is larger-growing, with strikingly variegated leaves. GH

Plectranthus australis
Mat-forming plant with crinkled leaves and pale mauve spring flowers. Good, fast-growing cover for large areas.

Vinca major (GREATER PERIWINKLE)
This frost-hardy plant with dainty blue flowers can be grown in the sub-tropics if given a cool, shady spot and watered frequently. GH

Viola hederacea (NATIVE VIOLET)
A delicate Australian groundcover which bears purple flowers throughout the year. GH

Groundcovers for damp areas

Gunnera magellanica
Succulent plant which forms a dense mat. Full sun. GH

Lobelia membranacea
Suckering, fast-spreading Australian groundcover with blue flowers. GH

Mimulus repens
Prostrate plant with many white flowers. Full sun.

Pratia pedunculata
Australian matting plant with tiny blue flowers throughout the year. GH

Selaginella SPP.
Moss-like plant with ferny foliage. Semi-shade. Variegated forms available.

Viola hederacea

Climbers used as groundcovers

Certain vigorous climbing plants are particularly suited to covering steep banks where they can trail on the ground, forming a dense cover, or hang over retaining walls. They include:

Allamanda cathartica (sun)
BOUGAINVILLEA (sun)
Calliandra tweedii 'HORIZONTALIS'
Ficus pumila (small banks only as this is rather slow growing, sun or shade)
HONEYSUCKLE (*Lonicera* SPP.) (sun or light shade)
IVY (*Hedera helix*) (shade)
STAR JASMINE (*Trachelospermum jasminoides*)
See also pages 115–21.

6
A productive garden

Fruit

HOT-CLIMATE GARDENERS ARE FORTUNATE in being able to grow a wide range of tropical and sub-tropical fruit trees at home. Exotic fruits which were once unknown to us, such as the sapote and carambola, now take their places in the garden alongside old favourites such as citrus and mango. As well as being productive, these trees are also ornamental.

No special skill or knowledge is required to grow tropical exotic fruit trees. For the most part treat them as you would any tree or shrub, with a little extra care during fruiting. The main thing to remember is that if you grow fruit trees you are required by law to protect them against fruit fly. Home gardeners who don't do so are assisting the spread of this major pest of commercial orchards.

The following fruit and nut trees have been selected as being the most popular and easiest to grow in a hot climate. I have mentioned some varieties but new, improved varieties are regularly being introduced to the market, sometimes, but not always, replacing old favourites, so it is always worthwhile discussing your choice with your local nursery. Unless stated otherwise, most of these trees can stand some dry periods in areas where there is reliable summer (and some winter) rainfall.

AVOCADO (*Persea americana*)
MEXICO AND GUATEMALA

Avocados can be grown in many parts of Australia and have long been a garden favourite. Dwarf varieties are particularly recommended. You need plant only one tree provided it is an 'A'-type pollinator. The avocado tree has an odd habit — its flowers change sex every day, some in the daytime, some more shyly at night. 'A'-type varieties change during the middle of the day so there is overlap of male and female flowers on the tree at that time, thus facilitating pollination. The best known avocado variety in Australia is 'HASS', a tall growing tree which requires deep soil and is also frost tender. Dwarf types 'RINCON' and 'WURTZ' bear a pear shaped and sized fruit in the second year.

FRUITS Rounded, oval or pear-shaped. Green, or green-turning-dark mauve to almost black

CULTIVATION Good drainage. Rich, well-composted soil. Fertilise young trees with a high-nitrogen fertiliser at the recommended rate (usually about 100 g a tree) every three months in the growing season, increasing to about 3 kg at maturity. Over-fertilising with nitrogen will produce too much foliage at the expense of fruit; apply a small amount in late spring, the main feeding in mid-summer and another small amount in late summer. Avocado trees can withstand dry periods but will only set good fruit if adequately watered. Young trees need regular, deep watering. Plant only accredited nursery trees free from root rot diseases. Subject to anthracnose in tropical areas, see page 228.

CARAMBOLA (*Averrhoa carambola*) also known as FIVE CORNERED FRUIT
INDONESIA AND TROPICAL ASIA

This is a very decorative fruit with five, large, yellow-golden segments which have been described as tasting somewhere between a peach, an apple and a pear. Although tropical in origin, and still preferring plenty of warmth and humidity, the carambola grows well in the sub-tropics. Trees bear usually in the second year, sometimes not until the third year. Fruit set can be adversely affected by wind, particularly dry winds, which stops pollination, so protection is crucial. Grafted varieties from Florida and Asia are excellent for home-growing. All varieties produce some fruit without pollination but the recommended varieties are self-pollinating and buyers should ask for these; namely 'Fwang Tung', 'Thai King', 'B8', 'B6', 'Arkin' and 'Hart'.

CULTIVATION In the sub-tropics plant between mid-spring and mid-summer. Water well at establishment and ensure adequate water thereafter. Light, not overly rich soil will do. Add some manure once or twice a year, plus late spring, mid-summer and late summer dressings of low-nitrogen NPK at about 100 g a tree.

CUSTARD APPLE AND CHERIMOYA (*Annona atemoya* and *A. cherimola*)
SOUTH AND CENTRAL AMERICA

There has been some confusion about the name of what Australians regard as the common custard apple. *A. atemoya* is a species name invented in this country for our hybrid custard apple which is actually a cross between *A. squamosa* and *A. cherimola*. Although in true nomenclature the name *A. atemoya* should not exist, let alone represent a hybrid species, it has been accepted internationally for the Australian custard apple types and is now used to describe 'Hillary's Pink Mammoth' and 'African Pride'.

The cherimoya is a cold-tolerant custard apple and the variety 'Deliciosa' has been documented as tolerating cold down to –6°C for up to three hours. Most cherimoya varieties will tolerate down to –3°C (air temperature) but need stem protection from ground level frosts. Leaves are hairier than those of other custard apples, which assists the cold-hardiness. The fruits are bigger and the tree itself is bigger and very vigorous, which can be a disadvantage in a small garden. It takes 4–5 years to set fruit. Same pruning technique and regime as for custard apples.

Today's custard apple varieties give some fruit in the second year. 'Hillary's Pink Mammoth', sometimes wrongly called 'Bullock's Heart' in South-East Queensland, is a particularly early-bearing selection of 'Pinks Mammoth', the best-eating cultivar.

CULTIVATION Deep, humus-enriched, very well-drained soil. Plenty of water is required, particularly during flowering and fruit-setting, which means watering during the cool season. Atemoyas are particularly prone to dehydration and should never go without water for long. Fertilise young trees with animal manure and about 50 g of high-potassium fertiliser applied once a month from the start of spring all through summer. The rate should be increased to the rate of 1 kg per year of age each year, with no further increase after the tree reaches maturity at 10 years.

The main disease which attacks custard apples or cherimoyas is the root disease, bacterial wilt, in hot tropical conditions. Ask for grafted trees on resistant rootstock.

PRUNING The secret to good-cropping custard apples is regular pruning of young plants to force a compact tree with multiple branches. A light spring pruning is followed by regular pruning during the summer growing period, but this must be done the right way. New branches should be cut to about 30 cm, removing the top two leaves. A new bud develops underneath the leaf stalk (not in the axil or angle between the leaf stalk and stem, as is the case with most plants). This 'underside' development offers protection to the tender bud so it is important that these trees have good wind protection, particularly during winter, as exposed leaf buds can be cold-damaged.

DAVIDSON'S PLUM (*Davidsonia pruriens*)
AUSTRALIA

This is a rainforest tree which produces plum-sized, blue-black fruits which are edible. Trees which have been improved by selection and have sweeter fruits than bush-grown types can sometimes be obtained from nurseries. Otherwise, the fruit is rather sour but can be stewed for pies and other fruit dishes, preserved as jam or made into wine or cordial.

CULTIVATION Plant in a sheltered position in light, humus-enriched soil which has been given additional fertility with animal manure or compost. Though further fertilising is not really necessary, growth will be faster if the young tree is given three or four dressings a year of a balanced NPK fertiliser, at the rate recommended for trees and shrubs. Water well during establishment, and give occasional deep soakings during very dry periods. Pruning is unnecessary though tip pruning when young will improve bushiness.

FIG (*Ficus carica*)
ASIA MINOR AND THE MEDITERRANEAN
Figs are usually grown only in dryish, mediterranean-type climates. However, varieties such as 'RED CONADRIA' have been evolved to grow in the tropics and sub-tropics. 'RED CONADRIA' is a well-flavoured variety which matures early and has the longest picking season of any fig. The secret for good fruiting is pruning each branch back hard to two base buds in July each year, trimming the whole tree to about ½–1 m. A good garden performer.

CULTIVATION Plant in winter in light, humus-enriched soil. Water well at establishment but thereafter only sparingly, during long, dry periods. No watering is required in winter unless the season is unusually dry. If the planting hole is well-prepared with about 10 g of animal manure and/or compost, dug well in, you will probably not need to fertilise again until the following season, when further manure or a 2–kg application of balanced fertiliser should be applied. Where soils are very poor, or growth very fast, an occasional light side-dressing of NPK fertiliser should be applied during the growing season.

PRUNING Tip-prune in spring, then prune fairly thoroughly after fruiting, removing old, crowded branches and long stems.

GUAVA (*Psidium guajava*)
TROPICAL SOUTH AMERICA

The Indian-bred guava fruits during winter when there is no fruitfly activity. Summer-fruiting Hawaiian varieties can be protected by bagging the fruit. Cherry guavas are popular and crop twice a year; the yellow cherry guava is a dwarf and ideal for the home garden, with a very sweet fruit. Guavas are yellow when ripe, up to 5 cm in diameter, with creamy-white or pink flesh. Unripe, still-green fruits can be picked and cooked.

CULTIVATION Plant during warm weather. Any fertile soil will do but growth is best in a light, humus-enriched soil. Fertilise with a high-nitrogen (22:5:8) NPK mix. Apply just before flowering, and as this depends on the variety, see if this information is available on the label. As a general guide, fertilise in early spring at the rate of about 1 kg, then again in late summer before fruit sets. Water well during establishment and during long, dry periods. Will withstand some waterlogging.

PRUNING Guavas should be well pruned in spring for shape and size, after all danger of frost is over. Trim into a bush or vase shape, keeping plenty of the small, fruit-bearing twigs which grow inside the canopy.

JABOTICABA (*Myrciaria cauliflora*)
BRAZIL
This is an excellent garden specimen with neat foliage; very good for landscaping. The fruits are a bit like large grapes, dark and purplish, with a thick skin and white flesh. Quite tasty and refreshing. Jaboticabas take about 3–4 years to fruit in the sub-tropics and 2–3 years in the tropics. Fruiting depends on tree size — the tree needs to be 1½ to 2 m high with a 5cm diameter trunk at base for fruiting to start.

CULTIVATION Jaboticabas are heavy potassium feeders so dressings of potash should be given. Otherwise they should be treated much like citrus in cultivation.

LYCHEE (*Litchie chinensis*)
CHINA
LONGAN (*Euphoria longan*)
In many ways alike, lychees, longans and the similar rambutan are all members of the same family. The longan is a stronger tree and grows better in a cold climate but at the same time is more frost-susceptible than the lychee. The lychee has a rougher and more pimply skin and a red fruit; that of the longan is a yellow-to-brown caramel colour. The longan fruit, though sweet, tends to be something of an acquired taste and the lychee is generally considered superior as a fresh fruit. Longans flower and produce fruit in 2–3 years. Lychees are mostly sub-tropical; they do need a cool rest period in autumn before flowering to optimise fruit set. Both trees are varietal specific to climate but there are no varieties available which fruit in all appropriate climates every year. Lychee 'KWAI MAY' (or 'B3') does best.

CULTIVATION Any moderately fertile soil. Care is needed in fertilising lychees. They only require one-sixth of the nutrients required by other fruit trees; if over-fertilised they tend to go yellow — whereupon gardeners tend to think more fertiliser is needed which can kill the tree. Beware dolomite and lime with lychees, which prefer acid soils. Instead, gypsum can be used to supply calcium because it doesn't alter soil pH. Take care with organic manures which can burn if used excessively. The best regime is a light dressing per tree of about 30 g of 15:4:11 NPK every month, increasing to about 50 g a dressing until tree is bearing. Then apply about 500 g when fruit is almost ripe, and again about two weeks after picking. Lychees and longans will grow in sun or light shade but need protection from strong wind.

MACADAMIA (*Macadamia integrifolia* and *M. tetraphylla*)
AUSTRALIA

Everyone knows Australia's only significant indigenous edible horticultural export and the nuts are a part of our national cuisine. What is less well known, however, is that macadamias make excellent garden shade trees, particularly if pruned for bushiness when young. And despite their rainforest origins, they will tolerate long dry periods. Macadamias are attractive, with long, pendulous white or pink flower spikes. They are easy to grow and most of today's varieties bear in about the third year. Many varieties are now available though those available to the home gardener tend to be limited. Small, compact-growing forms which can be pruned for yield and form are best.
CULTIVATION Plant in well-drained soil which is at least a metre deep. In the home garden, where soil is reasonably fertile and perhaps dressed twice a year in spring and autumn with animal manure or compost, no other fertilising is required. If soil is very infertile, or you want really heavy nut crops, you can apply a nitrogen-rich citrus fertiliser at about 3 kg a tree. When grown in red volcanic soil, macadamias can suffer from phosphate deficiency (where this is not readily available). But in other soils, macadamias, being members of the Proteaceae, family can take up phosphate too readily, so low-phosphate fertilisers only should be applied. The trees need plenty of water at establishment but after that should do well enough with only seasonal rainfall. Sun or light shade. Protection is needed from strong winds. Although some commercial growers now prune heavily, pruning is not really required in the home garden, apart from some early tip-pruning to promote bushinesss.

MANGO (*Mangifera indica*)
EASTERN INDIA AND PARTS OF SOUTH-EAST ASIA
Mangoes need summer rainfall and a dry winter—spring) so that spring flowering can lead to fruit set. In Australia's hotter areas they are a common backyard tree which provides shade, has attractive flowers and new growth, is long living and — in a good year — can bear an abundance of delicious fruit. The most popular variety is 'KENSINGTON PRIDE', also known as the Bowen mango. The Kent × Kensington hybrid variety R2E2 is Australian-bred and less susceptible to cold. The dwarf variety 'PALMER' is a very good, reliable cropper and is ideal for the small home garden. Mangoes are usually grown from the coastal areas of central New South Wales northwards. Further south to about Wollongong the variety 'VALENCIA PRIDE' crops well.
CULTIVATION Mangoes like plenty of water in summer but should be watered sparingly for three months before flowering. Soil should be light and not overly rich; mango trees will stand some waterlogging. Ideal fertiliser mix is NPK 15:3:11, with a total annual application of about 500 g for each year of age, up to a maximum of 5 kg a tree at maturity. Apply to young trees in mid-spring and mid-summer and to bearing trees during early summer, when fruiting, and again in late summer. Grafted varieties are best and bear faster than seed-grown trees. Mangoes are subject to anthracnose in tropical areas, see page 228.

PAWPAW, PAPAYA (*Carica papaya*)
SOUTH AMERICA
This rather palm-like tree grows easily in hot climates, even in poor soils, though it does need good drainage and fertile soils will produce better quality fruit. Male and female trees are usually needed for pollination but self-fertile types are available to home gardeners. The pawpaw is a fast growing backyard tree which can be easily grown from a seed on damp cotton wool — though several seeds will be needed so that there is a good chance of raising male and female plants. Males produce long stalks of clustered small flowers; females have much larger, fleshier flowers on short stems.
CULTIVATION Plant in a well-drained situation, ideally on the protected northern side of a building and water well during establishment; first with at least 4 litres of water and then daily for at least a week thereafter, if weather is dry. Do not plant tree too deeply; just a couple of centimetres of soil covering the roots will do. Prepare soil by adding 2 kg Dynamic Lifter or similar plant food, 200 g gypsum, 5 g borax, 400 g dolomite and 20 g zinc sulphate. The following feeding regime is then recommended: for three months after planting apply 200 g per half m^2 of Dynamic Lifter every 2–3 weeks. Every couple of months from spring to the end of summer apply at the rate of 600 g per half m^2, and twice during the growing season, at the end of spring and at the end of summer, apply 5 g borax per m^2. Do not fertilise in winter and mulch only from spring through to early summer, after which bare ground is best. Even in good soils, particularly red soils, rich in iron, pawpaw trees can suffer boron and zinc deficiencies so remedy accordingly, though with only small doses at a time. Sometimes they also suffer from sudden

dieback, when foliage and stem turn yellow and wither. The only remedy is to cut the tree back to below the infected area; it has been known to grow back.

PERSIMMON (*Diospyros kaki*)
CHINA

The non-astringent varieties of persimmon from Japan can be eaten when green, crisp and crunchy. The fruit reaches maximum sweetness if left to colour fully on the tree, but if there are problems such as bird attack, it can be picked at half colour and still be eaten right away. Pollinators are not needed and one tree in the garden will fruit perfectly well on its own.
CULTIVATION Persimmons are suited only to the sub-tropics where they are best planted in winter; which is also the time they bear fruit. They are not fussy about soils but do best in a light, humus-enriched soil. Water well during estabishment. Fertilise in late winter and early summer with a high potassium 8:4:10 (approximately) NPK mix at the rate of about 500 g a tree.
PRUNING Prune tree to a vase shape, thinning out crowded branches and cutting back only a few of the shoots for later growth; don't prune too drastically or fruiting from the terminal buds on the previous season's growth will be much reduced.

SAPOTE — BLACK (*Diospyros digyna*)
MEXICO
When is a sapote not a sapote? When it is actually an evergreen persimmon, though commonly called black sapote. This is an attractive evergreen bearing large, green-skinned fruit with chocolate-coloured flesh which has a mild, sweet, vaguely chocolaty taste so that it can be used as a substitute for making chocolate-flavoured puddings. It is important to buy grafted self-pollinating varieties such as 'MOSSMAN' and 'BERNICKER'; new varieties are steadily becoming available.
CULTIVATION Much the same as for persimmons, though moisture requirement is higher and the tree should not go without water for long periods.

SAPOTE — WHITE (*Casimiroa edulis*)
MEXICO AND CENTRAL AMERICAN HIGHLANDS
This is no relation at all to the black sapote. Instead it is a highland-originating tree which will grow in Australia from Cairns to Tasmania — but it will only fruit well where it can have a cool, dry, dormancy period to initiate flowering. What it won't tolerate are desert conditions. It is important to buy grafted trees which are self-pollinating such as 'DADE', 'ORTEGO' and 'VISTA'. New varieties are being introduced. The white sapote is a truly delicious fruit, with a rich, banana-ish flavour and very smooth, creamy flesh. Usually fruits vary from green to yellow–orange in skin colour, from small mandarin to large navel orange in size.
CULTIVATION Plant in autumn in reasonably drained soil. Water well during establishment, after which seasonal rainfall should be enough. A light dressing of 250 g a tree of low nitrogen NPK mix will assist growth when the tree is young, perhaps for the first two years. After this, in reasonably fertile soils, additional fertilising is not usually necessary. Young trees need to be pruned back hard from time to time to encourage branching because they tend to be spindly, except 'DADE' which branches naturally.

FROST PROTECTION

Trees such as avocados, guavas, persimmons, black and white sapotes, carambolas, cherimoyas, figs and macadamias can be grown in mountainous or dry inland areas (provided plenty of water is available). However, frost protection of the stem is vital. Although many of these trees can take cold conditions, and even light frosts, heavy ground frosts will ringbark the main trunk and kill them. Frost on surrounding grass or mulch can also be deadly. Wrap the stem in hessian, old cloths, plastic or newspaper (minimum three-sheet thickness), tying or stapling the wrap back on to itself. Do this in late autumn and remove at the end of spring each year, for the first two winters or until the tree canopy protects the trunk. Thin-barked stems of very young trees may also need protection from sun-exposure; they can be wrapped in a light-coloured material or daubed with white paint.

PESTS AND DISEASES

Pest and disease control measures, both chemical and organic, can be found in the Plant Clinic, page 226. Don't be put off growing fruit trees by the number of pests and diseases to which they are susceptible. In the well-tended home garden, few if any of these problems will occur.

OTHER FRUITS

Citrus

So much has been written about citrus trees that it can be confusing for the home gardener, who just wants to grow a few trees with as little trouble as possible. So I will keep it simple, because growing citrus in a hot climate is actually a very simple business, provided a few guidelines are followed.

Citrus are heavy feeders if they are to bear good fruit, and require plenty of water during the growing and fruiting season. The secret to citrus growing is to plant them in light soil, enriched with compost. Their roots must be able to 'get away' readily and good drainage is essential. Most of the problems gardeners encounter with citrus, particularly lemon trees, is that their root are stunted or insufficiently drained. Plant citrus like roses, in a large, shallow hole with a mound in the middle over which the roots can be gently spread. The bud union should be well clear of the ground.

Regular fertilising is necessary. For best results use a high-nitrogen 22:5:8 NPK mix, or a special citrus food, applied at the rate of 250 g a tree, spread under the base of the tree and out beyond the foliage limit to feed the outer roots. This should be increased by a further 500 g each year until the tree is mature at 10 years of age, applied in late winter and late spring. Thereafter, an amount of 5 kg should be applied per tree each year.

Citrus trees usually bear in autumn and winter. They do not need pruning, except for an occasional tidying up. The more vigorous-growing lemon trees such as 'LISBON' will need more pruning as outlined below.

Citrus trees originate in the tropics and most do well there and in the sub-tropics. The best selections are:

GRAPEFRUIT Easy to grow in all warm climates, though trees bear best in hot, desert areas with irrigation. Still a reasonable tree for the tropics and sub-tropics. 'MARSH' is a popular variety.

KUMQUAT A tree which produces small, orange, citrus-type fruit good for pies and marmalade. Very decorative. Best-known varieties are the 'MARUMI' and the 'NAGAMI'.

LEMON The 'EUREKA' lemon is a good-tasting fruit which is best suited for tropical and sub-tropical areas, though the 'LISBON' runs it a close second. The most popular lemon available to home gardeners, however, is the 'MEYER' hybrid which has less flavour than the others. Lemons can be pruned lightly for shape when young and long, unsightly water shoots removed. A 'LEMONADE'-tasting lemon, developed in Brisbane, is a small-growing lemon variety which, as the name implies, makes an excellent drink.

LIME The Tahitian lime is better than the Mexican or West Indian 'key lime' type; fruits are large, juicy, yellowish and the tree is relatively trouble-free. Faster growing than lemons and mandarins.

MANDARIN The most popular citrus because of its good eating qualities. Healthy trees produce very heavy crops. Prune inside growth to allow better light penetration for fruit development. Suitable varieties include 'EMPEROR' (wet tropics), 'HICKSON' (coastal sub-tropics) and 'ELLENDALE' (drier inland areas).

ORANGE Oranges usually do best in hot but fairly dry areas, with irrigation. However varieties such as 'JOPPA' do well in sub-tropical gardens. The 'WASHINGTON NAVEL' and the 'VALENCIA' also do reasonably well and the late-bearing 'VALENCIA' carries fruit through to mid-summer.

PUMMELO, POMMELO Usually a better bearing tree than the grapefruit in the tropics and sub-tropics, where it does exceptionally well. Fruits are very large and good varieties include 'BOS RED', 'SUNSHINE' and the standard 'SHADDOCK'.

TANGELO A cross between mandarin and grapefruit or pummelo and very tasty. Best grown in warm coastal districts.

Common citrus problems

CITRUS LEAF MINER Spray with diazinon.
FRUIT FLY Fenthion spray
SCALE Carbaryl or white oil
BLACK SPOT Triforine
POOR ROOT DEVELOPMENT See planting information.
COLLAR ROT Keep mulch or litter clear of stem. Treat by scraping off affected bark and applying Bordeaux mixture.
LEAF YELLOWING Apply iron chelates; if problem persists ask your garden centre to recommend a trace element mixture.
LEMON SCAB Spray with Bordeaux and white oil when flowering starts, with follow-up treatment of Mancozeb and white oil when flowering finishes.
More information about chemicals and other pest/disease control methods is found in the Plant Clinic, page 226.

Melons

Though they do best in drier areas, with irrigation melons can be grown in the sub-tropics and sub-tropics.

ROCKMELONS Plant seed in mounds, and side dress with urea. Planting time for the tropics is autumn; all year in the sub-tropics. Variety 'HALES BEST' is the best-known variety and is resistant to powdery mildew, a common problem with growing rockmelons in humid climates. Several other varieties are available to the home gardener. Pick when the fruit can be plucked easily from the stem, after which fruits will not ripen further.

HONEYDEW MELONS This fruit has a greenish-white skin and green fruit. Cultivate as for rockmelons.

WATERMELON This will grow almost anywhere, with very little help, but for best quality fruit, cultivate as for rockmelons. Harvest when bottom of fruit starts to lose colour; to test for ripeness, tap the fruit which should give a hollow sound.

Vines

GRAPES Some varieties are more suitable than others for growing in the sub-tropics. If you buy from a local garden centre or specialist supplier this should present no problem; if you obtain the plant privately then be careful, because it may not be suited to your area. The vine should be planted in winter in a light, humus-enriched soil, next to some kind of support such as a pergola, trellis or fence. Water well to establish, after that, leave it to nature as grapes do well in areas with fairly low rainfall. Fertilising is unnecessary; perhaps just an occasional spraying of the young vine with a foliar fertiliser to help it on its way, but high-nitrogen fertilisers will encourage foliage growth at the expense of fruit. The main problem with growing grapes is fungal diseases such as powdery and downy mildew.

PASSIONFRUIT This combines an attractive flowering vine with delicious fruit. Outer skin is either purplish-dark and smooth, purplish-dark and wrinkly, or green and smooth.

Passionfruit vines need good drainage, plenty of sunshine and regular watering in dry periods. Use a high nitrogen balanced fertiliser, such as a citrus food, at the rate of about 2 kg a vine, in late spring, mid-summer and early autumn. Plant so that the vine can grow over a trellis, pergola or fence. Prune back well in spring. Varieties such a 'PANAMA RED' and 'PANAMA GOLD' are good garden performers with a very sweet flavour.

Vegetables

GROWING VEGETABLES in a hot climate is very rewarding. Crops can be grown year-round and do so with a speed which pleases even the most impatient gardener. There is a cost benefit too in that shop-bought vegetables usually become expensive in high summer. Above all, there is the pleasure of producing and harvesting crops in your own garden, which is the reason why most people grow their own vegetables in the first place. In many of us there remains an ancient urge to turn the soil in our gardens to productive use, and there is no more satisfying way of doing this than growing our own vegetables.

However, there are a few problems which are particular to vegetable production in a hot climate. The main problem is the heat itself, allied to humidity. Long periods of unrelieved sunshine and heat can sap the energy from many cool-climate vegetables, while humidity encourages the development of fungal diseases. Insect pests tend to be more plentiful in a hot climate and monsoonal deluges can severely damage crops. These factors all need to be taken into consideration when growing vegetables in the sub-tropics and tropics. In hot, dry, inland areas the main problems are too much sun and too little available water.

Like any other form of gardening, successful vegetable-growing depends on good planning. First, it is important to think of the gardener as well as the garden. Plan your garden so that most of the hard, preparatory work is done during the cooler season and confine hot season efforts to early mornings or evenings. Then, prepare the ground.

Experienced vegetable gardeners have their own particular ideas about such things as soil preparation, composting, types of fertilisers, mulches and so on. It is possible for two different gardeners to have developed totally different growing methods, yet still produce identically excellent crops. Such gardeners will also have come to terms with the vagaries of their local environment and climate. But to grow really healthy, good quality vegetables there are certain fundamentals which must apply, and I outline them here. The aim is to assist those gardeners who have never before tried their hand at growing vegetables, or perhaps have done so without success. These simple steps will help you find a way of doing things which suits your special circumstances.

DESIGN AND PREPARATION

The two essentials are good soil and drainage. By good soil we mean soil which is rich in humus and has a fine tilth so that it is easy to work. Dig over the designated growing area, with a spade or rotary hoe. Dig as deep as you can, down to the sub-soil, but don't dig into the sub-soil and mix it with the topsoil. All large clods should be broken up and the soil spaded and forked over until it is of a fine, crumbly texture. Then add bulk and nutrition in the form of animal manure (whichever is most readily available to you) or compost. Soil can also be bought in and worked over for vegetable growing, with the addition of compost or animal manure.

If you haven't already done so, this is the stage at which to plan the design of your vegetable garden. Design is very much a matter of individual preference, the one essential is that all parts of the bed or beds be easily accessible, without having to trample other plants. The most common designs for vegetable gardens are:

Some formal garden designs

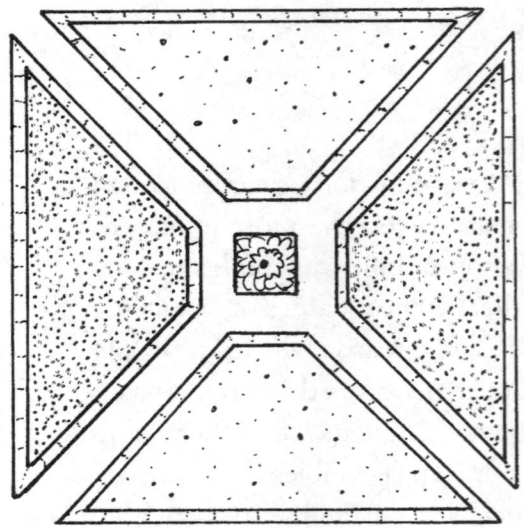

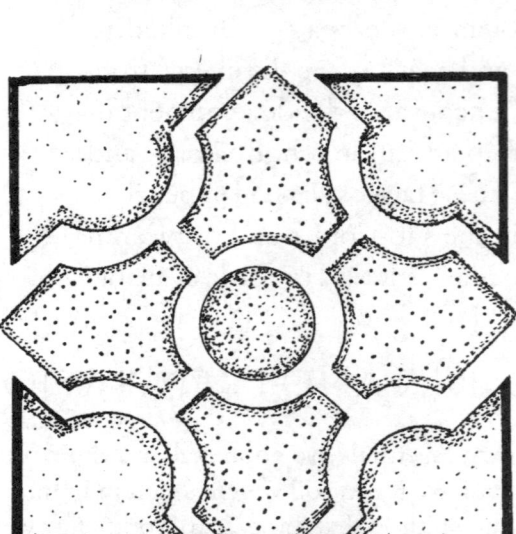

- A single very small bed with the centre easily accessible, or as large a bed as you like divided by pathways so that every plant can be reached. The single bed can be any shape. A narrow rectangle offers better access to plants than a square. A square or diamond-shaped bed can be neatly divided into four by two intersecting pathways offering good access; if the bed is very large, more pathways may be needed. A triangular-shaped bed offers ready access. Those who don't like straight lines in landscaping may favour a circular bed; again pathways may be needed for access.
- A single square, rectangular, diamond-shaped or circular bed with sufficient space in the middle for good plant access. The space can be paved or surfaced with gravel, sand or a mulch. This is a good idea if vegetable beds are part of an overall garden design because the effect can be made quite decorative, even to the addition of a garden seat or small pond.
- A series of separate beds; one for each type of vegetable, or for a couple of different vegetables grown in the same bed. This method is also used to stagger production of vegetables of the same type; for example, different beds can be used for lettuces or other vegetables planted over successive weeks—a common mistake made by novice vegetable growers is to plant for a single harvesting, then ending up with an over-supply of one vegetable at harvesting time. It is obviously better to stagger crops so that only a few of each type are planted—and later harvested—each week during the growing period. Separate beds, arranged to fit into the overall shape of the garden, offer easy access to individual plants and are also easy to cultivate. But they do take up a lot of space. The simplest method is simply to create beds by mounding up the soil. Beds can be edged with brick, concrete lawn edging or timber. Or they can be left with no edging at all, though it is customary to spade-cut the edges when the beds are surrounded by grass. This not only neatly separates the beds from the lawn, and discourages grass invasion, it also makes a small 'moat' which helps direct water into the area beneath the mound. Another method is to build up the sides of beds with brick or treated timber and fill the middle with soil. This method is often chosen when soil is brought in. These beds can reduce the amount of bending needed to tend plants as the sides of the bed can be sat on while planting, weeding and so on. This is an important consideration for older gardeners and it is possible (though expensive) to build beds up to waist height so that no bending at all is required.
- Steep banks can quite easily be made into terraces, with alternate rows of vegetables and pathways. Terraced beds have excellent drainage and are easy to work.

Gardening in a Hot Climate

Whichever design you choose, it is almost always advisable to raise vegetable beds above the surface of the garden to ensure good drainage.

When the soil has been well prepared, add a dressing of dolomite at the rate of about 200 g to the square metre; more in heavy soils. If soil is alkaline, 'sweetening' it with dolomite is unnecessary. A dressing of fertiliser should also be added; this should be a well-balanced mix of 5:6:4 NPK (nitrogen, phosphorus and potassium), at a rate of about 100 g a square metre, dug well into the soil up to about a week before planting. With row vegetables such as peas and beans, which also have seed which is very sensitive to fertiliser contact, scatter the fertiliser evenly along the furrow and cover with earth before sowing seed.

PLANTING

Vegetables are grown either from seed or seedlings. Vegetable seed packets contain very comprehensive planting instructions so there is no need for us to duplicate them here. Seeds can be sown in seedling trays or directly into beds. When buying seedlings from garden centres, you will find that they usually come with a label which provides some planting and cultural information.

Sow seedlings directly into the beds where they are to grow. Dampen the soil in the punnet so that you can take the plant out easily and it has some moisture around the roots. Make a small hole and place the seedling in it so that the roots are well covered and the leaves well clear of the soil. Refill the hole and gently firm the soil around the seedling. Then water. Planting is best done in the late afternoon or evening so that the tiny plant has a few hours of darkness to settle itself before the onslaught of morning sun.

Some vegetables are best planted just below the surface in rows, others in long furrows, still others need to be grown in small hills, mounded above the surface of the bed. Choko is a vine which can be planted anywhere, provided there is a support over which it can climb.

VEGETABLES PLANTED IN ROWS Broccoli, cabbage, capsicum, carrots, celery, eggplant, lettuces, okra, onions, parsnips, spring onions, silverbeet, tomatoes.

VEGETABLES PLANTED IN FURROWS Beans, peas, sweet corn, sweet potatoes. Sweet potatoes are planted as tuber shoots laid horizontal just under the surface of the ground, with tip cuttings protruding, about 30 cm apart.

VEGETABLES PLANTED IN SMALL HILLS Pumpkins, squash, cucumbers, zucchini

MAKING A SEEDBED

Seedbeds are necessary if you plan to grow future vegetables using seed harvested from previous crops. This is the 'no cost' method of ongoing vegetable production. Seedbeds are also useful if you want to stagger planting of purchased seed over successive weeks. A few seeds can be planted in the seedbed and, as seedlings develop, they can be planted out in small quantities.

The main advantage of a seedbed is that plants start life in one contained and protected area before being sent out to, as it were, face the harsher reality of the growing bed where it is not practical to protect a large area from sun and rain. The bed should be above ground, with protected sides. The soil should be very fine and of good quality, with plenty of organic matter. Sweeten and make fertile with dolomite and fertiliser at half the rate recommended for the main growing bed. Using a ruler and pencil, pen or stick, make straight furrows in which to sow the seed. An area which has light shade, perhaps from an overhanging tree, is ideal for a seedbed as it protects the tender young plants from too much sun and also the direct force of heavy rain. Otherwise, cover the bed with shadecloth attached to some kind of frame; either a frame at ground level which can be lifted off, or else an overhead shelter attached to upright posts. The latter method is more convenient; the former will offer added protection against pests.

The shadecloth should be of the lowest UV reading to allow plenty of light. A few days before planting, remove the shade so that plants have a chance to harden off.

Portable seedbeds are more versatile than those in-ground as they can be moved from one place to another and at planting times the seedlings can be transported directly to the bed. They can, for example, be placed outside during the day and put into a bush house or greenhouse at night. Portable seedbeds can be made cheaply out of wooden or polystyrene vegetable boxes, provided there are adequate drainage holes, or you can use plant pots, nursery seedling trays or egg cartons. Seedlings can be raised in shadehouses or bush houses, provided they get enough light and good air circulation.

There are two distinct points of view as to whether, in a hot climate, it is better to start vegetables in a seedbed or directly in the garden. One view is that seed sown in seedtrays shows a better germination rate and the vulnerable seedlings do better and grow faster if given this initial degree of care and protection. The other is that seedbed-grown seedlings tend to be 'soft' and tend to suffer from transplant shock, whereas those sown directly where they are to grow are acclimatised from the start to cope with exposure. Balancing one view against the other, it is fair to say that the average gardener, using today's especially formulated packet seed, can confidently sow direct into well-prepared garden beds without the extra work involved in using seedbeds. The easiest method of all, of course, is to buy in your seedlings.

Whether grown in seedbeds or sown directly into garden beds, you will need to thin out your seedlings as they develop, so that only the most vigorous remain, with plenty of room to grow.

CULTIVATION

Once seedlings start to grow, occasional side dressings of mixed fertiliser or urea will be needed with some vegetables (see the table on page 185). The growing plants will also need to be watered thoroughly; probably once a day but only if the soil just below the surface has dried out. The hotter and drier the weather, the more watering is required. Early morning watering is best; if watering in the evening, particularly during cool weather, confine water to the roots without wetting the foliage as this encourages fungal diseases. In very hot, dry weather, however, sprinkling foliage with water will reduce transpiration.

Mulching vegetables is particularly useful in a hot climate because it helps to retain moisture and stops the soil becoming baking hot. It also breaks up heavy rain drops and gives very young seedlings some protection from direct sun. Any organic material can be used, provided it has an open character which allows the plant to grow and permits air penetration. Straw and hay are ideal. Grass clippings are best used on top of a more open mulch as they tend to pack down and become squishy. Newspaper makes a good mulch and is often used in no-dig gardens, but it looks unsightly and has little nutritional value. Pine bark is a good mulch for vegetable gardens and yet is little used for this purpose. It can tend to acidify the soil, though very slowly, and the early application of dolomite will solve this problem anyway. Nut shells also make excellent mulches. The advantage of mulches like hay and straw is that they break down quickly and improve soil quality. This can be a useful ongoing process over the years and cuts down on the need for additional compost — see the section on organic growing, page 183. Black plastic is *not* a good mulching method in a hot climate as the soil beneath overheats; it also inhibits the even distribution of rainfall and overhead watering.

Weeds flourish at the expense of vegetable crops so regular and thorough weeding is needed. Mulches help repress weeds; weedicides are difficult to use in a vegetable bed, though weeding wands can be useful. Hand weeding is still the safest method; if done on a daily basis, perhaps while watering, it should not become too onerous.

PROTECTION

Where plant protection is concerned, prevention is better than cure, so the following points should be observed:

- ❖ Healthy plants are more resistant to insect attack and less vulnerable to disease. Keep them well fed and well watered.
- ❖ Today's hybrid seeds often come with built-in resistance to certain pests and diseases. Check the packet so that, if possible, you buy only those seeds which are resistant to the particular problems in your area.
- ❖ Rotate your crops, so that the same plant is not always grown in the same part of the vegetable garden. This prevents disease build-up and disrupts the feeding and

- breeding cycle of insects which feed on particular types of vegetables.
- The price of a good vegetable garden is eternal vigilance. Weed diligently, remove insects from plants regularly, pick off leaves which show evidence of insect infestation or disease, and immediately remove diseased plants.

When all else fails, you may consider resorting to chemicals. This is not a move to be taken lightly.

If insect depredation is so severe that it threatens the whole crop, and you feel chemical control is the only answer, then limit this to minimal use and carefully follow the instructions on the packet — for your own sake, as well as for the sake of the plant. Particularly note the withholding period — the time between applying the chemical and when the plant is safe to eat. Always wash chemically sprayed plants very thoroughly before eating.

The most common insect pests in vegetable gardens include beetles, bugs, caterpillars, aphids, bean fly, fruit fly, red spider mites and eelworm. For information on how to recognise and control them, turn to the Plant Clinic, page 226. Also included in this section is information on how to protect vegetables from bird and animal pests.

GROWING VEGETABLES IN CONTAINERS

Many vegetables can be grown successfully in containers. They include tomatoes (dwarf types), capsicums, chillis, eggplants, silverbeet, lettuces, radishes, spring onions and beans (which need large tubs or pots and a climbing frame). Container growing is ideal for home units and townhouses where the only available outdoor growing areas may be balconies, sunrooms, patios and courtyards — anywhere there is sufficient sunlight. There are even hybrid tomatoes bred especially for growing on patios.

Growing vegetables in pots, tubs, window boxes and other containers is often a preferred method for those who only want to produce a small amount of vegetables, or who don't want to face the rigours of outdoor growing in a hot climate. What is more, vegetables can make very attractive pot plants, particularly if decorative varieties are chosen, such as red-stemmed silverbeet, lettuces with frilled, colourful leaves, chillis and capsicums. These are obvious choices but the attractions of some vegetables may not be so obvious, for example the delicate, fern-like foliage of carrots looks surprisingly good in the pot.

The principles of growing vegetables in pots are the same as for any other plant and can be found in the chapter on container growing. However, vegetables do require some special consideration as follows:

- It is much easier to manage and protect vegetables in pots than it is in the ground, providing you are able to water and feed them regularly. In the garden, vegetables can, at a pinch, take care of themselves, relying on rainwater and naturally available soil nutrition. In the pot, they depend on human care.
- You will need to water daily during the growing season; the soil below the surface should not be allowed to dry out completely; at the same time over-watering will cause root problems and soil should not be sodden. Clay pots are porous so the soil inside dries out faster than in plastic or other non-porous containers.
- Vegetables in pots need frequent feeding because their roots cannot mine the ground for nutrition. Foliar sprays promote good growth for leafy and other vegetables; these can be used in conjunction with a balanced plant food applied to the soil.
- Pots containing seed or young seedlings can be placed in areas of light shade or part shade until the plant is sufficiently mature to take full sun. They should then be moved out of the shaded area because vegetables need long hours of sun to grow and produce good quality fruits and foliage. At the same time, on days of extreme heat and, perhaps, drying winds, you can move pots which are not too large back into the light shade area.
- Plants in pots are generally less accessible to insect attack but don't assume they are invulnerable. Red spider mite is a particular pest of pot plants and requires chemical control; caterpillars, grasshoppers, beetles and bugs are easy to spot and remove by hand.

Disease

While it can be relatively simple to control most insects without using chemicals, diseases in vegetables are caused by bacteria or fungi and these usually need chemical treatment, see the Plant Clinic, page 226.

ORGANIC GROWING

Growing vegetables organically means that no chemical fertilisers or insecticides are used in the garden at all. Even in the tropics, where insects and fungal diseases thrive, organic vegetable growing is practised with great success.

If you have enriched the soil well enough, it may be sufficient to sustain vegetable growth through one season, or else it can be enhanced with further applications of well-made compost. Where space permits, green manure can be applied by growing comfrey or a crop of nitrogen-fixing plants such as clover or *Dolichos lab-lab* which can then be dug into fallow beds. Actually, any plant waste can be dug into the soil as green manure. In a hot climate, nutritional elements break down fast, and today's vegetable hybrids require large amounts of nutrition; if you are not using chemical fertilisers then the soil must be made adequately fertile by organic methods.

Once a truly fertile soil has been established, and this may take several years, the garden should be nutritionally self-sustaining with minimum effort and input apart from ongoing mulching and the addition, perhaps, of occasional dressings of compost. In that early period, a steady nutrient build-up and tilth can be achieved by adding ingredients such as compost, animal manures, cotton waste, bagasse (from sugarcane) nut shells, mushroom compost, dolomite, blood and bone, seaweed, soybean and linseed meal, fish emulsion, rock sulphate and the residue of many commercially grown crops. A foliar fertiliser or compost 'tea' can be made by adding about 2 cups of compost to five litres of water. This can be sprayed on plant foliage. Add garlic or any other organic treatment to the liquid and you have a combined fertiliser and pest repellent.

Organic treatments are used to repel and control pests and diseases. Companion planting helps prevent problems by using certain insect-repelling plants to protect others. See page 20.

> *The principles of organic gardening*
> ORGANIC NUTRITION Home-made compost, animal manure and green manure are used to enrich the soil. Either singly or in combination.
> ORGANIC MULCHES These should be spread thickly over soil and around plants. As they break down they enrich the soil. Often the continuous breakdown of mulches such as straw and hay, plus the addition of some animal manure, is all that is needed to maintain sufficient soil fertility for growing vegetables.
> ORGANIC PEST AND DISEASE CONTROL This is based on the principle that healthy soil and healthy plants are resistant to insect attack and diseases. Organic treatments are used to repel nuisances. Eternal vigilance and the swift removal of insects and diseased plants is particularly important in the organic garden.

The same principles that are used for growing vegetables organically can be applied to the rest of the garden. Shrubs, trees, foliage plants and flowers can all be grown using only organic fertilisers, mulch and pest and disease controls. Once an organic garden is established, it is both cheaper and less arduous to maintain than a garden which requires traditional cultivation practices such as digging, together with constant applications of chemical nutrition and protection. For this reason it is recommended to hot-climate gardeners.

NO DIGGING

Apart from growing plants in containers, this is the ultimate effort-saver for hot-climate gardeners. It means exactly what it says — the soil does not have to be dug over. Instead, a growing medium is created by layered mulches. The method can vary; for instance Esther Deans, a Sydney pioneer of no-dig gardening, recommended alternate layers of newspaper, lucerne hay and straw. A 20–cm–deep layer of lucerne, preferably in wads peeled off a damp bundle, is laid over about 2 cm of newspaper. The lucerne is covered with a light dressing of fertiliser — either a rich compost, animal manure (including fowl manure pellets) or blood and bone. A third layer of 20–cm–deep straw is laid loosely over the top, with another light dressing of fertiliser. One bale each of lucerne and straw will make a 2 m × 2 m bed. If the ground beneath is very hard, a further cushioning of leaf litter, grass clippings or similar organic matter should be established.

Depressions are made in the straw and filled with handfuls of rich soil or potting mix. Seeds or seedlings are planted here — and that is all there is to it. The mulch layers break down in time to a rich soil with excellent tilth. In the meantime, plants thrive. Layered no-dig beds can be built up as high as you like, or can afford, edged in bricks, timber, steel roofing panels or whatever is available. Small, circular beds can be made in old car or truck tyres. Mulches recommended by other no-dig experts include peat, seaweed, nutshells, meadow hay, hessian bags, old carpet, even old clothes if they are made from natural fibres. Permaculture enthusiasts recommend a bottom layer of slashed weeds and grass, dressed lightly with gypsum or dolomite and fowl manure or blood and bone, topped with grass clippings, kitchen wastes and leaves. This is then covered with overlapped non-synthetic materials such as those already mentioned. The final touch, for aesthetic reasons, is a layer of sawdust, pinebark or some other cosmetic mulch. Yet another method involves putting compost or blood and bone on the cleared site, before the newspaper layer is laid.

Whichever method you decide to use, you will be able to grow healthy vegetables without having to put a spade in the ground.

A few more hints

- Several varieties of tomatoes are now produced for hot-climate growing, look for these types in the garden centre. 'GROSSE LISSE' remains the most reliable. Cherry and egg tomatoes do well in hotter climates.
- Grow a few non-hearting lettuces; leave them in the ground and pick off outer leaves as required.
- Don't over-fertilise plants. Fertiliser applied when lettuce hearts are developing will result in loose-leaved heads. In other, non-leafy, plants foliage will develop at the expense of roots, bulbs or fruit. It is quite enough to dress the soil thoroughly up to a week before planting, then side-dress as and if recommended in the table.
- Fertiliser is applied to the square (m²) or linear metre. Make sure it is well watered in and that seeds are not in direct contact with it.
- Substitute sulphate of ammonia for urea where soils are strongly alkaline. Use at the rate of 20 g per m².
- Some of the less common vegetables which are worth growing in a hot climate include cassava (a root vegetable with a floury texture and nutty taste), kohlrabi, endive (chicory), Jerusalem artichoke, daikon (Japanese radish), tatsoi (an oriental leaf vegetable, grown like lettuce), hakurei (a Chinese turnip-like vegetable with edible root and leaves). All except kohlrabi (plant in late summer–early autumn) and Jerusalem artichokes (spring) can be planted all year round.

FROST

Even in tropical and sub-tropical latitudes, frost can occur in mountain and dry inland areas. In these areas, plant seedlings only when all danger of frost is past, and sow seeds so that seedlings appear when the danger of frost is over. Seed packets usually contain planting information appropriate to the different climatic zones.

MANY VEGETABLES WHICH DO BEST in a cool climate can still be grown in the sub-tropics, or even the tropics. Try whatever takes your fancy; it may be that in your particular microclimate, or with your particular skill and dedication, you may be able to grow vegetables which are not generally considered suited to growing in a hot climate. The following table lists only those common vegetables which are considered the best for hot-climate gardens, together with information on planting time, harvesting time and recommended post-planting fertiliser application.

PLANTING GUIDE FOR SEED-GROWN VEGETABLES

T—tropics ST—sub-tropics

Vegetable		When to plant	When to harvest (weeks)	Fertiliser
Beans/(Dwarf)	T	late summer–late spring	8–10	Seeds should not be in direct contact with fertiliser.
	ST	All year		
(Climbing)	T	late summer–spring	10–12	
	ST	All year		
Broccoli	T	late summer–winter	12–16	Side dressing every 3–4 weeks. Add 10 g urea per m² when heads begin to form. Side dressing every 3–4 weeks. Add 10 g urea per m² when hearts develop. Add 10 g urea per m² when first fruits set.
	ST	All year		
Cabbage	T	late summer–spring	8–16	
	ST	All year		
Capsicum	T	All year	10–16	
	ST	winter–late summer		
Carrots	T/ST	late summer–spring	16–20	Fertilise several weeks before sowing.
Celery	T	summer–autumn	20–22	Apply soluble fertiliser weekly and side dressings of NPK 2–3 times during growth, with 10 g urea per m².
	ST	late spring–autumn		
Chinese cabbage	T	All year	8–10	Same as for cabbage.
	ST	All year		
Choko	T	autumn–spring	18–20	Side dress once with NPK or use foliar spray.
	ST	early winter–mid-spring		

Vegetables • 185 •

PLANTING GUIDE FOR SEED-GROWN VEGETABLES

Vegetable	When to plant		When to harvest (weeks)	Fertiliser
Cucumber	T	All year	8–12	Side dress with urea at 15 g a plant.
	ST	mid-winter–late summer		
Eggplant	T	All year	14–16	Side dress with urea at 15 g a plant when runners form.
	ST	early spring–late summer		
Leeks	T	mid-summer–early winter	12–20	Side dress with NPK every 4 weeks.
	ST	early autumn–early winter		
Lettuce	T/ST	All year, with different varieties	8–10 (approx.) are almost half grown.	Side dress twice with urea at 10 g per m² after thinning and when plants
Okra	T	All year	16–20	As for capsicums.
	ST	summer–end winter		
Peas (including snow peas)	T/ST	late summer–winter	14–16	Seed should not be in direct contact with fertiliser.
Pumpkin	T	All year	14–16	As for marrows.
	ST	winter–mid-summer		
Radish	T/ST	All year	6–8	
Silverbeet	T/ST	All year	8–12	Side dress with urea at 10 g per m² about every 3 weeks.
Spring onions	T/ST	All year	8–12	
Squash	T	All year	12–14	
	ST	mid-winter–summer		
Sweet corn	T	All year	18–20	Side dress with a nitrogenous fertiliser when about 60 cm high.
	ST	mid-winter–summer		
Sweet potato	T	mid-winter–late summer		
	ST	mid-winter–summer		
Tomato	T/ST	All year	8–14	Side dress with 10 g of urea a linear metre after first fruit set.
Zucchini	T	All year	8–14	Side dress with 10 g of urea per m².
	ST	mid-winter–late summer		

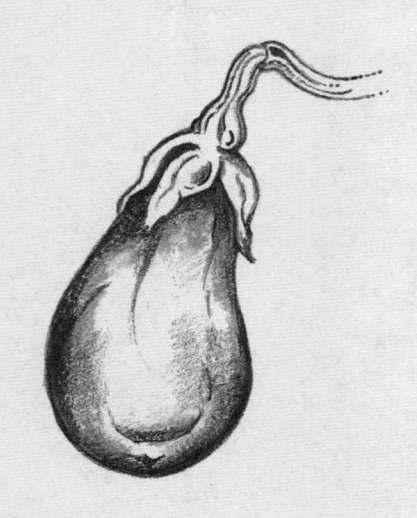

Herbs and spices

HERBS AND SPICES ENHANCE the flavour and nutritional quality of the food we cook and eat; without them food would be very dull indeed. While most spices come from hot parts of the world, many herbs come from cooler climates and are not easy to grow in the tropics and sub-tropics. In the sub-tropics, it is possible to grow some cool-climate herbs in winter only; to make up for this, warmth-loving herbs such as basil can be grown as a perennial.

For the purpose of this book I am using 'herbs' to include those plants commonly grown for culinary and medicinal purposes, and here I cover mainly culinary herbs, though some with known medicinal or perfumery qualities are included.

Herbs differ greatly in habit and requirements; one common requirement is good drainage. For this reason herbs are best grown on light, free-draining soils, in raised beds, mounds or rockeries. The more decorative herbs can be grown in the garden without any special place of their own; others can be grown among the vegetables. On the other hand, you may wish to create a special herb garden. This can be formal, laid out on traditional lines, with each carefully tended herb in its place. It can be semi-formal, with neat beds of different plants but lacking the intricate design of a formal garden. Or it can be quite informal, with herbs planted in mixed profusion and allowed to grow pretty well as they like. In fact herb gardens lend themselves to any kind of design. Beds can be round or square, rectangular or triangular, or shaped like a wheel with paths forming the 'spokes' and the plants grown in-between.

A few principles need to be observed.

- Tall growers should be planted at the back of beds, otherwise shorter plants will have no visual effect and may even be forgotten.
- Some herbs like acid soils, others prefer alkaline and the herb garden is a small area where both these needs must be met. It is often easiest to divide the garden into two sections, treating soil accordingly. If soil is predominantly alkaline, use acidifiers such as iron chelates to lower the pH in the area where acid-loving herbs are to be planted. If soil is too acid (most often the case in tropical and sub-tropical areas), apply dolomite before planting. Both treatments will need to be done annually. If your garden soil is neutral, or close to it, no treatment is necessary, except for plants with very specific needs. Fortunately, most herbs are quite tolerant of soil pH.
- Herbs like mint and parsley need plenty of water; others, such as rosemary, need very little. Unless you are prepared to spend long hours hand-watering plants according to individual needs, it is easier to group water-loving and dryland species so that they can be watered separately. Some herbs are marketed with colour-coded labels to show the different watering requirements.
- Because herb gardens require constant cultivation and frequent picking, like vegetable gardens, there needs to be ready access to all plants with pathways. Or you might design a large, central space paved, grassed or surfaced with gravel, which has a small pond, birdbath or garden seat, making the centre of the herb garden a place in which to relax, surrounded by delicious fragrances.

Herbs are usually bought as seedlings or well-grown pot plants. Many can also be grown from seed; when planting seed, follow the instructions on the packet. The following herbs are easy to grow in a hot climate. Soil preference, if important, is stated as 'acid' or 'sweet'.

BASIL (*Ocimum* SPP.)
Annual or perennial. One of the great herbs of Italian cooking. Spicy flavour. In a hot climate basil does best in a sunny position (sub-tropics) or light shade (tropics and dry inland) position. Any reasonably fertile but sweet soil. Companion plant with tomatoes.

Available varieties include SWEET BASIL (the basil most commonly used in cooking), BUSH BASIL (very easy to grow anywhere, including sand dune gardens), OPAL BASIL (very decorative dark-leaved basil), CAMPHOR BASIL (a moth repellent) and LEMON BASIL.

BORAGE (*Borago officinalis*)

An annual with large, edible but slightly prickly leaves and blue flowers. The leaves taste rather like cucumber and can be used in soups, salads or, with flowers, to decorate fruit drinks. Flowers can be used to decorate salad or fruit dishes, or frozen into ice blocks, adding a colourful touch to iced drinks. Sun. Any soil. In hot climates borage will often continue growing for another year; or else it will self-seed and come up again — often prolifically in favourable conditions.

CATNIP (*Nepeta cataria*)
A perennial which grows to about 1 m and produces long spikes of white and purple flowers. Makes a good border plant. Its scent, though not particularly interesting to humans, is popular with cats. Tea made from the leaves is said to have soothing, mildly sedative qualities (it used to be given to restless babies). Lemon-scented catnip is also available. CATMINT (*Nepeta mussini*) is a smaller-growing plant with greyish-green leaves. Nepetas will grow in sun or light shade. Any non-acid soil.

CHIVES (*Allium schoenoprasum*) 
Onion-like perennials with delicate, hollow, grass-like edible leaves. Garlic chives (*Allium tuberosum*) are larger-growing and have coarser, flat-bladed, garlic-flavoured leaves. Both are excellent in salads and many hot dishes. Best in full sun, though in the tropics the more delicate true chives should be grown in light shade.

DILL (*Anethum graveolens*)
An annual with slender branches and delicate yellow flowers with an aniseed flavour. Very similar in use and flavour to fennel, though less sturdy. Leaves and flowers can be used in cooking, seeds are flavoursome too and used to flavour vinegar for pickling. Dill is also an effective aid to digestion. Good soil. Full sun.

ELDERBERRY (*Sambucus nigra*)

A large, deciduous shrub or small tree which does well in the sub-tropics. Large, flat flowerheads can be picked for making wine or cooked in fritters. Berries are also used to make wine or jam. Good, fairly sweet soil. Sun or light shade.

FENNEL (*Foeniculum vulgare*)

A tall-growing, sturdy perennial which grows just about anywhere, including alongside the road. A declared noxious weed in some areas. Yellow flowers and leaves can be used in cooking. Any soil. Full sun. FLORENCE FENNEL or finocchio (*Foeniculum* var. *azoricum*) is grown for its flavoursome root used in Italian cooking. One of the easiest herbs to grow.

GOTU KOLA (*Centella asiatica*)
A pretty little groundcover perennial with deep pink flowers. Leaves can be eaten in salads. This plant is often grown for its alleged properties in granting longevity and alleviating arthritis. True or not, the plant contains useful vitamins and minerals, and can be safely ingested. Leaves can be eaten raw, or made into a tea.

HOREHOUND (*Marrubium vulgare*)

A perennial which grows so prolifically it has been declared a noxious weed in some areas. Although not very attractive, particularly when covered in dried seedheads, this plant does very well in hot, dry areas. It is not fussy about soil or position. Leaves are used to make horehound ale, and also a tea which allegedly helps cure coughs and soothe sore throats.

LAVENDER
Lavandula dentata, French lavender, will do well in the sub-tropics though may die back during long wet seasons. GREEN LAVENDER (*L. viridis*) and the dwarf ITALIAN LAVENDER (*L. stoechas*) can also be grown in the sub-tropics. Lavenders are grown for their fragrance, either in the garden (where they make a good hedge or border plant) or in sachets and pot-pourris. Best in sandy, sweet, very well-drained soil. In very light soil, bulk out with compost. Sun.

LEMON BALM (*Melissa officinalis*)
Perennial with upright stems and mint-like leaves. Flowers are small and white. The lemon-flavoured leaves can be used in many sweet and savoury dishes. Rich, sweet soil. Sun or part shade.

LEMON GRASS (*Cymbopogon citratus*)
This great mainstay of Thai cooking is a clumping, perennial grass which grows to about 1 m tall. Easy to grow provided it has year-round heat and good drainage. If leaves are yellowish or pale, apply a light dressing of high-nitrogen fertiliser. Sun.

MARJORAM (*Origanum majorana*)
A perennial with small, oval, flavoursome leaves, used extensively in cooking. Dainty pink, white or mauve flowers help make this a good border plant. Full sun. Rich, sweet soil. Plenty of water.

MINT (*Mentha* SPP.)
The several species of mint grow well in any reasonably fertile soil with plenty of water. In hot climates they do best in light shade. Range of mints includes SPEARMINT, PEPPERMINT, PENNYROYAL, PINEAPPLE MINT, APPLEMINT, VARIEGATED APPLEMINT, BASIL MINT, GINGER MINT, JAPANESE MENTHOL and EAU-DE-COLOGNE MINT which is useful for perfume sachets or putting in clothes drawers. VIETNAMESE MINT has a hot, spicy flavour and does particularly well in the tropics.

NASTURTIUM (*Tropaeolum majus* and *minus*)

Trailing and dwarf nasturtiums can both be grown in the herb garden for vivid colour if desired, though they are also popular as groundcovers and basket plants. *T. minus* is easier to control. The leaves are delightful in salads, soups and other dishes, while the seeds are a good substitute for capers. Flowers are also edible. Any reasonably fertile, sweet, well-drained soil. Sun or light shade. Usually grown from seed.

OREGANO (*Oreganum vulgare*)
Very similar to marjoram, except it has a more creeping growth habit and leaves are darker. Does best in light, sweet, sandy soils with low fertility. Full sun.

PARSLEY (*Petroselinum crispum*)
Common parsley has tightly curled foliage, whereas the foliage of Italian parsley is more open. Parsley is the herb most frequently used in cooking, and in the largest quantities, so it is useful to grow. In a hot climate it should be grown in light shade, and given plenty of water. However, despite opinions to the contrary, parsley does *not* like wet feet and soil must drain freely. Any fairly rich soil, but feed with liquid manure if soil fertility is not high enough.

ROSEMARY (*Rosmarinus officinalis*)
Rosemary can only be grown in the sub-tropics, and inland in tropical latitudes, if it is given full sun and very well-drained soil that is neither too fertile nor too acid. A good seaside plant which thrives on sand dunes. The small, needle-like leaves are fragrant and can be used in lamb dishes as well as sachets and pot-pourris. An attractive border shrub or low hedge.

SAGE (*Salvia officinalis*)
Sage is a woody plant with flavoursome greyish leaves. It needs dry conditions and is therefore not ideal for hot, humid climates. In the sub-tropics it can be grown if given very good drainage in a sandy soil, preferably on high ground where there is no build-up of humidity.

THYME (*Thymus vulgaris*)
This small, creeping or upright herb is not easy to grow in hot, humid areas and needs to be given the same conditions as sage. It is probably best placed in a sunny rock garden and allowed to creep over a hard surface. The leaves are used in many dishes.

WORMWOOD (*Artemisia absinthium*)
A bushy shrub with aromatic leaves which makes a good small hedge. It has insect repellent qualities but is of no culinary use, despite being used to flavour certain alcoholic drinks. It is easy to grow and not fussy about soil conditions. Not a plant for the tropics, but does well in the sub-tropics.

YARROW (*Achillea millefolium*)
This is an easy-to-grow herb with attractive foliage and flowers but very limited use. Many claims are made for it as a medicinal plant and it is usually grown for this purpose, and because it is one of the traditional garden herbs. Tolerates any reasonably fertile soil; needs plenty of water and full sun.

Spices

CARAWAY (*Carum carvi*)
Biennial or perennial plant which produces a profusion of white flowers that can be harvested as seeds in the second year. The distinctively flavoured seeds are used in cakes, breads and many dishes. Any light, reasonably fertile soil which is not too acid. Sun.

CARDAMON (*Elettaria cardamomum*)
A tropical biennial which produces sweet-flavoured seeds used in Indian and Indo-Chinese cooking. Added to hot milk, they make a soothing bedtime drink. Needs rich, sweet soil which is not allowed to dry out. Shade.

CHILLI (*Capsicum annuum* and *C. frutescens*)
Chillis are the bright red seed capsules and seeds of shrubs which range in height from 60 cm to more than 1 m. They can be used as ornamentals but have rather sparse foliage, so are generally confined to the hot-climate herb garden. They are not too fussy about soil, needing very good drainage but only reasonable fertility. Water only during prolonged dry periods after establishment. The seeds and capsules burn the palate and are used in a range of hot, spicy dishes.

CORIANDER (*Coriandrum sativum*)
A tall-growing annual for the back of the herb bed, with large, flat, white-to-pink flowerheads. Seeds are used in cooking and can be ground for mixing with other spices into curry dishes. The leaves can be used in salads and pickles. Plant where there is morning sun and afternoon shade (part-shade) in any well-drained soil.

7
Pottering about

Gardening in containers

CONTAINER PLANTS OUTDOORS

Plants grown in containers depend on humans for their food and water, which means they take more time and trouble than those grown in the ground. However, this effort is often outweighed by the advantages.

- Container-grown plants are mobile and can be differently placed according to weather, season or the gardener's wishes.
- They are readily accessible.
- Fertilising, pruning, weeding, deadheading and other practices are easier.
- Trees and shrubs which might be otherwise too large for a small garden can be grown in large tubs which contain their roots.
- Delicate plants which might not thrive in an open garden can do well in containers placed appropriately to take advantage of shade, shelter, warm and cool spots.
- Container-grown plants brighten up patios, verandahs and indoor areas.
- They can be used to create instant plant colour and interest while in-ground gardens are being established.
- Although container plants need regular watering, particularly if under cover, water is easier and less wasteful to apply.
- Given adequate lighting, container plants can be worked on at night, which is a boon for busy people who have no available time during the day for gardening. Gardening at night can be very pleasant in hot weather.

Most in-ground garden effects can also be created with containers and can be easier to maintain. For example formal or informal styles can be created by arranging pots in rows and formal patterns, or in loose groupings of mixed plantings. 'Avenues' of tubbed palms, conifers or other trees can lead to a doorway or some other feature, while in-ground hedges or trees may in time overwhelm the path or driveway and require extensive pruning. A tropical or rainforest effect can be created around a swimming pool in pots which can be moved further back as plants grow and threaten to overhang the water. Floral effects can be maintained throughout the year with regular interchanges of containers; rose gardens, herb gardens, even vegetable gardens can all be container-grown.

In a hot climate there are two added advantages to growing plants in containers. One is that it is easier on the gardener who does not have to spend hours labouring over large areas in the sun but can instead work cleanly and comfortably on the patio, in the bush house, indoors or wherever else the containers have been placed (large, hard-to-move specimens grown in full sun outdoors can be worked on in the early morning or evening). The other is that it is easier on the plants, which can be placed to avoid extreme weather conditions such as heat or violent drenchings from tropical downpours.

If it can be grown in the ground, it can be grown in the pot! That is the only guide you need to select plants for container gardening. Trees, shrubs, annuals, perennials, fruit trees, Australian natives, roses, climbing plants, palms, cacti, herbs and vegetables are all potential pot plants. Consult the plant lists in this book or your local garden centre.

SUN OR SHADE

This is a matter of commonsense. The same principles apply as with in-ground plants; sun-loving plants can be used in open areas while shade-lovers are for verandahs and other covered areas. Most of the popular indoor and under-cover foliage plants are shade-lovers but almost all plants can be grown indoors for short periods, or if given adequate light.

The section on indoor plants deals with light levels (page 197): the same principles apply to undercover indoor/outdoor areas.

POTS

The type of pot you use depends on your taste. As a general guide:

- Plastic pots hold water better than clay pots.
- Unglazed clay pots have porous walls and are therefore less likely to waterlog than plastic pots.
- Glazed pots retain moisture better than unglazed pots.
- Dark-coloured plastic absorbs heat more than light-coloured plastic. When placed in direct sun, the sides of plastic pots can become so hot that they can damage or retard plant roots. (This can actually be used as a 'natural' method of root pruning, to encourage top growth, but unless you are a very skilled gardener I wouldn't advise it.)
- If you are placing a plain plastic pot inside a decorative pot, as is common practice, make sure *both* pots are free-draining.

POTTING MIXTURES AND FERTILISERS

There is a bewildering range of potting mixes available. It is important to buy the best: that is, a mix of quality ingredients which has been well composted and aerated. The resulting medium should be dark, rich-looking, fine and not too dry to the touch. It will usually contain controlled-release fertiliser, identifiable as small yellow or yellowish-white grains. A good deal of scientific research has gone into creating today's potting mixes to ensure that they are well-balanced, do not dry out too readily, are free-draining and permit aeration around the roots. The safest course is to select a name brand potting mix manufactured by a well-known, reputable garden products company, which has the ingredients and other information clearly listed on the bag. Beware of very cheap mixes by unknown manufacturers.

Different plants will require different fertilising regimes but all will require more feeding than they do in the garden, including cacti whose native soils may be dry and sandy but are usually rich in certain nutrients. Liquid fertilisers which are sprayed onto the foliage are easy to use with container-plants, though they may encourage leaf growth rather than flower growth. They should not be applied to furry-leaved plants such as African violets.

Controlled-release fertilisers especially formulated for container plants are excellent. Many quality potting mixes contain controlled-release fertiliser which will last up to about four months. As fertilisers break down more quickly in a hot climate, you may need to start adding fertiliser earlier than indicated on the packet. In any case, the feeding regime should be boosted with liquid fertilisers during the summer period to stimulate root development and leaf growth. All plants have a dormancy period, usually in winter, when little or no fertiliser should be applied.

Plants in containers need to be watered more frequently and more carefully than plants in the ground. Plants in the open, where evaporation is faster, require more water than plants under cover. More frequent watering is needed when weather is hot. Beyond this, just how much water container plants require is a vexed question. Some plants have higher water needs than others; for example, just as in the garden, those with large, fleshy leaves need more water than those with small, fine, needle-like leaves. So it is important to understand individual plant needs. With some, such as spathiphyllums and anthuriums, the soil should never be allowed to dry out completely; with others, such as bromeliads and aralias, the top 3–4 cm of potting mix can be allowed to dry out before watering. With plants designed to collect water, for example, aechmea bromeliads, some water should be left in the central rosette and changed (if it hasn't evaporated) every couple of weeks. No plants should be allowed to become waterlogged as this will cause wilting, leaf drop and eventual death. Cacti and succulents need far less watering than most other plants, and none at all in winter, but will benefit from an occasional good soak of the soil during summer and early autumn.

It is a good idea to set up a watering regime, once or twice a week, or more, or less, as conditions dictate. To make this easier, group plants with similar water requirements. But no regime should be too rigid; the easiest way of testing whether a container-grown plant needs water is to stick your finger into the top few centimetres of soil and see whether it is dry. If it is, water is needed. If you don't trust your own judgement, put moisture meters in the pot. Plants themselves will soon show you whether they need water, because their leaves, and sometimes their stems, may wilt but by this time too much damage may have been done.

To water efficiently the soil needs to be thoroughly soaked then drained efficiently. For this reason, the saucer on which you have placed your pot can create problems because it can cause waterlogging and encourage root diseases. In hot weather the evaporation rate of water from saucers is higher. The heat encourages fungal disease development in stagnant water, so if you must use saucers, fill them with coarse gravel or small stones so that the plant roots cannot come directly in contact with the water. Water in the saucer will also increase humidity which may promote disease.

Potting mix has a habit of forming a hard crust or pan on the top, inhibiting water penetration. This can be particularly troublesome with hanging baskets, where the water just runs off the sides. Top-dressing the pot with bark, other coarse material, gravel or small stones will prevent this problem. Where possible, it is a good idea to give potted plants a good soaking in a bucket or some other container full of water. Azaleas, with their high water requirements, benefit particularly from this treatment. Ferns like it too, because their often tangled root systems make it hard for water sprinkled from above to penetrate.

Container-grown plants, whether grown indoors or under cover on patios, can become sickened by a continual diet of town water, with its high content of mineral and other additives. It is a treat for them to be placed outside in the rain now and again. If this is not possible, a good flushing through with water from some other (clean) source will help keep plants in perfect health over a long period. Annual flushings are necessary anyway to remove the salts which accumulate in potting media from fertilisers.

An irrigation system, which may be needed to drip-water large plants to soak to the bottom of their roots, will simplify the time-consuming business of watering. Automatic timers will make it even easier.

Drainage

One of the advantages of growing plants in containers is that you can ensure they have excellent drainage. This means the pots, tubs, baskets, window boxes, old wheelbarrows, coppers or whatever containers are used must not only have enough drainage holes to start with but that these are kept free of obstruction. Check this frequently.

It is still acceptable to fill the bottom of large containers with crocking or stones. The theory is that this helps prevents soil compacting and encourages free drainage but tests show that it has no real effect on the plant. Using broken pieces of polystyrene as crocking and through the mix will help reduce the weight of the pot.

Repotting

The plant itself will tell you when it needs repotting. When the plant is obviously too big for the pot it is in, when the roots are protruding from the drainage holes, or it is showing obvious signs of being root-bound (stunted growth, smaller-than-normal leaves, sparse and straggling growth are common signs), then moving up to a bigger pot is due. Even plants which do not outgrow their pots need to have their soil changed occasionally. On average, once a year is enough; repotting can be traumatic for plants particularly for plants in large containers.

Repotting small container-grown plants is fairly simple. Soak the soil thoroughly first, then loosen around the sides of the pot with a sharp instrument, taking care not to damage the roots. Small, plastic pots can be tapped to loosen soil but this is not feasible with clay pots. Then ease the plant gently out of the old pot and place it in the new, which you have already part-filled with fresh mix. When repotting large plants, it is important not to damage the roots or stem by indulging in what can become a tug-of-war. Soak the soil thoroughly, loosen it at the sides and remove as much of it as possible with a trowel until the top of the root ball is exposed. It should then be possible to remove the plant, gripping the root ball and the base of the stem. Further watering of the root ball may be helpful but it is important to keep a good covering of soil around the roots.

If you want to inhibit top growth and root development, now is the time to trim roots back carefully with sharp secateurs. This has a 'bonsai' effect on the plant and those treated in this way can live for years, if properly cared for.

Plant problems

Container-grown plants are generally subject to the same pests and diseases found in the garden, unless they are covered in a bush house or indoors. Even in a protected environment, aphids, scale, red spider mite and mealy bugs, as well as the occasional caterpillar, can pose problems. See page 226.

If plants show signs of wilting, this may be due to either over or underwatering so check the soil and take action accordingly. Poor growth, pale leaves, leaf drop, lack of flowering can all be signs that a plant needs more light. They may also indicate that the plant is not being sufficiently fed.

HANGING BASKETS

The main point to remember about hanging baskets is that they dry out faster than other containers, which means more frequent watering. For this reason, it is sensible to make use of plants with relatively low water requirements such as trailing geraniums, BLACK-EYED SUSAN (*Thunbergia alata*), portulaca, nasturtiums, DUSKY CORAL-PEA (*Kennedia rubicunda*). Water-retaining crystals will also help keep moisture in the potting mix. Although baskets can be watered in the usual way, it can be difficult to water those which are hung above head height adequately; for this reason an occasional thorough dunking in a container of water is a good idea.

Basket-grown plants need more regular feeding, too, because nutrients tend to break down or become leached out quickly, while at the same time plants crowded into a small amount of growing medium swiftly use up all the nutrients. Controlled-release granules or liquid fertilisers are the most suitable; both should be applied at about double the frequency for other container plants. With liquid feeds wet the soil first so that the fertiliser soaks in, rather than runs over the edge. The most popular liners for hanging baskets are sphagnum moss and coconut fibre, though other materials such as plastic and polyfoam are available. The mix in hanging baskets should be changed more frequently than in other containers because it becomes poor and sours more quickly.

Care needs to be taken that sun-loving plants in hanging baskets are not blocked from receiving sufficient sunlight by overhead shade. Do not hang delicate plants in exposed areas where they can become sunburned, dehydrated or suffer flower and foliage damage; during high winds (especially cyclones) it is wise to take hanging baskets down and move them to a more sheltered position to prevent the plants being damaged.

WINDOW BOXES

Window boxes are often a good way of growing a selection of winter, spring and early summer annuals in a hot climate. They require only small amounts of good soil, are easily manageable and can be protected from weather extremes such as tropical downpours. Window boxes must carry a great weight of water at certain times, as well as soil. Use the same potting mix as you would use in any other container. One point to bear in mind when selecting plants is that exposure is critical. For example, window boxes on the southern side of the house will receive very little sun or possibly no sun at all if there is a large overhang. Boxes on the northern side will receive sunlight for much of the day (depending on overhang and time of year). Those on the eastern side will receive morning sun only, while those on the western side will receive the direct force of the afternoon sun. Thus shade-loving plants can be planted on the southern side; sun-lovers on the northern side; most plants (except those requiring full shade) on the eastern side and only plants which are very heat and sun-tolerant on the western side.

CONTAINER PLANTS INDOORS

Many plants which are commonly grown indoors, under low light conditions, come from warm, humid rainforests and are therefore easier to grow in the tropics and sub-tropics than they are in colder climates. Room temperatures do not need to be artificially raised, humidity is naturally present for much of the year, and there is plenty of bright, natural light. However, plants grown indoors do have some specialised needs.

TEMPERATURE

The plant list on page 199 consists of those which can be grown easily in the sub-tropics and tropics, without artificial heating. This range can be increased with the addition of cool-climate plants where rooms are airconditioned. This must be maintained all year round except during cold days in the sub-tropical winter. Some of the less tropical plants on this list may show signs of wilting in very hot weather, in which case they should be well watered and cooled by fans. Fans also help disperse extreme humidity which can adversely affect some plants such as cacti. In the sub-tropics, when winter temperatures seem likely to fall below 10°C, very tropical plants should be moved into warm corners, well away from open windows and draughts.

Most indoor plants need moderate to high levels of humidity, and in the tropics and during most of the year along the sub-tropical coast this is available. Misting with a fine spray may be necessary in dry times, or for very tropical plants, though furnishings may have to be protected. Furry-leaved plants such as rex begonias and African violets should not be sprayed. Grouped plants will maintain a higher humidity level, particularly if containers of water are placed around them.

GENERAL CARE

Indoor plants need to be spelled outdoors occasionally. This depends on the plant; any plant which shows signs of stress when other remedies have failed should be taken out of doors for a 'rest' in more natural conditions. Plants don't like abrupt changes of position or temperature; when seasonal movement is necessary, do this gradually over a few days. Don't move plants in and out of doors when there are sharp differences in temperature between the two.

Most plants need pruning for shape and size. Soft-stemmed plants and those which need more bushiness should be regularly tip-pruned. Dust should be regularly washed from plant leaves (except those with furry surfaces); just plain, tepid water is best. Soapy water (not strong detergents) can be used if leaves are particularly dirty or covered with residue; there are also special chemical leaf cleaners available but these need to be used sparingly and with great care.

LIGHT

As already outlined, the basic selection and care of plants grown indoors is mainly a matter of commonsense and differs little from cultivating pot plants outdoors. One major difference, however, is the need to provide adequate light. Though overwatering is often said to be the main problem with potted plants, lack of light actually accounts for most plant losses indoors.

For successful indoor growing, the precise light needs of individual plants must be correctly estimated before placing them. As a general guide, those which grow naturally in shade are the easiest to grow indoors, and usually require less specialised lighting. Large-leaved, dark-coloured, fleshy jungle plants which are found naturally in the deep shade of the rainforest are best for the darker corners. By contrast, some palms, though successful indoors, need quite a lot of light to grow. The less light a plant gets, the lower the temperature should be, so keep poorly lit areas cool and apply less water and fertiliser.

The first step is to make the most of whatever natural light is available, or can be made available. Obviously, the main sources of natural light indoors are windows. In broad terms, plants with highest light needs should be placed near windows and those with lowest needs placed furthest from them. Of course, it is not quite that simple. Much depends on which way the windows face. A north-facing window means great variation in light throughout the year, with plenty of it during winter when the sun is low in the sky and not too much direct light in summer when the angle of the sun is sharper and higher. An east-facing window favours most plants throughout the year because of its direct morning light. A west-facing window means a lot of hot, direct sunlight on a summer afternoon. A south-facing window means relatively low but constant light levels throughout the year. Obviously, the higher the amount of sunlight received through a window, the hotter the atmosphere for plants. And there are variations which need to be considered also. Only plants with low-light needs should be grown where the light source depends on a window with a southern exposure. Plants with fairly low light requirements will require protection from late morning sun near an east-facing window. Most indoor plants, except for cacti and those with succulent foliage, will suffer if left for long periods near a west-facing window.

The following list of popular indoor plants gives desirable window exposures but these are rough guides only. So much depends on individual house conditions. Governing factors might include the colour of the internal walls, the amount of overhang on windows, the influence of foliage outside, density and cleanliness of window glass, and, of course, the size of the windows.

Skylights are an excellent way of adding extra light to a room to encourage plant growth. Like windows, the density and angle of the light admitted will depend on the size, position and nature of the skylight. Skylights light the southern side of a room, with sunlight moving from east to west during the day. The bright shaft of sunlight beamed down through a skylight can be too strong for low-light plants and can also generate a great deal of heat, so take care to place plants which can't tolerate these conditions out of the direct light source.

Natural light from windows and skylights can be modified by means of curtains, blinds and shutters. And, of course, plants may need to be moved during the year to take advantage of seasonally changing light intensity, or to escape its full force. Having learned the amount of light required by individual plants, it is then necessary to estimate fairly accurately the amount of light in different areas where plants are to be grown accurately. This can be done using a special meter, which gives light readings in footcandles, a term used to measure the light received on surfaces such as plant leaves. Most plants require between 500 to 1000 footcandles though flowering plants may require a minimum 1000 footcandles. Lux is the term used for measuring the light itself, as beamed from its source. A camera lightmeter can be used to estimate light accurately, though it requires a sound understanding of light-measuring principles in photography and how to translate this into footcandles.

Rather than use meters, many indoor plant growers find it easier to try to develop an understanding of light intensity through experience. A bit of experimentation in the home will soon show whether a plant is happy or otherwise in a certain spot; if it is not, and it has been well-fed, adequately watered, is not too hot nor too cold, then the chances are it is suffering from too much or too little light. Try moving it, using the commonsense knowledge you have gained in the garden to tell which plants, e.g. spathiphyllums, prefer low light and which others, e.g. cacti, need strong light.

There are several quite simple ways of enhancing natural light in the house. These include:

❖ painting walls a matte white (this actually reflects light better than a gloss paint)
❖ using fine net curtains which reflect and disperse light over a distance
❖ using mirrors, mirror tiles or other reflective surfaces. Even aluminium foil can be effectively used in small areas for this purpose; it can be wrapped around pieces of timber or other hard material to form panels which can be placed so as to reflect light from a natural (or artificial) source.

Most people only want to grow a few plants in the house for decoration. They will want to take advantage of natural light, generally boosted by the normal household lights, and there will be no need to go to the expense and trouble of providing extensive artificial light. For those who regard indoor plant growing as a hobby, for those who live in apartments where natural light is limited, and for those who live in houses with heavily shaded rooms — as is not uncommon in hot climates — artificial light will be necessary to grow most indoor plants.

This is usually provided by either incandescent or fluorescent lighting placed to encourage plant growth; that is, most light should come from overhead, to simulate natural conditions as much as possible. Plants which are given up to 18 hours a day artificial light can grow and flower; but even for plants with low light needs, a minimum of 10 hours a day is necessary wherever natural light is insufficient. The day-length of artificial light may need to be seasonally adjusted to suit certain plants; for example, zygocactus (schlumbergera) will not flower if given light levels in excess of natural day length.

Special indoor lighting which actually fosters plant growth can be used. These lights are incandescent or fluorescent lights modified to emphasise the blue, red and far-red light rays which plants need for growth and flowering.

Almost any style of lighting can be used, to suit plant location and home decor. Lamps, individual bulbs, banks of lights, fluorescent strips, recessed and concealed lighting of all kinds, lights concealed in the tops of plant hangers will create a range of different effects. Wattage depends on the degree of natural light (or lack of it) and individual plant needs. Reflectors can be used to increase light or diffuse it over a wider area.

Incandescent bulbs and lamps emit a lot of heat which can damage plants if placed too close. A minimum of about 30 cm distance is desirable. This is not a problem with fluorescent lights which provide more than twice the amount of light as incandescent bulbs for the same wattage. The business of growing plants under artificial light is quite complicated and if you plan to do this extensively then it might be wise to seek the advice of an indoor plantscaper who can tell you precisely what will grow where and how much light is needed.

Finally, where a large number of plants are dependent on artificial light for long periods, I suggest you consider installing automatic timers: they are more reliable than the human memory.

Although some plants have very specialised lighting requirements, most can be roughly grouped into those with light requirements which are low (about 3 m from a well-lit window to a level where it is just possible to read a book), medium (up to about 2 m from a well-lit window, where it is easy to read small print) or high (up to 1 m from a well-lit window, with some direct sunlight, or else perhaps very bright sunlight filtered through light outdoor foliage). This is a rough guide only, but is helpful for those who want to grow a few plants indoors without going to a lot of expense and trouble.

You will find lighting information in the chart below as well as guides to suitable exposures. An additional *(D) denotes a plant which will take direct sunlight. Notable features are also included, for example whether a plant is a tree, shrub, foliage plant or flowering plant.

As I have said, any plant can be grown indoors given the right conditions. This means that flowering perennials and annuals which are not usually considered as indoor plants can be grown indoors if given plenty of light; preferably a combination of natural and artificial light. Like cacti, these can take direct sunlight provided this is not so prolonged and intense (e.g. an afternoon western exposure) that plants become burned or dehydrated. Kitchen windows are popular spots for flowering annuals; vegetables can also be grown indoors with good light.

LIGHT REQUIREMENTS FOR INDOOR PLANTS

Exposure
N — North
E — East
S — South
W — West
*(D) — direct sun

Light
L — low
M — medium
H — high
VH — very high

Special features
F — foliage
Fl — flowering
T — tree
S — shrub

Name	Exposure	Light	Features
AFRICAN VIOLET	N, E, S	H	Fl
Aglaeonema SPP.	N, E, S	L	F
Anthurium SPP.	N, E	M to H	Fl
Aralia sieboldii (syn. *Fatsia japonica*)	N, E, S	M	F
Araucaria SPP. (Bunya, Hoop & Norfolk Pines)	All	M	T
Ardisia SPP.	N, E, S	H	S
ASPIDISTRA (*Aspidistra eliator*)	E, S	L	F
Bamboos	N, E, W	H	F
Begonias (Rex and fibrous rooted)	N, E	M	F
(bedding or wax)	N, E, W, *(D)	H	Fl
BLACK BEAN, MORETON BAY CHESTNUT (*Castanospermum australe*)	All	All	F and Fl
Bowenia SPP. (BYFIELD FERN)	All	All	F

Gardening in Containers

Name	Exposure	Light	Features
Bromeliads	N, E, W	M, H	F and Fl
Cacti (and most succulents)	N, E,*(D)	H	F and Fl
Caladium SPP.	N, E, S	M	F
CAPE YORK LILY (*Curcuma australasica*)	E, S	L to M	Fl
Clivia SPP.	E, S	All	Fl
Coleus SPP.	All	L to M	F
CROTON (*Codiaeum* SPP.)	N, E, W,*(D)	M	F
Cycas SPP.	N, E, W,*(D)	H	F
Cyclamen SPP.	E	H	Fl
DAVIDSON'S PLUM (*Davidsonia pruriens*)	N, E, W	M to H	F
Dieffenbachia SPP.	E, W, S	M	F
Dipladenia SPP.	N, E, W,*(D)	H	Fl
Dizygotheca elegantissima (FALSE ARALIA)	N, E	M	
Dracaena SPP.	All	M	
Elephant's Ears (*Colocasia esculenta* (TARO) and *Alocasia microrrhiza* SPP.	E, S	L to M	F, Fl

Ferns

Name	Exposure	Light	Features
Asparagus SPP.	All	M to H	F
Birds'-nest ferns (*Asplenium* SPP.)	E	All	F
Davallia SPP. (Hare's-foot ferns)	E, S	L to M	F
Donkey's Tail (*Sedum morgananianum*)	All	H	F
KING FERN (*Todea barbara*)	All	All	F
Maidenhair ferns (*Adiantum* SPP.)	E, S	L	F
MOTHER SPLEENWORT, HEN AND CHICKEN (*Asplenium bulbiferum*)	E, S	L	F
Nephrolepis SPP.(ruffled or fishbone ferns)	E, S	L to M	F
Pteris SPP. (brake ferns)	E, S	L to M	F
Figs (*Ficus* SPP. inc. Rubber Tree and benjamina varieties)	N, E, W,*(D)	M to H	F
Fittonia SPP.	E, S	All	F
Fuchsia SPP.	N, E	H	Fl
Ginger, Shell (*Alpinia* SPP.)	E, S	All	F, Fl
GOLD-DUST TREE (*Aucuba japonica*)	All	M	F
Impatiens SPP. (BUSY LIZZIE)	E, S	M to H	Fl
Ivies (*Hedera* SPP.)	All	M, H	F
Ixora SPP.	All	H	Fl
JADE TREE (*Crassula portulacea* syn. *argentea*)	All	H	F
Kalanchoe SPP.	N, E, W	H	Fl
KANGAROO VINE (*Cissus antarctica*)	All	All	F
Monstera deliciosa (Fruit Salad Plant)	All	L to M	F
Nandina domestica 'NANA' (DWARF SACRED BAMBOO)	E, S	All	F
Orchids (most species)	N, E	H	Fl
Cattleya SPP.		VH	

Palms

Name	Exposure	Light	Features
ALEXANDRA PALM (*Archontophoenix alexandrae*)	All	All	F
ATHERTON PALM (*Laccospadix australasica*)	N, E, S	L to M	F
DWARF DATE PALM (*Phoenix roebelinii*)	N, E, W	M to H	F
FAN PALM (*Licuala ramsayi*)	All	All	F
Kentia palms (*Howea* SPP.)	All	All	F

Name	Exposure	Light	Features
Lady palms (*Rhapis* SPP.)	N, E, S,*(D)	L to M	F
Lepidozamia SPP.	N, E, S,*(D)	All	F
Parlor Palm (*Chamaedorea elegans*)	N, E, S	L to M	F
Solitaire Palm (*Ptychosperma elegans*)	N, E, S	L to M	F
Walking Stick Palm (*Linospadix monostachya*)	N, E, S	All	F
Palm lilies (*Cordyline* SPP.)	All	L to M	F, Fl
Peperomia SPP.	All	All	H
Poinsettia (*Euphorbia pulcherrima*)	N, E, W,*(D)	H	F
Pothos (*Epipremnum aurum*)	All	All	F
Philodendron SPP.	All	L to M	F
Prayer Plant (*Maranta* SPP.)	N, E, S	All	F
Randia SPP. (native gardenias)	N, E, S	L to M	S, Fl
Silky Oak (*Grevillea robusta*)	All	H	F, L
Spathiphyllum SPP.	E, S	L	F, Fl
Staghorns (*Platycerium* SPP.)	E, S	M	F
Swedish ivies (*Plectranthus* SPP.)	All	All	F
Tillandsia SPP. (Air plants)	N, E, W,*(D)	H	F
Tree ferns (*Cyathea* and *Dicksonia* SPP.)	E, S	All	F
Umbrella Tree (*Schefflera* SPP.)	All,*(D)	All	F
Wandering Jew (*Tradescantia fluminensis* and *zebrina*)	All	M	F
Zebra Plant (*Aphelandra squarrosa*)	N, E, W	M	F
Zygocactus (*Schlumbergera truncata*)	N, E, W	M to H	Fl

NB As a further guide, most plants with variegated leaves need at least medium light.

DAY-LENGTH REQUIREMENTS FOR FLOWERING

Many flowering plants have exact requirements in the length of daylight required to initiate flowering. Some are easy to deal with: tuberous begonias, for example, need about 14 hours of daylight all year; others are quite complicated, the different species of cattleya orchids each have different requirements. Day-length refers to the amount of daylight normal for the time of year. As artificial light extends day-length for indoor plants, those which require short day-lengths to initiate flowering need to be taken out of the house for the critical period (usually 6–8 weeks) of bud development or else kept in a room where no lights are used at night. Plants with these requirements usually also prefer cool temperatures during the bud-setting period; otherwise although flowers should develop they may not last very long.

A few of the more popular indoor flowering plants with their day-length requirements are listed below as a general guide.

Indoor flowering plants

African Violet	Day-neutral plants which flower best with 14–16 hours of light each day
Azalea	Constant low-light (35 to 50 foot-candles—fc) or six weeks in autumn, then 500 to 1000 fc until about 3 weeks before flowering (sub-tropics)
Begonia (tuberous, wax)	14 hours of day-length each day Short day-length incubation period is not necessary but plants which are given up to 14 hours of darkness for about 6 weeks will show improved flowering
Cattleya Orchid	Normal day-night length for time of year, even under artificial light
Impatiens	Same as for African violets
Kalanchoe	14 hours of darkness each day for 6 weeks
Poinsettia	14 hours of darkness each day for 6–8 weeks. Best when given long spells outdoors at the warmest time of year
Zygocactus	12–14 hours of darkness for 8 weeks.

INDOOR PLANT PROBLEMS

Plants grown indoors are subject to fewer pests than in the garden. Most common pests are mealy bugs, scales and aphids. Red spider mites can be a nuisance with palms. Controls are the same as for all plants grown in containers or in-ground in the garden; however, the more intense degree of cultivation and observation given to indoor plants makes it easier to use non-chemical control methods. For instance, any stray caterpillars may be readily picked off by hand while infestations of scale and aphids can be treated by spongeing the leaves with soapy water. Serious infestations of mealy bugs are difficult to control even with chemicals; often the best treatment is to take the plant outdoors until the problem disappears.

Plants grown indoors are prone to the same problems as container plants. They may also show signs of stress from being placed too close to a window in full sun (leaf scorching, drying out, wilting) or near a lamp or some other heat source. Airconditioning will dry plants out unless they are regularly misted. The first step in solving these problems is to remove the plant as quickly as possible (but not so quickly as to cause trauma), to a more natural environment in a sheltered spot out of doors or in a bush house. If plants don't recover, look for other causes such as waterlogging, lack of water, pest infestation or disease. Plants which lose their colour are usually suffering from lack of adequate light.

Shadehouses and garden sheds

SHADEHOUSES

SHADEHOUSES PROTECT PLANTS FROM THE SUN and are used mainly by gardeners who grow orchids, ferns and other shade-loving plants. They are also useful places for propagation, raising seedlings and potting up or potting on plants for use elsewhere, as well as sheltering house plants being spelled.

It is possible to have shadehouses professionally erected, but as construction is relatively simple and kit forms are available, most gardeners prefer to put up their own. Materials (or kits) can be obtained from hardware stores or specialist suppliers. The main material used is knitted polyethylene shadecloth over a frame of galvanised steel, timber or PVC piping. Shadecloth comes in various ratings based on its ability to block out ultra-violet light, ranging from 30–90 per cent. An average garden shadehouse has a 70–80 per cent roof and 50 per cent sides. The roof variation depends on the position of the shadehouse: one which is exposed to hot sun all day in the tropics will certainly require 80 per cent, while 70 per cent is adequate for a shadehouse in the sub-tropics which receives some shade during the day. These differences are not very important, and either block rating will do.

You can choose from a range of decorator colours: plants will grow as well under shades of beige, brown and mixed colours as they do under plain green. Black and white are less suitable for domestic use; black and dark colours absorb light while white reflects it. Today's knitted shadecloth resists fraying and unravelling when cut and gives excellent tear resistance and 'burst' strength. This means it can withstand quite a lot of abuse, including strong wind and hail. A peaked roof is cooler than one which is flat and it will better deflect weather. A flat top will collect debris and may also hold water during heavy rain, which can cause sagging. If you must have a flat roof, make sure it has plenty of battens or steel mesh across the top to hold it rigid. Fastening accessories should be of best quality, resistant to rust.

Siting your shadehouse is important. The sun-blocking effect can be greatly increased by placing it on the southern side of the house, or where it is shaded by trees. This will have an adverse effect on many plants which still need adequate light to grow. It is also wise to avoid siting a shadehouse where it is exposed to constant strong winds (such as near the beach).

Shadehouses can be very adaptable. You may wish to erect them so that the sides can be rolled up or the top rolled back. They can function as simple plant houses, without doors and open along one side, or as completely enclosed structures with doors made of shadecloth on a solid frame or just tied at the sides. If the shadehouse is to shelter a valued plant collection, or delicate seedlings, it needs to be as secure as possible against weather and insect pests. Collections, for example, ferns or orchids, need to be seen to be admired, and require constant tending. For this reason the shadehouse must be large enough to house a growing collection without overcrowding the plants or preventing easy access to them. Probably many specimens will be suspended from the roof, which means room must be left to walk between them.

Two useful adjuncts to a shadehouse are electrical outlets, for a wide range of uses, and a watering system. These need to be included in the initial planning.

The warm, shaded, sheltered, humid shadehouse environment is ideal for plants such as orchids and ferns but it can also be a breeding ground for pests and diseases, so hygiene is very important. Unused plant pots should be well washed for re-use, it is even worth soaking them in disinfectant or one of the solutions used for sterilising babies' bottles before re-use. Clear away all debris, keep the corners tidy, benchtops clean after use, and remove all dead and dying foliage promptly. Unused pot saucers filled with stagnant water are breeding grounds for harmful fungi and mosquitoes. Avoid overcrowding, which cuts down air circulation.

Structures to shade and shelter plants can be built out of other materials besides shadecloth. These are traditionally known as bush houses and may be constructed from plain timber or timber trellis according to the gardener's own design and needs. These can look very decorative, particularly when attached to the house so as to be easily visible. They are suitable for growing most ferns, a range of shade-loving plants, and many orchids. They are also suitable places for spelling indoor plants. Unlike fully enclosed shadehouses, bush houses do not provide a protected, fairly controlled environment.

Use well treated timber; even if you build your bush house of odds and ends they should be weather-treated or the structure is likely to rot and collapse before very long.

FERNERIES

These are usually attached to a house in order to be readily visible from it and can be a good way of using otherwise awkward niches. For example, a semi-enclosed space with house walls on two or three sides, such as is sometimes found outside dining rooms and bedrooms, makes an ideal fernery because it can be easily and inexpensively roofed over with shadecloth (unlike hard material, shadecloth allows moisture from natural rainfall to pass through, which is good for the plants). The other side (or sides) can also be enclosed with shadecloth if desired, or perhaps walled with lattice. A partly enclosed patio, too, can make an excellent fernery. Other plant collections, such as orchids, can be housed in this way. Ferneries established on western walls will need adequate protection from afternoon sun. Those on southern walls will have a low natural light level. An irrigation system is desirable in ferneries to provide adequate water at regular intervals. If not, a tap must be handy for hand watering.

SHEDS

A few hints for hot-climate gardeners! Most garden sheds manufactured today for the home gardener are the steel or aluminium, self-erect type. The alternative is timber, which is more attractive but also more expensive. The metal sheds can be very hot inside, so if you are planning to spend any time in there (rather than just using it as a place to store tools), then a window will improve ventilation.

Most sheds have sliding doors which open wide. If possible, position the shed so that the doorway faces south or east to take advantage of prevailing breezes and give some protection against hot afternoon sun. It will also be cooler if storage cupboards or benches are placed along the western and/or northern sides and work benches on the eastern and/or southern sides.

UV block levels recommended for particular plants

30%	50%	70%	80%
Cutflowers	Azaleas	Ferns	Ferns
Hydroponics	Seedlings	Indoor plants	Indoor plants (low light level)
Seedlings	Orchids	Orchids	
Strawberries		General purpose	
Vegetables			

Propagating your own plants

IN THE PAST, DEDICATED GARDENERS used to raise their own plants from seeds or cuttings taken from plants in other gardens, or sometimes from the wild, because this was the only way they could obtain certain desirable plants. Today, of course, the range of plants available in nurseries is vast enough to satisfy most gardeners; however there are still those who enjoy the challenge and satisfaction of propagating plants at home. The majority of them are gardeners who prefer to raise vegetables, annuals and some perennials from seed, which is certainly cheaper than buying seedlings. Others may collect or breed certain plants as a hobby.

A hot climate offers certain advantages to home propagators. Artificial bottom heating for seedlings is not usually necessary, unless you wish to strike cuttings in the sub-tropical cool season. The ground is always warm enough for transplanting seedlings outdoors, or for sowing seeds where they are to grow. Above all, the rapid growth rate of young plants satisfies even the most impatient gardener.

On the other hand, high heat and humidity increases the dangers of fungal diseases such as damping off, in which seedlings just keel over and die, while some cold-climate plants just will not germinate at very high temperatures.

The two propagation methods commonly used by home gardeners are seeds and cuttings. A third, layering, is briefly described. Grafting requires the acquisition of certain skills and the right equipment. This does not put it beyond the ability of home gardeners but it is not a common enough practice to be included here.

SEEDS

The seed that we buy in packets from garden centres and other retail gardening outlets is easy to sow, easy to grow and especially formulated to produce reliable, high-quality plants. There is also the added advantage of sowing information on the packet.

If you take seed from garden plants, or the wild, it is important to understand the different germination requirements. Some seed only remains viable for a very short period; most very fine seed, which looks like dust in the hand, is of this nature. Seeds with hard coats, on the other hand, usually retain viability for months, perhaps years. In between these two extremes are many variations; if you don't know how long a particular seed is likely to remain viable, it is safest to sow it right away. You will soon know if it is not viable because there will be no germination.

Treatments for different seeds

HARD COATS: Scarify or nick the water-impervious surface, preferably opposite the 'eye'; seen (sometimes with great difficulty) as a tiny mark or depression in the coating.

Banksias and some other plants have very hard, usually large and dark-coloured, seed coats which need heat to burst them before germination. This can be done over a gas or charcoal barbecue, or in the oven, until the pods burst. *Don't leave the seeds on the heat, or in the oven, any longer or they will cook.*

FLESHY COATS: Soak in clean, tepid water for 24 hours before sowing.

FINE, DUST-LIKE SEEDS: No especial treatment but may be easier to mix with a fine sand before sowing.

SEEDS WITH WINGS: Remove wings before sowing.

Most garden plants today are hybrids and seed taken from these, or their many cultivars, is unlikely to produce a plant with exactly the same qualities as the parent. This may not matter too much; you will still get a satisfactory plant, but seed from a 'true', non-hybridised source is a better bet. By the same token, seeds from plants which have been cross pollinated by natural methods (mostly birds and bees) may yield plants with a mixture of characteristics. This can be a problem with vegetables if the dominant characteristics result in a poor plant. So vegetables intended for seed harvesting need to be isolated or protected in some way (perhaps by netting).

If you begin your home propagating career with bought seeds, as most of us do, and then progress to collecting your own, don't be disappointed at the slower (often much slower) germination rate. Businesses which produce seed commercially cater for the impatience of home gardeners by coming up with a product which germinates much faster than its counterparts in nature.

A step-by-step seed-raising guide

1. Buy a specially-formulated seed-raising mix or make your own. A suggested hot-climate mix is 2 parts of sterilised soil (a fine loam) or river sand to 1 part of peatmoss, thoroughly mixed in a bucket, with a teaspoon of dolomite and a dose of balanced fertiliser. A liquid fertiliser diluted at half strength is easy to use at the rate of about 500 ml to a 5–litre bucket. With a solid compound, a teaspoonful in the same quantity of water will do. Spraying the mix with a copper oxychloride fungicide will help prevent damping off.
2. Select your containers. Anything with good drainage will do, though shallow containers are best. Seedling punnets are ideal and make later pricking out easy, particularly the single cell types.
3. Make sure containers are hygienic to guard against disease. Whether you use old plant pots or traditional, neatly constructed seed boxes, they must be washed very clean. An extra precaution is to sterilise with one of the solutions used for babies' bottles.
4. Level and slightly firm the mix. Sow very light seed evenly on the surface. Sow larger seed in drills made by running your forefinger or an implement along the surface in a straight row, making a shallow depression or press them individually into the mix. Cover and firm lightly. Roughly speaking, a seed should be covered by about its own depth of mix. Sowing too deeply is a major cause of non-germination so seeds should be only just below the surface.
5. Mist seedlings with a fine spray of very clean water. Cover with glass or plastic to retain moisture and protect seed. Keep in a shaded low-light area.
6. Once seeds start to sprout, remove all coverings immediately.
7. Spray lightly each day with a mist of water. Don't over-water but don't let the soil become too dry, either.
8. When the real leaves start to appear, as distinct from the one or two seedling leaves which sprout first, gently transplant seedlings where they are to grow.

If sowing directly into the ground where plants are to grow, make sure the soil has been first worked to a fine tilth. Don't choose a time when heavy rain is obviously imminent or the seeds may be washed out of place. If the plants are to grow randomly, as in a wilderness or certain areas of a cottage garden, the seed can be broadcast with the hand, then lightly raked over. Otherwise, make drills with your forefinger or some implement, cover the seed lightly with soil and firm gently into place. Once the seedlings develop, they can be thinned out to allow room for others to grow. Weaker plants can be thrown away, others planted elsewhere.

CUTTINGS

Plants can be produced vegetatively from other plants by taking cuttings. It is a simple and quick way of obtaining a lot of plants of one type and shrubs are nearly always propagated this way. Cuttings can be taken from just about any part of the plant, from root to tip. Home gardeners are most likely to take cuttings from the stem of the plant and this can be done in three ways:

Hardwood cuttings (shrubs)

These are usually taken in the cooler months from old growth. The area where leaf stems meet the main stem is called a node, often noticeable by a slight ridge or swelling, and tiny buds in the space (axil) between the two stems. With large shrubs, cuttings of up to 30 cm long should be taken by making a cut just below a node. If you are taking a tip cutting, this is the only cut necessary; if a section of stem then make the second cut just above another node. Leave a small amount of leaf growth either at the tip or the top node but remove all lower and larger leaves. If top leaves are large, cut them in half, leaving only the bottom half. This allows photosynthesis to take place but reduces the amount of energy needed to sustain a large amount of vegetation.

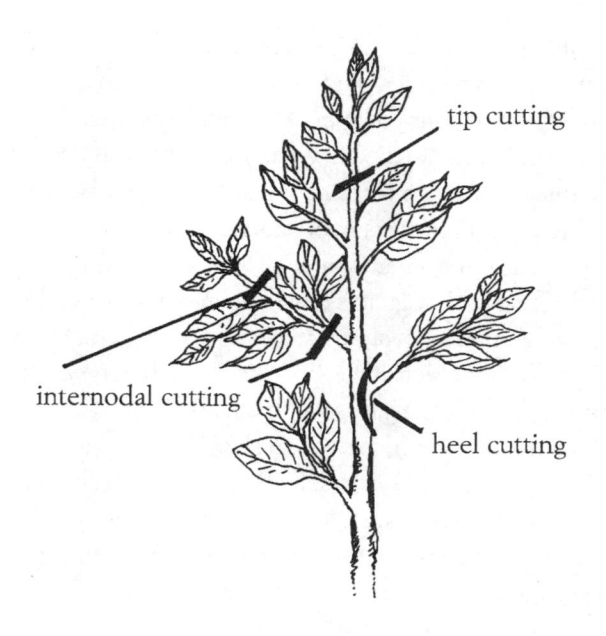

Half-ripe cuttings (shrubs)

These semi-hardwood cuttings are taken from the softer sideshoots and other current season's growth sections. They should be up to 10 cm long.

Softwood and tip cuttings (herbaceous plants and some shrubs)

The same method as for hardwood cuttings, except that the stem material is soft and fleshy, or in the case of shrubs taken from the new tips of the plant, and the cuttings are up to 7 cm long.

With all these cuttings, you require a very sharp knife or pair of secateurs to make a straight, clean cut across the stem. Or, with cuttings taken from a side shoot, a slightly diagonal cut can be made to include a 'heel' or small section of the older branch stem.

Potting your cuttings

Any kind of deep container can be used for striking cuttings and some can be stuck straight into the ground. Hardwood cuttings can be stuck into a trench of free-draining soil or a sand and soil mix until they strike, or placed in containers. Softwood cuttings should be placed in a container of high quality compost or half compost–half sand or vermiculite mix. Softwood cuttings need to be kept warmer than do hardwood cuttings. Half-ripe cuttings and tip cuttings of azaleas, camellias and other woody plants should be planted into a container of peat and sand mix (usually a 2:1 mix ratio), or a mix of sand and peaty compost. Cuttings generally stand a better chance of rooting if they are first dampened at the base and dipped into one of the hormone powders obtainable from gardening retail outlets. This powder should be used up quickly and not stored for too long, as it loses strength.

The potting medium should be well moistened before use, after which cuttings can be gently but thoroughly watered once. In hot weather, give them a light misting once or twice a day but over-watering will cause rotting. Don't panic if the stems and leaves droop a bit at first; this is common with softwood cuttings, and with the remaining leaves of hardwood cuttings. No real watering of the soil should take place until the cuttings are sprouting and planted out.

Some cuttings need to be kept permanently humid (but not wet). The simplest way is to cover them completely with a clear plastic bag, supported on a frame (wooden skewers are suitable, or twisted wire) to keep it clear of the foliage. The bag can be secured to the pot with a rubber band.

As cuttings start to develop roots under the soil or potting mix, so they will also produce leaf growth. Once this occurs, they can be planted wherever required.

SUCKERS

Not all plants strike easily from cuttings. Instead, some plants such as allamanda, ixora and brunfelsia can be propagated from suckers which grow from the roots, close to the main stem. The old root is cut with a knife near the sucker on the side of the plant. This, with the remainder of the root attached, should be potted. This method has the advantage of an already developed root and growing tip.

LEAF CUTTINGS

Some soft-leaved plants can be propagated by leaf cuttings. With African violets, a healthy leaf, complete with stalk, is carefully plucked off the parent stem and the stalk is stuck into a peat and sand mix so that the underside of the leaf lies flat. New roots will form at the juncture of leaf and stalk.

With Rex begonias the stalk is cut close to the leaf base, leaving only a stub, and the veins on the underside of the leaf are gently cut with a very sharp knife, with spacings of a couple of centimetres between cuts. The leaf is then secured flat on top of the mix, which should be kept just slightly moist but never over-watered, until the new roots develop. Leaf cuttings need tem-peratures of at least 16°C; where temperatures are lower, then heated propagation frames are necessary.

LAYERING

Plants with runners can be propagated by pegging or tamping down nodes or the terminal bud into garden soil or putting them over pots containing soil. As soon as the roots appear, the 'new' sections are severed from the main runner to form new plants. If a pot is used, the new plant can easily be transplanted elsewhere. Many climbing plants are propagated using this method but although it is easiest to do with plants that have long runners or stems, it can also be used for many other plants which have bottom branches near the ground, including azaleas. With these shrubs, bend the selected branch or incise with a sharp knife up to 7 cm lengthwise, just below a selected bud, to inhibit sap flow. Layering is best done in summer, when rooting can take place fast, before the stem section can rot in the ground. Use a non-flowering branch or runner.

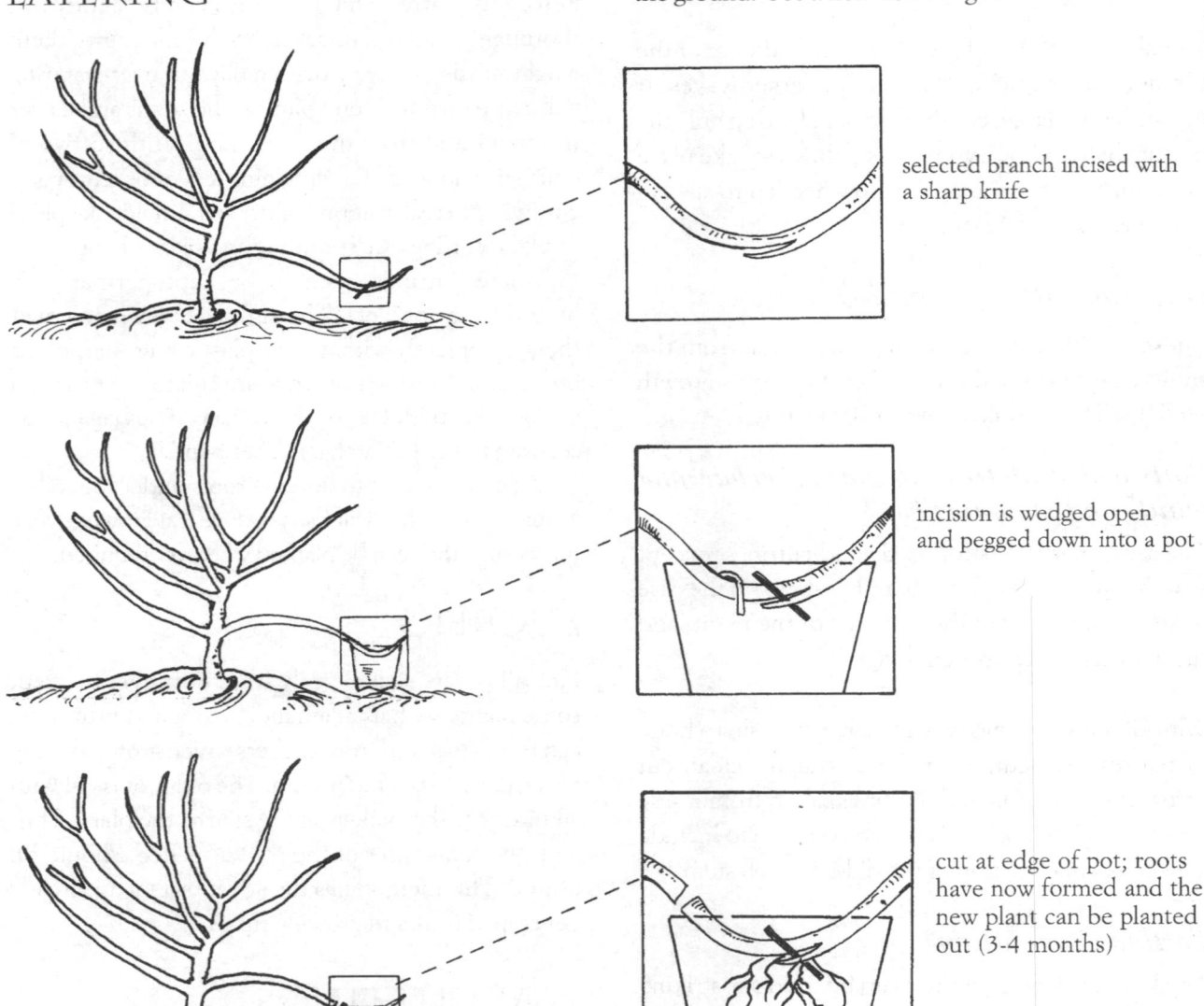

selected branch incised with a sharp knife

incision is wedged open and pegged down into a pot

cut at edge of pot; roots have now formed and the new plant can be planted out (3-4 months)

DIVISION

Plants with bulbs, corms, rhizomes and fibrous roots can be separated by division. This means digging up plants which have grown into large clumps and either pulling or cutting them apart. With some very large or difficult clumps, garden forks or spades can be used to drive down through the centre and force the clump first in half and then into the desired sections for replanting. The time to undertake plant division is the cool season when plants are dormant or not growing strongly.

Clumps of bulbs or corms (similar to bulbs but with the new sections developing on top of the old) are dug up, carefully separated and planted separately. Although bulbs are traditionally lifted and stored in winter, in a warm climate they are generally replanted in the ground after division. On the other hand if you are growing cool-climate plants, they will do best if placed in the fridge for a few weeks before it is time to plant them out again.

Some tubers, such as those of dahlias and begonias, are cut vertically through the centre, then given a dusting of dolomite or talcum powder to seal the wound. Each section should have a shoot, and the cut pieces are planted out in the usual way. Tubers are also treated this way, by being cut into sections and planted out separately.

Root and bulb division is not only an easy way of propagating plants, it is also a useful way of reducing the size of large clumps of plants such as cannas and agapanthus.

Still other plants, notably cacti and some ferns, produce little 'baby' plants called offsets. These also form on some bulbs, above the soil line. Offsets can be easily removed and planted out.

Plants propagated from seed

Most annuals and vegetables
BASIL
BORAGE
CHICORY
DILL

Plants propagated from cuttings

Most woody stemmed shrubs and trees
HELIOTROPE (CHERRY PIE)
PELARGONIUM (GERANIUMS)
REX BEGONIA (leaf cuttings)
Roses (floribunda, hybrid tea, miniature and climbing roses)
ZYGOCACTUS

Plants propagated by division

Agapanthus SPP.
Aloe SPP.
Babiana SPP.
Cyrtanthus SPP.
GARLIC
Iris SPP.
Lachenalia SPP.
LILIES (*Lilium* SPP. in general)
ORCHIDS (either of fibrous roots or offsets)
Phormium SPP. (NEW ZEALAND FLAX)
Sedum SPP. (STONECROP)
Sempervivum SPP.
Stokesia SPP.

Either/or plants

Agave SPP. — seed or division
Ajuga SPP. — seed, cuttings or division
BASIL — (contrary to common belief) can be propagated by tip cuttings, though seed is the more usual method
TUBEROUS-ROOTED BEGONIAS — seed, softwood cuttings and division
CHAMOMILE — seed, cuttings or division
CHIVES — seed or division
Clivia SPP. — seed or division
CHRYSANTHEMUMS — seed or cuttings.
Crinum SPP. — seed or division and offsets
CROWN OF THORNS (*Euphorbia milii*) — cuttings or seed
DAY LILY (*Hemerocallis* SPP.) — seed or division
Echeveria SPP. — leaf cuttings or division
Erigeron SPP. — seed or division
FENNEL — seed or division
FLAME LILY (*Gloriosa* spp.) — seed or division
FREESIA — seed or division
Gaillardia SPP. — seed, cuttings (half-ripe) or division
Hippeastrum SPP. — seed or division
Hosta SPP. — seed or division
Hymenocallis SPP. — seed or division
Kalanchoe SPP. — seed or cuttings
Kniphofia SPP. (Torch Lily, Red Hot Poker) — seed or division
LEMON BALM — seed or division
Lobelia SPP. — seed or division
Lobivia cactus — seed or cuttings
Mammillaria and *Mammilopsis* cactus — seed or division
MARJORAM — seed or layering
MINT — division, cuttings or seed
Muscari (GRAPE HYACINTH) — seed or division
Polyanthus SPP. — seed or division
Ranunculus SPP. — seed or division
ROSEMARY — seed or cuttings (half-ripe)
RUE (seed or cuttings)

Sage — seed or cuttings (half-ripe)
Salad Burnett — seed or division
Senecio spp. — seed, cuttings, division
Tansy — seed or division
Tarragon — division or cuttings
Thyme — seed or cuttings
Violet — seed or division
Wandering Jew (*Tradescantia* spp.) — seed or division
Zantedeschia (Arum Lily) — seed or division

Ferns

These are mostly propagated by spores, which is hard for the home gardener to do. However, the following fern species can be propagated by rhizome division or by removing and planting offsets which appear on the parent plant.

Asplenium
Blechnum (offsets)
Davallia
Dicksonia (offsets)
Nephrolepis
Platycerium (division of root buds)
Polypodium
Polystichum (division of crown)
Pteris (division of crown or rhizomes)

Adiantum and *Lygodium* spp. can be propagated by layering (see page 208). Peg down a joint (or node) which has a centre bud.

8
Caring for your garden

Before you start—the importance of soil and drainage

THE GOOD EARTH

In sub-tropical and tropical regions of Australia, including the arid areas, the kind of humus-rich sandy loam ideal for gardening is rare indeed. So we have the choice either of putting up with whatever soil is on the block and limiting plantings to those which can thrive there, or improving the soil to suit a wider range of plants.

For quick results, a heavy, hard or shaly soil should be thoroughly worked over. This is best done with machinery because the digging required will be very hard work in a hot climate unless you are very young, fit and keen.

Organic material such as compost and well-rotted manures should be added and the surface mulched. Then continuous top mulching of the soil with organic matter will bring about sufficient improvement to begin plantings within a few months. Frequent mulching over the years will bring the soil to a permanently manageable consistency, with plenty of nutrition. Clay can be effectively lightened with gypsum, often marketed under names such as 'claybreaker'.

It is not always necessary to work over an entire garden. You may prefer to put in plantings of species suited to the local soil (these may be exotics as well as indigenous plants) in most of the garden and only improve the soil in special areas such as flower beds, vegetable and herb gardens. Another alternative is to bring in quality loam from outside; this may be expensive by comparison but gives quick results — provided the soil is from a reliable source. When buying soil, make sure the supplier understands what it is for and, if possible, visit the site from which it is to come. The best suppliers have well-organised sites where soils and other growing media are extracted and blended; soils from these suppliers are likely to be appropriately sterilised, weed free and without large lumps. Soils from less reputable sources may contain contaminants, weeds and large clods which are hard work to break down.

The no-dig method discussed on page 184 is also worth considering for flower gardens. How to improve sandy soils, particularly the deep, loose sands common to coastal dunes, are discussed on page 43. The rich, red soils so popular with vegetable growers can be heavy enough to give many young garden plants a slow start. Sand or a lighter loam, or plenty of compost, can be dug into individual beds to help plant roots establish themselves.

Soil pH

Soils are either acid, neutral or alkaline in nature and this is measured on a pH scale ranging from 1–14. Neutral medium is at pH 7; acid soils range *below* pH 7; alkaline soils range *above*. The closer soil is to neutral, the more suitable it is for a range of plants. Some plants, however, require fairly acid soils while others come from alkaline soil habitats. Azaleas are among the best known acid-loving plants, others include camellias, vireya rhododendrons, ferns, most rainforest and heathland plants, orchids and food plants such as tomatoes and strawberries. Many common annuals, by contrast, prefer a fairly alkaline soil. Soils in hot, wet climates tend towards acidity, while some hot, dry, inland areas have soils which are alkaline. Where a higher acidity level is required, sulphur in a variety of forms readily available from garden centres is the chemical remedy, applied directly to or around the plant. Mulching over a long period, particularly with highly acidic materials such as pine bark, pine needles, sawdust and leafmould lowers the pH level of soil, that is, makes it more acid, as does the natural mulching which takes place in shrubberies and rainforest gardens. The pH level can be raised, or 'sweetened' by adding dolomite, and this is nearly always necessary when growing annuals, many herbs and certain vegetables.

You can text soil pH with easy-to-use kits available from garden centres. Hydrangeas are also reliable monitors of soil pH levels because their flowers are blue on acid soils and pink on alkaline soils. A predominance of mauve flowers, pink *and* blue flowers and those which seem indeterminate between the two indicates a neutral soil. Hydrangeas can be made to bloom either blue or pink by acidifying the soil or making it more alkaline.

DRAINAGE

Poor drainage is responsible for many garden problems; particularly root rot diseases which cause healthy plants to wilt, keel over and die suddenly. Internal drainage schemes just to improve garden conditions are usually too difficult and expensive for most householders, though if your block has severe problems they will have to be considered. In areas where there is heavy monsoonal rainfall and soil does not drain freely, relatively simple planting methods can overcome drainage problems.

To test your drainage, dig a hole at least 20 cm deep and fill it with water. The rate at which the water disappears gives you an idea of the drainage capability of your soil (this will vary in different parts of your garden, so dig several holes). If the water takes more than five minutes or so to disappear, the area is not suitable for all but a small number of plants which tolerate waterlogging.

There are several ways of overcoming this without expensive underground drainage. For small areas, raised flower beds filled with free-draining soil will be adequate. Rockeries are equally well-drained. Individual trees should be planted in a mound above the ground, rather than in a deep hole. Large mounds should also be made to plant groups of trees and shrubs. It is best if the soil beneath the mound is first turned over to a depth of up to 300 mm, though this is not strictly necessary unless it is very compacted. You will need to get rid of any stoloniferous or bulbous weeds first, including any solid grass cover, see pages 231–2 and 233; the quickest method is to spray with glysophate or some other grasskiller. The mound can consist of as much of the original topsoil as possible (if suitable, otherwise imported soil can be used), mixed with plenty of humus and lighter material such as river sand. This will give a friable, nutritious soil base.

Mounds are an excellent way of growing many native Australian plants which require excellent drainage, for example grevilleas. Many of the more shallow-rooted species will find sufficient growing room in a large mound; deeper-rooted plants will be well established, with plenty of well-drained areas through which they can spread, before having to establish themselves in the less well-drained soil below. Obviously, the bigger the mound, the better the drainage; the larger the plants, the bigger the mound. Mounds also help to slow down and/or direct water runoff to the rest of the garden. Here it can be allowed to drain away, or possibly used in some way. To conserve water within the mound itself, rip the earth horizontally across the fall of the mound to catch and hold water long enough to give plants a good drink.

Clay soils are poorly drained and can be improved with both gypsum, as already mentioned, and by mixing in a load or two of river sand or very sandy soil.

Planting

SELECTING PLANTS

BOOKS AND MAGAZINE ARTICLES will identify the type of plants you would like to grow and whether they are suitable for your garden. Visit garden centres, because new plants are being introduced all the time. Plants in books may be out of date or otherwise not available but a good garden centre will always have suitable substitutes as well as some plants not listed in your books. Garden centres do not stock a full range of available plants year-round; there is a good deal of seasonal variance. Always ask for a plant which you can't see, because they may be able to order it for you.

Make sure the plant you buy is healthy. Sick plant symptoms include drooping, withered or twisted foliage, leaf-yellowing and spots on leaves. Some plants have naturally light green foliage; one whose foliage appears unnaturally pale is usually easy to spot. Beware, also, plants with roots extending through the drainage holes, they have been in the pot too long. If the plant looks really healthy, and you are planning to plant or re-pot it right away, this is not much of a problem, although you will need to gently trim the roots before planting. The same goes for moss on the surface of the potting mix. This can indicate neglect, but if the plant looks healthy then it probably is worth buying.

Always buy enough plants at one time to do a particular job. For example, if planning a hedge or a border, don't buy so few plants that you have to space them unrealistically. Avoid the temptation of buying one of every plant you see. It is usually better (except with trees and larger shrubs) to plant more than one of each.

Selecting plants can be a frustrating business. First, there are so many plants from which to choose that selection can be a formidable task. Then, having decided (with great difficulty perhaps) on exactly what you need, you find they aren't available. It is still better to do your homework as to which types of plants best fit your garden scheme — but don't be afraid of impulse buying either. It is one of the great delights of being a gardener, even if you do sometimes come home with an 'unplanned' plant and wonder where on earth you are going to put it.

PLANTING SEEDS AND SEEDLINGS

There is more to planting than just shoving a plant in the ground and hoping it will grow. Different plants require different techniques, as do different soils.

Annuals, many perennials and most vegetables are grown from seed or seedlings, either purchased or raised in your own shadehouse. They require a bed of good soil worked to a very fine tilth because they are too delicate to thrive in ordinary, unimproved garden soil. If soil is very acid, a light dressing of dolomite will be required every couple of years.

Some seeds, if not raised to seedling stage in the shadehouse, can be planted directly into the ground. In a hot climate where soil compacts readily and heavy rain may fall, an additional top dressing of seed-raising mixture gives them a safer start. Sowing information is found on page 133. Again, because of strong sunlight and heavy rain, it helps to cover the bed with a fine net or a thin layer of open, light mulch such as sugarcane trash until the first leaves are safely above ground. Seedlings are sold in punnets either with flat bottoms or individual cells. The latter are easier (though usually more expensive) because the bottom of the cell can be lightly squeezed and the plug pulled out gently, ready to pop into the planting hole. Seedlings in flat-bottom punnets have to be prised apart and you need to take care not to damage delicate roots.

Seedlings are best planted with a handful of potting mix because even well-worked soils can dry out and harden quickly in hot weather. The beds should be covered with a very fine mulch immediately after planting. This helps deflect heavy rain from compacting the soil and also stops surface soil cracks.

TREES AND LARGE SHRUBS

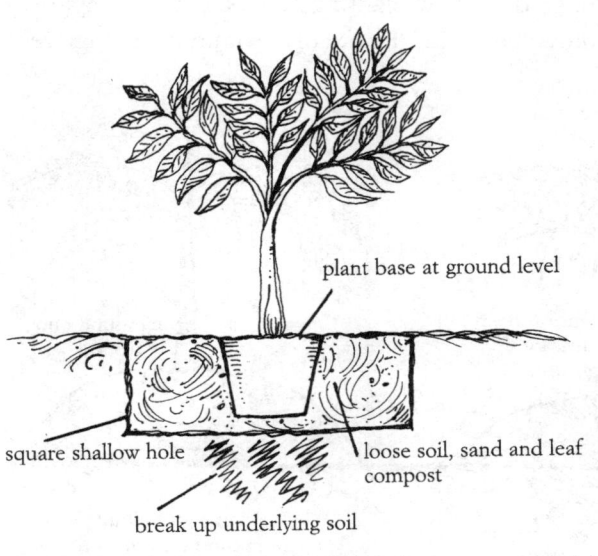

Good site in light, well-drained soil

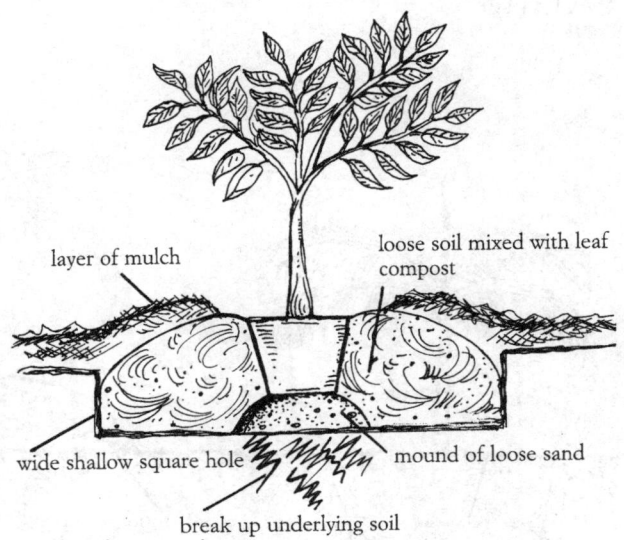

Hard or heavy soil

In good soils, dig a wide, shallow hole, deep enough so that the base of the plant is at ground surface level. The already well-soaked plant should be removed gently from the pot by squeezing and tapping the bottom. Despite what has sometimes been said to the contrary, it does no harm with larger plants to grip them at the base and help ease the rootball gently from the pot. Place the plant in the hole, then fill the hole almost to the top with water. When it has drained away, fill in around the plant with soil, firming the top gently with your hands. Pile the soil up a little in a circle around the plant to create a saucer which will hold water. Top with compost and/or mulch. With most soils it is also beneficial to place a few centimetres of potting mix at the bottom of the hole and mix some in with the soil. This lightens the mix, allowing plant roots to get away quickly, and also provides some nutrition. If you don't use potting mix, add a handful of well-rotted manure, blood and bone, a light dressing of fowl manure (not too close to the plant stem) or a small amount of controlled-release fertiliser to the base, working it lightly into the topsoil. Most nursery-bought plants come with fertiliser clearly visible around the top of the pot; however as the age of this fertiliser is unknown to the gardener it is better to provide a little supplementary feed as outlined here, particularly as the fertiliser break-down rate is fast in hot and humid conditions.

Planting in very hard, heavy soils requires a slightly different technique. Dig a shallow hole which is squared at the corners to give the roots a better chance (square holes are actually better for all trees and shrubs because the roots are encouraged to spread to the corners). Loosen soil at the bottom. Make a mound in the centre at the bottom, similar to the technique used for bare-rooted plants such as roses. The soil of the mound should be loose and gently firmed by hand. Place the plant at the top of the mound and hold it in place while filling the hole. Add potting mix, mushroom compost or a similar growth-enhancement medium to the soil. River sand can also be used to lighten the soil mix. Very hard or clayey soil must be broken down into crumbs. Mound up the soil mix until the plant is firmly in place; if the natural soil is clayey then any heavy clods which couldn't be broken down can be placed here to hold down the soil. Make a saucer-shaped depression around the plant at soil level to hold water. Fertilise as already suggested and cover with mulch.

With advanced trees and shrubs, a similar method can be used by which soil at the base of the hole is loosened, lightened with sand and compost if necessary, and a low, flat mound is made on top of it, high enough to hold the plant so that its base is at soil surface level. In heavy and hard soils, plenty of sand, leafmould or compost must be added to the soil around the plant to ensure good drainage and free root penetration.

PALMS

so that it is clear of the soil surface. Don't bother to loosen the soil surface. The palm will depend for its nutrition, stability and drainage on the mound; this principle is almost identical to that used for the mound plantings outlined above. Palms stuck into holes in clay soil are likely to expire from root rot.

TRANSPLANTING

First prune the plant back to about a third its size. Then cut around it vertically along the drip line, preferably up to a month before the plant is to be removed. Feeder root growth within this circle can be stimulated by feeding with an appropriate agent.

It is important that you have dug and thoroughly prepared the new planting hole before you begin. To remove the plant dig deeply around it, taking great

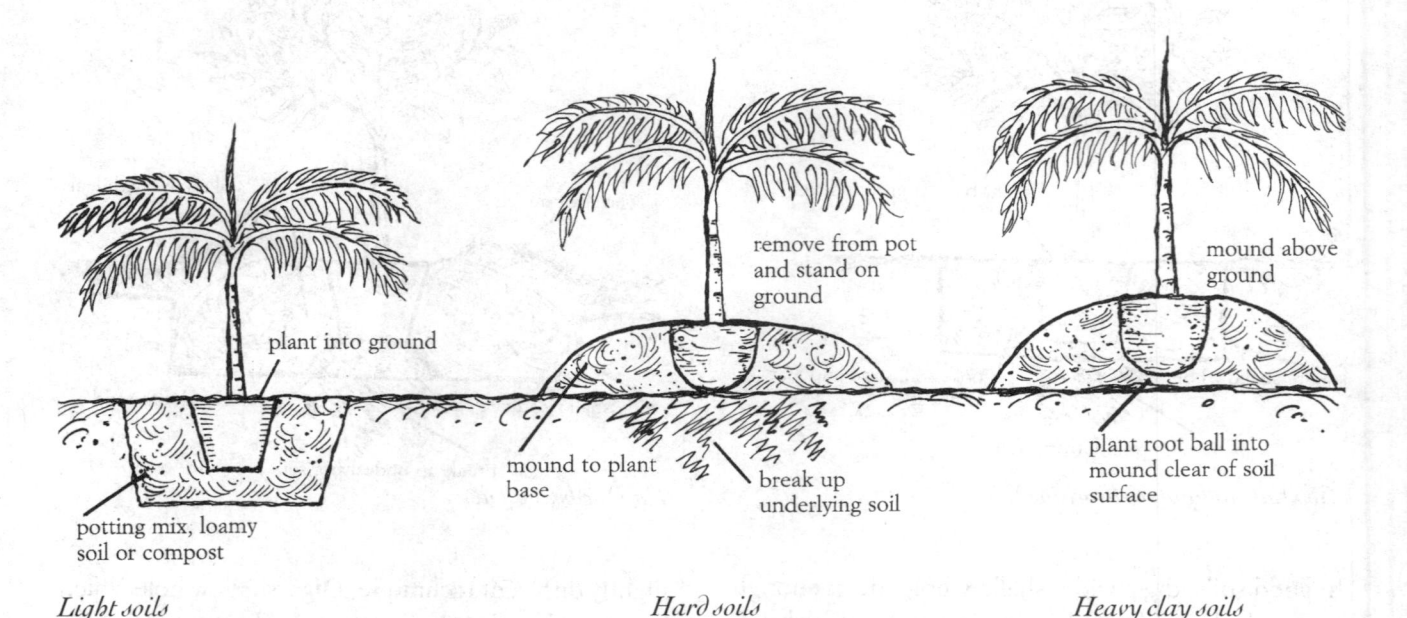

Light soils — *Hard soils* — *Heavy clay soils*

In the light, free-draining, sandy soils natural to most palm habitats, palms can be planted into the ground, along with plenty of potting mix, loamy soil or compost. Mushroom compost is particularly good and easy to handle. Nutrients should be added unless they are fairly fresh in the pot.

In hard soils, enriched earth should be mounded to the height of the plant base when it is removed from the pot and planted on the ground. The soil beneath should be loosened, provided it is fairly free-draining.

In very heavy clay soils, earth should be mounded above ground level and a hole made for the root ball

care not to damage the root ball. If this is large and heavy, you will need to wrap it in plastic sheeting or sacking to carry it to its new location. Water it in well and then every day for a month (the larger the plant, the more water it will need) and at least twice a week after that until the first signs of new growth appear. In clay soils, test that the water is draining away each day; if the soil remains waterlogged then reduce the watering rate. On very sandy soils, transplanted plants such as xanthorrhoeas will need to be watered every day for about three months.

The best time to move plants in a hot climate is during the cool season.

PLANT PROTECTION

Very young plants often need protection against strong winds which can break or bend them out of shape. Unless conditions are very severe, either temporarily or permanently, it is best to leave plants to fend for themselves. They develop stronger, widespread root systems to anchor themselves firmly if they are not staked. Artificial supports discourage strong root development and also encourages weak stem development.

If plants must be supported, there are two common alternatives. A stake can be driven into the ground about 15 cm from the stem, which must not be able to rub up against it. Nor should a stout stake be able to shade the stem. The plant is tied to the stake with a soft material such as stockings or rag (not wire or other hard material which can cut the stem). Chrysanthemums, tall dahlias and other flowering plants which almost always need staking can be tied with string. A better method for trees and large shrubs is to place three stakes in the ground and fasten (or guy) the plant to them with one or more soft ties which hold the stem firmly in place. Multi-stemmed shrubs rarely need staking but young trees may do so, particularly if they are fairly advanced, with long, slender stems. Stakes should only be left in place until the plant has established itself; no more than one year even in very windy areas.

Young plants can also be protected with grow-tubes, which are staked around the plant above ground level. These provide protection from sun, wind, children, animals and other likely causes of damage. Use only white-coloured grow tubes in a hot climate; black material absorbs heat and green can cause sunburn. Hessian can also be used to protect plants in this way but will break down fast in sun and rain. White plastic shopping bags are sometimes used but look untidy.

Watering, feeding and mulching

WATERING

PLANTS NEED WATER TO GROW; it plays an essential part in the manufacture of plant food and can constitute up to 90 per cent of plant weight. Water is absorbed mostly through root hairs but also through the leaves. In hot, dry weather the transpiration rate is higher, meaning more water is needed to keep stems and leaves from wilting. Dry weather conditions and waterless soil can cause plant roots to die, which will retard plant growth, or kill the plant if water is not supplied.

Just how much water should be lavished on the garden depends on the type of garden, soil type (sand or clay) and, of course, weather conditions. Hot areas which experience summer rainfall are usually able to keep watering to a more moderate level than those with hot, dry summers. Nonetheless, dry periods can be experienced even in mid-summer in the tropics.

Most gardeners like to have a watering routine and this can be affected by local authority requirements. Most in-ground plants, like pot plants, only require to be watered when the top few centimetres of soil surface are dry. Over-watering can make plants over-sappy and spoils them for withstanding droughts. On the other hand, many young palms, fleshy-leaved plants and small, shallow-rooted flowering plants need daily watering in hot weather. Annuals and small perennials may need watering twice a day in summer — but see the list of flowering annuals and perennials which mainly need to be watered only once every couple of days, page 126.

A great variety of irrigation systems are available to spare gardeners the task of constant watering. These can be linked to automatic timers, in line with local authority watering regulations. Irrigation methods vary from sprinklers to sprayers, tricklers and drippers. Each method has something to be said for it, depending on the planting area. It is obviously wasteful, for example, to use sprinklers on large shrubs when tricklers and drippers can reach straight to the roots. Lawns benefit from occasional deep soakings but it is generally easiest to sprinkle the surface, even though much is lost to evaporation and surface sprinkling discourages deep root development. Gardeners are usually advised to water the base of plants when possible, rather than sprinkling overhead, not only to conserve water but to avoid fungal problems which can be encouraged by wet foliage overnight. This advice is less important in a climate where heat quickly dries the leaves, even at night, and humidity is a common condition; in fact, most tropical-type plants are accustomed to night-time rainfall and like to have their leaves refreshed. Unfortunately, it is not feasible to run different types of irrigation outlets on the same pipeline, so different lines need to be laid to different areas of the pipeline. Some systems, which consist merely of lengths of black plastic pipe, nozzles and a control mechanism, are quite easy to install in the home garden and they can easily be concealed by mulch or among plants. But if you find all this confusing, consult either a contractor or your local supplier. Whoever designs the system should be a member of the Irrigation Association of Australia.

Here are a few hints:

- Sprinklers should not waste water on paths, driveways or other hard surfaces so position them accordingly.
- Large-droplet nozzle sprinklers are best in windy locations.

- You will need a multi-programme controller for different areas of the garden, for example lawns and shrubberies.
- For a comprehensive system, plumbing should be done by a qualified person.
- Be sure you know the application rate of different outlets in your system so that the controller can be scheduled.
- As a general rule, use micro irrigation in garden beds and drippers on native plants.
- Check regularly for nozzle blockages and see that spray patterns are working (foliage growth and similar changes can alter patterns). Also check for leaks and loose fittings.

CONSERVING WATER

Water has become so costly that most householders are aware of the need not to waste it. Whatever method you use for watering your garden, a few tips on water conservation will save you money.

- Don't over-water your lawn; the more you do so, the more dependent on water it will become. Less frequent watering encourages a deeper root system and healthier grass. If a lawn has become too dry it will show this by wilting and loss of colour; a thorough watering will soon put it right. Once a week should be quite enough, even in hot weather.
- In areas with long, dry periods choose a more water-efficient grass such as 'Dawson', 'Greenlees Park' or 'Wintergreen'. See page 167.
- Water after sundown and before 8 a.m. to minimise evaporation.
- Group plants with high moisture requirements so you don't waste water on those which require less.
- Plant water-efficient plants. These can be identified by their small, often tough and narrow or hairy leaves, and light-coloured foliage. Many Australian native plants are particularly water-efficient. Plants with very fleshy leaves and stems, such as cacti and succulents, are also adept at storing available water. See the section on gardening in hot, dry areas on page 51 for lists of water-efficient plants.
- Plants with deep root systems are more water-efficient than those with shallow systems.
- Mulch heavily to reduce water loss from the soil.
- Irrigation systems with automatic timers save water because they only operate for a set time. Turn them off in wet weather.

FERTILISER

Little and often is the important rule about fertilising plants in a hot climate, where plants tend to feed more greedily while at the same time the breakdown of nutritional elements in garden fertilisers is fast. If you live in the tropics, unless a fertiliser is specifically labelled for your area, it is best to increase the frequency of doses slightly over that recommended on the packet. Don't increase the actual dosage because this is both wasteful and potentially damaging to the plant.

Some plants are bred to be fed, that is the hybridising process to produce improved plants results in cultivars which depend on constant, correct feeding to perform well. Most annuals and vegetables fall into this category, as well as many of the perennials commonly sold today in nurseries. Such plants tend to do best with chemical or commercially available organic plant foods because they contain a balanced mix of the major and minor (trace) elements required for healthy growth. They should be planted in soil which has been prepared to a good state of nutrition with animal manures and well-composted vegetable matter.

Many shrubs and trees thrive in enriched soils with regular additions of animal manures and compost. With most species, feeding is only necessary with young plants, say up to two years old. Once the plant is making good growth, it should be able to get its nutrition from the soil without human assistance. In very infertile soils, or if the plant shows signs of stress, fertilisers should be given and in such cases a dose of quick-acting chemical fertiliser is usually the best solution, with further dressings of organic material to increase soil fertility and improve soil structure. First, check that the plant is not diseased or suffering from lack of water — symptoms can be similar.

Nitrogen is one of the most important elements required by plants for vegetative growth and leaf colour. Most commercially available plant foods are based on a ratio of nitrogen (N), phosphorus (P) and potassium or potash (K). This ratio will vary according to the requirements of certain types of plants; a typical all-purpose fertiliser might contain the ratio 5:7:4; that is 5 per cent nitrogen, 7 per cent phosphorus and 4 per cent potassium. One especially formulated for Australian natives in the Proteaceae family, such as grevilleas and banksias, will have a lower (4 per cent or under) ratio of phosphorus. Complete fertilisers will also contain the correct amount of trace elements such as calcium, iron, magnesium, manganese, sulphur, copper, boron and molybdenum.

TYPES OF FERTILISERS

Controlled-release granules

Osmocote and Nutricote are two very familiar granular fertilisers which feed plants for long periods from one application by making nutrition available to plant roots as required. They are so easy to use they are popular with nursery operators as well as home gardeners — it is very difficult to make a mistake with this type of fertiliser. Different formulations are available for indoor plants and container plants, outdoor plants, Australian natives and other growing requirements, and the period of activity may be different with each formulation, but is always clearly labelled. As I have already said, you may need to apply more often in hotter climate. One warning; the granule coating usually outlasts the nutritional elements it protects, so even if you see the granules still lying around the base of the plant or in the soil, don't assume they are still active.

Other controlled-release fertilisers

These include pills, tablets and spikes. Their action is similar to that of the granules, though the breakdown rate is usually faster and more subject to the elements, such as heavy tropical storms. Like the granules they are easy and clean to use.

Dry chemical fertilisers

These come in a wide variety of brands, usually in powder or granule form. Information for specific plant use, application instructions and chemical formulation are contained on the packet. As so many brands are available, it is best to choose one which has very clear information. Over large areas they can be cheaper and easier to apply than controlled-release types, though more frequent applications are usually necessary.

Liquid chemical fertilisers

These are usually applied as foliar sprays and are particularly useful for container plants, hanging baskets, annuals and small perennials, and as 'starters' for climbing plants. They can also be applied to plant roots but are slower and more difficult to use over large areas than either controlled-release or dry chemical formulations.

Dry organic fertilisers

These embrace a wide range of products, from cow pats and horse dung available in the field to those which are commercially manufactured, such as pelletised fowl manure. They include not only excreted animal products but also those made from animal blood, bone, hoof and horn. All gardens benefit from regular (annual or otherwise, depending on soil) dressings with organic fertilisers because they improve the soil structure and add nutrition. Even if you depend mainly on inorganic fertilisers for plant growth, the soil will need organic enrichment. 'Natural' organic material from farms and stables is excellent for this purpose but it will also contain weed seeds, possibly harmful chemicals also, and the nutritional value will be less reliable than commercially processed organic manures.

Liquid organic fertilisers

The animal wastes used in dry fertilisers, as well as seaweed, kelp and other aquatic products, are processed into liquid fertilisers, often boosted by additional trace elements. They are used in the same way as chemical liquids. When using liquid products it is particularly important *not* to exceed the recommended dose.

Single-element products

Major and minor elements are available singly but even experienced gardeners and professionals use these with extreme care. A common product like urea (a nitrogenous by-product of animal waste), often used to green lawns and foliage, can create problems, either by burning foliage or by over-dosing adjacent flowering plants with nitrogen.

FERTILISING FACTS

- *Always* study the information on the packet before buying, to make sure you have selected the fertiliser best suited to your purpose. When in doubt, go for plant foods formulated for a specific purpose, such as azaleas, Australian natives, shrubs, flowering plants and so on.
- Plant foods with a very high nitrogen content promote vegetative growth, sometimes at the expense of flower development. They are usually formulated for foliage plants and lawn. Special formulations are available to encourage flowering. An all-purpose fertiliser is still the best bet for most garden situations but those formulated for specific plants are very reliable.
- *Always* read the instructions carefully before applying fertiliser. It is safer to under-feed than over-feed plants, but under-feeding is also a waste of time and money.
- To be on the safe side when fertilising Australian native plants, use the plant foods specially formulated, and clearly labelled, for that purpose. Native plants require less fertilising than exotics as a general rule, particularly those which occur naturally in low-fertility soils.
- The best time to fertilise shrubs and most garden plants is in late spring or early summer, just before the onset of storm rains. Another application can be made in late summer but this depends on the type of fertiliser used and plant requirements. Annuals do best in hot climates with fortnightly applications of a weak liquid spray to ensure adequate nutrition; small, flowering perennials may benefit from similar treatment, or from fairly regular applications of bloom-inducing formulations.
- If you fertilise just before a summer deluge the dosage will be considerably weakened, or the fertiliser washed away from target areas, and a further application will need to be made shortly afterwards.

COMPOST

Compost is made from organic materials which are broken down into a humus which can be used to enrich soil and improve its structure. The more varied the materials used, the richer the compost is likely to be. There are as many ways of making compost as there are gardeners but basic principles are:

- Don't use meat, fish or seafood scraps because they smell and attract flies and animals. Only very experienced composters can make use of such wastes, otherwise your compost heap is likely to be declared a health hazard!
- Material should be fairly small and soft in texture; large branches and very woody material will need to be chipped, perhaps with an electric 'muncher'.
- The heap(s) must be turned regularly for aeration.
- Compost must be protected from heavy rain or the composting process will be inhibited and the heap is likely to become a soggy mess.

An easy method

Put down a layer of vegetative kitchen waste and cover with a layer of grass clippings and other small, non-woody garden waste. Each layer should be about 10–12 cm deep. Add a 2 cm layer of fowl or other manure. This is the basis of a simple compost heap and can be built up into several layers as desired. Additional layers of materials such as straw, sawdust, other organic mulch and shredded paper will make even better compost, spreading the manure between each group of materials. When piled up closely together, micro-organisms break down the mix until it is of a dark, crumbly consistency for garden use. The process is accelerated by heat and moisture within the heap. A small amount of chemical fertiliser can be added between two of the layers to enrich the heap and the top layer covered with a sprinkling of blood and bone. Lime added to the heap will sweeten the compost and cut down odour, but don't add it to compost which is intended for azaleas, rainforest species and other acid-loving plants.

If odour is likely to be a problem, cover the heap with a layer of soil. Well-made compost which contains no large amounts of strong-smelling ingredients (such as some fresh animal manures and wastes) should not smell. Generally, larger heaps make better compost because the greater density of material allows more heat to build up within. But small heaps no higher than your kneecap can be turned into satisfactory compost.

Lightly water the completed heap but cover against wet weather. Turn over thoroughly twice, at 2–3 week intervals, moistening each time, then leave until ready. This should take about three months. Whatever method you choose, it is important to allow enough time for heat to build up within the heap as this process burns off any weed seeds or disease in the material.

Compost containers

- Wooden bins
- Old fuel or bulk food drums (well cleaned-out)
- Manufactured polythene bins; polythene or metal tumblers
- Wire-mesh bins (round or square)
- Almost anything you can think of which will hold a sufficient amount of material and allow it to be regularly turned over by fork, spade or handle.

Manufactured compost containers come in various types, with differing methods of operation. Instructions for use come with the product. In general terms, tumblers have handles which are an easy way of aerating the mix; at the same time they allow the right amount of heat to build up at the centre of the compost.

Keeping compost in a contained area (or bin) makes it easier to handle but is not strictly necessary. Some gardeners merely make layered piles of composting material, turn them regularly with a garden fork and protect them from heavy rain. This can make very good compost though it looks rather untidy.

A traditional way of having compost always available for garden use is the three-bin system. Whatever the type of container used, one bin contains compost in the making, to which materials are added, in layers, until the bin is full. The second bin contains completed layers undergoing the composting process. The third bin contains completed compost for use. The bins can thus be constantly rotated.

Manufactured compost

Compost can be purchased from retail outlets in bags. This is easier, though much more expensive, than making your own and is certainly suitable for small areas such as beds of annuals. Particular types of compost are available, the most common being mushroom compost. This is limited in nutritional

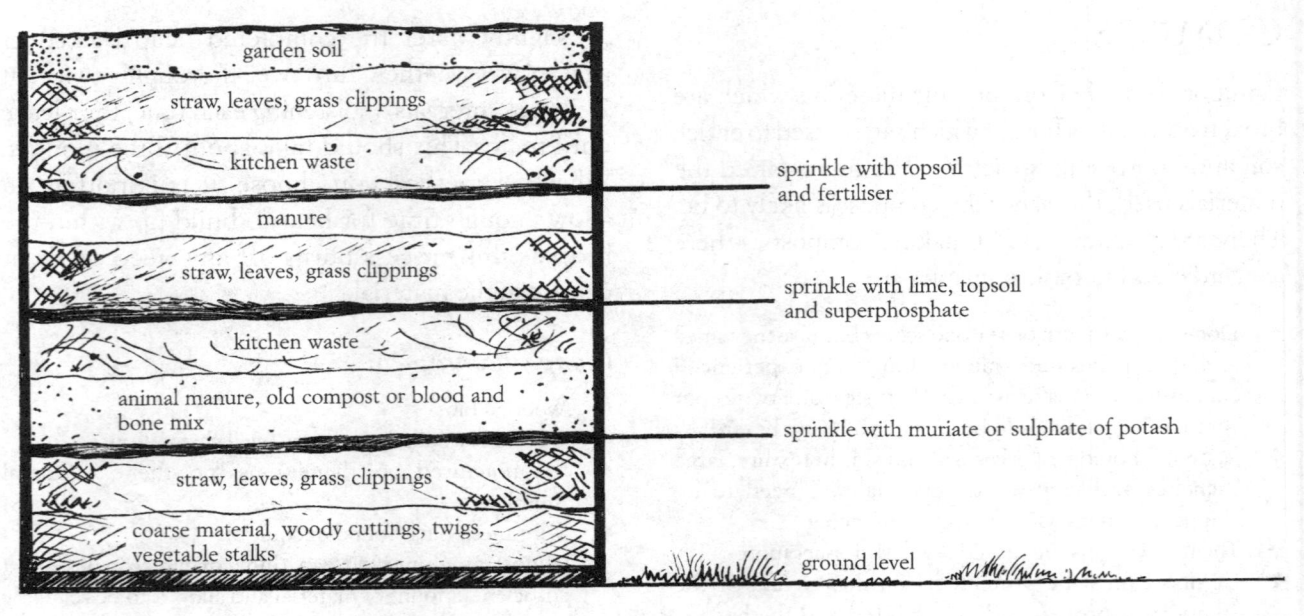

There are many ways to make compost. In practice the arrangement of layers will depend on type and availability of materials. A suggested method of making compost includes some essentials. These are a coarse bottom layer, animal manure, old compost or blood and bone as a 'starter', and a top cover of soil. As an alternative to animal manure, use sulphate of ammonia at a rate of 1:50 compost by weight.

value but useful for improving soil structure and adding to the soil when planting shrubs and trees, particularly palms. It is, however, alkaline so should not be used for azaleas or plants which like acid soils.

MULCHING

Mulching is a process by which the surface of the soil around plants is covered with a layer of material which serves to retain moisture, to protect the soil from compaction, to reduce temperature variations (thus keeping the soil cool or warm, as required), to prevent soil erosion and to suppress weeds. 'Soft' mulches from plant material also add nutrition to the soil as they break down.

Types of mulches available include: straw, pinebark and chips, nutshells, lucerne, bagasse, sugarcane trash*, newspaper, cotton waste.

You can gather your own mulch, if you wish. Naturally available mulches include:

- Leaf litter (from your own or a neighbour's garden, *not* from the forest!)

* A highly-recommended mulch for hot-climate gardens. The residue known as 'bagasse' is a lighter-textured mulch which is better dug into the soil surface as a compost, where it breaks down to an excellent dark soil mix.

- Bracken (very acid)
- Pine or casuarina needles
- Lawn clippings
- Garden waste (such as shrub prunings) put through an electric 'muncher' to speed breakdown.

Drawdown

Most mulches will cause a degree of nitrogen deficiency (in a process known as nitrogen drawdown) in the soil around plants. This is particularly severe, over a longish period, with pine bark and nutshells. Compensate by applying a high nitrogen fertiliser.

Hard mulches

Gravel and stones make excellent hard mulches to protect plants and provide most of the other mulching benefits. They do not become over-humid in hot, damp weather and are useful for soft-stemmed plants which require particularly good drainage, for example frangipani and pawpaw trees. Hard mulches look tidy and suit certain themes very well, such as cactus and mediterranean-style gardens. They do not, of course, break down and improve soil structure and fertility so may need to be used with soft mulches or compost underneath.

Mulching hints

- It is generally better to mulch large areas of the garden rather than each plant. Not only is this easier, it improves the overall garden soil nutrition.
- Keep mulch away from plant stems, or it may cause them to rot. This is particularly important in hot, humid climates.
- Sawdust, grass clippings and similarly fine material can become very slimy in wet weather or they can stick together to form a solid barrier which prevents rain reaching the soil. Poke them about a bit periodically to prevent this happening, though not so much it will allow weeds to come through. Or mix grass clippings with coarser mulching material.
- The mulch immediately around plants needs to be fairly open, to allow oxygen and rain to penetrate to the soil and the plant roots beneath.
- Some plants, particularly the more delicate annuals, as well as cacti and succulents, react against the strong toxins in pinebark and sawdust. Always use these mulches with caution except around large shrubs and trees; don't put them too close to plant stems. Otherwise, store the mulches for a few weeks before use, by which time the toxins should have been leached away.
- Don't be mean with soft mulches but spread them at least 10 cm deep and top up as required. The only exception to this is in areas where creeping groundcovers must make headway; here only a very light mulch dressing is suitable.

Making your own potting mix

An easy-to-make mix which suits most hot-climate garden plants is:
60% coarse river sand
40% peat moss (or appropriate substitute such as coconut fibre reduced to a peatlike consistency)
plus, per 10 l bucket,
65 g controlled release fertiliser
75 g dolomite (except for acid-loving plants)

The traditional John Innes potting mix, formulated in England, is:
7 parts sterilised and sieved loam
3 parts peat moss
2 parts coarse sand
to which is added the base John Innes fertiliser:
2 parts hoof and horn meal
2 parts superphosphate
1 part sulphate of potash

This basic recipe (known as John Innes No. 1) can be made richer by doubling (John Innes No. 2) or trebling (John Innes No. 3) the amount of base fertiliser to each 20 l of mix.

Pruning

SOME GARDENERS, PARTICULARLY THOSE WITH A FORMAL GARDEN TO MAINTAIN, are never happier than when snipping and trimming. The result is very tidy and elegant, but it does involve a lot of hard work. For those who don't care for this kind of work, it is nice to know that the types of flowering shrubs and foliage plants typical of hot climate gardens rarely need anything more than an occasional light trim of outer foliage, for good form and health. Generally it is not strictly necessary to undertake a pruning regime unless:

- Plants have grown too tall for their position and need their tops lopped.
- Plants look sparse in foliage and 'leggy' in their lower regions. Pruning promotes bushiness.
- Foliage has become obstructive or the plant is too rampant — not an uncommon problem with hot-climate shrubs.
- A plant needs help recovering from defoliation by insects, disease, drought or some other stress. A severe pruning is a good way of restoring plants to good health and often a better appearance than before.
- An old plant, particularly a tree, needs renovating.
- Pruning is required for improved flowering.
- Shrubs or trees are being grown as a hedge.

Most tropical and sub-tropical fruit trees only require a light pruning to form a good shape when young, and occasional pruning after that to maintain shape. Pruning is done with secateurs, a knife or a pruning saw — these should be sharp and in good condition. Sterilise with bleach or disinfectant before use. In humid weather, seal cuts with a tree wound-dressing, available from garden centres.

FRUIT TREES

If you are ambitious enough to try growing fruit trees that are strictly speaking cool-climate trees, they will need pruning to promote fruiting and allow light and air into the centre of the tree, as well as to reduce foliage growth to facilitate picking. Apples should be pruned in winter, nectarines and peaches in mid-summer, mulberries and citrus after fruiting. Branches should be cut so that an open bowl shape is achieved, with branches growing up and out.

During the first year after the tree has been planted, cut back the leader or central shoot to the level of a strong branch about 80 cm from the base of the tree, leaving about three well-spaced branches below the cut. This helps the young tree develop a good shape for the future. In the following years, cut back branches and shoots by about half to healthy, outward facing buds. Prune some of the older sideshoots back to the main stem to promote new shoots. All old, useless and weak growth should be removed; branches which cross each other in the centre of the tree should also be removed so that the centre stays open.

Make a neat, non-ragged downward cut at a 45–degree angle to the stem about 4 cm above an outward-facing bud, and sloping away from it, so that water will not collect there and possibly encourage disease. This works with plants with alternate buds;

where buds are paired then the cut must be almost straight across, with just enough slope so that water runs off it. It is best to promote new growth from outward buds so that the plant grows in that direction and centre growth doesn't become too dense.

Observe whether flowering takes place on new (the current season's) growth or old, woody growth. The latter should only be pruned when flowering is over. (Use this same principle with pruning climbers.) Trees which flower on new growth should be pruned in the cool season. For more on individual fruit tree pruning, see page 172.

ORNAMENTAL SHRUBS AND YOUNG TREES

Lightly cut back outer growth all over the plant using straight, clean cuts. Remove dead wood. Remove or cut back branches which obstruct people traffic, interfere with other plants or are in any way becoming a nuisance.

TIP-PRUNING

Most young plants benefit from tip-pruning to make them bushy, including Australian natives. This simply means pinching off the growing tips between your thumb and forefinger. Trees and large shrubs in containers can also have their height controlled in a similar way, by constantly pinching out the top shoot. This will encourage bushier branching further down.

RENOVATION

If an old tree needs renovating, do not do this too severely in one treatment, or the tree will be harmed. Instead, prune away old, dead, useless material over a period of weeks, then cut back branches gradually, until you achieve the desired shape. You can seal small cuts with tree wound-dressing though most arboriculturalists no longer recommend this treatment.

NATIVES

Native shrubs often tend to be leggy in the home garden and show a sparseness of foliage at lower levels. A light pruning after flowering will make these plants bushier and keep them in good health. Acacias, leptospermums and grevilleas should be regularly pruned to prolong life.

REMOVING SUCKERS

Some plants produce suckers or water shoots from the base, and these should be cut off at the bottom once the main growing season is over, or they may inhibit later flowering on the main shoots. Thorny plants such as roses and bougainvillea are particularly prone to producing such shoots.

The plant clinic

IF YOU STOPPED TO THINK about the number of dangers and diseases which exist in the world, you might become so frightened and discouraged you would never get out of bed again! Yet, except for extreme hypochondriacs, most people are sensible enough to get on with the business of living without worrying overmuch about health, bar taking a few sensible precautions and seeking expert help when necessary. It is much the same with plants.

Although there are a bewildering number of pests and diseases which can attack plants, for the most part they go through their life cycles without succumbing to either problem. You only have to look around any average suburb to see how easily gardens flourish, even when they are neglected.

Vigilance is one of the secrets of overall garden health. In a hot climate, those who like to take a quiet stroll around the garden usually do so in the early morning or evening, when it is cooler. This is the time to look for problems, always remembering the old saying that an ounce of prevention is worth a ton of cure.

Getting expert help for sick plants is never easy. Some nursery and garden centre staff are very knowledgable about plant problems; others are not. Radio programmes, newspaper gardening columns and plant clinics at garden shows are other sources of information. But let's face it, very few people have the time and inclination to take advantage of these sources; for the most part, they leave the plant to die or to recover by itself. Indeed, in hot climates especially, the diseases that kill plants often work so fast that by the time the problem is noticed, let alone identified and a remedy found, it is too late. It is the same with insect attacks: swarms of beetles or caterpillars can arrive and defoliate a plant within a breathtakingly short space of time. You can, however, take comfort in the fact that while insects proliferate in a hot climate, so do plants. Usually they recover quickly from insect attack, or else another plant will grow quickly in their place. The rampant lushness of tropical gardens is a testimonial to this.

Besides vigilance, the other two secrets of overall garden health are generally said to be recognition (of problems) and prompt action. But playing doctors and nurses in hot weather is hard work; and the many different problems which exhibit similar symptoms make accurate diagnosis and treatment difficult. So the best general advice is to let nature take its course as much as possible, and be prepared to replace a few plants now and again. Having said that, for the sake of those gardeners who are prepared to take the trouble to tackle garden problems, for those who are losing a lot of plants to the same problem, and for those who find their particularly precious plants at risk, some of the most common pests and diseases are identified here, with some suggestions for their treatment.

First, a few preventative measures:

- ❖ Weed regularly to prevent a build-up of growth which deprives garden plants of water and nutrients.
- ❖ Give plants adequate water and fertiliser; healthy, well-fed plants are less likely to succumb to disease and are better able to recover from insect attack.
- ❖ Hygiene helps prevent development of fungal diseases. Keep pots clean, make sure home-made compost is adequately sterilised, immediately remove affected plants. Leave area fallow for a while before planting anything else. Wet soil and humidity are conducive to fungal diseases.
- ❖ Don't fight nature by insisting on placing the wrong

plants in the wrong spots. Don't expose delicate plants to strong winds, salt spray or extreme heat, nor plant sun-lovers in shade and shade-lovers in full sun.

- Remove rubbish and plant debris in which diseases and harmful insects can lurk.
- Make sure the specimens you buy are healthy; even a novice gardener should recognise trouble signs such as lifeless or yellowing foliage (unless of course the foliage is meant to be yellow!), leaves which are otherwise blotched or covered in a foreign substance, weedy growth at the top of the plant, roots growing out of the bottom (indicating the plant has been too long in the pot, or else roots may be exposed to disease).
- Plant fruit trees at wide enough intervals so that foliage is not touching. This helps prevent the spread of problems from one tree to another and allows free passage of air which reduces the risk of fungal disease.
- Help prevent the development and spread of fungal diseases by not wetting plant foliage in the evening. This is particularly important with roses.

RECOGNISING INSECT PESTS AND DISEASES

Symptoms	Cause
Foliage	
Black spots	Black spot
Bronze discolouration of leaf	Red spider mite
Holes in leaves	Caterpillars, beetles
Leaf distortion	Aphids, caterpillars
White, downy growth under leaves	Downy mildew
White, powdery residue on leaves	Powdery mildew
Rusty pustules on underside of leaf (sometimes on top)	Rust
Small, raised scales on underside of leaf	Scale
Tunnels or streaks (usually yellowish) in leaves	Leaf miner
Webbing or rolling of leaves	Caterpillars
Yellowing or browning	Root rot
Flowers	
Holes in petals	Beetles
White (or pale) flecks on flower petals	Thrips
Whole plant	
Holes in stem	Borers
Dying	Root rot Nematodes

Symptoms	Cause
Seedlings	
Stem collapse	Damping off
Wilting leaves	Wilt
Fruit	
Black, sticky residue on leaves	Sooty mould
Flower death in avocadoes and mangoes	Anthracnose
Fruit falling early	Fruit fly/Fruit spotting bugs Anthracnose
Holes with brown edges on fruit larvae	Codling moth
Maggots	Fruit fly
Vegetables	
Bronzing of foliage	Red spider mite
Brown spots on leaves	Leaf spot
Downy, pale tufts under leaves	Downy mildew
Holes in leaves	Cabbage moth and white butterfly caterpillars
Powdery, white film on leaves	Powdery mildew
Small insects on leaf undersides	Aphids
Tunnels or streaks in leaves	Leaf miner
Lawns	
Brown patches	Brown patch Dollar spot White curl grub African beetle
Chewed grass blades	Lawn grass caterpillar and various insects

INSECT TYPES

APHIDS Tiny insects with soft, sometimes woolly bodies coloured black, white, brown or green, which cluster under leaf surfaces, in buds and on young shoots. They suck plant sap, distorting leaves, stems, buds, flowers and roots and can also spread virus diseases from plant to plant. A pest of brassicas, carrots, beans, some flowers such as chrysanthemums and roses.

BEETLES These small, hard-bodied insects come in all colours. They chew plant leaves and stems, and include the common pests, pumpkin beetle (dull orange, or orange with four black spots) and 28-spotted ladybird (orange with 28 black spots), not the beneficial ladybird which preys on aphids. Heavy infestations can be a problem in vegetables and ornamentals.

BORERS Beetles which bore tunnels in plant stems, making them brittle and eventually causing a branch or the whole tree to fall. Susceptible species include citrus and several rainforest trees. Signs are small piles of sawdust, often near the edge of a hole. Prune out infested stems as quickly as possible and destroy the caterpillars. Paint Bordeaux mixture on trees in spring, to deter egg laying by the parent moth.

BUGS These are usually larger than the typical beetle, often with beautifully coloured and curiously shaped shells. Some types of bug chew leaves and stalks, often causing wilting of plant stalks and young shoots, while others suck the sap, causing destruction of plant tissue and subsequent wilting. Bug types include the green vegetable bug (adults with green, shield-shaped backs, young bugs are black with yellow and white spots) and harlequin bugs (orange and black pattern). Most types of plants can be susceptible, though they rarely do more than mild damage.

CATERPILLARS (GRUBS) Certain moths lay their eggs on leaf undersurfaces and produce larvae which chew plant leaves, stems and fruits. Caterpillars are easy to recognise and remove by hand. Armyworm, sometimes known as cutworm, is a green, brown or striped caterpillar which bites clean through seedling stems, given them the appearance of having been cut. Usually found in large numbers. All plants can be susceptible to one type of caterpillar or another.

FRUIT FLY The great pest of orchards, having originated in Queensland and spread widely elsewhere. A little larger than the average housefly, they are reddish–brown in colour with some yellow colouring. They lay eggs in most tree-borne fruit (including tomatoes) and some vegetables such as capsicums. The maggots are prolific and destructive. Preventative spraying is legally required. Dak pots are used by commercial growers to indicate the presence of flies but they do not control them. Chemical baits are available which can be dabbed on to the bark of trees, but this is better used as an adjunct to spraying, rather than an alternative.

LEAF MINERS Tiny larvae which burrow through leaves, causing obvious tracks (or mines) and yellowish, brown or white discolouration. Trees, some shrubs such as azaleas and a few perennials are affected.

MEALY BUG Very small, waxy, six-legged, insects. Only males have wings and resemble scale insects. They can produce masses of white, waxy threads with a fluffy appearance around buds or in leaf axils. A pest of citrus, indoor plants and some flowering plants.

NEMATODES (EELWORMS) Tiny worms which live parasitically on plant roots, causing swellings (galls) which harm plant growth. Susceptible plants include tomatoes, cabbages, lettuces, ginger and gardenias.

RED-SPIDER MITES (TWO-SPOTTED MITE) Tiny pale green mites with dark markings on sides. Unthrifty, mottled or burned-looking foliage is a symptom. Attacks flowers, leaves and vegetables, as well as indoor plants. Affected plants may lose their leaves and die.

SCALE INSECTS Tiny grey, black, yellow or orange insects which suck sap. They make waxy coverings or scales which give leaves a discoloured appearance. White egg masses may also be visible and the leaf surface is covered with a sticky substance, often blackening with soot mould. Trees, shrubs, fruits, climbing plants and even cactus can be affected.

SLUGS AND SNAILS These can damage vegetables and flowers; their presence is signified by slime trails. Commercial baits are available, usually in the form of blue or green granules.

THRIPS Tiny, yellow, brown or black, soft-bodied, winged insects which distort leaves and cause them to wither, and inhibit bud development in flowers. First signs are a silvering of the leaf or petal. Flowers also turn brown and wither. Pale-coloured roses are particularly susceptible. Also affects vegetables and fruit trees. Can even be a nuisance with washing on the clothes hoist!

DISEASES

ANTHRACNOSE A fungal disease which attacks many hot-climate edible plants including avocadoes and mangoes. Symptoms are flower death and premature fruit drop. Preventative spraying is required.

BLACK SPOT Very dark-coloured spots with uneven edges, common on rose leaves, particularly in humid weather.

BROWN PATCH AND DOLLAR SPOT These are similar-appearing lawn problems in which brown, dead patches of grass appear. Dollar spot is smaller and both are caused by fungi, mainly in hot and humid weather. A similar browning-off effect can be caused by grubs of the African beetle which destroy grass roots.

DAMPING OFF Fungal problem of seedlings in which the stems first darken and then collapse. All seedlings are susceptible.

DOWNY MILDEW A soft, pale fungal growth on leaf undersides. Plants appear unhealthy.

POWDERY MILDEW Similar to downy mildew except that fungal spread resembles a fine, whitish powder on the upper leaf surfaces.

ROOT ROT Plants which show signs of yellowing or browning foliage, leaf and stem wilt, or else die suddenly may well be suffering from this common fungal problem which attacks many trees and shrubs. In the home garden, grevilleas are particularly susceptible. Good drainage is a must and susceptible plants should be planted in earth mounds above normal ground level. Chemical controls are not very effective in the home garden; drenching of the ground with fungicides such as Bordeaux or Mancozeb may help.

RUST Orange pustules on leaf underside, usually with a matching yellowish patch on the upper surface. A problem of damp and humid weather conditions, particularly if foliage is sprayed with water. Unchecked spread leads to death of foliage. Susceptible plants include geraniums, roses and mint.

SOOTY MOULD This is a black residue which often sticks to the so-called honeydew on leaves, produced by aphids and scales. The effect is a sooty substance covering leaves and stems of many ornamental and native tree and shrub species, including citrus. It does no great harm in the short term but looks unsightly and restricts photosynthesis if left unchecked. Control aphids and scale and the problem will go.

VIRUSES Like humans, plants occasionally suffer from virus diseases. Symptoms tend to be similar to those caused by various other pest and disease problems, which makes a virus problem very difficult to diagnose. If a sick plant has been properly watered and fed, and does not respond to standard treatments for other problems such as fungus diseases, then it may have a virus disease. The only thing to be done is throw the plant away if it fails to recover. Do not plant a similar plant in the same spot.

WILT Soft-stemmed plants are susceptible to various wilts, usually caused by fungus (though bacteria can also cause wilting). Tomatoes are the most susceptible vegetable plants; symptoms are a yellowing and wilting of bottom foliage, spreading upwards until the whole plant begins to droop. Spotted wilt in tomatoes is a virus problem which causes small brown spots on young leaves, bronzed spots or rings between veins on larger leaves and brown streaking of stems, as well as blotched fruit. Young plants can die. There is no sure remedy for wilts; plants should be removed.

ORGANIC PEST AND WEED CONTROL

The best gardeners are those who rely as little as possible on chemicals or, better still, do without them all together. Natural methods of controlling insects, plant diseases and weeds are time consuming but kinder to the environment; a garden should be a growing place, not a killing ground. Wilderness gardens, that is those gardens which, once established, are allowed to grow as much like natural bushland as possible, with minimum care, are easily cared for using organic methods only. But for the majority of enthusiastic gardeners who like smooth lawns, neat flower beds, well-placed shrubs, lots of flowers, gardening with no chemical help at all is quite a challenge.

For those prepared to take up the challenge, we offer some natural alternatives.

Insect pests

Most organic insecticides have to be home-made, although garlic spray is now commercially available. They are usually potent only for about 24 hours, particularly in hot weather.

Buttermilk spray

(Red spider mites)

½ cup flour
2 l water
1 tb buttermilk

Mix flour and water into a paste, add buttermilk. Spray on affected plants to smother mites and eggs.

Chamomile tea

This herb is traditionally known as the 'plant doctor' and a tea made by steeping the leaves in water for 48 hours, then straining and pouring on plants, is supposed to help sick plants recover. It is also said to control damping off in seedlings.

Chive tea

(Downy and powdery mildew)
Make and use as for wormwood tea below.

Garlic

This is a noted repellent of aphids and a simple way of getting rid of these pests on roses and other plants. Plant (or scatter, as an interim measure) garlic plants and garlic chives around the garden. Or you can make a spray as follows:

Garlic spray 1

(Aphids, cabbage white butterfly, caterpillars, snails. Also said to assist in the prevention of downy mildew)
100 g chopped garlic bulbs or equivalent in processed garlic
50 ml kerosene
soap
water

Mix garlic and kerosene. Leave for 48 hours and then add 600 ml water and 10 g pure soap flakes or grated bar soap. Strain and dilute to the rate of 1:100 (one part mix, 100 parts water).

Garlic spray 2

1 bulb garlic, chopped
50 ml vegetable oil
soap
water

Steep garlic in oil for about 48 hours. Strain and add ½ l of water in which 7g of soap flakes have been dissolved. Dilute at the rate of 1:45.

All-purpose garlic-based insect repellent and fungicide

1 garlic bulb or 2 tb chopped garlic
1 onion
1 large whole chili or 1 tb chopped or powdered chili

Chop everything finely, soak overnight in 2 cups of water, dilute to the rate of 1:5.

Nicotine solution

(Most insects, including slugs and snails)
Approx. 125 g cigarette butts (twice the quantity needed if these are filter tips)
4½ l water
30 g soap

Boil up cigarette butts in water for about 30 minutes. Add soap flakes or grated bar soap, strain and allow to cool before use. Spray or pour over plants to kill insects.

Pyrethrum spray

1 tb pyrethrum flowers
3 l water
washing soap

Boil water and pour over crushed flowers. Add some ordinary washing soap. Allow to steep for a while (about half an hour) then strain. Kills most insects. Pyrethrum is available from some herb growers.

Soapy water

(Aphids and scale. Also said to repel mealybugs, leaf-cutting insects and red spider mite)

Mix up a solution of 30 g soap flakes or grated bar soap in 1 l warm water to spray, dab or splash on plants infested with aphids. Rinse off with tepid water if used as a treatment for scale and aphids.

Wormwood tea

(Aphids, beetles, cabbage white butterflies, slugs, fruit fly)
100 g wormwood leaves, chopped and crushed
1 l warm water

Soak leaves in water overnight, stir well, then dilute to the rate of 1:5.

Fruit fly baits

One method of controlling fruit fly is by using traps, baited in various ways. The idea is to attract the flies away from the fruit. The more trees you have, the more traps you'll have to set, the more traps you set, the more effective the level of protection. At least in theory. In practice, fruit flies are often present in such numbers that they go for the baits and the fruits! Nonetheless, baits have proved effective. They can consist of many substances, with an emphasis on sweet things and yeast: sugar or honey in water, bran (preferably lightly sweetened), a pinch of yeast in water, vegemite dissolved in water, fruit peel, beer or ginger beer (home brews are best as they are more yeasty).

Traps can be purchased or made from any re-usable container such as soft drink bottles or plastic milk bottles. They can be filled to about one third with the bait, then suspended from trees or any other structure with the cap downwards. The other end should be pierced with a few small holes, just large enough to admit the flies. An effective trap is made by cutting off the top section of the bottle, reversing the capped neck so that it makes a tunnel and taping this in place. The cap should be replaced by gauze or fine wire mesh so that larger, hungry insects can't enter.

Quite a lot of insects can be trapped with sticky, sweet substances laid around the garden. However, these can also trap beneficial insects such as bees and parasitic wasps.

Netting

One of the simplest ways of protecting young seedlings and vegetables from attack by pests is to cover them with netting. In the case of seedlings, this can simply be draped over sticks or secured so that it is not blown about by the wind. Most vegetables except tall-growing species can be grown under frames of fine netting or white shadecloth. These are quite simple to make. Netting must be fine enough not to block sunlight. Tall-growing species can be covered just by draping with netting during vulnerable periods (e.g. fruiting), or more elaborate frames can be devised. Netting also deters birds from feeding on fruit.

Snail control

Slugs and snails will be deterred by a scattering of wood ash, coarse sand or crushed eggshells around plants or flowerbeds. They are also said to dislike sawdust. Wormwood tea (see recipe) poured on the ground should repel them, while citrus halves placed here and there will attract them overnight for easy disposal next day.

INTEGRATED PEST MANAGEMENT

A garden rich in different plant species will attract a great variety of insects, many of them beneficial in that they prey on pests. Control spraying — even using organic ingredients — can kill 'goodies' as well as 'baddies', so it should only be used when helpful predators (which also include birds and reptiles) cannot prevent pests from getting out of control. Nicotine spray, for example, will kill most insects, good and bad. Where possible, use target-specific sprays which will help rather than harm beneficial insects. And, as with all problems, deterrents are better than fatal solutions.

BENEFICIAL INSECTS include ladybird beetles (prodigious eaters of aphids), praying mantises, lacewing flies (colourful flying insects with orange eyes) and parasitic wasps (these are not easily confused with the wasps that build nests around houses and sting humans).

Insect-eating birds eat caterpillars, grubs, beetles, grasshoppers and other nuisances. It therefore makes sense to plant as many bird-attracting species as possible, with emphasis on prolifically flowering native species such as callistemons and grevilleas. This is all part of the organic philosophy of working with, rather than against, nature. Dipel is the brand name of a biological control spray made from the bacteria *Bacillus thurengiensis*. It is a fairly specific killer of caterpillars but doesn't harm beneficial insects.

NATURAL WEED CONTROL

Nature abhors a vacuum and, as gardeners know to their cost, will readily fill it with weeds. So a dense growth of garden plants is a most effective way of suppressing weed growth. Unplanted areas are natural weed targets. Groundcovers are excellent suppressors and can be planted over much of the garden, except flower beds and vegetable patches (and even here, spreading plants like pumpkins can be planted to grow amongst taller growing species).

DEEP MULCHES will suppress some weed growth but the tough, long-stemmed weed species common to hot climates will battle their way through. Many weeds, too, have such strong and efficient root systems that they can grow in minuscule amounts of organic matter, such as found on the top of rocks, tree stumps, pinebark and mulch.

Boiling water will kill weeds and is a particularly useful remedy on hard surfaces such as pathways and paving. Many strong, household chemicals such as borax and ammonia can be dabbed on to individual weeds to kill them—such remedies are sometimes suggested by organic gardeners but they are still a chemical solution to an organic problem.

Use barrier plantings of deep-rooted plants such as lemon-grass and clumping grass species to help prevent invasion from outside the barrier. Solid materials such as timber, metal or plastic can be placed as a barrier in the ground, at a sufficient depth and height above ground to prevent weeds from growing over or under. Sprinkler systems encourage weed growth by spraying water indiscriminately. Drip systems encourage garden plants while denying water to weeds during dry periods.

Soil solarisation will kill weed seeds in the soil in a heavily infested area which is to be planted. This is best done at the height of summer, when the sun is hottest. Clear plastic sheeting is laid over the area to be sterilised and the ground is watered either just before or during (by drip irrigation) the process. The sun's heat will kill seeds, pathogens and other life forms in the soil underneath. The sheeting must be held firmly in place. The longer the plastic is on the ground, the greater its effect, but a minimum of four weeks is recommended. Obviously, shaded areas are unsuitable. Soil solarisation is not an easy task for the home gardener to undertake properly, nonetheless for those willing to try it can be an effective way of sterilising a small area such as an annual or vegetable bed. Ground in which plants have died from fungal disease can also be treated this way.

BIOLOGICAL METHODS

Many plants, including edible species, contain chemicals which are toxic or unpleasant to others. This form of chemical warfare can be used to advantage by gardeners.

For example, if the stumps of plants of the cabbage family are left in the ground, weeds tend to avoid the area. Cucumbers and pumpkins grown among vertical-growing species will smother weeds and deter them with their own form of chemical warfare. Potatoes contain a substance which prevents the germination of some other plants, including many weeds. Wormwood (*Artemisia absinthium*) is a weed inhibitor.

WHEN ALL ELSE FAILS — CHEMICAL CONTROL

To spray, or not to spray, that is the question.

This is not a move to be taken lightly. Chemicals can create more problems than they solve; for example, by killing some types of insects they allow for the unnatural build-up of others, thus creating an imbalance. Further chemicals may be needed to kill those other insects if they become a nuisance. At the same time, plants are discouraged from using their own natural biological controls, or resistance. Birds and those beneficial insects which prey on pests can also be harmed by chemicals. The whole business of chemical use in the garden becomes an endless, potentially harmful cycle.

Yet many gardeners cannot bear to see prize specimens under attack and perhaps the results of many hours of loving labour being destroyed. There is sometimes, too, a responsibility not to allow problems to spread around your own garden and further abroad. Fruit fly is perhaps the best known of these problems and one which requires preventative spraying for the sake of commercial growers. Roses and other flowers, too, nearly always require chemical treatment at certain times of year against a variety of problems if they are to be worth growing at all. The rule should be, then, to use chemicals as little as possible and (with very few exceptions which require preventative measures) only in response to a correctly identified problem. Also, when possible, use garden-friendly controls such as derris, pyrethrum or organic sprays.

MANY DIFFERENT CHEMICAL CONTROLS have been formulated for particular insect pests and diseases. These are available at garden centres under a variety of brand names; the details of target, treatment method and chemicals used are on the packet. Directions for use should be followed exactly and protective clothing worn when applying chemicals harmful to humans. Though these are rarely available now for garden use, it still pays to take care. When spraying edible plants, please note recommended withholding periods, that is, the period after spraying before the fruit or vegetable can be eaten.

The following chart is a guide to treatments for common pests. Brand names change from time to time so check packets for actual chemical content.

Common brand names and their chemical content include:

Bordeaux mixture	copper hydroxide
Bugmaster	carbaryl
Derris dust	rotenone
Dipel	bacterial spray (bio-insecticide)
Folimat	omethoeate
Grubkil	chlorpyrifos
Harola	lime sulphur
Karathane	dinocap
Kelthane	difocol
Lawngrub killer	diazinon, cyfluthin or trichlorfon
Lebaycid	fenthion
Malathion	maldison
Nemacur	fenamiphos granules
Rogor	dimethoate (should not be used on citrus fruit)

Some common fungicides for the treatment of fungal diseases

Bayleton
Daconil
Fongarid
Mancozeb
Zineb

Pest	Treatment
anthracnose	Mancozeb
aphids	rotenone, pyrethrum, dimethoate
azalea petal blight	Bayleton
beetles	pyrethrum, derris, carbaryl, maldison, Lawn Beetle Killer (for African beetle and white curl grubs in lawns)
black spot	triforine, rose dust, lime sulphur
brown patch (lawns)	Mancozeb
cabbage moth larvae	carbaryl, cabbage dust, rotenone, Dipel, pyrethrum
caterpillars	carbaryl, rotenone, maldison, pyrethrum
damping off	prevent by dusting or watering seedlings with a watering fungicide or Bordeaux. If seedlings collapse, drench soil with Bordeaux or Fongarid.
dollar spot	triademefon, Bayleton
downy mildew	copper spray or fungicide
fruit fly	dimethoate, fenthion
lawn grass caterpillars	diazanon
leaf miner	dimethoate, fenthion
mealy bugs	white oil diluted in water 1:40 (1:100 for indoor plants), ornethoeate, fenthion, maldison, dimethoate
nematodes	fenamiphos
powdery mildew	dinocap, Bayleton, combined insect and fungus killers for roses
psyllids	carbaryl, maldison, omethoate
red spider mites	difocol, fenthion
rust	Mancozeb or other fungicide
scale insects	carbaryl and white oil mixed spray, fenthion, maldison. dimethoate
thrips	fenthion, maldison, dimethoate
white butterfly	same as for cabbage moth

WEEDS

A WELL-TENDED GARDEN is rather like a civilised society; full of well-bred, refined, highly cultivated inhabitants whose pleasant lifestyle can only be maintained by the ministrations of servants and the vigilance of a strong army. Rather like Rome, before the decline and fall. The gardener functions as both servant and soldier, caring for and protecting those within his or her charge. Weeds are the barbarians at the gate, ever ready to overrun the delicate garden plants and steal their sustenance if not kept at bay.

WEEDS FALL BASICALLY INTO THREE TYPES: grass-like plants such as paspalum, nut grass and Mullumbimby couch; creeping, small-leaf plants such as oxalis (with little yellow flowers) and clover (with rounded white flowerheads); broad-leaf weeds with fairly large, coarse-looking leaves such as thistles, dandelion, chickweed and lamb's tongue. All are easy to spot as they appear of their own accord among cultivated specimens. Not only do they look unsightly but they rob other plants of water and nutrients, and will overrun them if left unchecked.

The simplest method of weed control in a well-tended garden is to remove them by hand during regular daily or weekly checks. They are usually easy to pull out of soft, mulched and watered garden soil and, if dealt with regularly, never become a problem. However, busy people with large gardens cannot always maintain an efficient hand-weeding regime. For them, and others who find this method onerous, chemical control is the answer.

Chemical weed control in the home garden is not as harmful to the environment as insecticide spraying, which fills the air with often dangerous chemicals and can interfere with the balance of nature. By comparison, responsible and restrained weedicide use can rid the environment of trouble-some exotic weed species which could not realistically be controlled otherwise. Weedicides are simple to apply, either as a spray or with a long-handled wand. Weeds in lawns are particularly easy to spot as they stand out distinctly from the lawn grass.

The most commonly used chemical weedkiller is glyphosate, sold under brand names such as Round-up or Zero. This is easily sprayed on nuisance plants and leaves no residual effect in the soil. Instructions on the packet should, of course, be followed carefully. Glyphosate is a non-selective weedkiller and drifting spray can kill nearby garden plants. Even in a light breeze, the spray can drift a surprising distance, so spraying should only be done on windless days. As an extra precaution, it is simple to make a sprayguard using a handle of some kind (an old broom handle or long, stout stick is ideal) and attaching a piece of some rigid material (one gardener I know uses a piece of corrugated perspex) to one end, to act as a barrier when held in front of susceptible plants during weed spraying.

Glyphosate and other weedkillers can also be applied in concentrated form using a long-handled wand, readily available from gardening shops and hardware stores. Even this concentrated application may not be enough for persistent weeds growing through hard surfaces such as drives, pathways and paved courtyards. There are strong weedicides available especially for this purpose, with residual effects in the soil which prevent rapid regrowth. In very heavy rain, this residue may wash into adjacent areas, threatening plants.

Lawn weeds

Selective weedicides are also available; as the name applies these are targeted at specific plants, rather than greenlife in general. They are used mainly in lawns to control common problems such as bindii, clover, creeping oxalis, Mullumbimby couch and a variety of broad-leaf weeds and non-lawn grasses. Most of these can be controlled with a chemical mix which is sold under a variety of brand names which clearly indicate its function; for example, Lawn Weeder or Clover Killer. Paspalum and Mullumbimby couch are harder to control and will need a chemical such as Antipas; however this should not be used on blue couch, kikuyu grass or buffalo grass, all of which are commonly used hot-climate lawn grasses. Non-selective weedicides such as glyphosate can also be used on lawn weeds but must be applied with great care only to the particular weed, otherwise the lawn grass will be killed. A safer solution is to use broad-spectrum specific weedkillers to deal with most weeds, and remove paspalum and Mullumbimby couch by hand. As a final caution, when you go shopping for lawn weedkillers, read the information on the packet very carefully, to make sure you buy exactly the right product for the job.

SOMETIMES A GARDENER is faced with a big problem, such as killing off unwanted bamboo (the type with spreading, underground rhizomes), sugarcane or lantana. First, the offending plant should be chopped back as much as possible, then the remaining stem area chopped about a bit to expose inner tissue. A heavy concentrate of glysophate is usually effective to kill the plants, particularly if poured on rather than sprayed. Other herbicides are also available. However, if a large area is involved, and an appropriate herbicide is not readily available from the local garden centre, it may be useful to employ a contract sprayer, perhaps first contacting the Department of Agriculture, or Primary Industries, for advice.

Index of botanical names

Bold type for the page number indicates a major entry; italic type indicates a photograph.

Abelia 54, **95**, 108, 163, 164
Abutilon 108, 163
Acacia 25, 54, 59, **74**
   A. baileyana 70
   A. concurrens 46, **74**
   A. elata 74
   A. fimbriata **74**
   A. floribunda 164
   A. harpophylla 55, 164
   A. iteaphylla 70
   A. leuclada spp. *argentifolia* **74**
   A. longifolia 47, 49, 70
   A. melanoxylon 55, 164
   A. o'shanesii **74**
   A. pravissima 64
   A. sophorae 46
Acalypha 25, 27, 30, 31, 108, **146**, 164
   A. nemorosa 146
   A. wilkesiana 29, 146, 163, 164
Acanthus 55
   A. mollis 48, **126**
Achillea 55, 132
   A. clavennae 142
   A. millefolium **190**
Acmena 35, **86–7**
   A. hemilampra 46, 87
   A. smithii 46, 87
Acoelorrhaphe wrightii 89, **92**
Acokanthera spectabilis 47
Acronychia imperforata 46
Actinotus helianthi 48
Adenium obesum **95**
Adiantum 27, **153**, 200
Agapanthus 48, 59, **135**
Agapetes serpens 108
Agathis robusta 35
Agave 54, 59
Ageratum 134
Aglaeonema 27, 34, 35, **146**, 152, 199
Ajuga 54, 151, **169**
Alectryon coriaceus 46
Allamanda 30, 33, 42, 63, 64, 117
   A. cathartica 25, 31, **117**, 170
   A. neriifolia 31, **95**
Allantodia australis 153
Allium **188**
Allocasuarina 55, 84, 164
   A. torulosa 55
   A. verticillata 46
Alloxylon flammeum 30, 35, **74**
   A. wickhamii 74
Alocasia 27, 57, 58, 65
   A. macrorrhiza 35, 42, **135**, 200

Aloe vera 54
Alpinia 27, 30, 31, 35, 42, 48, **130**, 200
Alstroemeria aurea 136
Alternanthera 14, **146–7**, 163
Alyssum 55, **134**, 142
Amaranthus 54, **134**
Anacharis 40
Anethum graveolens **188**
Angelonia angustifolia **126**
Angophora costata 48
Anigozanthos 48, 54, 55, 58, 142
Annona 173
Anthemis 54, **134**
Anthurium 27, 151, 199
Antigonon leptopus 59, **117–18**
Antirrhinum **134**
Aphelandra 31, **95**, 201
   A. squarrosa 95
Aralia sieboldii, syn. *Fatsia japonica* 150, 199
Araucaria 83, 199
   A. heterophylla 48
Archontophoenix alexandrae 65, **91**, 93, 200
   A. cunninghamiana 91
Ardisia 27, 108, 199
   A. pachyrrhachis 35
Arenga pinnata **92**
Aristea 136
Aristolochia elegans 59, 117, **118**
Artemisia 20, 54
   A. absinthium 163, **190**
   A. schmidtiana 'Nana' **169**
Arundo donax 155
Asparagus spp. 153, 200
Aspidistra elatior 27, 151, 199
Asplenium 27, 35, 35, 58, 153, **156**, 200
   A. bulbiferum 200
   A. nidus 27
Astartea 142
Aster **127**
Atriplex 46, 70
Aucuba japonica 151, 200
Austromyrtus 47, 163, 164
Averrhoa carambola **172–3**
Azalea 27, 58, **95–6**, 97, 108, 163, 164, 201, 212
Azolla 40

Babiana 48, 140
Backhousia anisata 20, 54, 75
   B. citriodora 20, 25, **74–5**
   B. myrtifolia 54, 55, 75
Baeckea 'Sparkles' 47
   B. virgata 54, **96**, 142, 163
Bambusa 156, 163, 164
Banksia 46, 54, 69, 70, 205
   B. dentata 54
   B. ericifolia 46
   B. integrifolia 46, 55

Barklya syringifolia 31, 35, 42, **75**
Barleria cristata 30, **96**
Bauera 45, 65
   B. rubioides 108, 164
Bauhinia 30, **75**
   B. blakeana **75**
   B. corymbosa 121
   B. galpinii 30, 54, **96**
   B. purpurea 75
   B. variegata **75**, 77
Baumea articulata 40
Beaumontia grandiflora 31, **116**, 118
Begonia 27, 30, **126–7**, 146, **147**, 148, 197, 201
   B. semperflorens 27, 59, **134**
Berberis 'Ruby Glow' 163
Bergenia ciliata **127**
Bismarckia nobilis 93
Blandfordia 65
Blechnum **153**
Borago officinalis **188**
Borassus flabellifer 93
Boronia megastigma 45
Bothriocloa macra 53
Bougainvillea 25, 29, 30, 31, 33, 49, 55, 58, 64, 108, 115, 117, **122–5**, 164, 170
Bouvardia longiflora (syn. *humboldtii*) 31, **96**
Bowenia **156**, 199
   B. serrulata 35, 42, 156
   B. spectabilis 35, 42, 156
Brachychiton 21, 84
   B. acerifolius **78**
   B. discolor 79
   B. diversifolius 70
   B. gregorii 54
   B. populneum 70
   B. rupestris 54, 70
Brachyscome 44, 45, 48, **127**
   B. multifida 64
Bractantha 48, **128**, 142
Brahea 93
Bromeliad 27, 31, 33, 34, 35, 42, **159–60**, 199
Browallia, see *Streptosolen*
Brunfelsia 30, 31, 33, 108, 164
   B. pauciflora **96**
Buckinghamia celsissima 25, 30, 42, 73, **75**, 163
Buddleia 54, 58
Butia capitata 93

Caesalpina ferrea **80**
   C. gilliesii 30, 54
Caladium 35, 57, 58, 146, **147**, 199
Calamnus 93
Calathea 26, 27, 34, 35, 42, 146, **147**
Calendula **134**
   C. officinalis 55

Calliandra 30, 42, 59, 64, **96**
   C. haematocephala **96**
   C. schultzei 96
   C. surinamensis 96
   C. tweedii 'Horizontalis' **96**, 170
Callistemon 25, 54, 55, 59, **75**, **98**, 164
   C. 'Harkness' 65
   C. 'Little John' 142
   C. salignus 48
   C. viminalis 48
Callitris 70
   C. collumellaris 54
   C. glaucophylla 46
Calothamnus 55
Camellia **98**, 108, 212
Campsis grandiflora 55, 121
Canavalia rosea 45
Canna 48, **138**
   C. indica 30, 31, 55
   C. iridiflora 142
Capsicum **190**
Carex 40, 155
Carica papaya **175–6**
Carpentaria acuminata 91
Carum carvi **190**
Casimiroa edulis **176**
Cassia artemisioides 55
   C. brewsteri **75–6**
   C. fistula 31, **76**
   C. javanica 31, 33, **76**
   C. 'Paluma Range' **76–7**
Castanospermum australe 199
Casuarina 164
   C. cristata 54
   C. equisetifolia 46
   C. glauca 46, 65
   C. littoralis 54
   C. torulosa 65
Cattleya 143, 144, 145, 200, 201
Celastrus orbiculatus 55
Celosia **134**, 142
Centella asiatica **189**
Centranthus ruber **126**
Cerastium tomentosum 55, 64
Ceratonia siliqua 54
Cestrum 108
   C. elegans **98**
   C. nocturnum 31, **98**
Chamaecyparis 84, 163
   C. lawsoniana 163
Chamaedorea costaricana 92
   C. elegans 92
   C. erumpens **92**, 200
Chamaelaucium uncinatum 54, **100**
Chamaerops humilis 48, 54
Chinobambusa 156, 163
Chlorophytum comosum 151
Christella dentata **153**
Chrysalidocarpus 48
   C. lutescens aurea **92**

Index of botanical names • 235 •

Chrysanthemum 55, 128, 217
   C. frutescens 48, 59, **127–8**
   C. x *superbum* 59, **128**
Chrysocephalum **128**, 142
   C. apiculatum 48, **169**
Cinnamomum camphora 84
Cissus antarctica 25, 27, 31, 34, 35, 118, 200
Cistus 48
Clarkia (syn. *Godetia*) 134
Clematis aristata 27
   C. microphylla 55
Cleome 134
Clerodendron 118
   C. nutans 118
   C. paniculatum (syn. *fragrans*) 31, 98
   C. philippinum 98
   C. splendens **118**
   C. thomsonae 118
   C. ugandense **98**, 108
Cleyera japonica 151
Clianthus formosus 55
Clivia minata 26, 27, 31, 48, 138, 199
Clothamnus 108
Clytostoma 121
Cocos nucifera 48, 91
Codiaeum 27, 35, 42, 58, **147–8**, 199
Coleonema 47
Coleus 27, 30, 58, **147**, 199
Colocasia 35, 42, 65, 199
Colvillea racemosa 77
Combretum 121
Copernicia glabrescens 93
Coprosma 25
   C. x *kirkii* 'Variegata' 48, 151, **169**
   C. repens 47, 70, **147**, 163, 164
Cordyline 21, 27, 29, 30, 34, 35, 42, 65, **147**, 149, 200
Coreopsis 54
Coriandrum sativum **190**
Correa alba 46, 47
   C. 'Dusky Bells' 142
Cortaderia 155
Corymbia, see *Eucalyptus ficifolia*
Cosmos 134
Costus 140
Cotoneaster horizontalis 54
Crinum 48, 138, 142
Crotalaria 108
   C. agatiflora 30, **98–9**
Crowea 142
Culcita 153
Cupaniopsis anacardioides **82**
Cuphea 58, 64, 142
   C. hyssopifolia **99**, 142
   C. ignea 99, 142
Cupressus 83, 84
   C. glabra aurea 163
   C. lambertiana 83
   C. macrocarpa 163
   C. sempervirens var. *stricta* 54
   C. torulosa 163
Curcuma australasica 27, 35, **138**, 199
Cyathea 27, 65, **154**, 201
Cycas 25, 49, **156–8**, 199
   C. angulata 156
   C. armstrongii **156**
   C. cairnsiana 156

C. circinalis **158**
C. media **156**
C. neocaldedonica 158
C. revoluta 42, 158
C. rumphii 158
Cymbidium 143, 144
Cymbopogon 155, **189**
Cyperus 155
   C. alternifolius 40
   C. exaltatus 40
   C. involucratus 65
   C. papyrus 65
Cyrtomium **153**
Cyrtostachys lacca syn. *renda* **92**, 93

Dahlia **127**, 134, 217
Dampiera 45, 55
   D. hederacea 170
   D. linearis 142
Danthonia 53, **169**
Davallia 27, **153**, 200
Davidsonia pruriens **173–4**, 199
Delonix regia 8–9, 31, 48, **81**
Dendrobium 143, 144, 145
Dennstaedtia davellioides **153**
Dianella 27, 35, 42, **138**
   D. intermedia 138
   D. tasmanica 142
Dianthera nodosa **128**
Dianthus 55, 132, **134**, 142
Dicksonia 27, **154**, 201
Dictyosperma album 92
Dieffenbachia 26, 35, 42, **148**, 199
Dietes 138
   D. bicolor 42, 136, 138, 142, 155
   D. grandiflora 142
   D. vegata 138
Dillwynia sericea 54
Diospyros **176**
Dipladenia 27, 30, 31, 49, 58, 115, 117, 199
   D. sanderi 118
Dizygotheca elegantissima **148**, 199
Dolichos 55
Dombeya natalensis 77
Doodia 27, **153**
Doryanthes excelsa **138**
   D. palmeri 35
Doryanthes, see *Mesembryanthemum*
Dracaena 29, 42, 93, **150**, 199
   D. draco 25, **93**
   D. fragrans 150
   D. marginata 93, 150
Drejerella 99, 108
Dryarna fluvius 53, 169
Dryopteris **153**
Duranta 42
   D. 'Aussie 2000' 163
   D. repens 58, 150, 163
   D. 'Sheena's Gold' 108, **150**, 163

Echeveria 55, 142
Elaeocarpus 46, 54
Eleagnus 47, 54, 151
Elettaria 151, **190**
Erigeron 45, 55, 127, **169**
   E. karvinskianus 48, 142, **169**
Erodium 142
Erythrina 84

E. caffra 78
E. crista-galli 78, 85
E. lysistemon 76
E. speciosa 78
E. sykesii 78
E. variegata 78
E. vespertilio 54, 78
Escallonia macrantha 163
Escholtzia californica 54
Eucalyptus 55, **78**, 84
   E. caesia 78
   E. camaldulensis
   E. citriodora 78
   E. cladocalyx 70
   E. ficifolia 48, **78**
   E. forrestiana 55
   E. leucoxylon 55, 70
   E. maculata 70
   E. platypus 55
   E. ptychocarpa **78**
Eucharis 132, 140
Eugenia 86, 87
   E. braziliensis 86
   E. reinwardtiana 27, 46, 87
Euodia, see *Melicope*
Euiodiella muelleri 81
Euonymus **150**, 163
   E. fortunei 54, 150, 163
   E. japonicus 150
Eupatorium megalophyllum 27, **99**, 108
Euphorbia milii 54, 55, **99**, 142
   E. pulcherrima 31, **106**, 108, 163, 200
Euphoria longan **174–5**
Eupomatia laurina 27, 35
Euroschinus falcatus 46

Faradaya freycinetia 31
   F. splendida 35, **118**
Fatsia japonica **150**
Feijoa sellowiana 47, **99**
Ficus 65, 84, 200
   F. carica **174**
   F. macrophylla 65
   F. pumila 21, 25, 27, 64, **118**, 169, 170
Fittonia 27, 151, 200
Foeniculum **188–9**
Frankenia pauciflora 45
Freesia **128–9**, 209
Fuchsia **99**, 108, 200

Gaillardia 132, 134
Galphimia glauca 30, 31, 59, **100**, 108
Gardenia jasminoides syn. *grandiflora* 29, 30, 31, **100**, 108
Gazania 127
   G. ringens 48, 55, 64, **169**
Geranium 'Johnson's Blue' **169**
Gerbera **128**
Gleditzia triacanthos 54
Glochidion ferdinandii 46, 164
Godetia, see *Clarkia*
Gomphrenia 54
Goodenia hederacea **169**
   G. ovata 70, 169
   G. rotundifolia 169
Gordonia axillaris 30, **100**, *101*
Grevillea 25, 42, 47, 54, 55, 58, 63, 64, 70, 100, 169, 219
   G. baileyana 42, 100
   G. banksii 46, 49
   G. curviloba 169

G. 'Honey Gem' 44
G. juniperina 169
G. lanigera 'Mt Tamboritha' 169
G. 'Ned Kelly' 54
G. robusta 48, 54, **82**, 84,100, 200
Gunnera magellanica 142, 151, **170**
Gypsophila elegans 54

Hakea 25, 55
   H. florulenta 47
   H. gibbosa 47
   H. leucoptera 55
   H. salicifolia 70
   H. trineura 54
Hardenbergia violacea 27, 55, 115, **118**, **169**
Harpullia pendula 54, **79**
Hedera helix 27, 64, 170
Hedychium 27, 31, 48, **130**
Helianthus 55, 132, 135
Helichrysum, see *Bracteantha*; *Chrysocephalum*
Heliconia 29, 30, 31, **130**, 132
Heliotropum arborescens **100**
Helipterum 55, 59
Helmholtzia 65, 140
Hemerocallis 137, **139–40**
Hemigraphis 27, 35
Heteranthera 40
Hibbertia 45, 64, **170**
   H. obtusifolia 142, 170
   H. ovata 170
   H. scandens 45, 48 55, 170
   H. serpyllifolia 170
Hibiscus 29, 30, 47, **110–12**, 164
   H. rosa-sinensis 31
   H. tiliaceus 30, 46, 70
Hippeastrum **138**
Holmskioldia sanguinea **101**
Hosta 27, 31, 42, 57, 58, **150**
Howea 200
   H. fosteriana 93
   H. longifolia 45
Hoya 31
   H. australis 27, 49, 118
   H. carnosa 27, **118**
   H. macgilvrai 118
Hydrangea macrophylla 27, 58, **101–2**, 108, 213
Hymenocallis **139**, 142
Hymenosporum flavum 59

Impatiens 27, **130**, 200, 201
Ipomoea horsfalliae 31, **119**
   I. purpurea 117, **119**
Iresine 150
   I. herbstii 27, 150
   I. lindenii 150
Iris 40
Ixora 27, 30, 31, 42, 60, **102**, 108, 200
   I. chinensis 102, 164
   I. coccinea 102, 164

Jacaranda mimosifolia 31, 33, 54, **79**, 84
   J. semiserrata 79
Jacobinia, see *Justicia*
Jagera pseudorhus **78–9**
Jasminium 119
Juniperus 48, 54, 83, 84, **169**
Justicia carnea 26, 27, **102**, 108
   J. guttata 99

Kalanchoe 129, **130**, 200, 201
Kennedia rubicunda 45, 121, 196
Kerria japonica 108
Kigelia pinnata 33
Kniphofia **130–1**
Kohleria 27, 155
Koelreuteria paniculata 54, **79**
Kunzea 45, 64

Laccospadix australasica 93, 200
Lagerstroemia indica 31, 33, 48, 54, 58, **79–80**, 84
    L. speciosa 80
Lagunaria patersonii 46
Lantana camara 102
    L. montevidensis 48, 64, **102**, 142, **169**, 170
Lathyrus odorata 121, 135
Lavandula 55, 163, **189**
Lepidosperma 155
Lepidozamia 25, 27, **158**, 200
    L. hopei 35, 158
    L. peroffskyana 35, 42, 158
Leptospermum 25, 44, 54, 58, **102**
    L. brachyandrum 65
    L. flavescens 45
    L. laevigatum 46, 65, 614
    L. petersonii 20, 102
    L. 'Pink Cascade' 54, 142
    L. scoparium 'Horizontalis' 48
Licuala ramsayi 65, 92, **93**, 200
Ligustrum ovalifolium 163
Limonium 48, 135
Linospadix monostachya **93**, 200
Liriope spicata **131**, 169
Litchie chinensis **174–5**
Livistona 48, 65, **92**, 93
Lobelia **131**, 134, 142
    L. alata 131
    L. cardinalis 131
    L. membrenacea 170
Lobularia maritima 55, 134, 142
Lomandra longifolia 42, 65, **139**
Lonicera 64, **119**, 170
    L. nitida 163
Lophostomon confertus 84
Lupinus 134
Lychnis chalcedonica **131**
Lycopodium 153
Lycoris **139**
Lygodium 154

Macadamia 174
Macaranga tanarius 46, 70
Macrozamia 55, **158**
Malpighia coccigera 31, **102**, 108
Malvaviscus arboreus **102–3**
Mandevilla 30, 31, **119**; see also *Dipladenia sanderi*
Mangifera indica 84, **175**
Maranta 35, **150**, 200
    M. leuconeura 27
Marrubium vulgare **189**
Medinilla magnifica 30, **103**
Megaskepasma erythroclamyx 30, **103**, 108
Melaleuca 25, 44, 48, 54, 55, 84, **103**, 150, 163, 164
    M. armillaris 55
    M. bracteata 103
    M. compacta 55
    M. incarna 45

    M. leucodendron 65, 70
    M. linariifolia 48, 65
    M. quinquinervia 46, 65, 70
    M. 'Revolution Gold' and 'Revolution Green' 103, 163
    M. viridiflora 65
Melastoma affine 49, 65, **103**, 108
Melia azedarach 46, 54, 70, **82–3**, 84
Melicope elleryana 42, 65, 78, **81**, 84
Melissa officinalis **189**
Mentha 27, **189**
Mesembryanthemum 45, 48, **131**, 169
Metrosideros 25, 47, **81**
    M. excelsa 46, 81, 163
    M. kermadecensis 49, 81, 163
    M. queenslandica 81
    M. thompsonii 46
Michelia champaca 81
    M. figo 103
Microlaena stipoides 53, **169**
Microlepia **154**
Microsorum **154**
Mimulus repens 132, **170**
Mirabilis jalapa **131**
Monstera deliciosa 27, 30, 35, 58, **150**, 200
    M. friedrichsthali 35, 150
Murraya paniculata 25, 30, 31, 47, 70, **103**, 163
Mussaenda 30, 31, 42
    M. erythrophylla **104**
    M. frondosa 104
    M. philippica 104
Myoporum floribundum 55
    M. insulare 70
    M. parvifolium 49, 55, **170**
    M. viscosum 70
Myrciaria cauliflora 174

Nandina domestica 27, **150–1**, 163, 164, 200
Nepeta **188**
Nephrolepis 27, **154**, 200
Nerine **139**
Nerium oleander 30, 47, **104**, 164
Nierembergia repens **170**
Nolina recurvata (syn. *Beaucarnea recurvata*) 93
Normanbya normanbya 93

Ocimum 58, **187**
Oenothera **170**
Onoclea 154
Ophiopogon 58, 155, **169**, 170
Oreganum **189**
Orthosiphon aristatus **104**, 105
Osmunda regalis 154
Osteospermum 48, **128**
Otacanthus caeruleus 102

Pachystachys coccinea 104
    P. lutea 30, 31, 57, 59, **104**
Pandanus 29, 46, 58, **93**
Pandorea 25, 27, 49, 59, 108
    P. jasminoides 117, **119**
    P. pandorana 119
Passiflora 119
Pawlonia tomentosa 54
Pelargonium 48, **128**, 142
Pellaea falcata **154**
Pennisetum alopecuroides 55, 65, **170**

Pentas lanceolata 27, 30, 31, 42, **104**
Peperomia 27, 151, 200
Persea americana 172
Petrea volubilis 48, **119**
Petroselinum crispum **189**
Phaleria clerodendron 27, 31, 35
Philodendron 26, 27, 30, 31, 34, 58, 121, 200
Phlebodium **154**
Phoenix 54, 90
    P. canariensis 49, 91
    P. dactylifera 54, 91
    P. reclinata 54, 91
    P. roebelenii 91, 200
Phormium 151
Phyla nodiflora 48, 53, 55, 169
Phyllostachys 156, 163
Physostegia virginiana 65
Pilea cadierei 151, 170
Pinus 84
    P. canariensis 54, 70
    P. halepensis 54
    P. mugo 54
    P. nummulariifolia **170**
    P. pinea 54
    P. pinnaster 54
Pisonia 151
Pittosporum 81, **104–5**, 164
    P. crassifolium 104
    P. eugenioides 104
    P. phylliraeoides 55
    P. revolutum 104
    P. rhombifolium **81**
    P. tenuifolium 104
    P. undulatum 104
Pityrogramma 154
Platycerium 27, 154, 201
Plectranthus 151, 201
    P. australis **170**
Plumbago auriculata 30, 42, 47, 59, 70, **105**, 163
Plumeria 31, 48, **79**, 80
    P. obtusa 79
    P. rubra 79
Poa labillardieri 54
Podocarpus elatus 48, 84
Polyanthes tuberosa **131**
Polypodium 154
Polystichum 154
Portulaca 44, 45, 48, 55, 64, **135**, **170**, 195
Portulacaria afra 27
Pothos 35, 121
Pratia pedunculata 142, **170**
Primula 131
Pseuderanthemum 151
Pseudosasa 156, 163
Psidium guajava 174
Pteris 154, 200
Ptychosperma elegans 49, **93**, 200
    P. macarthurii 93
Pultenea pedunculata 170
    P. spinosa 170
Pyrostegia venusta 25, 31, 49, 55, 59, 117, **119–20**, 120
Pyrrosia rupestris 154

Quisqualis indica 30, 31, 33, 119

Radermachera sinica 81
Randia 27, 30, 31, 35, 42, 200
Ranunculus 40, 142
Raphiolepis indica 47, **106**, 163, 164

    R. umbellata 106
    R. x delacouri 47, 106, 163
Ravenala madagascariensis 29, **93**
Ravenea glauca **92**
    R. hildebrandtii 92
    R. moorei 92
    R. robustior 92
Restio tetraphyllus 40, 65, 155
Rhagodia 46, 70
Rhapis 201
    R. excelsa **92**
    R. humilis **92**
Rhododendron lochae 114
Rondeletia amoena **106**, 163, 164
    R. odorata 106
Rosmarinus officinalis 55, **190**
Roystonea regia **91**, 93
Rudbeckia 55, **128**
Ruellia macrantha **106**
Russelia equisetiformis 47, 59, 64, 70, **106**

Sabal 49, 88, **92**
    S. domingensis 54, 92
    S. palmetto 92, 93
    S. uresana 93
Saintpaulia 27, **126**
Salvia 48, 131, 135
    S. elegans 55, 135
    S. involucrata 131
    S. officinalis 55, 131, **190**
Sambucus nigra **188**
Scaevola 45, 48, 55, 142, **170**
Schefflera actinophylla 42, 59, 70, 84, 151
    S. arboricola 34, 42, 59, **151**, 201
Schelhammera multiflora 35
Schinus areira (syn. *Schinus molle*) 54, 70
Schotia brachypetala 31, **81–2**
Scolopia braunii 48
Sedum 48, 55, 142, 200
Selaginella **154**, **170**
Sempervivum 48, 55, 142
Senecio 55, 142
Shinobambusa 156, 163
Solandra maxima 30, 31, 49, 117, 121
Solanum jasminoides 49, **121**
Spathodea campanulata 74, 84
Spathiphyllum 26, 27, 34, 201
Stenanthemum scortechinii 55
Stenocarpus sinuatus 35, **82**
Stephanotis floribunda **121**
Stokesia laevis 48, 132
Strelitzia reginae 29, 30, 31, 48, **132**
Streptocarpus 132
Streptosolen jamesonii 30, 31, **106**, 164
Syagrus romanzoffianum syn. *Cocos plumosa* 49, **92**, 93
Syngonium 27, 35, 151
Syzygium 35, 46, 70, **86–7**, 108
    S. banksii 46
    S. australe 87, 163
    S. erythocalyx 87
    S. francisii 87
    S. jambos 86
    S. leuhmannii **87**, 163
    S. oleosum 48
    S. wilsonii **87**, 163

Tabebuia 31, **82**
Tagetes 55, **134**

Tamarix aphylla 47, 54, 55, 70
Tamarindus indica **82**
Tapeinocheilos ananassae 27, 31
Tecomanthe hillii 31, 49, **121**
Tecomaria capensis 30, 31, 42, 49, 64, 70
Themeda triandra 55, **169**
Thevetia peruviana 59, 70, **82**
Thuja **83–4**, 163
Thunbergia 121
    T. alata 58, 117, 121, 196
    T. grandiflora 117
    T. mysorensis 30, 31, 117, **121**
Thymus 45, 55, **190**
Tibouchina 30, 31, 33, **107**
Tipuana speciosa 42, 82, 84
Todea barbara **154**, 200

Tradescantia fluminensis 27, 48, **170**, 201
    T. zebrina 170, 201
Tropaeoleum majus 55, 134

Utricularia australis 40

Vallisneria 40
Verbena 132
Viburnum odorotissimum 107, 163
    V. tinus 47, 54, **107**, 163, 164
Victoria amazonica 40
Villarsia reniformis 40
Vinca major **170**
Viola 134
    V. hederacea 27, 48, 132, **170**
    V. odorata 132

Vireya 27, 31, 33, 113–14, 212
Vitex trifolia 47, 54

Washingtonia filifera 54, **93**
    W. robusta 48, 54, **91**
Waterhousea 35, 65, **86–7**
Watsonia **139**
Wedelia trilobata 63, 64, **128**, **170**
Westringia 25, 164
    W. fruticosa 46, 47, **107**, 163
    W. 'Wynyabbie Gem' 54, 55
Wisteria 117, 121
Wodyetia bifurcata **91–2**

Xanthorrhoea 25, 48, 55, 58, 70, 151, 216

Xanthostemon chrysanthus 31, 35, **79**
    X. whiteii 79
    X. youngii 79
Xeronema 132

Yucca 55
    Y. filamentosa 25, 46

Zamia 49, **158**
Zantedeschia **139**, 142
Zauscheria 142
Zea mays 155
Zephyranthes **139**
Zingiber 31, **130**
Zinnia **135**
Zoysia **169**
Zygocactus 201

Index of common names and general topics

If you cannot find a plant listed under its common name, please look in the index of botanical names. See also the plant lists in chapters. Bold type for the page numbers indicates a major entry; italic type indicates a photograph.

acid-loving plants 212
African Lily **135**
African Tulip Tree 59, **74**, 84
African Violet 27, **126**, 193, 197, 199
Alexandra Palm 90, **91**, 200
algae 39
alkaline-tolerant plants 55
Allamanda 25, 29, 30, 31, 33, 42, 63, 64, 95, 117, 170
Aluminium Plant **170**
American Cotton Palm 91
Angelwing, *see* Begonia spp.
Angels' Wings 147
Arabian Jasmine 119
Aralia **150**
Arum Lily **139**
Aspidistra 199
Aster 127
Austral Lady Fern **153**
Avocado 172

Baby's Breath 55
Bamboo 42, 65, **155–6**, 163, 164, 199
Bangalow 48, 91
barley straw 39
Basil 20, 58, **187**
Belah 54
Bhutan Cypress 163
Bird of Paradise 29, 30, 31, 48, **132**
bird's nest ferns 27, 35, *35*, 58, 153, 154, 200
Black Bamboo 163
Black Bean 199
Black Palm 92
Black-eyed Susan 58, 196
Bladderwort 40
Bleeding Heart Vine 118
Blue Butterfly Bush **98**
Blue Lilly Pilly **87**
Blue Sage 27
Boobialla **170**
Bookleaf Pine 163
Borage **188**
Bottle Palm 91
Bottle Tree 54, 70
Bottlebrush 48, 54, 55, 65, 59, 75, **98**, 142
brake ferns **154**
Brazilian Cherry 86
Brazilian Red Cloak **103**
Brisbane Laurel 104
Brisbane Wattle **74**
Bromeliad **159–60**
Broom 55
Browallia 106

Brush Box 84
Burrawang 158
Bush Pea **170**
Busy Lizzie 27, **130**, 200, 201
Byfield Fern 35, 42, 156, 199

Cabbage Tree Palm 92
Cactus 55
California Poppy 55
Camphor Laurel 84
Canary Bird Bush 98–9
Canary Island Date Palm 49
Cape York Lily 27, 35, **138**, 199
Carambola **172–3**
Caraway 190
Cardamon 190
Cardinal Creeper 119
Cardinal Flower **131**
Carob Bean 54
Carpentaria Palm 48, **91**
Carpet Bugle 55, **169**
Cashmere Bouquet 98
Cast Iron Plant 27
Catmint 188
Catnip **188**
Cat's Whiskers **104**, *105*
Cheese Tree 164
Cherimoya 173
Cherry Pie, *see* Heliotrope
Cherry Satinash **87**
Chilean Jasmine 27, 30, 31, 48, 115, **118**, 199
Chilli 190
Chinese Hat **101**
Chinese Lantern 108, 163
Chive **188**
Christmas Bells 65
Chrysanthemum 127, 209
Cigar Flower
Citronella 155
Citrus **177**
climbing plants 21, 27, 30, 31, 49, 55, 58, **115–21**, *see also* Bougainvillea spp.; vines
Clivia 26, 27, 31, 48, 138, 199
Coconut Palm 48, 90, **91**
compost 221–2
Condamine Couch 48, 53, 55, **169**
Coneflower 128
Conifer 25, 54, 58, **83–4**, 163
Cook Island Pine 83
Cooktown Orchid 145
Coral Pea 55, 195
Coral Tree 54, 76, **78**, 84
Coral Vine 59, **117–18**
Coriander 190
Cotton Palm 48, **91**
Creeping Charlie **170**
Creeping Fig 27, 64, 118, 169, 170
Crepe Myrtle, *see* Pride of India
Croton 27, 29, 35, 42, 58, **147**, 199

Crown of Gold 31, 35, 42, **75**
Crown of Thorns 54, 55, **99**, 142, 209
Crow's Ash 54
Cuban Royal Palm **91**
Cup and Saucer Vine 27
Cunjevoi Lily 35, 42, **135**, 200
Custard Apple **173**
cuttings **206–8**, 209
Cycad 42, 49, **156–8**
Cypress 54, 83, 84, 163

Daisy 48, 55, 58, **127–8**
Davidson's Plum **173–4**, 199
Day Lily *137*, **139–40**, 209
Dill **188**
diseases 90, **228–9**, 233
Drejerella, *see* Shrimp Plant
Donkey Tail 200
Dragon Tree **93**
dry areas 51–5
Dumb Cane 26, **148**
Dusky Bells 142
Dusky Coral-pea 196
Dutchman's Pipe 59, **118**
Dwarf Date Palm 91
Dwarf Poinciana 54
Dwarf Umbrella 34, 42, 59, 151

Eel Grass 40
Elderberry **188**
Elephant's Ear 35, 199
Elkhorn 27, 35, **154**, *157*
Emu Bush 55
European Fan Palm 48
Evening Primrose **170**
Everlasting, **128**

False Aralia **148**
Fan Flower 45, 48, 55, 142, 170
Fan Palm 92
Fennel 20, **188–9**
ferneries 204
ferns 27, 35, 58, 153, 200
fertiliser 194, **220–1**
Fig 42, 65, 66, (edible) **174**, 200
Fijian Firebush 146
fire **69–70**
fire retardant plants
Fishbone Fern 27
Fishtail Fern **153**
Fishtail Palm 91
Flamboyant, *see* Poinciana
Flame Tree **78**
Flax Lily 138
Floss Flower **134**
Foambark **78–9**
Four O'Clock Plant **131**
Foxtail Palm **91**
Fragrant plants 29
Frangipani 29, 31, 33, 42, 48, 70, 79, *80*
Fraser Island Creeper 49, **121**
Freesia 118, 298
fruit **172–8**, 224–5
fruit fly 230

Fruit Salad Plant 150

Geraldton Wax 54, **100**
Geranium 20, 48, 58, **128**, 142, 169
Ginger, ornamental 27, 30, 31, 35, 42, 48, **130**, 200
Gold Dust Plant 200
Golden Biota 83
Golden Candles 30, 31, *57*, 59, **103–4**, 108
Golden Cane 29, 88, 90, **92**
Golden Cup 30, 31, 48, 117, **121**
Golden Penda 31, 35, **79**
Golden Privet 70, 163, 164
Golden Rain Tree 54, **79**
Golden Shower 31, 76
Golden Silver Wattle **74**
Golden Water CLub 40
Gotu kola 189
Granny's Bonnet **126**
Grape **178**
Grapefruit **177**
grasses 42, 53, 55, 155, 167
Grass Tree 25, 49, 55, 58, 70, **151**, 216
Greater Periwinkle **170**
Green Biota 83
Gristle Fern **153**
groundcovers 53, 168–70
Guava **174**
Guinea Flower 45, 48, 55, **170**
Gum, *see* Eucalyptus spp.
Gymea Lily **138**
Gypsum 165, 213

hare's foot fern 27, **153**
heathland 43, 47, 49
hedges, 55, **162–4**
Heliotrope **100**, 209
Herald's Trumpet **118**
herbs 187–90
Honey Locust 54
Honey Myrtle, *see* Paperbark
Honeydew **178**
Honeysuckle 25, 64, 117, **119**, 164, 170
Horehound **189**

Indian Hawthorn **106**
insect repellents 20, **229–30**
Ivory Curl Tree 25, 30, 42, 73, **75**, 163
Ivy 27, 170, 200

Jaboticaba 174
Jacaranda 31, 33, 54, **79**
Jade Plant 27, 200
Jasmine 25, 49, 119
Javanese Velvet Plant 27
Johnstone River Apple **87**
Jointed Twig Rush 40
Juniper 48, 54, 83, 84, **169**

Kangaroo Grass **169**

Kangaroo Paw 48, 54, 55, 58, 142
Kangaroo Vine 27, 31, 34, 35, **118**, 200
Kentia Palm 200
King Fern **154**
King Orchid 145, *145*
Krempin, Jack 91
Kumquat **177**

Lacy Ground-fern **153**
Lady Palm **92**, 201
Lavender 30, 55, 163, **189**
lawns 25, 58, **165–8**, 218–19, 231; *see also* grasses
layering 208
Leichhardt Bean **75–6**
Lemon **177**
Lemon Balm **189**
Lemon-scented Tea Tree 20, **102**
Lemon Scented Myrtle 20, 25, 54, 55, 74 75
Leopard Tree 79
Lilly Pilly 25, 27, 35, 46, 48, 65, 70, **86–7**, 163
Lily 135, 136, 138, 139, 209, 210
Lily of the Nile, *see* African Lily
Lipstick Palm **92**
Lime **177**
Liquidambar 84
Little Boy Blue **102**, 108
Longan **174–5**
Lupin 134
Lychee **174**

Macadamia 175
maidenhair ferns 27, **153**
Maltese Cross **131**
Mandarin **177**
Mango 84, **175**
Marguerite 48, 59, **127–8**
Marigold 55, **134**
Marjoram **189**
Marmalade Bush, *see* Browallia
Marsh Marigold 40
Matt Rush 59, 65
Melon 177, 178
Mexican Cigar Flower **99**
Michaelmas Daisy **127**
Milfoil (Water)
Miniature Umbrella Tree **151**
Mint 20, 27, **189**
Mint Bush 55
Mirror Plant **147**
Mist Flower **99**
Mock Orange 25, 30, 31, 47, 70, **103**, 163
Mondo Grass 25, 59, 155, **169**
Morning Glory 119
mulch 222–3

Nardoo 40
Narrow-leaved Lilly Pilly **87**
Nasturtium 55, **134**, **189**, 195
Native Frangipani 59
Native Guava 27, 35
Native Violet **170**
New Zealand Christmas Tree 81
New Zealand Flax **151**, 209
Night Jasmine 29, 33, **98**
no-dig gardening 184–5
Norfolk Island Pine 48

Oleander 30, 47, 58, 104

Orange **177**
Orange Trumpet Vine 25, 31, 48, 55, 59, **119**, *120*
Orchid 27, 33, 35, **143–5**, 209
Oregano **189**
organic gardening 183–4
Oyster Plant **126**

Pagoda Flower 98
Palm Lilies (cordylines) 21, 27, 29, 30, 34, 35, 42, 65, 147, 200
Palmetto 49, **92**
palms 25, 42, 48, 54, 58, 67, 70, **88–93**, 157, 158, 216
Pampas Grass 155
Pansy **134**
Paperbark 25, 44, 45, 46, 48, 54, 55, 65, 70, **103**, 150, 163
Parlour Palm **92**, 201
Parrot Feather 40
Parrot Leaf 147
Parrot Pea 54
Parsley **189**
Passion Flower **119**
Passionfruit **178**
Pawpaw **175–6**
Peacock Plant 147
Pepper Tree 54, 70
Persimmon 176
Peruvian Lily **136**
pests 90, **227–8**, 229–30, 231, 233
Petticoat Palm 91
Philippine Violet **96**
Philodendron 26, 27, 30, 31, 34, 200
Piccabeen Palm 91
Pickerel Rush 40
Pine 54, 70, 83, 84, 163
Pineapple Guava 47, **99**
Pineapple Sage 55, 135
Pink, *see* Sweet William
Pink Cassia 31, 33
Pink Euodia 42, 65, **81**, 84
Pink Jasmine 119
Pink Lasiandra 103
Pink Silky Oak **74**
Plum Pine 48
Poinciana **8–9**, 29, 31, 48, **81**
Poinsettia 31, 33, 58, **106**, 108, 163, 164, 200
Polka Dot Plant 27
Polyanthus **131**
Pondweed 40
Pony Tail Palm **93**
pools 37–9
Poplar 84
Port Wine Magnolia **103**
Pot Marigold **134**
Potato Vine **118**, 121
Pothos 200
potting mixes **193–5**, 223
Powder Puff 30, 42, 59, 64, **96**, 170
Powder Puff Lilly Pilly **87**
Prayer Plant 200
Pride of India 25, 31, 33, 48, 54, 58, **79–80**, 84
Princess Palm 92
propagation **205–10**
Pummelo **177**
Purple Coral Vine **118**
Purple Wreath **119**
Pyalong Gold, *see* Bush Pea

Pyrethrum 20, 230
Queen Palm 49, **92**
Queensland Golden Myrtle 81

rainfall 11, 16, 65, 67
Rain Lily **139**
Rain of Gold 30, 31, 59, **100**
Rangoon Creeper 30, 31, 33, 119
rasp ferns 27, **153**
Red Hot Poker **130–1**
Red Spur Valerian **127**
Rex begonia, *see Begonia* spp.
Rock Felt Fern **154**
Rock Orchid, *see* King Orchid
rockeries 142
Rockmelon **177–8**
rocky ground 45
root problem trees 84
Rosemary 54, 55, 64, **190**
rose 121, 140, 141
Rough Tree Fern 154
Royal Fern **154**
Running Marshflower 40

Sacred Bamboo 27, **150–1**, 163
Sage 27, 49, 54, **190**
Saltbush 46, 70
Sapote 176
Scarlet Flowering Gum **78**
screening plants 42, 164
Screw Palm **93**
Sealing Wax Palm **92**
Seaside Daisy 169
seed 205–6, 209
shade-loving plants 26–7, 93, 108
Shasta Daisy 59, 64, **128**
She Oak, *see* Casuarina
Shrimp Plant **99**, 108
Showy Parrot Pea 54
Sickle Fern **154**
Silky Oak 48, 54, **82**, 84, 100, 200
Silver Saw Palmetto **89**, **92**
Singapore Daisy 63, 64, **128**, **170**
Singapore Holly 31, **102**
Snapdragon **134**
Snowballs 55
Snow in Summer 55
Soft Bracken **153**
Soft Tree Fern **154**
soil pH 15–16, 43–4, 51–2, 166, 212, 213
Solitaire Palm **93**, 201
Spear Lily 35
Spider Flower **134**
Spider Lily **138**, **139**
Staghorn 27, 35, 154, *157*
staking 217
Star Jasmine 170
Statice 48, **135**
Stonecrop 48, 55, 209
storms 65, **66–8**
stormwater 39, 65
Sturt's Desert Pea 55
Sugar Palm **93**
sugarcane 164; *see also* mulch
Sunflower 55, 132, **135**
Sun Jewells, *see Portulaca*
Sun Plant 135, 170
Swamp Bloodwood **78**
Swamp Cypress 65

Swan River Daisy 127
Sweet Pea 117, 121, 135
Sweet Pittosporum **104**
Sweet William **134**

Tamarind **82**
Tamarisk 54, 55
Tangelo **177**
Tapioca Plant 59
tassel ferns **153**
Tea Tree 20, 25, 44, 46, 54, 58, 65, **102** (Leptospermum), **103** (Melaleuca), 142; *see also* Paperbark
temperature 11
Temple Bamboo 163
Thyme **190**
Tipu Tree **82**
Traveller's Palm 29, **93**
tree fern 25, 27, **154**
Tree Waratah **74**
Tropical Magnolia 81
Trumpet Tree **82**
Tuberose **131**
Tuckeroo **82**
Tulipwood 54, **79**
Turk's Hat **102–3**

Umbrella Tree 34, 42, 59, 70, 84, 151, 201

Valerian 127
vegetables **179–86**
Veldt daisy **128**
vines (fruit) 178
Violet 132, 210
Vireya 27, 31, 33, **113–14**, 212

Walking Stick Palm **93**, 201
Wallaby Grass **169**
Wandering Jew 48, **170**, 200
water conservation 48, 52, 53, 219
Water Gum **87**
Water Fern 40
Water Starwort 40
Water Trumpet 40
Waterlily 39, 40
Watermelon **178**
Wattle, *see Acacia* spp.
Waxflower, *see* Geraldton Wax
Wax Plant 27, 31, 48, 118
Weeping Grass 53, **169**
Westringia 25, 46, 48, 54, 107, 163
Wheel-of-Fire Tree 35, **82–3**
White Cedar 46, 54, 70, **82**, **84**
White Potato Vine 121
Willow 84
Winter Pink 142
Wisteria 117, 121
Wonga Vine 59, 119
Wormwood 20, 163, **190**

Yarrow 154, **190**
Yedda Hawthorn 106
Yellow Bladderwort 40
Yellow Poinciana 31
Yesterday-Today-and-Tomorrow 25, 30, 31, 33, **96**, 108

Zamia 156, 158
Zebra Plant 95, 147, 200